# Great Dates in Russian and Soviet History

# Great Dates in Russian and Soviet History

General Editor Francis Conte

 Facts On File®

AN INFOBASE HOLDINGS COMPANY

**Great Dates in Russian and Soviet History**

Translation copyright © 1994 by Facts On File

Some material in this volume was originally published in *Les Grandes Dates de la Russie et de l'U.R.S.S.*, a volume in the Larousse series *Les Grandes Dates*, © Librairie Larousse 1990.

Facts On File, Inc.
460 Park Avenue South
New York NY 10016

**Library of Congress Cataloging-in-Publication Data**

Great dates in Russian and Soviet history / general editor Francis Conte.
    p.  cm. — (Great dates)
Translated from French.
Includes index.
ISBN 0-8160-2687-4 (alk. paper)
I. Conte, Francis.  II. Series.
DK36.G74  1993
947'.002'02—dc20                    93-20364

A British CIP catalogue record for this book is available from the British Library.

Facts On File books are available at special discounts when purchased in bulk quantities for businesses, associations, institutions or sales promotions. Please call our Special Sales Department in New York at 212/683-2244 or 800/322-8755.

Text design by Robert Yaffe
Jacket design by Catherine Rincon Hyman
Composition by Facts On File/Grace M. Ferrara
Manufacturing by the Maple-Vail Book Manufacturing Group
Printed in the United States of America

10 9 8 7 6 5 4 3 2 1

This book is printed on acid-free paper.

# CONTENTS

# PREFACE

Great Dates in Russian and Soviet History is intended to meet the need for an accessible source of information on the primary events, people and ideas that have shaped the complex history of the region. Like other volumes in the Great Dates series, it is designed for a wide audience: informed and interested lay readers; students, researchers and teachers; and professionals in journalism, government and related fields. The choice of materials reflects a broad view of Russian and Soviet history, one that encompasses science, technology and culture as well as more traditional political, diplomatic, military and economic developments.

The basic structure of the book is a chronology of key dates in Russian and Soviet history from earliest times to the present. Each chapter addresses a distinct time period. Within each chapter, chronological entries are organized under categories relating to political and institutional life, foreign affairs, economy and society, religion, civilization and culture, and science and technology. As appropriate, special categories for major events are included. Each chapter opens with a synopsis of its time period. In addition, selected political and governmental terms are defined in a glossary at the rear. The comprehensive index will help to further guide the reader through Russian and Soviet history and current events.

# A NOTE ON THE RUSSIAN CALENDAR

## Two Systems of Dating

This volume uses the double dating system that was employed in Russia for centuries. Until October 5, 1582, the Julian calendar was used throughout the Christian world. On this date, the Roman Catholic Church instituted a new calendar, the Gregorian calendar (after Pope Gregory XIII), a system that was 10 days ahead of the Julian calendar. With these two systems in effect, the date under the Julian calendar (called the "old style") was always indicated first, followed by the date under the Gregorian calendar (the "new style"). The discrepancy between the two calendars was 10 days on Friday, October 5 (15), 1582. The discrepancy increased to 11 days in February 1700, to 12 days in February 1800, and to 13 days in February 1900.

New Year's Day: Until 1492, the calendar year in Russia began on either March 1 or September 1. After 1492, in accordance with the tradition of the Byzantine Church, the first day of the year was fixed as September 1. By decree of December 15, 1699, Peter the Great transferred the first day of the calendar year to January 1, beginning with January 1, 1700.

## Change of Era

By the same decree, Peter the Great substituted the Christian Era for the Byzantine Biblical Era that began with the date deemed to mark the creation of the world, fixed at September 1, 5509 B.C. To correspond with the Christian Era, it is necessary to subtract 5509 years for dates between September 1 and December 31, and to subtract 5508 years for dates between January 1 and August 31. In addition, in the texts of this period, the millennium is rarely indicated.

## Change of Calendar

Despite all these other changes, Peter did not abandon the Julian Calendar, which remained the official calendar of the Russian Church and state until February 1, 1918. On this date, the Soviet government adopted the Gregorian calendar, but the Russian Orthodox Church continues to use the Julian calendar.

# The Eastern Slavs Before Christianization

The Slavs are a people of Indo-European origin. Starting most likely from the northeastern slopes of the Carpathian Mountains, they gradually colonized central and eastern Europe along a large swath running from the upper Vistula River to midway down the Dnieper River. Around A.D. 500, the Slavs began to divide into several distinct tribes that participated in the Great Migrations. Disrupting the entire continent of Europe, these vast movements of peoples sounded the death knell for the Classical World and opened the door for the eventual emergence of modern Europe.

The Slavic tribes began to disperse after reaching the region of the Dnieper River. Although some decided to settle there, others continued to migrate, some toward the southern steppes, others toward the forests of the upper Volga or to the shores of the Baltic. By the second half of the 9th century, the time when the Kievan state came into existence, the Eastern Slavs had formed two distinct groups: one inhabiting the middle Dnieper region, the other the region around Novgorod. In the south, the Slavs were in contact with peoples of Persian origin; in the north, they interacted with Baltic, Finnish and Scandinavian peoples.

The Varangians, a tribe of Vikings that had originated in Scandinavia, lived in the midst of the regions inhabited by the Eastern Slavs. The Varangians played a crucial role in the regions' political and economic development: They contributed to the unification of the Slavic tribes under princely leadership and they began the commercial exploitation of the rivers of the regions, creating a trade route that eventually extended from the North Sea to the Black Sea (the famous "route from the Varangians to the Greeks" described in the *Primary Chronicle*, one of the first written accounts of Russia's earliest history). After installing themselves at Novgorod, the Varangians embarked on the conquest of Kiev. The capture of the city by Oleg marked the birth of the Kievan state, which continued to develop through the end of the 9th century.

Kiev's development was greatly affected by its proximity to the Byzantine Empire, which served as a commercial outlet and a civilizing influence. Through their contact with the Byzantine Empire, the Slavs and the Varangians became aware of the broader geopolitical situation, and they managed to exploit this knowledge by becoming the intermediaries between northern Europe and Byzantium. Meanwhile, Prince Oleg's successors consolidated the Kievan state, conquering neighboring peoples and creating an administrative structure geared, in particular, to the collection of tribute. During the second half of the 10th century, Sviatoslav pursued a policy of conquest and extended the state's territory to the detriment of the Khazar Empire and the Volga Bulgarians. Upon the accession to power of his son Vladimir, Kiev was a state to be reckoned with by both West and East.

# Early Chronology

## 3rd–7th Centuries

Under the pressure of the great movements of peoples and the great invasions that swept through eastern Europe (those of the Goths, the Huns and then the Avars), the Slavic tribes fanned out and divided into three principal groups:

- The Venedi, whose territory constituted a vast triangle that ran along the length of the Carpathian Mountains and extended to the upper Vistula River in the west, to the Dnieper River in the east, and to the Pruth River in the south

- The Antes (made up of Slavs and of Persian-speaking Sarmatians), who lived along the shore of the Black Sea between the Dniester River and the Dnieper

- The Sloveni, who crossed the Danube River and spread throughout the Balkan peninsula

## 8th–9th Centuries

The Slavic peoples occupied half of Europe just prior to the emergence of that continent's great states. To the north and east, they had reached the region of Novgorod and the Volga River; to the west, they had pushed, on occasion, as far as Kiel, Bamberg and Linz; to the south, their habitations extended all the way to Crete. The Southern Slavs became the Yugoslavs and the Bulgarians. The Western Slavs became the Poles, the Czechs and the Slovaks. The Slavs of the north and of the Baltic region were gradually absorbed by the Germanic peoples. As for the Eastern Slavs, they split up into the Russians, the Ukrainians and Belorussians, the three Slavic peoples who inhabit the lands of the former Soviet Union.

## Circa 750–800

Scandinavian Viking tribes (the Varangians) penetrate to the Middle Volga region.

## Circa 800

Direct contacts are established between the Khazar Empire (whose capital, Itil, was situated at the delta of the Volga) and the Scandinavians, who commercially exploited four of the region's key river routes (the Volkhov, the Ilmen, the Lovat and the Volga).

## 839

According to the *Bertinian Annals*, a delegation of Varangians calling themselves "Rhos" arrive at the court of the Frankish Emperor Louis I. The *Pri-*

## Eastern Europe and Central Asia c. 800

*mary Chronicle* will later declare "the Slavs and the Russes" to be the same people, noting that it was from the Varangians that the Russes got their name even though they were of Slavic origin.

### Circa 850–900

According to the *Primary Chronicle*, Slavic and Finnish tribes invite three Varangians (Rurik, Sineus and Truvor) to reign over Novgorod, Belozersk and Izborsk, respectively.

## 856–860

The Varangians Askold and Dir conquer Kiev.

## 860

With the concurrence of the Slavs of Kiev, the Varangians organize the first maritime expedition against Constantinople. With the emperor Michael III away, the invaders easily lay siege to the undefended city, only to be dispersed by a violent storm. The Byzantines attribute their good fortune to the intercession of the Virgin, and the episode will be celebrated in their Church's traditional holiday of Pokrov (the Veil).

## 867

Patriarch Photius founds a bishopric for the Slavs and the Varangians, who had converted to Christianity in 860 as a result of their contact with Byzantium.

## 878–882

The Varangian Oleg, ruler of Novgorod, conquers the city of Kiev and founds the Kievan state. His power (as indicated by taxation records) will soon extend from Novgorod to the basin of the Pripet River and to the heart of the Dniester region in the southwest.

## 883–885

Oleg conquers the Drevlianians, the Severians and the Radimichians, Slavic tribes inhabiting the region to the north of Kiev.

## 898

The Magyars march on Kiev from the northwest.

## 907

Oleg leads an expedition against Constantinople. The campaign against the city involves a land attack and a naval assault (with 2,000 boats). The outcome of the fighting is favorable to the Byzantines.

Following the engagement, Constantinople enters into its first treaty with the Slavo-Varangians. The treaty, which deals primarily with commercial relations, makes Russian exports to Byzantium (primarily wax, honey, furs and slaves) exempt from customs duties. Russian merchants are permitted to conduct business in Constantinople and are granted monthly subsidies while in residence there.

## 911

The treaty concluded in 907 with the Byzantines is complemented by a new agreement setting out certain obligations owed by the Russians to the Byzantine emperor. The agreement includes a mutual nonaggression pact.

## 913

Prince Oleg dies and is succeeded by Igor.

## 915

The *Primary Chronicle* mentions the arrival on the steppe of the Pechenegs, a nomadic people of Turkic origin allied with Byzantium.

## 941

Igor attacks Constantinople and suffers a severe defeat. The Russian flotilla is repulsed by "Greek fire" (an incendiary compound projected through copper pipes).

## 943

The Russians conduct a victorious campaign against Persia's Transcaspian provinces.

## 944

The Byzantines conclude a new treaty with the Russians. The clauses relating to commercial relations are more restrictive than those of the treaty of 907. The Russians undertake to assist the Byzantines militarily in protecting Chersonesus (a Byzantine possession within the borders of the Kievan state) and in the event of an attack on Byzantine territory by the Bulgars.

## 945

The Drevlianians murder Prince Igor, who had demanded an increase in tribute. Olga, his widow, becomes regent and establishes an administrative network for the collection of tribute.

The *Primary Chronicle* notes the presence at this time of a church, St. Elijah, in Kiev.

## 957

Olga is received in Constantinople by the Emperor Constantine VII Porphyrogenitus. She is accompanied by a large delegation, including 22 merchants.

## 957?

Olga converts to Christianity, taking the Christian name Helen. (The *Primary Chronicle* mentions the event taking place during the year 955, but this date does not seem credible because as late as 957 the Byzantines knew Olga only by her pagan name.)

## 959

Olga dispatches a delegation to the Court of Emperor Otto I at Frankfurt am Main in an effort to develop commercial ties with central Europe.

## 959–960

A flurry of diplomatic activity takes place between Kiev and Byzantium as Constantinople appeals to the Russians to organize an expedition against Crete. (Crete will be reconquered from the Arabs in 961.)

## 960

Otto I sends Bishop Adalbert to Kiev.

## 961–962

Led by Varangian aristocrats grouped around Prince Sviatoslav, Olga's son, a pagan reaction breaks out in Kiev. Olga cedes power to Sviatoslav.

Bishop Adalbert is poorly received in Kiev, and his mission ends in failure.

## 963

Sviatoslav leads campaigns against the Khazars, from whom he takes the city of Sarkel, the Kuban River area and the foothills of the Caucasus Mountains. He extends his power to the principality of Tmutarakan and conquers the Viatichi, which had been the sole remaining Slavic tribe paying tribute to the Khazars.

## Circa 965

Sviatoslav leads an expedition against the Volga Bulgars, sacking their capital, the Great Bulgar. He then conducts a new campaign against the Khazars, ravaging their capital, Itil; this will lead in a short time to the breakup of the Khazar Empire.

## 967

As a result of their campaigns, the Russians control the entire Volga-Caspian Sea trade route and have become the masters of the Don Ossetians as well as of other Eastern Slavs.

## 968

At the request of Nicephorus Phocas, the Byzantine emperor, Sviatoslav undertakes a major campaign against the Danube Bulgars. The Russians conquer the Bulgars's capital and take their ruler, Boris, prisoner. Sviatoslav makes plans to transfer his capital to Pereyaslavets.

## 969

The Pechenegs lay siege to Kiev.

Olga dies. Sviatoslav confers the administration of Kiev to his eldest son, Iaropolk;

the territory of the Drevlianians to his second son, Oleg; and Novgorod to his youngest son, Vladimir.

**970**

After having fought the Bulgars on behalf of the Byzantine Empire, the Russians move against the emperor himself, ravaging the environs of Constantinople. They are defeated, however, by John Tzimisces and are forced to abandon the Balkans 2.

**971**

The Byzantines sign a new treaty of assistance and nonaggression with Sviatoslav. The commercial clauses of the treaty of 944 are reaffirmed.

**972**

During his return voyage to Kiev, Sviatoslav is murdered by the Pechenegs.

His eldest son, Iaropolk, becomes prince of Kiev.

**973**

Iaropolk sends a delegation to the Court of Otto I, in Upper Saxony.

**977**

The murder of Sviatoslav (972) provokes a civil war between his three sons over the succession to leadership of the Kievan state. Oleg is killed and Vladimir is forced to flee into exile in Scandinavia, where he takes refuge at the Court of Olaf Tryggvasson, king of Norway.

**979**

With the help of Varangian mercenaries, Vladimir returns to Kiev and has his half brother Iaropolk assassinated.

# Chapter 2  980–1174

# The Expansion and Decline of Kiev

The reign of Vladimir inaugurated a new stage in Russian civilization. Kiev became a Christian state, and the Russians, adopting the Byzantine liturgy, assimilated the ancient Judeo-Christian culture. As in all of the recently Christianized Slavic states, the conversion occurred on the initiative of the prince, and politics was an essential consideration: In states characterized by scant ethnic or cultural homogeneity, conversion was part of a prince's effort to create an ideological cohesiveness that would facilitate the strengthening of his power. In the particular case of the Rus, the introduction of Christianity hastened the fusion of the Varangians and the Slavs. Moreover, by his conversion the Kievan prince obtained recognition from the Western powers and confirmed his alliance with Byzantium, from which he had solicited assistance for the development of his Church.

The rapid adoption of Christianity in Kiev is one of the more remarkable features of 11th-century Russia. It greatly contributed to the growing influence of the Kievan state and to the diffusion of a new culture that manifested itself, above all, in the construction of churches and in the dissemination of the written word. In the latter area, the presence of literate Bulgarians (who took refuge in Kiev after the annexation of their country by Byzantium) was a key factor: They were responsible for introducing the Cyrillic alphabet into Russia.

The growth of Kiev's influence in the 11th and 12th centuries was also facilitated by the state's territorial expansion, especially to the northeast, and by its increased control over the Baltic region. But Kiev's expansion remained partial: Territorial gains could not be consolidated because of the state's structural weaknesses.

The history of the Kievan state was marked by numerous clashes among competing princes, clashes that spurred the development of complex rules of dynastic succession. The system of succession from brother to brother, in which the claim of the eldest son was equal or superior to that of his father's third brother, provoked perpetual conflict for the title of grand prince of Kiev. Whoever held that title had authority over the entire territory of the Kievan state.

The strife over succession encouraged the emergence of new principalities, and at the same time resulted in a significant push to colonize new territories. In the middle of the 12th century, a new power center constituted itself around the principalities of Rostov, Vladimir and Suzdal. Its rapid growth fed the ambitions of its princes, who soon emerged as rivals of the grand prince of Kiev. In 1169 Andrei Bogoliubsky seized the historic center of the Rus. Pillaged and ravaged, Kiev was unable to restore its ancient power before the arrival of new invaders, the Mongols.

# Politics and Institutions

## 980

Vladimir, grand prince of Kiev, institutes an official pagan cult.

## 981

Vladimir seizes Czerwen and Przemysl, increasing his power in the west.

## 983

A campaign against the Iatviags (a Lithuanian tribe) opens to the Rus the river routes of the Niemen, the Bug and the Vistula in the direction of the Baltic Sea.

## 985

A new Russian expedition against the Volga Bulgarians ends without a decisive victory but results in a treaty of friendship and commerce. The commercial accord will be vital to the Russians because Kiev will be able to profit from the regular trade relations the Bulgarians have developed with the Arabs.

Upon his return from this expedition, Vladimir has idols erected in the hills of Kiev and offers a solemn sacrifice to the god Perun.

## 987

Russo-Byzantine talks are held. Basil II, the Byzantine emperor, solicits Vladimir's assistance in combating the rebellions of Bardas Phocas and Bardas Skleros in Asia Minor. Vladimir agrees on the condition that he receive the hand in marriage of Anne, sister of the emperor. The marriage is approved by Constantinople on the condition that Vladimir accept baptism.

## Late 987–Early 988

Vladimir converts to Christianity and is baptized (probable date).

## 988

A Russian flotilla is dispatched to Constantinople to buttress the armies of Basil II.

The entire population of Kiev is baptized.

## Winter 988–989

Vladimir lays siege to Kherson, a Byzantine city on the lower Dnieper, which he captures thanks to the treachery of the local bishop. (The expedition may have been intended to convince the emperor to fulfill his agreement to send his sister Anne to Russia.)

## 989

After an initial setback at Chrysopolis, the Byzantine army and Russian forces vanquish Bardas Phocas at Abydos, in Asia Minor.

Anne and Vladimir are married.

## 992–997

The Pechenegs invade the environs of Kiev and are repulsed.

## End of the 10th Century

Turov is established on the Pripet River and made the capital of a principality created by Vladimir for his adoptive son Sviatopolk.

## 1000–1001

Pope Sylvester II and Prince Vladimir exchange delegations.

## 1006

Kiev enters into a new treaty with the Volga Bulgars.

## 1007–1014

Russian troops provide renewed military support to the Byzantine emperor in his campaigns against the Balkan Bulgars.

## 1014

Iaroslav, son of Vladimir and prince of Novgorod, refuses to pay the tribute that is due to the Kievan state.

## 1015

Vladimir sends his son Boris to fight the Pechenegs while he sets off on a campaign against Iaroslav. Taken ill, Vladimir dies in Berestovo on July 15.

Sviatopolk takes power with the assistance of Boleslaus I of Poland, his brother-in-law and ally. In return, Sviatopolk accords Boleslaus the southwestern region of the country. Sviatopolk has his half-brothers Boris and Gleb assassinated. A cult develops very quickly around these two martyr-princes who accepted death without resisting, their actions becoming models of submission to the will of the eldest.

## 1018

The Poles intervene in Kiev to support Sviatopolk against Iaroslav.

## 1019

Iaroslav defeats Sviatopolk and becomes the ruler of Kiev.

## 1024

The city of Iaroslav is founded on the Volga River.

## 1025 or 1026

Iaroslav and his brother Mstislav the Brave, prince of Tmutorokan, agree to divide the realm. Iaroslav will govern Kiev and the region west of the Dnieper, and Mstislav will rule Chernigov and the land east of the Dnieper.

## Circa 1030

A line of fortifications is established along the Ros River as an outpost of the Kievan Slavs against the nomads of the steppe.

## 1031

Iaroslav takes part in a war against Poland to reconquer the southwestern lands ceded by Sviatopolk to Boleslaus.

## 1032

The king of Norway, Harald Sigurdsson, comes to Kiev and marries Elizabeth, a daughter of Iaroslav. A treaty is signed by the prince of Kiev and his new son-in-law to provide for the defense of the northern frontier.

## 1036

Mstislav the Brave dies, leaving Iaroslav ruler of the entire Kievan state.

## 1037

A Russian victory over the Pechenegs ushers in nearly 25 years of peace within the Kievan state. Hostilities will reemerge with the arrival in the region of the Kipchaks, or Cumans, whom the Russians call the Polovtsy.

## 1038

The future king of Hungary, Andrei I, takes refuge in Kiev, where he marries Anastasia, a daughter of Iaroslav.

## 1043
Iziaslav, Iaroslav's son, marries Elizabeth, daughter of Mieszko II, the king of Poland.

## 1043-1046
The last war between Kiev and Byzantium takes place. It results in a treaty that renews the commercial relations sanctioned in the accords of 944.

## 1048
Henri I of France sends a delegation to Kiev to ask for the hand of Anne, a daughter of Iaroslav.

## 1051
*May.* Henri I of France and Anne of Kiev are married at Reims.

## 1052
The Byzantine-Russian alliance is strengthened by the marriage of Iaroslav's son, Vsevolod, to the Byzantine princess Anne, daughter of Constantine IX Monomakh.

## 1054
Iaroslav the Wise dies, and his son Iziaslav succeeds him as prince of Kiev. Iaroslav's will disinherits Vseslav of Polotsk, his grand-nephew, and Rostislav of Novgorod, his grandson; outraged, these two foment unrest.

## Circa 1060
The political independence of Prince Vseslav is affirmed by the creation of a diocese at Polotsk.

## 1061
The Kievans win a victory over the Cumans.

## 1066
Vladimir Monomakh, grandson of Iaroslav, marries Anglo-Saxon princess Gyda, daughter of Harold II.

## 1067
Rostislav of Novgorod is poisoned in Tmutorokan by a Byzantine agent.

## 1068
The forces of Iziaslav are defeated by the Cumans.

Outraged by the conduct of Iziaslav with respect to the Cumans, the Kievan populace revolts and proclaims Vseslav of Polotsk prince of Kiev. Vseslav, however, is captured by his cousins and then kidnapped by the Poles, whose assistance had been sought by Iziaslav.

## 1073
Iziaslav is driven from Kiev by his brothers. He takes refuge in Poland and then in Germany, where he appeals unsuccessfully for assistance from Pope Gregory VII.

## 1076
The death of Sviatoslav, son of Iaroslav, opens the way for Iziaslav to return to Kiev.

## 1078
Iziaslav is assassinated by his nephew, Oleg Sviatoslavich of Chernigov.

## 1078-1093
Vsevolod, third son of Iaroslav, reigns as prince of Kiev.

## 1091
The Tmutorokan region gains its freedom from the authority of the Kievan princes.

## 1093-1113
Reign of Sviatopolk, son of Iziaslav, as prince of Kiev.

## 1096
The Cumans attack Kiev and succeed in entering the city.

## 1097–1100

Congresses of princes, led by Vladimir Monomakh (son of Vsevolod), meet in Lübeck in 1097 and in Vitichev in 1100, in an effort to end conflicts over succession. The passing of titles from father to son is instituted, except for the title of grand prince of Kiev, which continues to be governed by the former rules, whereby brothers succeed brothers but the claim of the prince's eldest son is equal or superior to that of the prince's third brother.

## 1103

A congress of princes is convened to devise a plan for the common defense of the borders on the steppe.

## 1111

Vladimir Monomakh wins a great victory over the Cumans.

## 1113

A popular revolt erupts in Kiev against the financial policies of Prince Sviatopolk. The populace appeals to Vladimir Monomakh, who becomes prince of Kiev and takes legislative action to regularize tax collection.

Mstislav, son of Vladimir, becomes prince of Novgorod.

## 1115

Oleg Sviatoslavich of Chernigov, an enemy of Vladimir, dies.

## 1116

The Kievans win a new victory over the Cumans.

## 1117

Vsevolod, son of Mstislav, becomes prince of Novgorod.

## 1125

Vladimir Monomakh dies.

## 1125–1132

Mstislav, son of Vladimir, reigns as grand prince of Kiev.

## 1130–1136

Very tense relations persist between the Novgorodian oligarchy and the state of Kiev.

## 1132–1139

Iaropolk II, son of Vladimir, reigns as grand prince of Kiev.

## 1136

Vsevolod Mstislavich is expelled from Novgorod by decision of the *veche*, an assembly of adult males. This marks the beginning of Novgorodian independence.

## 1139–1146

Vsevolod II Olgovich, grandson of Sviatoslav, reigns as grand prince of Kiev after having ousted Viacheslav, who was to have succeeded his brother Iaropolk II. This provokes a lasting conflict between the descendants of Sviatoslav and those of Vladimir Monomakh.

## 1146–1154

Iziaslav II, son of Mstislav, reigns as grand prince of Kiev. (In choosing Iziaslav, the Kievans rejected Igor Olgovich, Vsevolod II's brother.)

## 1147

Igor Olgovich, who had become a monk, is assassinated by the Kievans.

A regional chronicle first mentions Moscow, which was founded by Yuri Dolgoruky, son of Vladimir Monomakh and the first independent prince of Suzdal.

## 1149–1151

A struggle takes place between Iziaslav II and his uncle Yuri Dolgoruky, prince of

# Spread of Religion in Eastern Europe and Central Asia

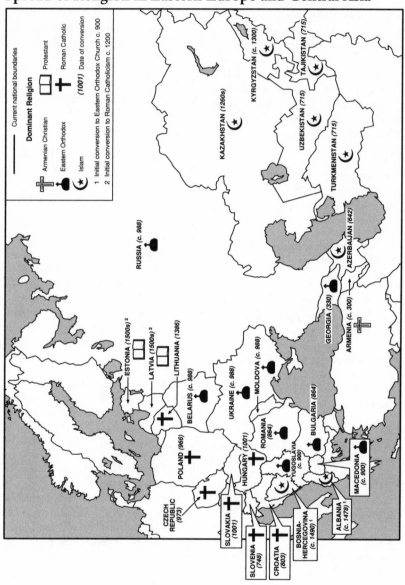

Rostov-Suzdal, for the title of grand prince of Kiev.

## 1151

A war is waged between the forces of Iziaslav II, the grand prince of Kiev who is allied with Hungary, and those of Vladimirko of Galicia.

## 1154–1157

Yuri Dolgoruky reigns as grand prince of Kiev. His son, Andrei Bogoliubsky, takes the title of prince of Rostov-Suzdal and reinforces his new capital, Vladimir, on the Kliazma River.

## 1167–1169

Mstislav II Iziaslavich of Volynia reigns as grand prince of Kiev.

## 1169

*March.* Andrei Bogoliubsky captures and pillages Kiev, placing his younger brother Gleb in charge of the city. Andrei strips Kiev of its political supremacy (symbolized by the title of grand prince, which he takes for himself and transfers to his own principality of Vladimir). This marks the beginning of the decline of the Kievan state.

## 1170

The Suzdalians are defeated at Novgorod.

## 1171

Upon the death of Gleb, Andrei Bogoliubsky gives the city of Kiev to the Rostislaviches of Smolensk; Roman is made the prince of Kiev.

## 1173

Mstislav the Brave, prince of Smolensk, revolts against Andrei Bogoliubsky.

## 1174

Andrei Bogoliubsky is murdered by his boyars in his palace at Bogoliubovo. The assassination reflects the rivalry between the new capital, Vladimir, and the former centers of the principality, Rostov and Suzdal.

# Religious and Cultural Life

## 988

The Kievans are baptized at the insistence of Vladimir.

The Greek Theophylact is nominated metropolitan of Kiev (probable date).

## 990–996

The Church of the Dormition (also known as the "Church of the Tithe") is constructed in Kiev.

## 996

Vladimir inaugurates the Church of the Tithe, to which he gives "one-tenth of [his] goods and one-tenth of the revenues of [his] cities." He assigns priests from Kherson to serve in this church, and he has the remains of his grandmother, the future Saint Olga, interred there.

## Circa 1000

The dioceses of Belgorod and Novgorod are established.

## Early 11th Century

Chernigov becomes the residence of Mstislav, brother of Iaroslav, and a diocese is established there.

## 1007

Vladimir warmly receives Bruno de Querfurt (the future Saint Boniface), who passes through Kiev on a journey to the Pechenegs.

## 1018

After the conquest of Bulgaria by the Byzantine Empire, a number of literate Bulgars find refuge in Kiev. Bringing their liturgical books with them, the Bulgars will play an essential role in the diffusion of writing among the Eastern Slavs by introducing the use of the Cyrillic alphabet.

## Circa 1023

A school is established at Kursk.

## 1024

Pagan demonstrations take place in Suzdal, and many women are killed. The city of Iaroslav is established on the Volga River.

## Circa 1030

Iaroslav creates a school for clergy and laymen in Novgorod.

## 1030–1035

The Church of the Savior is constructed in Chernigov. The remains of the city's founder, Mstislav, will be interred there in 1036.

## 1034

A treaty between Iaroslav and the Byzantine Emperor recognizes the jurisdiction of the patriarch of Constantinople over the Russian Church. (The existence of this treaty is disputed by some historians.)

## Circa 1035–1039

Theopempt is nominated metropolitan of Kiev (he is the first metropolitan to be verified by sources).

## 1036

Iaroslav names the literate Russian Luke Jidiata bishop of Novgorod at the time of the installation of his son Vladimir as prince of the city.

## After 1036

The diocese of Yuriev (Kaniev) is established.

## 1037–1041

The Cathedral of St. Sophia of Kiev is constructed.

## Circa 1040

The compilation of the first portion of the *Primary Chronicle* begins.

## 1045–1050

The Cathedral of St. Sophia of Novgorod is constructed.

## 1049

The Russian monk and theologian Hilarion drafts his sermon "On Law and Grace," a panegyric to Vladimir.

## 1051–1054

Hilarion is made metropolitan of Kiev by Iaroslav, without the accord of Constantinople.

The monasteries of St. George, St. Irene and St. Demetrios are founded in Kiev.

The earliest portions of *Russian Justice* are drafted.

## After 1051

After a long stay at Mount Athos, the hermit Anthony, originally from Chernigov, installs himself in a cave in the hills of Kiev.

## 1052–1053

At Vychgorod, the Church of SS. Roman and David is constructed to house the remains of Boris and Gleb.

## After 1054

A diocese is established at Pereiaslavl, a Russian outpost city on the steppe.

## 1055

The metropolitan Ephrem, named by Constantinople to replace Hilarion, suspends Luke Jidiata of Novgorod for three years.

## 1056–1057

The "Ostromir Gospel," the oldest Russian manuscript, is copied from a Bulgarian original.

## Circa 1060

The patriarch converts the bishoprics of Chernigov and Pereiaslavl into metropolitanates, in recognition of their role in the fight against the Cumans.

The diocese of Polotsk is created, and a church dedicated to Saint Sophia is built there. The hermitages situated in the caves of Kiev transform themselves into one of the first cenobitic communities under the direction of Barlaam.

## 1065

Theodosius founds the Monastery of the Caves in Kiev.

## 1068

Anthony, a monk, is chased out of Kiev by Prince Iziaslav because of his encouragement of a revolt that had forced the prince to temporarily flee the city.

## 1070

The Vydubetsky Monastery is established south of Kiev.

## 1071

Revolts directed by the *volkhvy* ("sorcerers") break out at Suzdal; they are severely repressed by the prince.

## 1072

*Russian Justice* (short version) is promulgated.

Boris and Gleb are canonized at Vychgorod; their canonization is preceded by the writing of *The Lay of the Martyrs*.

## 1073

Anthony of the Caves, spiritual founder of the first Russian monastery, dies.

The first *Izborniki Sviatoslava*, a collection of Sviatoslav's writings, is compiled.

## 1076

Leonce, bishop of Rostov, is martyred during a pagan revolt.

The second *Izborniki Sviatoslava* is compiled.

## 1076–1089

With the mandate of the metropolitan John II Prodrom, the framework of the Russian Church is strengthened.

## 1077

The Abbey of the Caves is completed at Kiev.

## 1079–1085

The *Lectio*, which deals with the deaths of Boris and Gleb, is written by Nestor, a monk of the Caves.

## 1082

Metropolitan John II deplores the fact that communion is being ignored by soldiers taking part in border marches.

## 1086

A women's monastery dedicated to Saint Andrew is founded in Kiev. A cult for this saint begins to develop in Russia.

## 1086–1088

At the insistence of Princes Iaropolk and Sviatopolk, dioceses are established at Vladimir (in Volynia) and at Turov (in Polotsk).

## Circa 1088

The *Life of Theodosius* is compiled by the monk Nestor.

## 1089

The *Constitution of the Church* is compiled by Metropolitan John II.

## 1089–1090

The Cathedral of St. Michael is erected at Pereiaslavl.

## 1091

According to Russian sources, the last of the pagan revolts occurs at Rostov.

The remains of Theodosius are interred at the Abbey of the Caves in Kiev, and a new local cult develops.

## 1096

A new compilation of the *Primary Chronicle* is prepared.

Upon the death of its bishop, Isaiah, the diocese of Rostov is provisionally shut down.

## 1104–1109

The abbot Daniel journeys to Palestine.

## 1108

Theodosius, who is called "the head of all of the monastic orders in Russia," is canonized.

In Kiev, the Monastery of St. Michael ("with the golden roof") is founded by Prince Sviatopolk, who will be interred there.

Nicetas, bishop of Novgorod, dies.

## 1113

The collegiate of St. Nicholas is established in Novgorod by Prince Mstislav.

## 1115

The relics of Saints Boris and Gleb are moved to the new collegiate of Vychgorod.

## 1116

A revised version of the *Primary Chronicle* is prepared by Sylvester, a monk at the Vydubetsky Monastery, after Vladimir

Monomakh withdraws the commission to prepare a new version from the Monastery of the Caves.

## 1117–1119

A monastery dedicated to the nativity of the Virgin is built in Novgorod.

## 1119–1120

The Abbey of St. George is constructed in Novgorod.

## Before 1128

The Monastery of the Savior is founded in Polotsk by Evfrosinia, granddaughter of Prince Vseslav of Polotsk, who became a nun.

## Circa 1130

The first princely charters are granted for the monasteries of Novgorod.

## 1136

The diocese of Smolensk is established on the initiative of Rostislav, founder of the city.

## Circa 1136

Yuri Dolgoruky restores the diocese of Rostov, the seat of which had been vacant since the death of Isaiah.

## 1140

The Monastery of St. Cyril of Dorogozhich is founded in Kiev.

## 1147

A schism occurs between the metropolitanate of Kiev and the dioceses of Novgorod, Smolensk, Polotsk and Suzdal when Iziaslav II has Klim Smoliatich elected metropolitan of Kiev without the consent of the patriarch of Constantinople.

## 1149–1151

Klim is forced to leave Kiev.

## 1150

The relics of Igor Olgovich, who was murdered by the Kievans in 1147 soon after he had become a monk, are moved to Chernigov.

## Before 1152

The Varangian Church of St. Olaf is constructed in Novgorod.

## 1155

Klim is permanently expelled from Kiev by Yuri Dolgoruky, who asks the patriarch to name a new metropolitan; Bishop Constantine I is designated. Novgorod obtains ecclesiastical autonomy as a result of the loyalty of its bishop, Niphon, to the patriarchy of Constantinople during the schism with Kiev.

## 1156

Arcade, successor to Niphon, is the first bishop elected by the *veche* of Novgorod.

## 1158–1160

The Cathedral of Vladimir is constructed.

## 1158–1169

A conflict erupts between Andrei Bogoliubsky and the metropolitan over the creation of a metropolitanate at Vladimir. The Byzantine prelate reaffirms the uniqueness of Kiev as the "Metropolitanate of all Russia" and authorizes only the establishment of an episcopal seat at Vladimir.

## 1164

Andrei Bogoliubsky moves the icon of the Virgin of Tenderness, which had been housed at the women's monastery in Vychgorod, to Vladimir.

## 1165

Novgorod becomes a full voting archbishopric.

## Circa 1165

The Church of the Intercession is constructed on the Nerl River.

## 1166

Archbishop Elijah of Novgorod is instructed in the liturgical rites and disciplines.

## 1168

Abbot Polikarp of the Monastery of the Caves is condemned by Metropolitan Constantine II because of a quarrel over the obligation to abstain from eating meat on holidays.

## 1169

The patriarch recalls Constantine II, who had been tactless in his relations with the Russian clergy. With the support of Andrei Bogoliubsky, Polikarp becomes archimandrite.

The Russian Monastery of St. Pantaleon is founded on Mount Athos.

## 1170

The cult of the Virgin of the Sign emerges in Novgorod.

# Appanage Russia and the Mongol Conquest

The decline of Kiev, perceptible from the second half of the 12th century, continued during the years prior to the invasion of the country by the Mongols. During this time, Kiev's political rivals were able to significantly weaken the principality, and Kiev's economic prosperity, which had largely rested on its trade with Byzantium, also ebbed. Kiev's economic decline was attributable primarily to the insecurity of trade routes, which were constantly menaced by the presence of the Cumans, and to the waning of commercial activity throughout the Byzantine Empire.

The political and economic decline of Kiev encouraged the migrations of peoples and the emergence of new centers of power: Volynia and Galicia to the southwest, Smolensk and Novgorod to the north, and Tver and Vladimir-Suzdal to the northeast were, practically speaking, freed of their dependence on Kiev. By the end of the 12th century, the political center of gravity of the Kievan state had shifted to the northeast, to Vladimir-Suzdal, which had become one of the most powerful of the Russian principalities. Ruled by the descendants of Vladimir Monomakh, who had conquered Kiev and taken the title of grand prince, Vladimir-Suzdal owed its rapid development in large part to its control over the Volga trade route.

Despite the hegemonic designs of its princes, Suzdal was unable to assume the dominant role formerly played by Kiev, and the consequent disintegration of the Rus served to accentuate the political cleavages among the appanage principalities. The competing interests of the principalities, and the resulting conflicts, facilitated the conquest of the country by the Mongols. Following a preliminary campaign in 1223 that reached as far as the Kalka River (near the Sea of Azov), the Tatars (as the Mongols were called by the Russians) ravaged the entire territory between 1236 and 1240. The invasion was correctly perceived at the time as a cataclysm. It caused the ruin of every region of the country except Novgorod, provoked new mass movements of the population of Kiev toward less-menaced territories to the west, and isolated the north from the rest of the country.

Novgorod and Pskov, which had not been occupied by the Mongols, were attacked first by the Swedes and then by German knights from Livonia. These western invaders were defeated by Alexander, prince of Vladimir, who later bore the surname "Nevsky" on account of his victory over the Swedes on the banks of the Neva River. To the southwest, the principalities of Galicia and Volynia, sometimes united, sometimes separated, were in the midst of expansion under the dynasties of Daniel and Roman; increasingly, they shielded themselves from western influences. The ethnic differences between the Eastern Slavs—the future Ukrainians, Belorussians and Great Russians—were also becoming clear-cut.

During a century and a half, the state founded by the Mongols on the lower Volga—the Golden Horde—wielded its power over the principalities. It exploited the princely rivalries for its own gain, and it used the terror that it inspired to exercise its domination and to collect tribute. Little is known about this period, which was characterized by a general decline in activities and institutions. Only the Church was able to maintain itself as a unifying force, successfully preserving the feeling amongst the Russians of a shared cultural patrimony.

The principality of Moscow gradually supplanted that of Vladimir-Suzdal, from which it became separated in the first half of the 13th century. The creation of a dynasty (Daniel's) that turned out to be stable, and the extension of the principality through colonization of new lands to the north, provided the basis for Moscow's subsequent expansion beginning in the middle of the 14th century. But the key factor in the development of the principality was the activity of its princes: Rivals of their counterparts in Tver, they schemed with the Golden Horde to obtain the title of grand prince. After having handled the Tatars skillfully for a century, the Muscovites became sufficiently powerful to go on the offensive. In 1380, with the active support of the Church, they battled the Mongols of the khan Mamai at Kulikovo, near the Don River. The great victory won by Prince Dmitri (who later took the surname "Donskoi") marked the emergence of a new set of power relations in the region and pierced the myth of the invincibility of the Mongols. Although symbolic and short-lived, this victory was of fundamental importance to the emergence of a national consciousness that came to be associated with the principality of Moscow.

# The Principality of Vladimir-Suzdal

## 1174–1176

Rostov and Suzdal enter into conflict with Vladimir and Pereiaslavl. Rostov and Suzdal appeal to the nephews of Andrei Bogoliubsky, while Vladimir and Pereiaslavl appeal to his younger brothers and emerge victorious. Vsevolod III Iurevich (of the "Large Brood") takes the title of grand prince of Vladimir. As a result of this conflict, the principality of Vladimir gains preponderance over Kiev.

## Eastern Europe and Central Asia c. 1200

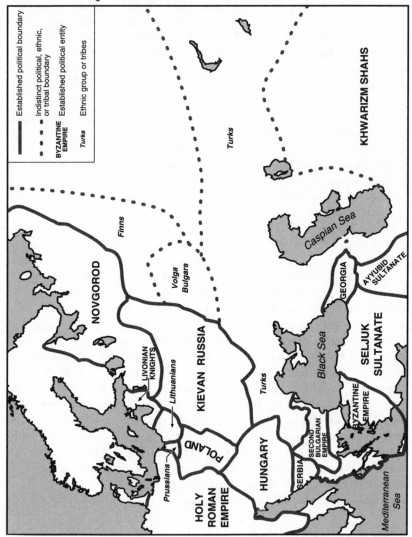

## 1200

The principality of Vladimir is strengthened by the creation of an episcopate for the city of Riazan, which Vsevolod detaches from the huge diocese of Chernigov.

## 1207

In Vladimir, Vsevolod imprisons the princes of Riazan and their family, who had rebelled against his authority. The population of Riazan, after having resisted the grand prince, is deported and the city is burned.

## 1212

Vsevolod III dies. In his will, he has designated his youngest son, Yuri, to succeed him. His eldest son, Constantine, does not recognize the decision of his father and enters into conflict with Yuri.

## 1214

The dissension in the principality of Vladimir leads to the creation of two separate dioceses, Rostov and Vladimir-Suzdal.

## 1216

Constantine, supported by Mstislav Mstislavich ("the Bold") and the Novgorodians, wins a decisive victory over his brothers on the banks of the Lipitsa River (in Poland) and takes the title of grand prince.

## 1219

Constantine dies and is succeeded by Yuri II.

# The Mongol Invasion

## 1223

*May 31.* The Mongols first appear within the borders of the Kievan state. The Cumans appeal to the princes of the southern territories to repulse the armies of the Mongol Subutai. The coalition is defeated on the Kalka River, near the Sea of Azov, but the Mongols turn back.

## 1237

A new invasion is launched by the Mongols, who cross the middle Volga and attack central Russia.

*December 31.* The Mongol army of Batu conquers Riazan; the population is exterminated and the city is burned.

## 1238

With the ravaging of Moscow by the Mongols, the principality of Vladimir is threatened. Grand Prince Yuri II withdraws to the northeast, beyond the Volga, but leaves most of his garrison in the city.

*February 7.* After a short siege, the Mongols storm Vladimir and massacre its populace.

*February 8.* Suzdal is occupied by the Mongols.

*March 4.* The Mongols set out in pursuit of Yuri II and annihilate his army on the Sit River. Yuri is killed in the fighting.

*March 5.* Batu marches on Tver and Torzhok, which he besieges, and penetrates the territory of Novgorod, but the thaw halts his offensive and the threat to Novgorod is averted.

## 1239

Batu's army joins the southern detachment of Mongka in the Don River valley, and the Mongols spend the year there.

## 1240

The Mongols go on the offensive again at the beginning of the summer. Batu sacks Pereiaslavl, Chernigov and the southern Russian principalities.

*December 6.* Kiev is conquered and destroyed, and all of its inhabitants are massacred.

Following the siege of Kiev, the Mongols ravage Volynia and Galicia. All of southern Russia is devastated.

Once the Mongols have conquered the principalities, the bishoprics of Pereiaslavl, Belgorod and Iuriev disappear.

## 1242

Informed of the death of the Great Khan Ugedey, Batu returns to Mongolia.

## 1243

Iaroslav, the son of Vsevolod, and prince of Vladimir since 1238, is installed by the Golden Horde as grand prince of Vladimir.

## 1246–1252

Andrei II, son of Iaroslav, reigns as grand prince of Vladimir.

## 1252–1263

Alexander Iaroslavich Nevsky reigns as grand prince of Vladimir.

## 1257–1259

The Mongols conduct a census of the Russians (with the exception of the clergy) to determine the tribute (*vykhod*) owed to the Golden Horde.

Numerous revolts are carried out by the Slavs against the Mongol occupation forces, and especially against the functionaries (*basmaks*) determining the tribute.

## 1263–1272

Iaroslav II Iaroslavich reigns as grand prince of Vladimir.

## 1272–1276

Basil Iaroslavich of Kostroma reigns as grand prince of Vladimir.

## 1276–1281

Dmitri Alexandrovich of Pereiaslavl reigns as grand prince of Vladimir.

## 1281–1283

Andrei III Alexandrovich of Gorodets reigns as grand prince of Vladimir.

## 1283–1293

Dmitri Alexandrovich of Pereiaslavl again reigns as grand prince of Vladimir.

## 1293–1304

Andrei III Alexandrovich of Gorodets again succeeds Dmitri as grand prince of Vladimir.

# The Principalities of Moscow and Tver

## 1147 (retrospect)

Moscow is mentioned for the first time in a regional chronicle.

## 1263

Alexander Nevsky gives Moscow to his son Daniel (1261–1303) as an appanage.

## 1301

Seized from the principality of Riazan, Kolomna (a territory that encompasses the inferior course of the Moskva River and its confluence with the Oka) is reattached to Moscow.

## 1303–1325

Yuri Danilovich, Daniel's son, becomes prince of Moscow and annexes the territory of Mozhaisk, taken from the prince of Smolensk.

## 1304–1318

Michael Iaroslavich of Tver reigns as grand prince of Vladimir.

## 1317 or 1318

Yuri Danilovich of Moscow marries the sister of the Great Khan; the Great Khan accords him the title of grand prince.

## 1318

Grand Prince Michael of Tver crushes the Muscovites and captures the wife of Yuri.

## 1319

Accused by Yuri of having poisoned the sister of the Great Khan, Michael of Tver appears at the Court of the Horde and is executed. Yuri's title as grand prince of Moscow is confirmed.

## 1322

The Great Khan gives the title of grand prince of Moscow to Dmitri

Mikhailovich of Tver (he of "the fearsome eyes").

**1324**

Yuri travels to the Court of the Golden Horde seeking a retrocession of his title.

**1325**

Yuri is murdered at the Court of the Golden Horde by Dmitri of Tver, who is immediately executed. Alexander of Tver, Dmitri's brother, becomes grand prince of Moscow, and Ivan I Danilovich (popularly known as Ivan Kalita) is recognized as a prince of Moscow.

**1326**

Peter, metropolitan of Kiev and of all Russia, installs himself at Moscow, which becomes the religious capital of Russia.

**1327**

Aided by the Muscovites, the Mongols devastate Tver. Alexander flees to Pskov, then to Lithuania.

**1328–1341**

Ivan I Kalita reigns as grand prince of Moscow. He is charged with determining the tributes owed to the Golden Horde by the other Russian princes.

**1337**

Alexander is authorized by the Mongols to return to Tver.

**1338**

Alexander of Tver is executed at the Court of the Golden Horde.

**1341–1353**

Simeon the Proud, son of Ivan Kalita, reigns as grand prince of Moscow.

**1353**

Simeon the Proud dies of the plague. His testament exhorts his heirs to obey Alexis Pleshcheyev, the future metropolitan.

Simeon's brother, Ivan II Ivanovich ("the Meek"), takes the title of grand prince of Moscow.

**1359**

Upon the death of Ivan II, the title of grand prince of Moscow falls to Dmitri of Suzdal; Metropolitan Alexis assumes the regency of the principality.

**1363**

With the support of the Muscovite boyars, Alexis obtains from the Golden Horde the title of grand prince for the young Dmitri, son of Ivan II. The dynasty of Daniel continues uninterrupted.

**1368**

Olgerd of Lithuania, allied with Michael of Tver (who has received the title of grand prince), ravages the environs of Moscow but does not succeed in taking the city.

**1372**

Olgerd suffers another defeat at Moscow.

**1374**

Moscow annexes Rostov.

**1375**

Michael of Tver surrenders to Dmitri and recognizes the preeminence of Moscow.

**1377**

Mongol forces led by Arab-Shah defeat the Russians on the banks of the Piana River and pillage Riazan and Nizhni Novgorod.

**1378**

*August 11.* Dmitri wins a victory over the Mongols on the Vozha River. Encouraged by this success, the prince attempts to form a league of Russian principalities against the occupiers.

**1380**

*March 8.* Dmitri, supported by the troops of some 20 principalities, inflicts a serious defeat on the army of Khan Mamai in the Battle of Kulikovo Field. This shatters the myth of the invincibility of the Mongols and marks the birth of a Russian national spirit. The victory, won near the Don River, gains Dmitri the surname "Donskoi."

## 1382

Dmitri Donskoi must submit to the new kahn, Tokhtamysh, who has captured and destroyed Moscow.

## 1389

Dmitri Donskoi dies.

# Novgorod

## 1195

A treaty is entered into with the Germans.

## 1206

Vsevolod III places his eldest son Constantine in charge of Novgorod.

## 1209

A revolt breaks out against the *posadnik* Dmitri (first civil magistrate of Novgorod), a loyal servant of Vsevolod III.

## 1216

Novgorod defeats Suzdal on the banks of the Lipitsa.

## 1222

Iaroslav Vsevolodovich seizes control of Novgorod from his brother Constantine.

## 1233

A treaty is entered into with the Germans.

## 1236

Alexander, son of Iaroslav, becomes prince of Novgorod.

## 1240

Alexander defeats the Swedes on the banks of the Neva River, earning him the surname "Nevsky." Soon after this victory he is dismissed by the *veche* of Novgorod.

## 1241

The Teutonic Knights capture Izborsk and Pskov, and threaten Novgorod.

## 1242

Alexander Nevsky is recalled by the *veche* of Novgorod to battle the Teutonic Knights.

*April 5.* Alexander Nevsky scores a definitive victory over the Teutonic Knights in a battle on the ice of Lake Chud (also known as Lake Peipus), near Pskov.

## 1245

Alexander Nevsky expels the Lithuanians from Novgorodian territory.

## 1259

The Novgorodians revolt against the census imposed by the Mongols. Judging them to be less dangerous than the western invaders, Alexander Nevsky protects the envoys from the Golden Horde.

## 1286

The Hanseatic League (a commercial league of northern European cities) establishes a branch in Novgorod.

## 1348

Pskov gains its independence from Novgorod and becomes a free city.

# The Principalities of Volynia, Galicia and Kiev

## 1153–1187 (retrospect)

Iaroslav Osmomysl Vladimirovich of Galicia, the only southwestern prince to attempt to subdue the boyars, reigns over Galicia.

## 1173, 1180–1181, 1194–1201, 1203–1204

Rurik Rostislavich reigns as prince, then as grand prince, of Kiev.

## 1185

Prince Igor of Novgorod-Seversk wages an unsuccessful campaign against the Cumans. This campaign inspires the famous poetic account *The Lay of the Host of Igor*.

## 1187

Iaroslav Osmomysl dies. Andrew of Hungary attempts to seize Galicia.

## 1187–1197

Vladimir Iaroslavich reigns as prince of Galicia.

## 1197

Roman, prince of Volynia since 1172, reunites Galicia and Volynia under his rule.

## 1202

The Kievans welcome Roman of Volynia, and Rurik Rostislavich flees.

## 1203

With the aid of the Cumans, Rurik Rostislavich takes and sacks Kiev.

## 1203–1204

Roman of Volynia wages a victorious campaign against the Cumans.

## 1205

Roman of Volynia is assassinated by the Poles. His sons being too young to succeed him, Galicia is torn by civil wars and suffers Polish and Hungarian interventions.

## 1214–1218

Intending to give Galicia to his son Koloman, Andrew II of Hungary tries to force it to submit to Hungarian and Catholic influence. To effect this, he proposes to place the territory under the jurisdiction of Rome, putting forward, for the first time, the notion of uniatism.

## 1221

Daniel, the son of Roman of Volynia, having come of age, becomes prince of Volynia.

## 1223

Dominicans who had come to Russia are expelled from Kiev by Prince Vladimir. (The expulsion reflects the strong reaction against the Roman Catholic Church that developed following the sacking of Constantinople by the Crusaders in 1204.)

## 1238

Galicia comes under the authority of Daniel of Volynia.

## 1240

Fleeing the Mongols, Michael of Kiev and Daniel of Volynia enter Hungarian territory. Daniel's attempt to mount a crusade against the Mongols fails. Following the devastation of western Russia by the Mongols, Daniel attempts to repopulate the region by bringing in Hungarian, Polish and German settlers. Lvov is founded and will replace Kiev as the center of commerce in the southwest.

## 1253
Daniel accepts a union with Rome and receives the royal crown from Pope Innocent IV. His son, Leon, marries Constance of Hungary.

## 1264–1301
Leon reigns as prince of Volynia.

## 1301
Leon dies. His death inaugurates a period of decline for Volynia and Galicia. Volynia will be gradually integrated into Lithuania. Galicia will be the subject of conflict between Poland and Hungary.

## 1349
The Poles take Galicia. This marks the beginning of Galicia's submission to the Kingdom of Poland.

## 1387
The Poles seize control of all of Galicia at the time of their victory over the Hungarians.

# Religious and Cultural Life

## 1173 (retrospect)
Evfrosinia dies in Jerusalem. She will soon become the patron saint of Polotsk, her city of birth, and, later, of all of Belorussia.

## 1184
The German Church of St. Peter is founded in Novgorod.

## 1190
Leontius of Rostov is canonized by John, his distant successor as bishop of Rostov. Leontius was martyred during a pagan revolt in 1076.

## 1192
Barlaam founds the Monastery of the Transfiguration at Novgorod.

## Circa 1200
The diocese of Riazan is created. The *Chronicle of Kiev* is compiled by Moses, abbot of the Vydubetsky Monastery.

## 1202–1206
Vsevolod of the Large Brood constructs the Monastery of the Nativity of the Virgin at Vladimir.

## 1206
The wife of Vsevolod of the Large Brood takes holy vows in the Monastery of the Dormition at Vladimir that she and her husband had founded.

## 1214
Suzdal and Vladimir are definitively separated from the diocese of Rostov.

## Circa 1220
The dioceses of Przemysl and Uhrusk-Chelm are created. Anthony, archbishop of Novgorod, is ordered by Metropolitan Michael to vacate his archepiscopal seat to become the head of the bishopric of Przemysl.

## 1226
Simeon, bishop of Suzdal and one of the authors of the *Paterikon of Kiev* (an anthology of the lives of the saints of the Monastery of the Caves), dies.

## 1228
Patriarch Germanus II sends a letter to the metropolitan of Kiev, Cyril I, reminding him of the ban on Russian princes interfering in ecclesiastical affairs.

## 1230
In a solemn service, the remains of Abraham of Smolensk are interred in the Church of the Dormition, in Vladimir.

## 1230–1260

Serapion, bishop of Vladimir, delivers sermons interpreting the Mongol invasion as a just punishment inflicted on the principalities for the fratricidal struggles among the princes.

## 1241

Memmon, the bishop of Przemysl, must flee the city because of his plotting against the prince. Captured by Daniel's troops, he is arrested while in possession of numerous articles of wealth—an example of the sort of abuse of power of which prelates were often accused.

## 1245–1247

The Franciscan friar John of Plano Carpini journeys to Russia and Mongolia. He seeks to convert the Mongols and to plan an eventual crusade against them.

## Before 1250

The diocese of Lutsk (in Volynia) is established.

## After 1250

The diocese of Tver is established.

## 1261

The diocese of Sarai (capital of the Golden Horde) is established.

## 1263

Alexander Nevsky, already considered a patron saint of the country, dies. He becomes the subject of a local cult, and a compilation of his life is written. (He will be officially canonized in 1547.)

## 1273

A synod of the Russian church takes place at Vladimir. The metropolitan of Kiev, Cyril II, establishes a set of rules at this synod that fix, in particular, the conditions that will govern the recruitment of priests.

## 1299

The abbot of the Monastery of St. George, at Novgorod, will henceforth hold the title of archimandrite. This solidifies the preeminence of the monastery in the local ecclesiastical hierarchy.

## Circa 1300

Metropolitan Maxim (1287–1305) moves from Kiev to Vladimir, marking the decline of the metropolitanate of Kiev.

## 1311

A chapel dedicated to Vladimir, "the Apostle of Russia," is consecrated at Novgorod. This is indicative of the belated emergence of a cult devoted to the first Christian prince that will develop steadily thereafter.

A council condemns a Novgorodian priest who had refused the monastic order.

## 1326

Peter, the metropolitan of Kiev, installs himself at Moscow, where he dies and comes to be venerated as a saint. Henceforth, all of the metropolitans "of Kiev and of all Russia" will reside at Moscow. Kiev will not reemerge as a metropolitan seat until the following century, when it is under Lithuanian domination.

## 1328

Theognost establishes the metropolitanate of Kiev at Moscow.

## Circa 1335

Sergius of Radonezh founds a monastery 40 miles north of Moscow. This will become the Monastery of the Holy Trinity-St. Sergius, one of the most important religious and cultural centers in the country.

## Second Half of the 14th Century

The first great Russian heresy appears. The *strigolniki* sect in Pskov and Novgorod will be repressed and wiped out at the start of the 15th century.

## 1355

Alexis is consecrated metropolitan.

## 1356

A synod, convoked by Patriarch Callistos I, confirms Alexis as the metropolitan of Kiev, although officially his metropolitan seat is at Moscow. The patriarch grants to Roman the title of metropolitan of Lithuania.

## 1361

Upon the death of Roman, Alexis obtains from the patriarch the suppression of the metropolitanate of Lithuania.

## 1370

The frescoes in the Church of St. Theodore in Novgorod are painted.

## 1377

The *Laurentian Chronicle* is written.

## 1378

Metropolitan Alexis dies.

Theopanes (Feofan) the Greek paints frescoes in the Church of the Transfiguration, in Novgorod.

# Chapter 4                                    1389–1533

## The Rise of Moscow

Following the victory of Dmitri Donskoi over the Mongols in 1380, the prestige of Moscow conferred on its prince a moral authority over the whole of northern Russia that contributed to the principality's emergence as the center of the future Muscovite state. The 15th century was characterized by the process of the "gathering of Russian lands," accomplished under the aegis of Moscow, whose rapid rise astonished contemporaries. The principality also benefitted in this enterprise from a favorable conjuncture: The gradual collapse of the Golden Horde and the dynastic stability of Moscow were key factors in the successes enjoyed by the Moscow princes. The growth of their power brought about the disappearance of the appanages, which laid the foundation for the establishment of a new, centralized Russian state.

During the first half of the 15th century, the Muscovites asserted their ambitions without decisive results. The Duchy of Lithuania and the principality of Tver remained Moscow's primary rivals, and frequent incursions by the Mongols maintained a climate of insecurity within the principality. It was during the reigns of Ivan III and Basil III that the great Muscovite expansions began. The conquest of Tver and of Novgorod by Ivan, and his victorious campaigns against Lithuania, allowed him to take control of many western Russian lands along the upper Oka River. Confirmed by Basil III, these acquisitions encouraged numerous appanages to voluntarily submit themselves to the new power in the region. These expansions reinforced the hegemonic designs of Moscow, which were reflected in the pretensions of its princes to complete sovereignty over all of Russia.

A new political ideology emerged at this time to reinforce the pretensions of Moscow. This ideology rested on the model bequeathed by Byzantium, whose fall in 1453 made Russia the guardian of Orthodoxy. Closely associated with princely power, the Church supported the centralizing policy of Moscow and encouraged the development of court ceremony, which was inaugurated during the reign of Ivan III. During his long reign (from 1493 onward, he called himself *gosudar*, or sovereign), the prestige of Moscow was solidified by the monumental construction of the Kremlin under the direction of Italian architects. Basil III, succeeding Ivan, completed this project.

# Domestic and Foreign Affairs

## 1389

Basil I Dmitrievich becomes grand prince of Moscow.

## 1392–1393

Basil I purchases Nizhni Novgorod from the Golden Horde.

## 1395

The armies of the Turk Tamerlane, after defeating those of the Mongol Tokhtamysh, threaten Moscow and ravage Riazan.

## Circa 1400

The Muscovites mount a victorious campaign against the Volga Bulgars and seize their capital, Great Bulgar.

## 1404

Vitovt, grand duke of Lithuania, annexes Smolensk and Viazma.

## 1408

A Russo-Lithuanian treaty is signed. Basil I agrees with Vitovt to fix the border between their two states at the Ugra River.

Many appanage princes of the western provinces transfer their allegiance from the grand duke of Lithuania to the grand prince of Moscow, recognizing the latter's new power.

Edigey, khan of the Golden Horde, attacks Moscow to punish Basil I for not paying tribute. The principality is devastated. The city of Moscow, however, is not taken, and Basil agrees to submit to the will of the khan.

## 1425

Basil I dies. Vitovt, grand duke of Lithuania and father-in-law of the late prince, becomes guardian of his son and successor, Basil II, whom he defends against the ambitions of Yuri of Galich, brother of Basil I.

The princes of Riazan, Pereiaslavl-Riazanski, Pronsk, Tver and Smolensk, as well as those of the western principalities (including Novoselsk, Odoev and Vorotynsk), swear allegiance to the grand duke of Lithuania.

## 1428

The prince of Pskov renews his allegiance to the grand duke of Lithuania.

## 1430

The death of Vitovt, grand duke of Lithuania, provokes an armed conflict between Basil II and Yuri of Galich, who claims the title of grand prince of Moscow based on the ancient Kievan rules of succession.

The fragmentation of the Golden Horde begins with the creation of the Crimean khanate, which is independent of the great khan.

## 1432

Novgorod accepts the protection of Svidrigailo, grand duke of Lithuania.

## 1434

Yuri of Galich dies. His sons, Basil the Squint-Eyed and Dmitri Shemiaka, continue the conflict with Basil II for possession of Moscow.

## 1436

The Khanate of Kazan is established.

## 1445

Basil II, vanquished by the Mongols of Kazan, is taken prisoner and must pay a very heavy ransom to gain his freedom. Important territorial concessions are made to several Tatar princes.

## 1446

Taking advantage of the discontent of the Muscovites (who are distressed by the concessions of Basil II to the Mongol princes and by Basil's heavy ransom), Dmitri Shemiaka captures Basil and blinds him.

## 1448

With the support of the Mongol princes Kasim and Iakub, Basil II retakes Moscow from Dmitri Shemiaka.

## 1449

Upon the demand of Basil II, the prelates of the Russian Church exhort Dmitri Shemiaka, under threat of excommunication, to abandon his designs on Moscow.

Casimir of Poland, menaced by Michael, son of Grand Duke Sigismund of Lithuania, signs a treaty of friendship with Basil II.

## 1450

Dmitri Shemiaka launches his last offensive against Moscow. He is repulsed with the assistance of the armies of the principality of Tver. Dmitri Shemiaka takes refuge in Novgorod.

## 1451

Mongol contingents in the service of Basil II assist the grand prince in repulsing the assaults of the Hordes of Kazan, Sarai and the Dnieper against the principality of Moscow.

## 1451, 1455 and 1461

Khan Ahmad of the Golden Horde leads unsuccessful campaigns against the principality of Moscow, which refuses to pay tribute.

## 1452

To repay him for services rendered in the struggle against Dmitri Shemiaka, Basil II offers a principality to the Mongol Kasim. It will be known as the principality of Kasimov. This is the first time a Mongol of the ruling dynasty recognizes Russian suzerainty.

## 1453

Dmitri Shemiaka is poisoned in Novgorod.

## 1456

An alliance is established between Moscow and Novgorod.

## 1462

Ivan III succeeds his father, Basil II, becoming grand prince of Moscow. He had already been serving as cosovereign with his blind father.

## 1463

Ivan III purchases the patrimony of the princes of Iaroslavl.

## 1465 and 1472

The Mongols conduct unsuccessful punitive campaigns against Ivan III, who has not been confirmed in his title by the great khan and who refuses to pay tribute.

## 1466

The Khanate of Astrakhan is created.

## 1471

Ivan III leads a campaign against Novgorod, which had just entered into an alliance with Casimir IV, king of Poland and grand duke of Lithuania. Defeated in a battle on the banks of the Shelon River, the Novgorodians are forced to pay an enormous tribute. The *posadnik* Boretsky is executed, and members of the boyar party are deported.

## 1472

Ivan III is remarried to Sophia (Zoe) Paleologue, the niece of the last Byzantine emperor, Constantine XI. By this marriage Ivan III inherits the imperial rights.

Ivan III acquires the city of Dmitrov, appanage of his brother Yuri who had died childless. He also seizes the territory of Perm, which is populated by the Permiaks, Finno-Ugric-speaking tribes that had previously been under the suzerainty of Novgorod.

## 1473

Ivan III allies himself with the Crimean khan, Mengli-Geray, in order to combat the Golden Horde.

## 1474

Ivan III purchases the remaining independent territory of Rostov.

## 1475

Novgorod revolts against the authority of Ivan III, resulting in a new intervention of Muscovite troops.

Ivan III sends an ambassador to Persia in search of potential allies for a move against the Golden Horde.

## 1478

Novgorod capitulates. A number of families are exiled.

The land-tenure system based on the *pomestie* is created: Having confiscated the patrimony of the boyars of Novgorod, Ivan III grants them the benefit of lands (*pomestiia*) in the Moscow region in exchange for their military service and their political loyalty.

## 1480

The Mongol domination of Russia is ended. Ivan III officially announces his refusal to give allegiance to the Golden Horde, and he allies himself with the Crimean khan to fight the great khan, who has the support of the Lithuanians. The armies face one another on opposite banks of the Ugra River, but a confrontation does not take place; the Mongols break camp and return to Sarai.

## 1483

To put an end to Mongol incursions, Prince Theodore Kombsky, the *voevode* (military governor) of Nizhni Novgorod, is charged with preventing the passage of Mongol tribes over Muscovite territory.

## 1485

After having recognized the suzerainty of Moscow, Michael of Tver signs a secret treaty of alliance with Casimir IV, king of Poland and grand duke of Lithuania. Ivan III discovers the existence of this pact and launches a campaign against the principality of Tver. The city, besieged, surrenders without resistance, and Michael flees to Lithuania.

## 1487

Ivan III installs Mohammed-Amin as khan of Kazan and obtains from him an oath of allegiance.

## 1489

Ivan III annexes Viatka, a northern state founded by emigrants from Novgorod and ruled by a *veche*.

## 1491

Ivan III has his brother Andrei the Big arrested for having refused to march against the Mongol hordes, and he confiscates Andrei's domains.

## 1492

Taking advantage of difficulties in the relations between Lithuania and Poland following the death of Casimir IV, Ivan III declares war on Alexander, grand duke of Lithuania, and invades the country with the assistance of Mengli-Geray, the Crimean khan.

## 1493

Ivan III takes the title of Sovereign (*gosudar*) of All Russia.

## 1494

Ivan III and Alexander, grand duke of Lithuania, sign a treaty. Alexander recognizes Ivan as sovereign of all Russia and marries Ivan's daughter Helen.

## 1495

Ivan III expels merchants affiliated with the Hanseatic League from Novgorod and confiscates their businesses.

## Circa 1500

Ivan III inherits a portion of the territory of the principality of Riazan, and receives the other portion under guardianship.

## 1500

The princes of Novgorod-Sversk and of Chernigov ally themselves with Moscow.

Ivan III launches a new campaign against Lithuania, under the pretext of wishing to insure that the Lithuanians respect the Orthodox faith of Helen, wife of Grand Duke Alexander.

## 1503

A ten-year armistice is agreed to by Ivan III and the grand duke of Lithuania. Alexander recognizes Muscovite control over Chernigov, Bryansk, Putivl, Gomel and most of the districts of Smolensk and of Vitebsk.

Moscow scores a victory over the Knights of the Livonian Order, who had attacked Pskov.

## 1505

Ivan III dies. His son, Basil III, becomes grand prince of Moscow. Basil inherits from his father three-quarters of the patrimony of the Muscovite state and obtains the rights of sovereignty.

## 1510

Basil III annexes Pskov.

## 1514

Basil III captures Smolensk from the grand duke of Lithuania.

## 1517–1524

Because of the treason of its leader, Basil III takes control of the last remaining independent territory of the former principality of Riazan.

In an effort to mediate the dispute between the grand duke of Lithuania and Basil III, Emperor Maximilian I of Germany sends his ambassador, Baron Sigismund von Herberstein, to Russia.

## 1519

The grand master of the Teutonic Order delivers a message to Basil III proposing that they join in a league that the Western powers hope will fight the Turks. Basil refuses this initiative.

## 1522

An armistice is agreed to by Lithuania and Moscow. Under its terms, Basil's acquisition of Smolensk is confirmed.

## 1523

The appanages (*udels*) of the princes of Sversk are annexed by Moscow.

## 1526

The second mission to Moscow of Baron Sigismund von Herberstein leads to the extension of the armistice with Lithuania. Maximilian's ambassador writes *Rerum moscovitarium commentarii*, a valuable account of his trip to Russia.

## 1531

Basil III seizes control of Kazan and installs there a khan loyal to Moscow.

## 1533

Basil III dies.

# Religious Life

## 1390–1406

Cyprian, a Bulgarian, reigns as metropolitan of Moscow.

## 1392

Sergius of Radonezh, founder of the Monastery of the Holy Trinity-St. Sergius and initiator of a monastic renewal in Russia, dies.

## 1395

The venerated icon of Our Lady of Vladimir is moved to Moscow as Mongol forces, led by Tamerlane, advance on the region. On the day of the icon's arrival, Tamerlane terminates the campaign and orders a retreat. The icon is thereafter considered the protectress of the city of Moscow.

## 1396

Stephen of Perm, evangelist of the Zyrians and the Permiaks (tribes of Finnish origin), dies.

## 1406

The first hagiographic compilation is prepared by Arsenios, a former monk at the Monastery of the Caves who became bishop of Tver.

## 1415

Vitovt, grand duke of Lithuania, tries to secure the election of Gregory Tsamblak, a Bulgarian, as metropolitan of Kiev. Photius, metropolitan of Moscow, protests, and Gregory is excommunicated by Constantinople.

## 1419

Gregory departs. Orthodox practitioners in Lithuania are again beholden to the metropolitanate of Moscow.

## 1439

The Union of Florence comes into existence at the Council of Florence. Under the union's terms, the patriarch of Constantinople recognizes papal supremacy. Isidore, the metropolitan of Moscow, adheres to the union in the name of the Russian Church.

## 1443

The Council of Russian Churches condemns the Union of Florence and deposes Isidore.

## 1448

A synod of the Russian Church designates Jonas, bishop of Riazan, to succeed Isidore as metropolitan, thereby disregarding the authority of Constantinople. This marks the de facto beginning of the independence of the Russian Church.

## Circa 1450

The Solovetsky Monastery is founded by Baarlam and Germanus, disciples of Sergius of Radonezh.

## 1451

Constantinople confirms Jonas as metropolitan of Russia.

## 1456

By recognizing Gregory, a disciple of Isidore, as metropolitan of Kiev, Casimir IV of Poland tries to weaken Moscow by splitting the Russian Church.

## 1459

A synod of the Russian Church refuses to recognize Gregory. This begins the schism between western Russian and northern Russian ecclesiastical authorities. Shortly, the metropolitan of Moscow will abandon the title of "metropolitan of Kiev and of all Russia" in favor of "metropolitan of Moscow."

The synod recognizes the right of the sovereign to confirm the metropolitan elected by the bishops.

**1470**

The heresy of the Judaizers begins in Novgorod. Adherents deny that Christ is the Messiah and reject the temporal authority of the Church.

**1499**

The first full translation of the Bible into Slavonic is completed. The project is realized through the efforts of Gennadi, archbishop of Novgorod, whose primary goal is to use it as a weapon in the struggle against the Judaizers.

**1503**

A dispute arises between Nilus of Sora (or Nil Sorsky), a hermit who advocates that the Church give up all material possessions, and Joseph, abbot of the Monastery of Volok, who takes the view that the Church ought to play a preponderant role in Russian life and defend its possessions in the name of its societal responsibilities. A Church council decides in favor of Joseph of Volok.

**1504**

A Church council condemns the Judaizers.

**1508**

Nilus of Sora dies.

**1515**

Joseph of Volok dies.

**1516**

At the invitation of Basil III, Maxim the Greek leaves Mount Athos for Moscow, where he is charged with organizing Greek manuscripts and reviewing the translation of Greek liturgical texts into Slavonic.

**1525**

Accused of dogmatic errors (including preaching in favor of Church reform) and of having gone beyond the functions that had been assigned to him, Maxim the Greek is taken away from Moscow and imprisoned.

# Civilization and Culture

**1395**

Theophanes the Greek paints frescoes in the Church of the Archangel in Moscow.

**1399**

Theophanes the Greek paints frescoes in the Church of the Nativity of the Virgin in Moscow.

**Circa 1400**

The *Story of the Massacre of Mamai*, an account of the expedition of Dmitri Donskoi against the Mongols, is written by an anonymous author.

**1405**

Theophanes the Greek and Andrei Rublev decorate the Church of the Annunciation in the Kremlin in Moscow.

**1408**

Andrei Rublev and Daniel the Black paint frescoes in the Church of the Dormition in Vladimir.

**Circa 1410**

Andrei Rublev paints an icon of the Holy Trinity, which is destined for the Monastery of the Holy Trinity-St. Sergius.

**Circa 1420**

The *Hypatian Chronicle* is compiled.

**1422–1427**

Andrei Rublev decorates the principal church of the Monastery of the Holy Trinity-St. Sergius.

## 1428–1430

Andrei Rublev decorates the Spasky Cathedral of the St. Andronic Monastery in Moscow.

## 1430

Andrei Rublev dies.

## 1442

Pakhomi Logofet, a Serbian scholar exiled in Moscow, compiles *Vladimir Polychron*. In this work, he expresses his sympathy for the unification of Russia under the leadership of Moscow.

## 1455

The *Chronicles of Tver* is compiled. The author attacks the ambitions of the principality of Moscow.

## 1466–1472

Athanasius Nikitin, a merchant from Tver, journeys to India. He will write an account of his voyage in *Wanderings Beyond the Three Seas*.

## 1474

At the invitation of Ivan III, the Italian architects and artists Aristotle Fiervanti, Pietro Solario, Alevisio Nuovo and Marco Ruffo come to Moscow.

## 1474–1479

Aristotle Fiervanti constructs the Cathedral of the Dormition in Moscow.

## 1490

Architects from Pskov construct the Collegiate of the Annunciation in Moscow.

## 1497

Ivan III promulgates a *Sudebnik* (legal code) for the entire country (its chief sources are the *Russkaia Pravda* and the Pskov *Sudebnik*).

## 1505–1509

Alevisio Nuovo reconstructs the Collegiate of the Archangel in Moscow.

## 1510

In a letter to Basil III, Philotheus (Filofei), abbot of the Monastery of St. Eleazar in Pskov, formulates the theory that Moscow is the Third Rome.

## 1532

The Church of the Ascension is constructed in Kolomenskoe, near Moscow.

# Muscovite Russia During the Reign of Ivan the Terrible

At the death of Basil III in 1533, his son Ivan IV was only three years old. Young Ivan's mother, Helen Glinsky, assumed the regency and ruled firmly, but her own premature death opened a nine-year interregnum, during which time the boyars took over control of the state (the "Boyar Regency").

Despite his youth, Ivan IV struggled for recognition as the leader of Russia. At the age of 16 he ended the period of boyar rule, had himself crowned, and assumed power in his own right. Surrounded by a group of enlightened counselors—including his tutor Metropolitan Macarius, Prince Andrei Kurbsky and Alexis Adashev—Ivan IV put forward an ambitious reform program during the early years of his reign. He called together the *Zemskii Sobor*, the first full meeting of representatives of Russian estates in the history of the country. He organized a central administration, including formal departments of war, finance and foreign affairs, which replaced a governing apparatus that until then had been rudimentary and chaotic. At the local level, Ivan IV put forward a reform plan whereby elected bodies were charged with overseeing the actions of centrally appointed governing officials.

This liberal period of Ivan IV's reign ended brutally with the establishment of the *oprichnina* (a special, extragovernmental regime through which the service nobility became the czar's docile instrument) and the defeat of the old aristocracy. Ivan IV, who proclaimed himself ruler by divine right, systematically used terror to assure his authority, thereby earning the epithet "the Terrible."

In foreign affairs, the expansion eastward and the attempt to conquer a maritime route to the Baltic Sea were the two focal points of Ivan IV's reign. With the triumphant seizure of Kazan and Astrakhan, the Volga River was opened to colonization and once again became a commercial waterway. Farther to the north, Russians crossed the Urals, and the epic struggle waged by the Don Cossack Ermak was a prelude to the annexation of western Siberia. To the west, however, the Muscovites suffered a series of reversals. In his effort to exploit the weakness of the Teutonic Knights in Livonia, Ivan IV came up against the ambitions of Poland and Sweden. His great adversary, Stephen Bathory, king of Poland, imposed the Peace of Iam-Zapolsky on Ivan IV, forcing him to cede Livonia to Poland. The Swedes, meanwhile, seized Estonia and the Gulf of Finland. Until the reign of Peter the Great, the Baltic would remain closed to the Russians.

## Russian Expansion in Europe (1533–1914)

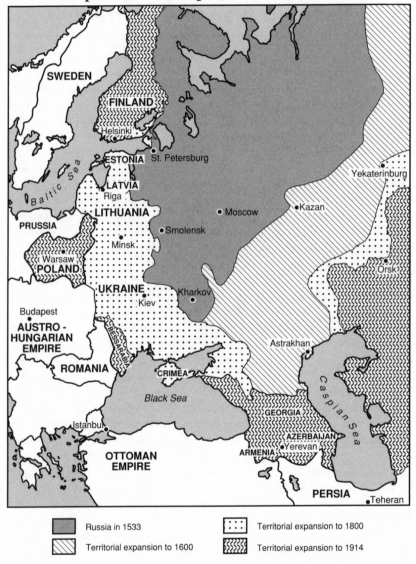

Russia in 1533

Territorial expansion to 1600

Territorial expansion to 1800

Territorial expansion to 1914

# Politics and Institutions

## 1533

When Basil III dies, his son Ivan IV is only three years old. Ivan's mother, Helen Glinsky, becomes regent, relying on the support of her favorite, Prince Telepnev-Obolensky. She attempts to continue the policies of Basil III and deals firmly with boyar intrigues. To assure the rights of her son, she has her two brothers-in-law imprisoned.

## 1538

Helen Glinsky dies (the Shuiskys and the Belskys, boyar families, are suspected of having poisoned her). This opens an interregnum, the "Boyar Regency," dominated by familial and clan rivalries.

## 1539

The Shuiskys are ousted by the Belskys.

## 1542

Ivan Shuisky returns to power, forcing Ivan Belsky into exile.

*December.* Ivan IV has Andrei Shuisky strangled.

## 1547

*January 7.* Coronation of Ivan IV, who adds to the title of grand prince that of czar. Ivan surrounds himself with able counselors: his former tutor Macarius, the priest Sylvester, Prince Andrei Kurbsky, and Alexis Adashev, all advocates of major reforms.

## 1550

The *Zemskii Sobor*, the first full meeting of representatives of Russian estates, is convened. The assembled deputies review with the czar the outlines of new administrative and judicial systems, and they set in motion the drafting of a new legal code. New governmental departments (*prikazy*) for finance, war and foreign affairs are established.

Limits are placed on the powers of provincial governors (*voevoda*). These officials will be subject to the control of elected assemblies, and they will be gradually replaced by the village mayors (*starosty*), who are also elected.

The first census is conducted, in order to better establish tax assessments.

*October.* Ivan IV issues a ukase (edict) organizing the czar's service: Domains in the Moscow region are allocated to 1,000 boyar sons, who will form the nobility of the capital and serve the sovereign.

## 1551

The Boyar Duma (assembly) is convened only intermittently. It is replaced by a restricted cabinet council composed of men in whom the czar has confidence.

## 1553

A political crisis arises out of a serious illness suffered by the czar. Contemplating the possible succession of power should he die, Ivan IV makes the boyars swear an oath to his son. Ivan's cousin Prince Vladimir, however, invokes his own rights to the throne and gains the support of a faction of boyars. Sylvester and Adashev, Ivan's advisors, seem to hesitate in offering their allegiance to the czar's son.

## 1555

The benefices of the boyars are abolished, in particular, the taxes they were permitted to deduct from those levied on behalf of the czar. Local administration and fiscal administration are reformed.

## 1560

*July.* Two of Ivan IV's chief counselors are disgraced: Adashev is banished from the Court and returned to the

Livonian army; Sylvester is forced to retire to a monastery.

*September.* The czarina, Anastasia Romanov, dies.

Adashev and Sylvester are tried; the former is imprisoned, the latter confined to Solovetsky Monastery.

## 1562

The system for the inheritance of estates is modified. Henceforth, princely domains, in the absence of male heirs, and boyar domains, in the absence of a will or of near heirs, will revert to the state.

## 1564

Prince Kurbsky, the last remaining counselor from the early period of the reign of Ivan IV (after the disgrace of Adashev and Sylvester and the death of Metropolitan Macarius in 1563), believing himself to be in danger, chooses to flee into exile in Lithuania.

*November 24.* The mock abdication of Ivan IV begins as the czar, accompanied by his second wife and a portion of his Court, leaves Moscow for Aleksandrov, northwest of Vladimir.

*December 25.* Ivan sends two letters to Moscow: The first, addressed to the people of the city, expresses his deep attachment to them; the second, sent to the metropolitan, criticizes the boyars and the clergy and announces the czar's intention to abdicate. The people beg him to return.

## 1565

*April.* The *oprichnina* (special political and police institutions loyal to the czar, and also a separate jurisdictional zone within Russia) is created. The country is divided into two zones: The first zone retains the former organizational structure, while the second zone (the *oprichnina*) comprises a domain re-

served for the service nobility. The former proprietors in this second zone are either indemnified or incorporated into the new system. This reform is accompanied by a bloody repression (3,500 boyars are executed).

## 1566

The *oprichnina* system is extended to cover more territory.

The *Zemskii Sobor* is convened for its second session in order to decide on the course to be followed in the war against Lithuania.

## 1568

*July.* Metropolitan Philip (of the Kolychev family of boyars) is put on trial after speaking against the *oprichnina* and refusing to bless the czar.

## 1569

Ivan IV has Metropolitan Philip strangled.

## 1572

Ivan IV prepares his will. It includes a political testament in which he counsels his successors on the art of governing. Ivan recommends firmness and justifies his violence as having been necessary.

## 1575

The episode of the false czar Simeon: Simeon Bekbulatovich, a Tatar from Kazan, is proclaimed "Czar of all Russia" and installed in the Kremlin, while Ivan IV, renouncing his titles and dignities, has himself called Ivan of Moscow and gives over his court to Czar Simeon. This situation persists for a year.

## 1581

In a fit of anger, Czar Ivan IV kills his eldest son, Ivan.

## 1584

*March 18 (28).* Ivan IV dies.

# Foreign Affairs and Colonization

## 1548

An expedition against the Tatars of Kazan is defeated.

## 1549

The Muscovites suffer a new defeat at the hands of the Tatars. They succeed, however, in founding a new city, Sviiazhsk, near Kazan, which effectively splits the territory of the khanate in two.

## 1552

*June.* After having reorganized his army and augmented his artillery, Ivan IV departs Moscow at the head of an army of 150,000 men with 150 canons on a campaign to conquer Kazan.

*October 2.* Under siege since August, Kazan falls.

## 1555

Sheremetev's force of 13,000 men is defeated by the Crimean khan.

## 1556

The Khanate of Astrakhan is defeated and annexed by Moscow.

## 1557

*February.* Ivan IV refuses to receive a Livonian mission.

*December.* An army of Tatars invades and ravages Livonia.

## 1558

Prince Wisniowiecki of Poland, allied with Ivan IV, defeats the Crimean Tatars at Azov, while the Russians, led by Adashev, attack the estuary of the Dnieper River.

*January.* The Russians launch a campaign against Livonia and besiege the fortified cities of Narva and Dorpat.

*May.* After refusing a truce offer, the city of Narva is assaulted and taken by the Russians.

## 1559

*October.* The grand master of the Livonian Order, Gotthard Kettler, signs an armistice with Ivan IV.

## 1560

*February.* The Livonian War resumes when Kettler, having entered into an alliance with Poland, breaks the armistice.

*August.* Prince Kurbsky crushes the Livonian army at Fellin. The Livonians call for Polish assistance.

## 1563

*February.* Already in control of Smolensk and Vitebsk, the Russians overrun the Palatinate of Polotsk. Russia and Denmark enter into an alliance against Poland and Sweden.

## 1569

Urged on by Poland, a Turkish-Tatar army menaces Astrakhan.

## 1571

The Crimean khan attacks Moscow. The city is pillaged and burned.

## 1575

Ivan IV refuses to put himself forward as a candidate for the vacant Polish throne, preferring instead to negotiate with Emperor Maximilian II for the dismemberment of Poland.

## 1579

*July.* Stephen Bathory, king of Poland, declares war on Russia.

*August.* Polish troops besiege Polotsk. Ivan IV takes refuge at Pskov and seeks to negotiate with Bathory.

## 1581

*February.* Russia launches a campaign against Bathory.

*March.* The Swedes make inroads into Livonia. At the behest of a Russian envoy, Pope Gregory XIII offers to mediate the conflict.

## 1582

In the service of the Stroganovs, Ermak, leader of the Don Cossacks, crosses the Urals with his forces. He defeats Khan Kuchum and begins the conquest of western Siberia.

*January.* The Peace of Iam-Zapolsky, under the terms of which Russia renounces Livonia, is signed. Because Sweden is not a party to this treaty, the Lithuanian-Russian border dispute remains open.

## 1583

*August.* An armistice between Russia and Sweden is concluded. Under its terms, Sweden retains all of the territory it conquered and takes Russia's only outlet into the Gulf of Finland.

# Economy and Society

## 1547

*June.* A severe fire occurs in Moscow. The palaces of the czar and of the metropolitan, the arsenal and many churches are destroyed.

## 1553

*August.* The Englishman Richard Chancellor, backed by London merchants in his effort to discover a northeastern passage to the Orient, is shipwrecked in the White Sea and brought to Moscow.

## 1555

An English commercial enterprise is founded in Moscow. Endowed with various franchises and privileges, it obtains a de facto monopoly over Russian foreign trade.

## 1558

Anikei Stroganov obtains from the czar important territorial grants on the Kama River and to the west of the Urals.

## 1578

Regular commercial relations are established between Antwerp and Russian ports on the White Sea.

## 1581

The first "forbidden year" is declared. The right of peasants to leave the domain on which they are tenants is suspended for one year. (This measure will be renewed each year until 1587.)

# Religious and Cultural Life

## Circa 1540

Macarius compiles the *Calendar of the Saints,* which will serve as the official calendar of the Russian Church until the time of Peter the Great.

## 1547

The *Domostroi* ("Household Manager") is compiled.

## 1551

The *Stoglav Sobor,* or Council of the Hundred Chapters, gathers in Moscow. It publishes the *Stoglav,* a code governing Church and secular matters.

## 1560

The merchant Basil Pozniakov, charged with the task of bringing financial assistance to the patriarch of Alexandria and to the archbishop of Mount Sinai, writes an account of his voyage.

## 1560–1580

The *Sloboda* (settlement) of Aleksandrov, the Church of St. Basil the Blessed, the Printing Office and the Falconer's Palace in Moscow, and the Kremlin in Kazan are constructed.

## 1563

Macarius writes his *Stepennaia kniga* (a dynastic history).

## 1564

The *Apostol* ("Acts of the Apostles") is published. It is the first book printed in Moscow by the Russian printers Ivan Federov and Peter Mstislavets, who had been trained by a Danish printer and sent to Russia by the king of Denmark at the request of Ivan IV.

## 1570

*May.* Jan Rokyta, a Czech adherent of the Bohemian Brethren, holds a public colloquium with the czar on the respective merits of Protestantism and Orthodoxy.

## 1581

The first Slavonic Bible is printed at Ostrog (in Volynia) by Ivan Federov.

## 1582

*February.* Antonio Possevino, a papal legate, visits Moscow. He proposes to the czar a union of the Roman and Orthodox churches and a crusade against the Turks.

## 1583

Ivan IV and Elizabeth of England exchange letters concerning the proposed marriage of Marie Hastings, niece of Elizabeth, to Ivan.

# Chapter 6                                    1584–1613

# The Time of Troubles

Upon the death of Ivan IV, his son Fedor was proclaimed czar. A simple man dominated by his religious beliefs, Fedor I left the governing of Russia first to his uncle Nikita Romanov, then to his brother-in-law Boris Godunov, both of whom had been counselors to Ivan IV. Godunov continued the policies of the former czar. With the support of the new class of service nobility, he managed to thwart boyars who intrigued to regain power (in particular, Basil Shuisky and Ivan Mstislavsky). In an effort to spur agricultural development, Godunov limited the freedom of movement of Russian peasants: A series of decrees, which gradually tied peasants to the land they were cultivating, became the point of departure for the new system of serfdom. During Godunov's tenure, the metropolitanate of Moscow was transformed into a patriarchate. He continued the eastern expansion of the realm, and, in the west, he reconquered from the Swedes a portion of Karelia at the mouth of the Gulf of Finland.

When Fedor died without leaving a direct heir, the *Zemskii Sobor* elected Boris Godunov czar. Shortly thereafter, however, there loomed the "ghost" of Dmitri, the son of Ivan IV and Maria Nagaia who had been murdered under mysterious circumstances: Gregory Otrepiev, a defrocked monk, began to pass himself off as the czarevitch. With the assistance of troops raised by Polish aristocrats, Gregory (the False Dmitri) marched on Moscow after the sudden death of Boris Godunov. Dmitri succeeded in deposing Fedor II, the late Boris's son, and proclaimed himself czar.

Compromised by his ties to Poland, Dmitri displeased the nobility by taking measures in favor of the peasantry and was deposed by Basil Shuisky, the "Boyar Czar." Other False Dmitris appeared, and Shuisky was deposed despite the support of Sweden, whose intervention he had encouraged. In a situation of extreme confusion, Ladislaus, the son of the king of Poland, Sigismund III, managed to have himself proclaimed czar of Moscow. Then, in an extraordinary burst of patriotism, a national militia drove the Poles out of the country. The *Zemskii Sobor*, meeting in Moscow, unanimously elected as the new czar Michael Romanov, grandson of Nikita, the brother-in-law of Ivan IV.

# Political and Military Affairs

## 1584

*March.* Fedor I, son of Ivan IV, becomes czar. He is surrounded by a council of guardians (Nikita Romanov, Boris Godunov, and Princes Ivan Mstislavsky, Ivan Shuisky and Bogdan Belsky).

*April.* Bogdan Belsky makes a bid for power against the other members of the council and is exiled as a result. Nikita Romanov achieves preeminence. Ivan's widow, Maria Nagaia, and her young son Dmitri, the younger brother of Fedor and the presumptive heir, are banished to Uglich.

*May.* The *Zemskii Sobor* meets and crowns Fedor czar.

## 1585

*April 14 (24).* Nikita Romanov dies.

*June.* The principality of Tver is reintegrated into the Muscovite state (it had been given as an appanage to "czar Simeon" by Ivan IV).

## 1587

*January.* Basil Shuisky and Ivan Mstislavsky carry out a plot against Boris Godunov.

## 1591

*May 6 (16).* Czarevitch Dmitri dies in Uglich: Boris Godunov is accused of having had him assassinated.

*June.* The *Sobor* meets to examine the Uglich affair. A commission of inquiry is led by Shuisky.

## 1594

Boris Godunov is named regent. The title represents official recognition of his de facto leadership.

## 1595

Russia signs an accord with Sweden, under which it receives a portion of Karelia and of the Neva River, and the southern coast of the Gulf of Finland as far as Ivangorod.

## 1597

*December 27 (January 6, 1598).* Fedor I dies.

## 1598

*January 7 (17).* Czarina Irina, widow of Fedor I, withdraws and decides to take holy vows.

*February.* The *Zemskii Sobor* meets, presided over by the patriarch of Moscow.

*February 8 (18).* Boris Godunov is elected czar.

*September 1 (11).* The new czar is crowned.

## 1599

Athanasius Vlasiev travels to the Court of Emperor Rudolph II in Prague.

## 1600

*August.* A Polish mission to Moscow results in a 20-year armistice signed by Leon Sapieha and Boris Godunov.

## 1601

*June.* Accused of having organized a plot against Boris Godunov, Fedor Romanov, son of Nikita, is arrested and imprisoned. His entire family is exiled, and he and his wife must take religious vows.

## 1602

Gustavus, the brother of the king of Denmark, arrives in Moscow. He becomes engaged to Xenia, the sister of Boris Godunov.

## 1603

The myth of the False Dmitri emerges: In Poland a young man, possibly the defrocked monk Gregory Otrepiev, passes himself off as the czarevitch Dmitri.

## 1604

The False Dmitri crosses the Russian border at the head of a Polish army. Many cossacks revolt and join him under the leadership of Hetman Khlopko.

## 1605

*January 16 (26).* The False Dmitri's army is defeated by Basil Shuisky at Dobrynichi.

*April 1 (11).* Boris Godunov dies. His son, Fedor II, ascends to the throne despite the hostility of the boyars.

*April–May.* An uprising occurs in the southwestern border provinces. The supporters of the False Dmitri proclaim the deposition of Fedor II, who is arrested and, shortly thereafter, assassinated.

*June.* The treason of Moscow's military leaders allows the False Dmitri to easily take the capital. Dmitri is crowned czar.

*November.* Dmitri is married by proxy to Marina Mniszech, the Polish daughter of the palatine of Sandomir.

## 1606

*January.* The Boyar Duma is converted into a senate. A Pole, Jan Buczinski, is charged with establishing a list of this body's future members. New offices are created on the Polish model, such as that of grand marshal of the crown.

*May.* Marina Mniszech arrives in Moscow. Marriage celebrations are held, and Polish diplomats hold talks with the boyars, who learn of secret concessions made by Dmitri to the Poles.

The concessions include the extension of the Uniate Church's jurisdiction to Muscovite territory, the cession of territory to Poland and the promise to transfer the Russian crown to Poland on the death of Dmitri.

*May 7 (17).* The boyars launch a coup d'état and depose Dmitri, who is then executed. The boyars appear in Red Square and propose the convocation of the *Sobor* and the temporary transfer of full power to the patriarch. The crowds, however, demand a new czar, and the boyars designate Basil Shuisky, who is elected by acclamation.

*May 22 (June 1).* Shuisky is crowned, swearing an oath in the manner of the Polish kings. He promises to govern with the Duma and the *Sobor*.

*June.* Czarevitch Dmitri is canonized in accordance with a manifesto of Basil Shuisky, who hopes by this measure to remove all legitimacy from the False Dmitri.

*Summer.* Upon word of the coup d'état, a rebellion begins in the region to the northeast of the Black Sea and in the province of Riazan. This rebellion extends the length of the Volga to Astrakhan, and unrest also occurs in Tver, Pskov and Novgorod. The peasants refuse to obey the Boyar Czar.

The cossacks in the Terek River region rebel in the name of a pretender son of Fedor I, the czarevitch Peter.

## 1607

*February.* The Romanov family, exiled under Boris Godunov, is rehabilitated.

*June.* A second False Dmitri appears, also supported by the Poles and the cossacks. Impostors multiply: A certain Fedor passes himself off as the nephew of Dmitri and leads a party of Don Cossacks; another pretender, claiming to be a son of Ivan IV, tries to take control of Astrakhan.

## 1608

*April–May.* Muscovite troops commanded by Dmitri and Ivan Shuisky, brothers of the czar, seeking to block the route of the second False Dmitri, are completely routed: 5,000 soldiers capitulate and swear an oath to the new pretender.

*June.* The rebel army marches to the village of Tushino, on the right bank of the Moskva River and within sight of Moscow, but is unable to enter the capital.

*July.* On order of Prince Sapieha, cousin of the chancellor of Lithuania, 20,000 Polish troops arrive to support the second False Dmitri.

*July 15 (25).* An armistice is signed between Russia and Poland on the basis of the territorial status quo. Sigismund III promises to recall all Polish soldiers in the service of the pretender.

*September.* Marina Mniszech comes to Tushino and pretends to recognize her husband (the False Dmitri) in the person of the second False Dmitri. Tushino becomes a sort of second Russian capital, in opposition to Moscow.

*November.* The czar appeals to the Swedes to assist Russia against the Poles.

## 1609

*February 18 (28).* An accord is signed at Vyborg between Shuisky and Charles IX of Sweden. In return for the abandonment by Russia of its claims to Livonia, Charles promises to send an expeditionary corps of 5,000 men to free Moscow.

*February 25 (March 7).* In an effort to put an end to the crisis, certain boyars, including Prince Gagarin, plot to depose Basil Shuisky. Their plot fails (as do new attempts in April and May).

*July.* Michael Skopin-Shuisky, nephew of Czar Basil, and the Swedish forces, commanded by Jakob de la Gardie, defeat the cossacks of the second False Dmitri near Tver.

*September.* Breaking the armistice signed with Russia the previous year, Sigismund III of Poland decides to lay siege to Smolensk. A conflict breaks out between the Polish royal army and that of Prince Sapieha at Tushino.

## 1610

*January.* Pressured by Russian and Swedish troops, Sapieha is forced to lift the siege of the Monastery of the Holy Trinity-St. Sergius, which his troops had been surrounding since 1608. Sapieha's precipitous retreat sets into motion a reaction against the second False Dmitri. Moscow is soon free. Hermogen, patriarch of Moscow, together with Abbot Dionysius of the Holy Trinity-St. Sergius Monastery and his bursar Abraham Politsyn, keep alive the spirit of national resistance.

*February.* Tushino sends a deputation to Smolensk. The representatives of the second False Dmitri propose to Sigismund III a treaty under which an association would be formed between Russia and Poland, with each country maintaining its current religious practices and institutions. Sigismund puts forward a counterplan that would require the installation in Russia of a system of representation on the Polish model.

*June.* A corps of 50,000 men, including Russians and Swedes, is defeated by the Poles outside Smolensk.

*July.* The boyars depose Basil Shuisky, who had lost his strongest supporter with the death of his nephew Skopin-Shuisky. They decide to hold power themselves, under the direction of Prince Mstislavsky, until the election of a new czar.

*August.* Ladislaus, the son of Sigismund, is elected czar by the boyars; the two other candidates had been the second False Dmitri and Michael Romanov. The boyars send to King Sigismund, near Smolensk, a great delegation that includes Fedor Romanov (who had taken the religious name Philaret). To gain recognition, Ladislaus will be required to convert to Orthodoxy and to agree to respect Muscovite institutions.

*September.* Polish troops take control of Moscow.

*December 1 (11).* The second False Dmitri is murdered by Tatars near Kaluga.

## 1611

*February.* Procopius Liapunov issues a manifesto calling on Russians to rise against foreign domination. National militias are organized to the north and east of Moscow.

*March 13 (23).* The Polish army, isolated in the Kremlin, is attacked by the national militias of Liapunov and Prince Dmitri Pozharsky. A French mercenary, Jacques Margeret, repulses the attack.

*May.* Riots break out in Moscow against the Polish garrison. Sigismund takes Smolensk. In the absence of the *Zemskii Sobor,* a national council is convened and a triumvirate (consisting of Liapunov and two cossack leaders, Trubetskoi and Zarutsky) is appointed to lead a provisional government. Radical agrarian reform is proposed. The assassination of Liapunov by cossacks puts an end to this tentative plan of reorganization, advanced in the face of the Polish presence at Moscow.

*October.* Kuzma Minin, alderman of Nizhni Novgorod, and Prince Pozharsky prepare a national uprising. Minin organizes a collection of funds to facilitate the raising of a new militia, which will be placed under the command of Pozharsky.

## 1612

*January.* Mutinies occur in the Polish garrison at Moscow.

*April.* Organizers of the Russian resistance send circulars to all of the Russian provinces, urging the convocation of a new national council.

*August.* Pozharsky's troops besiege Moscow. A Polish expeditionary force coming to the assistance of Czar Ladislaus is stopped by Pozharsky's troops at the gates of Moscow.

*October 17 (27).* The Polish garrison is forced to surrender, and Ladislaus flees. A provisional government led by Dmitri Pozharsky is installed.

## 1613

*February 11 (21).* The *Zemskii Sobor* meets in Moscow and elects Michael Romanov czar.

# Economy and Society

## 1584

The port of Archangel (Arkhangelsk) is created under the name Novokholmogory.

*July.* The *Sobor* passes a law barring the expansion of noble and ecclesiastical estates and abolishing the land and tax-related privileges of proprietors (*tarkhany*).

## 1585

The Russian colonization of Siberia continues. Ivan Mansurov constructs a fortress at the confluence of the Irtysh and Ob rivers.

## 1586

Tyumen is founded beyond the Ural Mountains. To the northeast, following the conquest of Siberian tribes, other new cities are built, including Tobolsk, which replaces Sibir (Isker), the former Tatar capital.

A new charter is issued to the Anglo-Russian company that controls foreign trade.

## 1592

The "right of departure" of peasants from their landlord (the St. George's Day law) is abrogated. This right had been curbed by the institution of "forbidden years" in 1581. In an effort to put an end to the constant movements of the population, as well as to assure the exploitation of the land and to limit brigandage, peasants are bound to the land. The "second serfdom" begins.

## 1594

A census is taken of all lands under cultivation, and all peasant laborers are registered.

## 1597

Registers of land, buildings and property are established, and a ukase mandates the pursuit of fugitive peasants.

## 1601–1602

Bad harvests and resultant famine claim 500,000 victims.

## 1602–1603

A cholera epidemic strikes Russia.

## 1605

*August.* The False Dmitri abolishes the restrictions placed on the "right of departure," limits voluntary enslavements and forbids searches for fugitive serfs.

## 1606

The first uprising of the lower classes in Russian history occurs under the leadership of a former serf, Ivan

Bolotnikov, who raises an army of peasants and cossacks.

## 1607

*March.* Basil Shuisky annuls the edicts of Dmitri and imposes new limitations on peasant rights.

*October.* Bolotnikov is defeated by Shuisky's troops at Tula.

# Religious and Cultural Life

## 1589

*January 17 (27).* The metropolitanate of Moscow is elevated to a patriarchate. Job, the first patriarch of Moscow, is consecrated by the patriarch of Constantinople.

## 1596

The White City is constructed in Moscow under the direction of Fedor Saveliev, a Muscovite architect.

*October 11 (21).* The Union of Brest-Litovsk is established: All Russian bishops in charge of dioceses in Polish territory agree to a union of the Roman Catholic and Eastern Orthodox churches in Poland. Under this agreement, the Orthodox Church recognizes the supremacy of the Pope but is permitted to maintain the eastern liturgy and a separate ecclesiastical hierarchy. This marks the birth of the Uniate Church, which is rejected by a major portion of the Orthodox faithful and clergy.

## 1605

Patriarch Job is relieved of his duties by the False Dmitri and replaced by a Greek, Ignatius.

## 1606

Ignatius is dismissed. The new patriarch, Hermogen, will become a hero of the resistance and will die in 1612 while in Polish captivity.

## 1612

Metropolitan Cyril of Rostov, replacing the imprisoned Hermogen at the head of the Church, presides over the national council and the provisional government.

## 1613

Cyril of Rostov crowns the new czar, Michael Romanov.

# Chapter 7                    1613–1682

## The First Romanovs

By the end of the Time of Troubles, Russia was in shambles. Disorganized and devastated by the Polish invasion, the country had lost almost half its population. Russian history under the first three Romanovs would be characterized by a slow and difficult recovery punctuated by serious social problems.

Michael Romanov struggled to reestablish order. He ended brigandage, which had developed into an endemic problem during the Time of Troubles, and he repulsed the cossacks. He conducted a new war against Poland, after which Ladislaus was forced to renounce his pretensions to the Russian throne. To improve the functioning of the administration and to make taxation more equitable, Michael I ordered a new property assessment and a new census, and he combatted abuses of the *voevoda* and provincial officials. In institutional terms, the last years of Michael's reign marked the apogee of the *Zemskii Sobor*, which became a sort of permanent national council and gave the Russian state the appearance of being a "parliamentary" monarchy.

Under the reign of Alexis I, large increases in taxation, coupled with the worsening condition of the peasantry, provoked a deep social crisis, evidenced by rioting in Moscow in 1648 and by the outbreak of a revolt led by Stenka Razin. The liturgical reforms initiated by the patriarch Nikon, who wanted to bring the Russian Church back in line with Greek traditions, provoked the opposition of the Old Believers led by Avvakum. This marked the start of a permanent schism. In the Ukraine, the cossacks under Bogdan Khmelnitsky rose up against Polish domination and appealed to the czar, who intervened on their side. Victorious, Russia annexed some important territories, including Smolensk, Kiev and the western bank of the Dnieper.

Fedor III was merely the nominal ruler during his short reign. Having no interest in affairs of state, he ceded his power to his counselors. One of these, Basil Golitsyn, revived the *Zemskii Sobor*, which had been dormant during the previous reign.

## Russian Expansion in Asia (1533–1914)

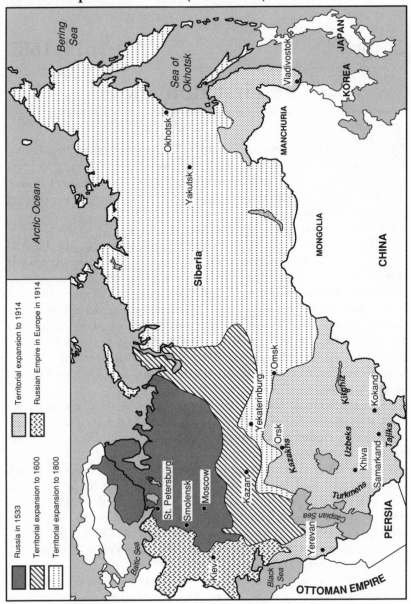

# Politics and Institutions

## 1613

*February 11 (21).* Michael Romanov is elected czar by the *Zemskii Sobor*, which becomes a kind of national assembly regularly convoked by the czar. The Boyar Duma remains as a privy council of the sovereign.

*May 1 (11).* The czar is crowned by Metropolitan Cyril in Moscow.

## 1614

*June.* A rebellion led by Marina Mniszech is ended. She is imprisoned and her son is put to death.

## 1615

A new *Zemskii Sobor* is elected.

## 1615–1616

Fiscal pressures increase. The Duma and the *Zemskii Sobor* vote for an emergency tax (20 percent on property and 120 rubles per estate). The Stroganovs loan the state 56,000 rubles.

## 1618

Freed by the Poles, Philaret Romanov, father of the czar, is elected patriarch and shares power with his son. Under Philaret's influence, from 1622 to 1633, the role of the *Zemskii Sobor* will be gradually reduced.

## 1619

*June.* The *Zemskii Sobor* takes a series of important steps: An inventory of taxable land is taken; peasants who had fled their land are encouraged to return; a special department is set up to deal with official abuses of power; a project to reform provincial administration, giving priority to elected assemblies, is put through; a national budget is established.

## 1621

The *Zemskii Sobor* issues a circular that encourages rural districts to resist the efforts of local officials to exact illegal taxes and corvées (unpaid labor).

## 1624

*September.* Marriage of Michael Romanov to the princess Maria Dolgoruky. Maria will die within months, and the following year the czar will marry Eudoxia Streshniev (the daughter of an obscure gentleman), who will be the mother of Alexis.

## 1626–1633

A series of very expensive military reforms are instituted: 5,000 foot soldiers, as well as cannon makers and instructors, are recruited from abroad, and arms are purchased from Holland and Germany.

## 1627

The powers and responsibilities of the magistrates and local tribunals are strengthened, usurping the prerogatives of the provincial governors (*voevoda*).

## 1628

Punishments are made more humane; a limitation is placed on the infliction of corporal punishment to recover debts.

## 1633

*October.* Philaret dies. Michael Romanov restores power to the *Zemskii Sobor*, convoking it during all crises.

## 1645

*July 2 (12).* Michael Romanov dies, and his eldest son, Alexis I, succeeds him. The accession to the throne is confirmed by a vote of the *Zemskii Sobor*. The new czar is only 16 years old, and his former tutor, Boris Morozov, exercises a de facto regency.

## 1646

The gradual elimination of the Boyar Duma, in favor of a council formed by the close advisors of the czar (the "Chamber Duma" or "Privy Council of Boyars"), begins.

The Department of Secret Affairs is established. Initially a secret police and secret tribunal, the department will evolve into an administrative oversight agency.

A census of households is conducted. Tax rates are increased, and a tax on salt is established.

## 1647

A code of military law is promulgated. The code is an adaptation of Holy Roman Empire legislation (the "Regulation of Charles V").

## 1649

*January 19 (29).* The *Zemskii Sobor* publishes a new legal code (*Ulozhenie*). Its nearly 1,000 articles reflect the essential content of the Code of Ivan IV, with new elements borrowed from the Lithuanian and Byzantine codes. Under its terms, peasants are definitively attached to the land, privileges of foreigners are abolished, and the Church is subjected more firmly to state control.

## 1650

*February–October.* The cities of Pskov and Novgorod revolt.

## 1652

A ukase broadens military recruitment to include additional social groups.

## 1653

Alexis ceases to convoke the *Zemskii Sobor* on a regular basis.

## 1669

New criminal legislation is enacted: Punishments are reduced, as are the powers of elected magistrates.

After the Peace of Andrusovo (1667), the Department of Foreign Affairs (directed by Afanasi Ordyn-Nashchokin) ceases to be responsible to the Duma and becomes autonomous.

## 1671

Artamon Matveev replaces Ordyn-Nashchokin as head of the Department of Foreign Affairs.

## 1674

*September.* The czarevitch Alexis dies. His younger brother Fedor becomes the new heir to the throne.

## 1676

*January 20 (30).* Czar Alexis I dies. Fedor III accedes to the throne. Actual power is exercised first by Artamon Matveev (until he is exiled to Siberia in July), and then by the clan of the czar's late mother, Maria Miloslavsky (who died in 1669).

## 1679–1682

The penal code is revised. Maiming is prohibited.

## 1681

*November.* Fedor III convokes the *Zemskii Sobor* to consult with him on the reorganization of the army.

## 1682

Inspired by Basil Golitsyn, and with the consultation of the *Zemskii Sobor*, the council of boyars and the high clergy, Fedor III abolishes the *mestnichestvo*, the system of aristocratic precedence in the civil and military services.

*April 17 (27).* Fedor III dies without an heir.

# Foreign Affairs

## 1613

*March.* A Russian delegation is sent to Warsaw, but Sigismund III gives no response to its overtures. Ladislaus does not renounce his pretensions to the Russian throne, and Philaret, father of the czar, is taken prisoner.

*July.* Polish forces attack Mozhaisk, Kaluga and Tula.

## 1614

The Swedes lay siege to Tula.

## 1615

*July.* Gustavus Adolphus, king of Sweden, is defeated at Pskov. The German emperor Matthias offers to mediate the Russo-Swedish conflict.

## 1617

*February 17 (27).* With the mediation of England, Russia and Sweden enter into the Peace of Stolbovo. The Swedes return Novgorod but keep Ingria (Ingermanland) and Livonia, as well as fortifications along the border. Free trade between the two countries is established.

## 1618

*December 1 (11).* Poland and Russia sign a 14-year truce at Deulino. Moscow abandons Smolensk without obtaining Ladislaus's renunciation of the Russian throne, and in return Russian prisoners are released.

## 1623

A French delegation comes to Moscow seeking an alliance against Poland and the Hapsburg Empire.

## 1626

Gustavus Adolphus seeks to ally himself with Russia against Poland.

## 1632

*December.* Following the death of Sigismund III, the czar declares war on Poland. The campaign of Smolensk takes place.

## 1634

*February 9 (19).* The Russians capitulate to the Poles.

*May 7 (17).* A permanent peace between Russia and Poland is established on the basis of the territorial status quo.

## 1637

The Don Cossacks seize Azov.

## 1646

*March.* A Russian delegation travels to Poland. The czar proposes to Ladislaus IV that the Dnieper Cossacks and the Don Cossacks be combined, and that Russian and Polish troops join forces to invade the Crimea.

## 1647

*June.* A Russian-Polish alliance begins military action against the Turks. The Poles battle the Turks in Turkey while the Russians fight them in the Crimea.

## 1648

*April 25 (May 5).* The Poles are defeated by the Zaporozhian Cossacks, led by Bogdan Khmelnitsky, on the Dnieper River in the Ukraine.

*September 10 (20).* The Poles suffer another defeat at Piliavtsy.

## 1649

*August.* Defeated at Zborov, Khmelnitsky signs a treaty with the Poles. (He will, however, resume hostilities in June 1650.)

## 1651

*September.* Khmelnitsky suffers another defeat at the hands of the Poles, and he signs the Treaty of Belaia Tserkov.

## 1652

The first confrontation between Russians and Chinese on the Amur River takes place following the expedition of Khabarov (1649–1651).

## 1653

*August.* With the intercession of Patriarch Nikon, Khmelnitsky asks for the assistance of the czar.

*October.* Despite the treaty signed with Poland, the *Zemskii Sobor* accepts the idea of an intervention on the side of the cossacks. Alexis confirms the ancient rights of the cossacks to administrative autonomy and the free choice of their hetman.

## 1654

*May.* The campaign against Poland begins.

*July.* Poland forms an alliance with the Crimean Tatars.

*September 13 (23).* The Polish garrison at Smolensk capitulates after a difficult siege. The *Rada* (the national assembly of the Ukraine) meets, on the initiative of Khmelnitsky, at Pereiaslavl. The Ukraine, under Khmelnitsky's control, recognizes the sovereignty of the czar.

## 1655

*August.* Russian and cossack forces lay siege to Lvov.

## 1656

*August.* Khmelnitsky dies. His successor, Vygovsky, is a partisan of Poland.

*October.* With imperial mediation, the Treaty of Vilna is signed. Alexis I will be offered the Polish throne on the death of Jan Casimir; in return, Alexis must abandon his conquests in Lithuania and the Ukraine and ally himself with Poland against Sweden.

Russia enters into its first negotiations with China.

## 1658

*September 6 (16).* The Treaty of Gadiach is signed by the cossack hetman Vygovsky and Poland. Under its terms, one-third of the Ukraine is to be established as a west Russian grand duchy that will join the Polish Commonwealth with the same status as Lithuania. In addition, the Union of Brest-Litovsk is abrogated and freedom for Orthodoxy is guaranteed. Russian troops invade the Ukraine and provoke an uprising against Vygovsky.

*December.* A three-year truce is signed by Sweden and Russia. Under its terms, Russian conquests in Livonia are guaranteed.

## 1659

*September–October.* Russian forces commanded by Prince Trubetskoi surrender to a coalition of Poles, cossacks and Tatars. Poland maintains its hold on the western bank of the Dnieper.

## 1660

A permanent Russian delegation takes up residence at The Hague.

## 1661

*June.* A permanent peace is signed by Russia and Sweden. Alexis renounces his conquests in Livonia.

## 1667

*January 30 (February 9).* Russia and Poland sign the Treaty of Andrusovo, a 13-year armistice. Poland retains possession of Vitebsk and Polotsk, and retains its rights in Livonia, but it cedes to Russia Smolensk and the surrounding region, as well as all of the eastern bank of the Dnieper; although Kiev is on the western bank, Poland temporarily cedes the city to Russia.

## 1668

The czarevitch Alexis is the candidate for election to the throne of Poland.

*August 25 (September 4).* A Russian delegation is in France. Potemkin meets Lionne and Colbert. The countries enter into negotiations for a free trade agreement. (Potemkin will visit France again in 1681.)

## 1675

Using Jesuit intermediaries, Russia enters into new negotiations with China in Peking.

## 1678

*August 3 (13).* An accord is reached between Poland and Russia, renewing the armistice of Andrusovo.

## 1681

The Treaty of Bakhchirisai ends the Russo-Turkish conflict. Under its terms, all the lands between the Don and the Dniester rivers are to remain unoccupied, and no towns are to be established in the territory between Kiev and the lower Dnieper.

# Economy and Society

## 1619

The city of Yeniseisk is founded.

## 1620

From 1600 to 1620 (the Time of Troubles), Russia has lost almost half its population. The population of Moscow has fallen by 33 percent.

## 1630

The government authorizes a Dutchman, Firmbrandt, to build a velvet mill.

## 1631

The state subsidizes the English industrialist Frank Glover to create workshops for goldsmiths and jewelers, in collaboration with the Russian merchant Ivan Martynov.

## 1632

The city of Yakutsk is established.

The government authorizes the Dutch industrialist Vinius to establish a cannon and cannonball foundry in Tula, with a labor force made up mostly of foreigners.

## 1641

The right of landowners to pursue fugitive peasants is broadened to encompass all provinces, but the statute of limitations is set at 15 years. The sale or transfer of peasants is made legal.

## 1643–1646

Peter Golovin, the *voevode* of Yakutsk, on the Lena River, sponsors an exploratory expedition led by Basil Poiarkov. The expeditionary party travels up the Aldan River, then follows the path of the Amur River all the way to its mouth, and, finally, follows the seacoast to the future site of Okhotsk.

## 1646

Commercial franchises granted to English merchants during the reigns of Ivan IV and Boris Godunov are revoked.

The czar orders the construction of a system of fortified cities in the provinces of Belgorod and Simbirsk.

## 1648

*June.* Rioting breaks out in Moscow as a result of increased taxation and the unpopularity of the czar's entourage. The crowd pillages the Morozov Palace and sets fires in the city.

## 1649

The town of Okhotsk is founded.

A new legal code definitively binds the peasantry to the land.

*January.* At the behest of Russian merchants, English merchants are restricted to the port of Archangel. The privileges of the English Muscovy Trading Company are abolished.

## 1650

A ukase prohibits peasants from any type of artisanal or commercial activity.

*February–October.* The cities of Pskov and Novgorod revolt.

## 1652

Irkutsk is founded.

## 1654

The "Little Russian" emigres who had fled to Poland found Kharkov.

An epidemic strikes (in certain regions, the mortality rate approaches 85 percent).

## 1656

A monetary crisis occurs. The government decides to coin a copper ruble to replace the silver ruble on a one-for-one basis, in order to save money for the treasury. (In the following five-year period, the government will coin five million copper rubles.)

## 1662

*June.* The inflation caused by the circulation of copper rubles provokes the "Copper Revolt." In Moscow, the revolt is mercilessly put down: 7,000 people are killed. In the provinces, agrarian troubles increase. A portion of the armed forces, under orders from Prince Kropotkin, joins the insurgents.

## 1663

*March.* A ukase puts an end to the minting of copper coins, which the government takes out of circulation.

## 1665

The task of establishing a mail service is conferred on a Dutchman, Johann van Sweeden. (Until this time, the postal department had only provided fresh horses and supplies to traveling functionaries.)

## 1666

Directed by the ataman Vaska, bands of cossacks ravage the provinces of Voronezh and Tula, rallying the peasants and serfs to revolt against landowners.

## 1667

*May.* The first commercial code is promulgated. Under its terms, retail trade is restricted to Russian merchants, and foreigners engaging in wholesale trade must use a Russian intermediary. The Department of Commerce is also established.

## 1668

Dutch engineers and artisans construct the first Russian naval squadron at the Dedinovo dockyards on the Oka River.

## 1669

*March.* The cossacks, led by Stenka Razin, attack the Persian flotilla on the east coast of the Caspian Sea.

## 1670

*June 12 (22).* Stenka Razin seizes Astrakhan. The city is pillaged and the *voevode* executed. Razin makes Astrakhan the base of his operations.

*July.* Razin travels up the Volga. Tsaritsyn, Saratov and Samara fall. The revolt broadens. The peasants leave their lands, become cossacks, and organize into bands that rampage through the regions of Simbirsk, Tambov and Nizhni Novgorod.

*October.* Stenka Razin is defeated at Simbirsk. The insurrection collapses.

*December.* Russian troops commanded by Prince Dolgoruky take the offensive against the insurgents.

## 1671

*January.* Pacification is achieved.

*May 27 (June 6).* Stenka Razin is executed in Moscow.

*November 16 (26).* Astrakhan is retaken.

## 1672

All commercial privileges of the clergy are suppressed.

## 1680

Foreigners are playing an increasingly important role in the Russian economy. The Dutchman Denis Jovis and the Dane Peter Marselis exploit the copper mines in the Olonets region of Karelia. A German, Tilmann Ackermann, builds forges near Kaluga. The Frenchman Mignot opens a mirror factory in Moscow. The technical personnel for all these enterprises are recruited from abroad.

# Religious and Cultural Life

## 1616

Dionysius, the archimandrite of the Monastery of the Holy Trinity-St. Sergius, organizes a working group to reform the Russian Church. Michael Romanov charges him with revising the liturgical texts, an enterprise that brings Dionysius up against the hostility of the conservatives, including the czar's mother. Dionysius will be imprisoned

but later liberated by Philaret upon the latter's return.

## 1633

A school is established at the Chudov Monastery (also known as the Monastery of the Miracle of the Archangel St. Michael), at the Kremlin.

## 1633–1634

Adam Olearius journeys from Germany to Russia. He will return once more to Russia in the course of a mission to Iran (1635–1639). The account of his travels (published in 1643) is one of the richest sources for the history of Russia in the 17th century.

## 1646

Nikon becomes archimandrite at the Novospassky Monastery in Moscow. He is noticed by the czar, who confers on him the duty of serving petitions. The czar sends Nikon to Novgorod to negotiate with the magistrates of the city.

## 1648

The Moscow Printing Office publishes Smotritsky's *Slavic Grammar*, which had been first published in Vilna (Vilnius) in 1619.

## 1649

The czar calls a Church council, which condemns the modifications of the rituals proposed by the "Hellenizers" (in particular, the requirement for singing in unison).

The prelate Epifanius Slavinetsky (who will die in 1675) begins to play an important role in Church life. He collaborates with Nikon in the translation of the works of the Church fathers and in the editing of a philological lexicon and a Greek-Slavic-Latin dictionary. Along with the Little Russian teachers recruited by Rtishchev, Epifanius attracts evergrowing numbers of students and comes into competition with the Greek school of Arsenios.

## 1652

*April.* Nikon is made patriarch of Moscow.

## 1653

Ignoring the decisions of the council, Nikon issues an amended book of psalms. Traditionalists protest to the czar. Nikon reprints the *Nomocanon.* The archpriest Avvakum, who opposes Nikon's efforts to revive the Church's Greek traditions, is arrested and deported to Siberia.

## 1654

Assembling a new council, Nikon obtains a unanimous vote ordering corrections in the liturgical texts and a condemnation of the two-finger sign of the cross.

## 1655

Arsenios Sukhanov, the superior of the Monastery of the Epiphany, returns from the West with 5,000 Greek manuscripts, which he intends to use against the "Old Believers," who oppose Nikon's reforms.

## 1656

Paul of Koloma, the last traditionalist bishop, dies. The lack of bishops will lead to the progressive disappearance of priests among the Old Believers. This, in turn, will bring forth two different trends: the *bespopovtsy* (literally, "those without priests") in the north and in Siberia, who will choose their own leaders; and those who will decide to return to the priests of the official Church.

## 1657

The archimandrite of the Solovetsky Monastery convokes an assembly of monks and priests (known as a "black council" or "people's council"). The assembly decides to remain faithful to the old books and addresses a supplication with this sentiment to the czar. The Solovetsky Monastery becomes a center of the struggle against the reformers. The patriarch sends instructions to all the dioceses enjoining them to exercise more care in the recruitment of clerics.

## 1658

No longer enjoying the czar's confidence, Nikon retires to the Monastery of the Resurrection (or "the New Jerusalem"), which he had founded. The metropolitan of Krutitsy, Pitirim, takes over the affairs of the patriarchate.

## 1659

Krizhanich, a Croatian priest and Catholic theologian who is also a historian and a grammarian, comes to Moscow to argue for Slavic unity. He will be exiled to Tobolsk, in Siberia, where he will write his principal works, including *The Russian Empire in the 17th Century.* Pardoned in 1676, he will settle in Poland.

## 1660

Czar Alexis convenes a council that condemns Nikon, but a retraction by one of the participants annuls the entire vote.

## 1661

Avvakum, upon his return to Moscow, is received by the czar and housed in one of the Kremlin monasteries.

## 1663

Alexis asks for the advice of the eastern patriarchs, who condemn Nikon.

## 1664

*August.* Avvakum, faithful to his ideas, is again exiled to Siberia.

## 1665

Simeon of Polotsk, a renegade White Russian (Belorussian), founds a school at the Zaikonospassky Monastery, where young foreign affairs officers are initiated into the secular knowledge required for their careers. In 1672 Simeon will become the tutor of the czarevitches Alexis and Fedor and of their sister Sophia. At heart a poet and a dramatist, Simeon is an ideal representative of the Kiev school.

## 1666

A new council condemns Nikon while approving the ideas of the Hellenizers.

## 1667–1671

Alexis has his residence at Kolomenskoe rebuilt by White Russian architects and artists.

## 1668

Alexis sends troops against the rebellious monks at the Solovetsky Monastery.

Molière's *Amphitryon*, a play that Potemkin brought back from Paris, is translated into Russian.

## 1668–1670

Polish artists travel from Kiev to decorate the czar's palace and the Golitsyn mansion. The influence of Polish art also appears in Muscovite iconography (the council of 1666 had criticized innovative tendencies in painting).

## 1670

A German drama group is formed in Moscow.

## 1672

Religious dissidents immolate themselves at Nizhni Novgorod. The number of such collective suicides will increase (37 incidents in 1691 will claim more than 2,000 victims).

## 1673

Rtishchev, partisan and protector of the Kiev school, dies. The Hellenizers regain a strong influence.

An opera hall is built in Preobrazhenskoe. *Esther*, based on Simeon of Polotsk's libretto, is staged there.

## 1674

The first textbook of Russian history, the *Sinopsis*, is published.

## 1681

The council meets and decides to create new dioceses to reinforce the influence of the official Church. The council also decides to establish a special police force to combat the dissidents, to whom it is forbidden to give shelter. The dissidents' hermitages and religious sites are destroyed.

A proposal for a Slavic-Greek-Latin Academy is put forward, in an effort to forge a synthesis of Greek and Kievan influences.

*August 6 (16)*. Nikon dies. (Fedor had just obtained from the eastern patriarchs an annulment of the condemnation that was declared against Nikon in 1666.)

## 1682

*March 31 (April 10)*. Avvakum and his followers are burned at the stake.

*May*. Revolt of the *streltsy*, an infantry corps established by Ivan the Terrible (the *streltsy* are strong supporters of the old religious and military traditions and favorably disposed to the Old Believers). The Old Believers support the revolt.

# Chapter 8                                    1682–1725

## Russia under Peter the Great

The reign of Peter the Great constituted a veritable revolution. Under Peter's rule, Russia attempted to break with its past and to turn toward the West. The founding of a new capital, St. Petersburg, symbolized the new course.

In 1689 Peter put an end to the regency of his half-sister Sophia, who had exercised power in the name of her half-brothers Ivan and Peter since shortly after the death of Fedor III. Feeling himself to be still too young and inexperienced to rule in his own right, Peter placed governing authority in the hands of his mother, Natalia Naryshkina, who exercised power until 1694.

Upon becoming master of the country, Peter set out to reform the state apparatus and to extend his own power. The central administration was reorganized: Ministerial colleges (agencies) were established, as was a private chancellery. In addition, the Boyar Duma was replaced by a Senate whose members were named by the czar and were charged with the management of judicial and financial affairs. At the local level, a pyramidal administrative structure was put into place, nationwide: At the top were the regional governments; in the middle, the provincial governments; at the bottom, the district governments. Social reforms were also carried out in the same spirit: The boyar class disappeared, to be replaced by a new service nobility organized in a hierarchical fashion and governed by the "Table of Ranks." Finally, the Church was reformed: The Holy Synod replaced the patriarchate, the clergy was transformed into a corps of functionaries and the Church was generally subjected to the authority of the state.

In the realm of foreign affairs, the major event of Peter's reign was the Great Northern War, which involved a struggle between Russia and Sweden for mastery of the Baltic region. After two decades of nearly uninterrupted conflict, Peter the Great was victorious over his great rival Charles XII and obtained Estonia, Livonia, Ingria and a portion of Karelia in the Treaty of Nystadt. To overcome his adversary, Peter had found it necessary to build a navy from scratch and to equip a modern army, which he recruited from the ranks of the nobility and the peasantry through a generalized conscription.

# Politics and Institutions

## 1682

*April 17 (27).* Upon the death of Fedor III, high dignitaries and the late czar's counselors rule out his brother Ivan, who was weak in body and spirit, and proclaim as the new czar Fedor's half-brother Peter, the son of Alexis I and Natalia Naryshkina.

*May–June.* Fedor's sister Sophia, exploiting the discontent of the *streltsy*, inspires them to revolt against the Naryshkina clan, several of whose members are murdered. Peter and Ivan are named "co-czars" under Sophia's regency.

*July 6 (16).* The double coronation of Ivan and Peter takes place, an event that is unique in the history of European monarchies.

*Summer.* Sophia is forced to temporarily abandon Moscow to the *streltsy*. After regaining control of the situation, she has Prince Ivan Khovansky, the leader of the *streltsy*, apprehended and executed.

## 1687

*July.* Ivan Mazepa is elected hetman by the Ukrainian *Rada.*

## 1689

*January.* Peter marries Eudoxia Lopukhina.

*September 2 (12).* With Ivan's assent, Peter ends Sophia's regency after she had planned a coup in an effort to take power in her own right. Sophia is consigned to a convent, and Basil Golitsyn, her chief advisor, is exiled to Kargopol. The regency is conferred on Natalia Naryshkina.

## 1690

Out of the "play regiments" of his adolescence in the village of Preobrazhenskoe, Peter creates the first regiments of the Preobrazhensky and the Semenovsky Guards. A third of their forces is made up of French Huguenots who had taken refuge in Russia.

## 1694

*January.* Natalia Naryshkina, the regent, dies.

## 1696

*February 8 (18).* Czar Ivan dies. Peter becomes the sole czar.

## 1697

*January.* The *streltsy* launch a new plot.

*March.* Peter leaves Russia for the West. His journey takes him to Königsberg, Berlin, Hanover, Cleve, Amsterdam and The Hague. He stays near a shipbuilding works in Zaandam, where he works as an ordinary laborer.

## 1698

*January.* Peter is in London. He meets William III and visits the Royal Society, the Observatory and the Mint.

*August.* Following his visit to Vienna, where he meets Emperor Leopold, Peter returns to Moscow.

*August–September.* The *streltsy*, who were transferred to Azov, near the Polish border, stage a revolt. General Alexis Shein stops them before they march on Moscow, and more than 200 are condemned to death.

*September.* The czarina Eudoxia, accused of complicity in the *streltsy* plot, is exiled to the Cloister of the Intercession in Suzdal.

## 1699

Peter orders the formation of a permanent army, which will be made up of serfs and enlisted men, to replace the seignorial militias.

The private chancellery is established. A series of ordinances are put forward governing the organization of municipalities. Elected municipal chambers are set up.

*March 2 (12)*. François Lefort, counselor and mentor to Peter the Great, dies.

## 1700

A governing council is created, which takes over the responsibilities of the Boyar Duma.

## 1701

Ordinances are promulgated that ban kneeling for the passing of the sovereign and taking off one's hat during the winter months while passing before the czar's palace.

## 1703

*May 16 (27)*. St. Petersburg is founded.

## 1705

Peter establishes the first obligatory military conscription in Europe. Clergy, civil servants, members of guilds and a portion of the peasantry are exempted.

## 1705–1706

An uprising occurs in Astrakhan.

## 1705–1711

The Bashkirs of the Ural region revolt against Russian officials.

## 1708

Local administration is reformed. Russia is divided into eight *guberniia* (governments): Moscow, St. Petersburg, Kiev, Kazan, Azov, Smolensk, Archangel, Siberia. (The number of governments is later increased to 11.) The governments are themselves divided into 50 provinces administered by governors, or *voevoda*. Each province is divided into several districts headed by commissioners.

## 1711

The Boyar Duma is suppressed and replaced by a nine-member Senate presided over by a secretary general, who is charged with handling matters in the czar's absence. Peter leaves Moscow to lead a campaign in the Pruth River region. The Senate will be reorganized in subsequent years and led by a chief procurator (1722). It will assure the continuity of power and will become the country's supreme judicial and administrative authority.

Czarevitch Alexis marries Charlotte of Wolfenbüttel.

## 1712

St. Petersburg is made the official capital of Russia, and Peter orders all of the high nobility to install themselves there. The relics of Alexander Nevsky, which had been housed in Vladimir, are transferred to St. Petersburg in 1724.

Beginning at this time, provincial governors will be assisted by councils elected by the nobility.

*March*. Peter marries a former Livonian servant, Martha Skavronsky, who will become Catherine I.

## 1714

New regulations governing nobles and noble estates are adopted. The *pomestie* system, whereby estates are granted in reward for services rendered to the czar, is made universal. The former system of hereditary estates (*votchina*) is merged with the *pomestie*. Henceforth, all noble estates are deemed to be by grant of the sovereign, but they are made hereditary and inalienable. The key regulation mandates the transmission of estates to a single son, his identity being left to the discretion of the testator.

Young noblemen are required to know how to read and write in order to marry, and they are barred from becoming officers unless they have attended military school.

## 1717

Peter the Great makes his second journey to the West.

*May.* In Paris the czar meets with the regent and visits the academies, the Sorbonne, the Observatory and the Opera. He meets Louis XV in the Tuileries.

## 1718

The ministerial departments are reformed: The former *prikazy* system (administrative bureaus) is replaced by nine colleges (agencies). Each college is administered by a council of 11 members.

The judiciary is reformed: The *voevoda* are stripped of their judicial powers; courts of primary and appellate jurisdiction are established in all provinces; appellate courts are established in important cities.

The fiscal system is reformed: The household tax and the tax on cultivated lands are replaced by a head, or poll, tax.

*February.* Czarevitch Alexis, around whom are grouped all factions opposed to Peter's policies and who had fled Russia, is brought to St. Petersburg. Appearing before an assembly of high lay and ecclesiastical dignitaries, Alexis is forced to renounce his rights to the throne.

*March.* The former czarina Eudoxia, accused of adultery, is exiled to a cloister on the banks of Lake Ladoga.

*June.* Alexis is condemned to death by execution but dies on the 15th (26th),

the victim of apoplexy or perhaps of the torture he had undergone.

## 1719

Peter, the czar's designated successor, dies.

## 1721

*October 11 (22).* Peter the Great is named emperor by the Senate and abandons the title czar.

## 1722

The Ukraine is deprived of all administrative autonomy. It loses the right to elect its hetman, and, henceforth, it is to be governed by the College of Little Russia.

A manifesto by Peter on the subject of dynastic succession is published: Henceforth, the sovereign is to be empowered to freely designate his successor.

Rules governing the functioning of the colleges are promulgated.

*January 13 (24).* The Table of Ranks is created. It establishes a hierarchy of 14 ranks for civil, military and court services.

## 1724

*May.* The empress Catherine is crowned.

## 1725

*January 28 (February 8).* Peter the Great dies without having designated a successor.

# Foreign Affairs

## 1686

Russia enters the Holy Alliance (with the Holy Roman Empire, Poland and Venice) against the Ottoman Empire.

*May.* Russia and Poland sign a treaty of "eternal peace." Under its terms, Poland renounces its claim to Kiev in exchange for a Russian promise of military assistance against the Tatars and a payment of an indemnity of 1,500,000 crowns.

## 1687

Carrying out the terms of the treaty with Jan Sobieski, king of Poland, Basil Golitsyn undertakes an ill-fated campaign against the Crimean Tatars.

## 1688

The Russians are defeated in the Crimea.

## 1689

The Russians sign the Treaty of Nerchinsk with China. Russia renounces its claims to the Amur River basin, but it obtains the right to engage in commerce with China.

## 1695

The Russians suffer a defeat at Azov in their war against the Turks and Tatars.

## 1696

A new campaign is launched against Azov: The Turks and the Tatars are defeated and the city is taken.

## 1698

*August.* A meeting between Peter and Augustus II of Poland takes place at Rawa. They discuss a Polish-Russian alliance against Sweden.

*October.* Johann Reinhold Patkul, spokesman for the Livonian nobility that opposes Swedish domination, solicits the assistance of Russia. He proposes that Livonia be partitioned between Russia and Poland.

## 1699

*January 16 (26).* The Peace of Carlowitz terminates hostilities between the Ottoman Empire and Russia, Poland, Austria and Venice. Russia obtains Azov,

but the agreement mandates an armistice of only two years. The Russian diplomat Emelian Ukraintsev is charged with the task of obtaining a definitive peace with Constantinople.

*November 1 (11).* A conference is held at Preobrazhenskoe between the czar and envoys from Poland and Denmark. A secret alliance against Sweden is agreed to.

## 1700

*July.* The Peace of Constantinople is signed by Russia and the Ottoman Empire.

*Summer.* The Great Northern War begins, pitting Russia, Denmark, Saxony and Poland against Sweden.

*November.* The Russians launch an offensive against Narva, and an army of 40,000 besieges the city. The siege is interrupted by the arrival of Charles XII, king of Sweden.

## 1701

Menaced by Charles XII, Augustus II of Poland enters into a new alliance with Peter at Birsen.

*June 22 (July 3).* A Russo-Polish army is defeated by the Swedes at Riga.

*December 18 (29).* Boris Sheremetev crushes the Swedes at Erestfer.

## 1702

*July 7 (18).* Sheremetev scores another victory at Hummelshof. Volmar and Marienburg fall as well. Livonia is ravaged. Admiral Fedor Apraksin's forces see action in Ingria.

*November 30 (December 11).* Peter the Great takes Nöteborg and renames the fortress Schlüsselburg ("Key to the Baltic"). With their conquest of Nienschanz, the Russians control all of the Neva River.

## 1703

*May.* Russia wins its first naval victory at the mouth of the Neva. St. Petersburg is founded.

## 1704

*August.* After a fierce assault, Narva falls to the Russians.

## 1705

*December 8 (19).* Johann Patkul, the "czar's commissar," is arrested in Vienna (he will be turned over to the Swedes, then condemned and executed, in 1707).

## 1708

*January.* The Swedes launch an offensive against Russia. Charles XII marches on Grodno.

*July.* The hetman of the cossacks, Ivan Mazepa, who was courted by the Swedes in 1705, takes their side against the czar. The cossacks, frustrated by the measures taken by Peter to limit their autonomy, revolt against the Russians.

*November.* Peter the Great issues a manifesto to the Ukrainians, advising them to elect a new hetman. Many cossacks rally to the side of the czar, and Ivan Skoropadsky is elected hetman.

## 1709

*June 27 (July 8).* Charles XII is defeated at Poltava.

*July.* A quadruple alliance is formed. Russia, Poland, Denmark and Prussia join forces against Sweden.

## 1710

*July.* Sheremetev overcomes resistance at Riga. Karelia and Livonia are occupied. Frederick, duke of Courland, solicits Russian protection and asks for the hand of Anna Ivanovna, the czar's niece.

*November 9 (20).* Under pressure from Charles XII, who has taken refuge in Turkey, the Turks declare war on Russia.

## 1712

*September.* The Allies besiege Stralsund.

## 1713

*March.* The Russians conduct a campaign in Finland and take Åbo.

## 1714

*July 27 (August 8).* The Swedish flotilla is defeated by the Russian navy at Hangö (Gangut). The Åland Islands are occupied.

## 1717

*August 22 (September 2).* A commercial treaty is signed by Russia and France.

## 1718

Charles XII dies in Norway.

## 1719

*July.* The Russian flotilla raids the Swedish coast and lands cossack troops who march on Stockholm.

## 1720

The Russian navy wins a victory in the Åland Archipelago.

## 1721

*August 30 (September 10).* With French mediation, the Treaty of Nystadt is agreed to by the Russians and Swedes. This treaty marks the end of the Great Northern War. Russia obtains definitive possession of Livonia, Estonia, Ingria, a portion of Karelia (including Vyborg) and a portion of southern Finland, in return for the payment of an indemnity of 2,000,000 crowns.

## 1722

*May.* With a fighting force of 100,000 men, Russia launches a campaign against Persia along the Caspian Sea.

**1723**

*September 1 (12).* Persia abandons to Russia all of the Caspian coast, including Derbent and Baku and the provinces of Shirvan, Gilan, Mazanderan and Astrabad (Gorgan). Turkey protests.

**1724**

*June.* Russia signs a treaty with Turkey at Constantinople, dividing the Caspian territories among the two powers.

# Economy and Society

**1693**

With the aid of Dutch sailors, Peter the Great founds a shipyard at Archangel.

**1696**

Peter embarks on the construction of a naval fleet. He constructs a shipbuilding facility at Voronezh, on the Don. Twenty-three galleys are put to sea.

**1697**

An edict is issued mandating the establishment of forges at Tobolsk, to supply the requirements of the army for guns and cannons.

**1698**

*August 19 (29).* Peter issues a ukase that forbids the wearing of beards and requires the wearing of European-style dress.

**1699**

Commercial and industrial companies are created and afforded monopolies.

*December 15 (25).* Peter issues a ukase concerning the reform of the calendar. Henceforth, the year will begin in January rather than in September, which was the traditional Byzantine custom. The Christian Era is substituted for the Byzantine Biblical Era. The use of the Julian calendar, however, is continued.

**1702**

The *terem* (a separate quarters for women in the homes of noblemen) is banned.

**1703**

A fortress is constructed at Oranienbaum, in the government of Kazan.

**1704**

The administration of state farms is centralized. Revenues rise from 299,000 rubles to 569,000 rubles.

The killing of deformed children and of children born out of wedlock is banned.

**1705**

The selling of salt and tobacco becomes a state monopoly.

**1706**

The raising of sheep in the Poltava region is officially encouraged.

At the czar's instigation, the metropolitan of Novgorod founds a home for abandoned paupers.

The first Russian military hospital is established in Moscow. It is equipped with a school of surgery, a center for the study of anatomy and a botanical garden.

State pharmacies are established in St. Petersburg, Kazan and Riga.

**1708**

A revolt led by Hetman Conrad Bulavin takes place in the Don region. Persecuted Old Believers, military deserters, ruined peasants, fugitive serfs and cossacks will fight against the army of the czar for nearly two years.

**1710**

The tax on households and cultivated land is revised. The number of properties liable for tax according to the 1678 census is reduced by 20 percent (40 percent in the north).

## 1712
A state stud farm is established.
*February.* The Commerce College is created.

## 1714
*February.* An edict is issued mandating compulsory, free education for the children of deacons and priests.

## 1715
A commercial treaty is signed with Persia.

The Commerce College is charged with the tasks of training Russian merchants and organizing trade missions to Italy and Holland.

Asylums are established in all major Russian cities.

## 1717
Free trade in wheat is established. A number of commercial privileges previously accorded to foreign merchants are revoked.

## 1719
All commercial monopolies are revoked.

An edict is issued declaring that prospecting for and extracting all varieties of metals will henceforth be free and accessible to all. Proprietors of land retain only a right of priority.

## 1722
A coal deposit is exploited for the first time.

## 1723
The state gives up its manufacturing monopolies and endeavors to lease them to individuals by offering favorable terms.

## 1724
The growth in commercial traffic at the port of St. Petersburg continues: 16 for-eign vessels in 1714; 53 in 1715; 119 in 1722; 180 in 1724.

## 1725
Construction begins on a canal linking the Neva to the Volga. (The canal will be completed in 1732.)

Russia's production of cast iron equals that of England.

# Religious and Cultural Life

## 1683
Two Greeks, the brothers Likhoudis, teach logic and Aristotelian physics in Moscow.

## 1686
The Slavonic-Greek-Latin Academy opens.

## 1690
Patriarch Joachim, who had directed a repression of dissidents during the regency of Sophia, dies.

## 1700
Following the death of Patriarch Hadrian, Peter leaves the patriarchal seat vacant and organizes a provisional administration for ecclesiastical affairs. A community of Old Believers settles near Olonets, in Karelia.

## 1703
The first Russian newspaper, *Vedomosti* (the "News"), commences publication in Moscow.

## 1705
Russian missionaries reach Kamchatka.

## 1710
*January 18 (29).* An edict is issued making official the usage of a simplified Cyrillic alphabet. The Old Slavonic alphabet is retained only by the Church.

## 1715

Inspired by the German philosopher and mathematician Gottfried Leibniz, Russians begin planning an Academy of Sciences modeled on the Academy of Berlin.

## 1716

The czar orders a census of the Old Believers and takes fiscal measures against them (the double soul tax).

## 1719

The "Spiritual Regulations," rules governing ecclesiastical affairs, are promulgated under the authority of Bishop Theophanes Prokopovich.

## 1721

*January 14 (25)*. The Ecclesiastical College (the future Holy Synod) is inaugurated. The patriarchate of Moscow is eliminated and replaced by a permanent assembly charged with the management of Church affairs and the control of the clergy.

## 1723

*August 10 (21)*. Death of Prince Dmitri Cantemir of Moldavia, who served Russia and authored the *Description of Moscow*.

# Chapter 9        1725–1761

# The Rule of the Favorites

Catherine I, Peter the Great's second wife, was placed on the throne by the nobility, who expected to share power with her. Very quickly, however, the Petrine institutional structure was shaken: The Senate lost some of its authority, while in the provinces the governors (*voevoda*) gained broader powers. During Catherine's brief reign, two of her favorites, Alexander Menshikov and Peter Tolstoy, shared power and imperial prestige.

Upon Catherine's death Peter II, grandson of Peter the Great, ascended to the throne, but his reign was also brief. With the accession of Anne I, the evolution of state structures seemed to accelerate. Before she could become ruler, the nobility had imposed on Anne the "Conditions of Mitava," which prohibited her from making any decision without the assent of an enlarged governing council. With the help of the Imperial Guards, Anne shook off this tutelage and imposed a tyrannical and arbitrary regime. She relied heavily on her German favorites—Count Burkhard von Münnich, Andrei Osterman and Ernst Bühren; the latter came to symbolize her regime (the *bironovshchina*).

Soon after the death of Anne I, Elizabeth I seized power in a palace coup that removed Ivan VI (the grand-nephew of Anne and her designated successor) from the scene. Elizabeth I reinstituted Petrine traditions by reestablishing the authority and the prestige of the Senate. Her minister, Peter Shuvalov, effectively promoted the development of industry and commerce by freeing economic activity. Because the support of the nobility was essential to the stability of her regime, Elizabeth I extended the rights and privileges of nobles and augmented the institution of serfdom.

In the area of foreign affairs, Russia's interventions in European conflicts increased during the period. For the first time ever, Russian contingents appeared on the Rhine. Anne and Elizabeth fought on the side of Austria against France and Prussia during the wars of succession between Poland and Austria. Russia's generals also played a decisive role in the Seven Years War: Russian forces defeated the Prussians on several occasions, occupying Berlin and pushing Frederick II to the brink of ruin.

# Politics and Institutions

## 1725

*January.* Succession problems arise upon the death of Peter the Great. The sole male heir, his grandson Peter, son of Alexis, is only nine years old. Partisans of reform favor Catherine, whereas their adversaries support the former czarina Eudoxia. After a compromise is reached between the aristocrats and the "new men" of the late emperor's entourage, the Palace Guard installs Catherine as empress.

*June.* Anna Petrovna, the eldest daughter of the empress, marries Charles Frederick, duke of Holstein-Gottorp.

## 1726

*February.* The Supreme Secret Council is established and takes over some of the powers of the Senate. Presided over by the empress, the Supreme Council has seven members, including the two powerful figures in Catherine's reign, Alexander Menshikov and Peter Tolstoy.

## 1727

*May.* Catherine I dies. Peter II, who is only 12 years old, becomes ruler. Menshikov, who by now has become all-powerful, sends Tolstoy into exile.

Nominations of officers in the army become the province of the Supreme Secret Council.

*September.* Alexander Menshikov is disgraced and exiled to Siberia. An aristocratic reaction ensues as the Dolgorukys, upon returning to power, seek to restore the former rights of the old nobility. The Imperial Court is returned to Moscow from St. Petersburg.

## 1728

The Supreme Secret Council gradually assumes additional powers. The colleges (government agencies) are made subordinate to the council.

The College of Little Russia (the agency administering the Ukraine) is abolished, and the hetmanate is reestablished.

The Supreme Council decides to convene a deputation in Moscow to complete the codification of the laws.

## 1729

*November.* Peter II is married to Catherine Dolgoruky.

## 1730

The law relating to primogeniture is abolished.

*January.* Peter II dies. Ignoring Catherine I's will, which had designated as eventual successors Peter the Great's daughters Anne and Elizabeth, the Supreme Council chooses Peter the Great's niece Anne Ivanovna, the widow of the duke of Courland. She agrees to accept a charter drawn up by Dmitri Golitsyn (the "Conditions of Mitava") that limits her powers in favor of the Supreme Secret Council. Members of the lower nobility are displeased with this state of affairs; they demand that the charter be broadened to their favor.

*February.* Exploiting the divisions in the nobility, Anne renounces the Conditions of Mitava and establishes autocratic rule.

*March 4 (15).* Anne abolishes the Supreme Secret Council and restores the Senate to its former power.

*April.* The Dolgorukys are driven from power.

*July.* A corps of cadets is established, and the military academy is abolished.

*October 18 (29).* A three-member Cabinet of Ministers is established; its functions are identical to those of the former Supreme Secret Council.

**1731**

Anne issues a manifesto designating as her successor the future child of her niece Anna Leopoldovna (the future duchess of Brunswick).

**1732**

The Imperial Court and the administration is moved back to St. Petersburg. An accounting commission is established to control the gubernatorial administrations.

Count Burkhard von Münnich modifies the system of military recruitment: There will be one recruit for every 350 peasants, with the possibility of payment in lieu of service.

**1734**

As part of a renewal of the policy of centralization, the elective hetmanate of Little Russia is abolished and replaced by a provisional commission.

**1735**

The authority of the Cabinet of Ministers is strengthened: In the empress's absence, its decrees will have the force of law.

**1736**

A law is adopted limiting the military obligations of the service nobility and permitting one son of each of these families to remain on his family's lands.

**1740**

*August 2 (13).* Birth of Ivan Antonovitch, son of Anna Leopoldovna.

*October 17 (28).* Anne I dies. Ernst Bühren (Biron), who becomes regent in the name of Ivan Antonovitch, takes the title of highness.

*November 8 (19).* General Münnich has Bühren arrested and imprisoned at Schlüsselburg. Anna Leopoldovna is proclaimed regent and Münnich takes the title of prime minister.

**1741**

*January.* Ministerial responsibilities are reshuffled, leaving Münnich with authority only over the military. The direction of foreign affairs is returned to Andrei Osterman.

*November 25 (December 6).* Elizabeth Petrovna, daughter of Peter the Great, stages a coup d'état. She issues a manifesto that bases her right to power on Catherine I's will. The emperor Ivan VI and his family are imprisoned.

**1742**

*January.* Osterman and Münnich are condemned to death, then pardoned and exiled to Siberia along with Bühren. Alexei Bestuzhev-Riumen assumes responsibility for foreign affairs.

*April.* Elizabeth I is crowned in Moscow.

*November.* Elizabeth issues a manifesto designating her nephew, the duke of Holstein-Gottorp, as her successor.

*December.* The Cabinet of Ministers is abolished, and the Senate is reestablished with 14 members. The Dolgorukys return to the Court.

**1743**

The Conference of Ministers (equivalent to the former Cabinet) is established. The Senate, however, maintains an important role.

*May.* A Bureau of Petitions is established.

**1744**

Elizabeth receives a delegation in Kiev seeking the restoration of the hetmanate and the abolition of the provisional commission that was established in 1734.

*March.* A decree is issued creating the government of Orenburg.

## 1750

*February.* Cyril Razumovsky (brother of Elizabeth's morganatic spouse, Alexis) is elected hetman. Russian officials leave the Ukraine, and responsibility for Ukrainian affairs is transferred from the Senate to the College of Foreign Affairs.

## 1755

Peter Shuvalov, named grand master of the artillery, undertakes a program of military modernization.

*April.* A commission to codify the laws is established.

## 1757

Military recruitment is reformed: Previously limited to the 10 governments of Russia, recruitment is now extended to Little Russia and to the Baltic provinces.

## 1758

*February.* Bestuzhev-Riumen, who had opposed a Russian alliance with France, is arrested. Michael Vorontsov takes over responsibility for foreign affairs.

## 1761

The Senate issues a proposal for the administration of the Ukraine. The proposal calls for Kiev to be detached from the province and transformed into the seat of a region that would be administered directly by the Senate.

*December 25 (January 5, 1762).* Elizabeth I dies.

# Foreign Affairs

## 1725

*March 31 (April 11).* During an audience with the French ambassador Campredon, Catherine I proposes a Franco-Russian alliance and the marriage of Louis XV to Elizabeth Petrovna, daughter of Peter the Great.

## 1726

*July.* Maurice of Saxony, who had been elected duke by the Courland Diet, is expelled from Mitava by the Russians.

*July 26 (August 6).* Russia becomes a party to the Treaty of Vienna, which was signed in 1725 by the Hapsburg emperor Charles VI and Spain. Russia puts 30,000 troops at the disposal of its allies, in exchange for their support in the event of a war with the Ottoman Empire.

## 1727

*February.* The Courland Diet confirms the election of Maurice of Saxony as duke, again rejecting Alexander Menshikov, whom Catherine had designated.

*August.* A permanent peace is established with China on the basis of the territorial status quo. Regular commercial relations are established.

## 1728

*July.* The Tatars attack Little Russia.

## 1731

The Kazakhs of the Lesser Horde accept Russian sovereignty.

## 1732

*June.* Franco-Russian negotiations continue, but Osterman, against the wishes of Bühren, insists on Russian fidelity to the alliance with Austria.

## 1733

*August.* Russia supports Augustus III as a candidate for king of Poland against France's candidate, Stanislaus Leszczynski.

## 1734

*June.* Fighting breaks out between France and Russia in the War of the Polish Succession. Anne sends a fleet to the Baltic, where it defeats a French squadron off Danzig.

## 1736

*May.* Münnich conducts a campaign against the Crimean Tatars.

*October.* A war begins between Turkish and allied Russo-Austrian forces.

## 1737

*March.* Bühren is elected duke by the Courland Diet. This election will be ratified by Augustus III in July.

## 1738

Franco-Russian relations are reestablished. Prince Cantemir travels to Paris.

## 1739

*September 18 (29).* The Treaty of Belgrade ends hostilities between the Russo-Austrian alliance and Turkey. As a result of Münnich's victories (at Azov, Ochakov and Jassy), Russia recovers Azov and Zaporozhe, which had been lost during the reign of Peter the Great.

## 1741–1742

A Russo-Swedish war breaks out.

## 1743

*January.* The Congress of Åbo is held.

*June 5 (16).* The Treaty of Åbo is entered into by Russia and Sweden. Under its terms, Sweden cedes to Russia the eastern potion of southern Finland (the provinces of Kymmengard, Wilmanstrand and Nyslott).

*December.* Franco-Russian diplomatic relations, which had been interrupted by the conflict with Sweden, are

reestablished. The French ambassador, the Marquis de La Chétardie, returns to Russia.

## 1744

*January 24 (February 4).* At the instigation of Bestuzhev-Riumen, a treaty is signed between Russia and Saxony; it results in Russia's indirect engagement in the Anglo-Austrian coalition. A new break in diplomatic relations with France takes place.

*December 28 (January 8, 1745).* Elizabeth accedes to the Treaty of Warsaw between Austria, Saxony, England and Holland.

## 1746

*May 22 (June 2).* An Austro-Russian treaty is signed. It establishes a defensive alliance in which each side pledges to provide 30,000 men in the event the other is attacked. Bestuzhev-Riumen, the principal architect of the alliance, receives 6,000 ducats from the Austrian emperor.

## 1747

*June 1 (12).* An Anglo-Russian subsidy agreement is signed. Under its terms, Russia will receive 100,000 pounds each year to arm its troops.

## 1748

*April.* For the first time in its history, Russia intervenes in a conflict in Western Europe by sending troops to the Rhine.

## 1756

*July.* France and Russia resume diplomatic relations.

*December 31 (January 11, 1757).* Russia accedes to the Treaty of Versailles, which established a Franco-Austrian alliance.

## 1757

*January 11 (22).* An Austro-Russian convention is entered into. Under its terms, the two countries agree that each will provide 80,000 troops in the event of war with Prussia.

*August 19 (30).* The Russian army, under the command of Stepan Apraksin and Peter Rumiantsev, crushes the Prussian contingent at Gross-Jägersdorf. Instead of taking advantage of his victory and occupying Pomerania, Apraksin retreats to Tilsit.

*December 30 (January 10, 1758).* Russian forces occupy Königsberg.

## 1758

*July.* The Russians lay siege to the Küstrin Fortress, the key to control over Brandenburg.

*August 14 (25)* The Russian army is encircled by the Prussians at Zorndorf; it manages to extricate itself but suffers heavy casualties.

## 1759

*February 25 (March 8).* A Russo-Swedish convention is entered into, with the participation of France and Denmark. The key objective of the agreement is to close off access to the Baltic Sea to all foreign warships.

*July.* Russian troops led by Count Peter Saltykov defeat the forces commanded by Prussian General Dohna at Palzig, thereby opening the way to the Oder River, to Frankfurt, and to Berlin.

*July 30 (August 10).* Saltykov and the Austrian forces under General Gideon von Laudon crush the army of Frederick II at Kunersdorf. Divisions amongst the allies hamper their ability to exploit the victory.

*September 28 (October 9).* Saltykov enters Berlin; the city capitulates and is pillaged. Berliners are forced to pay 1.5 million thalers to the Russian invaders.

## 1760

*March 12 (23).* An agreement is negotiated with Austria, whereby Russia will obtain the western bank of the Dnieper from Poland and Austria will receive western Prussia from Frederick II.

# Economy and Society

## 1725

*January.* Vitus Bering's expedition is launched.

## 1725–1727

State revenues decline from 10 million to 8 million rubles per year. (Ninety percent of the decline is attributable to the peasantry.)

## 1727

Bering discovers the strait separating Asia and America.

## 1729

Legislation is promulgated concerning bills of exchange. Taxes are reduced on certain products (including hemp).

A decree is issued providing for the free exploitation of mines in the region surrounding Tobolsk.

*April 22 (May 3).* A fire ravages the German quarter of Moscow.

## 1730

A bureau for horse breeding is established.

## 1731

A decree is issued making the nobility responsible for the collection of the head tax.

## 1733–1743

Bering makes a second expedition to survey the eastern shores of Siberia,

Kamchatka, and the Kuril and Aleutian Islands. He dies in Alaska.

## 1734

An office for the oversight of manufacturing is established.

Russians explore their northern coast, from the White Sea in the west to the mouth of the Kolyma River in eastern Siberia.

## 1737

Guards and patrols are established in Moscow to prevent fires.

## 1739

Price controls are placed on grain.

## 1740–1750

Cloth manufacturing is established at Voronezh. The merchant Pustolov obtains many special privileges from the state, including jurisdiction over his workers. A postal route is established between Moscow and Astrakhan by way of Tsaritsyn, along with a connecting route from Tsaritsyn to Kiev.

## 1741

Primary schools are established in the government of Kazan.

## 1748–1755

To prevent deforestation, forges, distilleries and glass factories within a 200-kilometer radius of Moscow are ordered to shut down.

## 1749

The first Russian oil field is discovered.

The College of Mines and Manufacture, which had been abolished in 1725, is reestablished.

## 1750

A naval academy is founded.

## 1752

The central government makes an effort to introduce silkworms into Little Russia and into the governments of Astrakhan and Orenburg.

## 1753

Tobacco farming, which had been suppressed under Peter II, is reestablished.

The territory of the Zaporozhian Cossacks, ceded to Russia under the Treaty of Belgrade (1739), is colonized.

Two banks are established: a commercial bank, with capital of 500,000 rubles; and a bank for nobles, with capital of 750,000 rubles, which will make loans at a 6-percent rate of interest.

*December.* Seventeen internal customs duties are abolished.

## 1754

An edict is issued authorizing wheat trade between Russia and the Ukraine.

Peter Shuvalov's proposal for the abolition of all internal tariffs is adopted.

## 1755

The export of hemp, liquor and leather is prohibited.

The right to import foreign products into Little Russia is prohibited. Henceforth, Russia will have the sole right to import goods into this region.

Several taxes that were a burden to local industry are abolished in Little Russia.

At the instigation of the scholar Mikhail Lomonosov, Ivan Shuvalov (brother of Peter) founds Moscow University and becomes its trustee. At the time of its establishment, the university consists of faculties of law, medicine and philosophy.

## 1759

Peter Shuvalov monopolizes the livestock and cattle trade. This leads to a six-fold increase in prices, from which he realizes an enormous profit.

**1760**
A decree is issued limiting the rights of masters over their serfs in criminal matters. Deportation is substituted for corporal punishment.

**1761**
The Senate decides to postpone a general survey of the empire, a project that had been launched by Peter Shuvalov.

# Religious and Cultural Life

**1725**
   *November 2 (13)*. The Academy of Sciences is established.

**1726**
In order to save funds, an edict is issued ordering the merger of the secular schools created by Peter the Great with seminaries.

**1727**
The Supreme Secret Council orders the publication of *The Cornerstone of Faith*, a work that defends a strict interpretation of Orthodoxy against all reformist tendencies.

**1728**
The *St. Petersburg News* is founded, inspired by English journals that combine miscellany with popular science.

**1730**
   *March.* Anne issues a manifesto ordering the clergy to scrupulously follow ritual practices and condemning reformist tendencies in the Church.

**1733**
Steps are taken to combat the Old Believers. The baptism of children be-

comes obligatory, and those convicted of proselytization are sentenced to forced labor.

**1733–1738**
Instruction at the Academy of Sciences is suspended.

**1735–1742**
Italian opera is introduced into Russia, and a permanent troupe, directed by the Italian composer Francesco Araia, is founded. His own opera, *The Force of Love and Hate*, is performed. The Frenchman Jean-Baptiste Landet founds a school of ballet; works by Hasse and Dalloglio are staged.

**1735–1765**
The rococo style of Francesco Bartolomeo Rastrelli dominates Russian architecture during this period, as evidenced in the construction of the Winter Palace and the Smolny Convent in St. Petersburg, and the reconstruction of the imperial residences at Tsarskoe Selo and Peterhof.

**1739**
A decree orders the establishment of a seminary in every diocese.
   Mikhail Lomonosov writes his ode "On the Capture of Khotin."

**1743**
Instruction in the catechism is made obligatory in all schools.

**1746**
Lomonosov begins teaching a popular course in experimental physics.

**1747**
Alexander Sumarokov, a student in the cadet corps, writes his play *Khorev*, a Russian tragedy with a historical theme that enjoys great success.

## 1752
The palace of the Kremlin, damaged in the fires of 1701 and 1737, is rebuilt.

## 1756
The first permanent theater opens in Russia. Directed by Alexander Sumarokov, the theater features the troupe of the actor Fyodor Volkov of Iaroslavl.

## 1757
Ivan Shuvalov founds the Academy of Fine Arts in St. Petersburg.

## 1758
The French painter Louis-François Lagrenée settles in Russia. He will become director of the Academy of Fine Arts.

# Catherine II and
# "Enlightened Despotism"

Elizabeth I chose as her successor her nephew Peter of Holstein-Gottorp, a great admirer of Frederick II. Upon his accession to the throne, Peter III broke the alliances that Elizabeth had entered into with Austria and France (he judged them to be not very beneficial to Russia) and allied himself with Prussia. He surrounded himself with German advisors, including Count Burkhard von Münnich, a former counselor to Anne who was called back from exile. With Russia threatened by the possibility of a return of the hated *bironovshchina*, Catherine, the czar's ambitious spouse, had no difficulty rallying the Guards, and, with the assistance of the brothers Orlov, she deposed Peter III.

A reader of Montesquieu and a friend of Diderot and Voltaire, Catherine II claimed to rule in the name of the Enlightenment. Her convocation of a Legislative Commission, in which deputies drawn from all social classes were called upon to create a new body of laws for the empire, is a spectacular manifestation of Catherine's reforming spirit. The actual results of her reign, however, failed to match her intentions. In reality, Catherine pursued the policies of Elizabeth. By her Charter of the Nobility, Catherine consolidated the privileges of the nobility, freed it of all obligations of service to the state and granted it absolute authority over the peasantry. In addition, serfdom was considerably extended; indeed, the institution reached an apogee of harshness under the "enlightened despotism" of Catherine the Great. In the economic sphere, she freed industry from those last vestiges of state tutelage that Peter Shuvalov had permitted to persist, thereby spurring an unprecedented development of productive capacity. The Pugachev Rebellion, which threatened for an instant to bring down the monarchy, and, above all, the fear engendered later by the French Revolution put an end to any remaining liberal impulses.

In foreign affairs, the Northern System envisaged by Nikita Panin (an alliance between Russia, Prussia and England against France and Turkey) allowed Catherine to carry out three partitions of Poland and to annex Lithuania and White Russia. In two wars against Turkey, Russia conquered vast territories at the mouth of the Dnieper and annexed the Crimea. These new territories were then opened to colonization under the authority of Prince Grigori Potemkin.

# Politics and Institutions

## 1761

*December 25 (January 5, 1762).* Upon the death of Elizabeth I, Peter III, son of Anne (the eldest daughter of Peter the Great) and Charles-Frederick, duke of Holstein-Gottorp, ascends the throne. (Peter III is married to his cousin Sophia of Anhalt-Zerbst, who became the grand duchess Catherine in 1745.)

## 1762

*January.* Peter III abolishes the Secret Chancellery and does away with torture.

*February 18 (March 1).* The "Manifesto of Freedom to the Nobility" is promulgated. Already relieved of service obligations by Elizabeth I, the nobility is now freed from military service as well.

*June 14 (25).* Peter III inaugurates a Lutheran church at Oranienbaum and proclaims the equality of rights between the Protestant and Orthodox churches. He also decides to secularize the property of the Church. These measures, as well as his switching of alliances, which places Russian troops at the disposition of Frederick II (who is preparing for a war against Denmark), cause widespread discontent, particularly among the Guard.

*June 28 (July 9).* A coup d'état against Peter III is carried out. Alexis and Grigori Orlov and Nikita Panin rally the Izmailovsky Regiment and other regiments of the Guard, who occupy strategic positions in St. Petersburg. Catherine is proclaimed empress.

*June 29 (July 10).* Peter III abdicates.

*July 6 (17).* Catherine issues a manifesto officially declaring the abdi-

cation of Peter III. Peter is murdered under mysterious circumstances by Alexis Orlov at Ropsha.

*August.* The Senate meets and ratifies the coup d'état.

*September 2 (13).* Catherine II is crowned in Moscow.

*September 21 (October 2).* The Khrushchev-Gurev plot is discovered. The plotters had intended to topple Catherine from the throne and replace her with Ivan VI, who had been overthrown by Elizabeth I in 1741 and is still imprisoned at Schlüsselburg.

## 1763

The General Staff is reconstituted. It must reestablish the regiments following the Seven Years War (1756–1763), create new munitions factories, construct arsenals and barracks, and mark military routes.

*January.* In response to complaints of the peasantry concerning the domains of the clergy, Catherine transfers authority over ecclesiastical property to the College of Economics.

*March.* Archbishop Arseni Matsievich of Rostov is arrested. Arseni had taken a public position against the secularization of ecclesiastical property, calling on the people to resist and demanding the return of Ivan VI.

## 1764

The hetmanate of the Ukraine is abolished and the administration of the region is conferred to a College of Little Russia presided over by Peter Rumiantsev. Serfdom is extended to the Ukraine.

Catherine launches a program aimed at secularizing the property of the clergy: 900,000 Church serfs become state peasants and benefit from more favorable living conditions. Many monasteries are closed. An edict of tolerance is issued in favor of schismatics.

The Senate is reorganized and becomes larger and more powerful (four specialized departments are created to expedite procedure). Alexis Viazemsky, chief procurator of the Senate, is named director of the Commission on Interior Affairs.

*July.* Catherine II journeys to Courland.

*July 4 (15).* Ivan VI is murdered during an escape attempt at Schlüsselburg.

## 1765

The "Manifesto on the Division of the Empire into Governments" is published.

## 1766

The Ural Cossacks revolt.

*December.* An imperial manifesto is issued calling for the election of an assembly to take up legislative reform.

## 1767

*June 26 (July 7).* The *Nakaz* ("Instruction") is published in Russian, French, German and Latin. It sets out Catherine's political theories, which are borrowed largely from Montesquieu and Beccaria, for the benefit of the Legislative Commission.

*July 20 (31).* The Legislative Commission has its first meeting in Moscow. It consists of 564 deputies, of whom 30 percent are nobles, 39 percent are city dwellers, 14 percent are state peasants, 12 percent are representatives of national minorities, and 5 percent are representatives of the state administration; one deputy is an ecclesiastic, and serfs are unrepresented. The Commission is presented with 1,441 registers of grievances.

Catherine makes an inspection tour of the territory of the government of Kazan.

## 1768

*May.* The State Council is established. Its initial members are Alexis Viazemsky, Count Jakov Sievers, Pavel Bibikov, the Orlov brothers and Alexander Cherkassov. It is charged, in particular, with the reorganization of the army and of the administration of the military, with an eye toward the next war against the Ottoman Empire.

*December 7 (18).* The Legislative Commission is disbanded without having produced any results.

## 1771

The Ural Cossacks revolt again.

## 1772

Siberian exiles revolt under the leadership of Mauritius Beniowski.

## 1773

*September.* The Pugachev Rebellion begins. A cossack who passes himself off as Peter III, Emelian Pugachev rallies the discontented serfs and ethnic minorities in the region of the Ural River and leads them north, inciting mine and manufacturing workers in the Urals before turning west. At Kazan the rebels head south, following the Volga and clash with imperial troops on several occasions. Catherine appoints Bibikov "dictator of the East" and charges him with the repression of the uprising.

## 1774

Provincial courts are reformed.

*March.* Driven toward the Caspian Sea by Mikhelson and Alexander Suvorov, Pugachev sees his forces rapidly dissolve.

*August.* Mikhelson crushes bands of Pugachev's rebels at Tsaritsyn and takes more than 18,000 prisoners.

*September 14 (25).* Pugachev is captured.

*December.* Pugachev is brought to trial in Moscow.

## 1775

The "Administrative Instructions" are published. The number of governments set up by Peter the Great to handle economic and military affairs had already increased from 8 to 20 by 1762. A new division of the empire now creates 51 governments, each with 300,000 to 400,000 inhabitants. The former provinces are abolished, and each government is subdivided into districts (*uezdy*) of 20,000 to 30,000 inhabitants. At each echelon, administrative, judicial and financial organs are separated. Nobles, city dwellers and free peasants are given their own tribunals. Masters are given sole authority over their serfs.

*January 10 (21).* Pugachev is executed in Moscow.

## 1783

*April.* Grigori Orlov dies.

## 1785

The "Charter of the Nobility" is published; it codifies the status of nobles and defines their rights, franchises and privileges. The Charter grants nobles considerable control over the regional governments and the district administrations, including the judiciary. Nobles are freed from any obligation of civil or military service to the state, and they are exempted from taxes and corporal punishment. Henceforth, nobles alone have the right to possess lands cultivated by serfs, over whom they are granted absolute power (peasants being deprived of all recourse to the imperial administration). Nobles are permitted to engage in commerce and industry.

A "Charter to the Towns" is also published. Under its terms, inhabitants of cities are divided into six classes: landed proprietors, merchants (who themselves are divided into three guilds according to their level of prosperity), artisans organized into occupational associations (*tsekhi*), independent artisans, "eminent citizens" (those practicing the liberal professions), and strangers and temporary residents. City dwellers are granted the right to elect a municipal duma (composed of six municipal councillors, one for each class) and a mayor.

According to a report by the Count of Ségur, the French ambassador to Russia, in 1785 the Russian army's fighting forces number 500,000 men, of whom 230,000 are regular troops.

## 1787

*February–July.* Catherine II tours the Crimea during a visit organized by Potemkin, who is charged with developing the region. The empress is accompanied by Emperor Joseph II of Austria, the king of Poland, and a host of foreign ambassadors.

## 1791

*December 5 (16).* Potemkin dies.

## 1794

Catherine convenes a council of high dignitaries of the empire. She declares her intention to prevent Grand Duke Paul from succeeding to the throne because of what she considers to be his bad character and lack of ability. Catherine designates her grandson Alexander heir to the throne.

## 1796

*November 6 (17).* Catherine II dies.

# Foreign Affairs

## 1762

*April 13 (24).* Peter III signs a peace treaty with Prussia.

*May 29 (June 9).* Russia enters into an alliance with Prussia. Eighteen thousand Russian troops, led by Count Zakhar Chernyshev, join Prussian forces in Silesia.

## 1763

*April.* Ernst Bühren is reinstalled as duke of Courland at Mitava after his rival, Prince Charles of Saxony, is removed.

## 1764

*March 31 (April 11).* A new treaty with Prussia is signed. The two countries agree to support the candidacy of Stanislaus Poniatowski, an intimate friend of Catherine II, for the Polish throne.

The Northern System, an alliance between Russia, Denmark and England, is brought into being.

## 1766

A treaty of friendship and commerce is signed with England.

## 1768

*February 18 (29).* In Poland, the Confederation of Bar, a patriotic, anti-Russian association, is formed to oppose King Stanislaus II (Stanislaus Poniatowski). Bloody confrontations occur between Poles and Russian troops.

*September 25 (October 6).* Urged on by the French foreign minister (the duke of Choiseul), who wishes to protect the integrity of Poland, Turkey declares war on Russia. Frederick II sends to the Russians the assistance that was promised in the treaty of 1764.

## 1769

*September.* In the Russo-Turkish War, Russian troops, following a series of reversals, conquer the fortress at Khotin, the key to controlling Moldavia. Alexis Orlov incites the Greek populace of the Balkans and concentrates his fleet in the Aegean Sea.

*October 1 (12).* Prussia and Russia reach an accord on the protection of Protestant and Orthodox dissidents in Poland.

## 1770

*July.* Alexis Orlov totally destroys the Turkish fleet, which had sought refuge in the Bay of Chesme.

*September.* With forces that are inferior in number to those of the enemy, Peter Rumiantsev crushes the army of the Turkish grand vizier. Frederick II and Emperor Joseph II of Austria, increasingly anxious about the increasing power of Russia, hold talks.

*October.* Peter Panin conquers the fortress at Bendery, in Bessarabia. Prince Henry of Prussia travels to St. Petersburg to propose that Prussia mediate the conflict between Russia and Turkey.

*December.* Akkerman (on the Black Sea), Braila and Bucharest are conquered by Russian troops.

## 1771

Russia troops occupy the Crimea. A Russian protectorate is established, which Constantinople does not recognize.

*March.* Prussia attempts to mediate the conflict between Russia and Turkey. Catherine II demands Moldavia and Wallachia.

*December 24 (January 4, 1772).* Catherine II and Frederick II enter into a secret agreement on the partition of Poland.

## 1772

*February 8 (19).* A secret agreement is entered into with Joseph II on the partition of Poland.

*April.* Meetings between Russian and Turkish officials are held at Focsani.

*July 25 (August 5).* The first partition of Poland occurs. Russia annexes the northern bank of the western Dvina River as well as the regions of Polotsk, Vitebsk and Mogilev.

*September.* Alexander Suvorov wins victories at Karasu and Kuchuk Kainarji, but Rumiantsev is defeated at Silistria and must retreat across the Danube River.

## 1774

*March.* Forced to fight on two fronts because of Pugachev's rebellion, Catherine II reduces the forces she has deployed against the Turks.

*July.* The Russo-Turkish War ends with the signing of the Treaty of Kuchuk Kainarji. Under its terms, Russia gains the mouths of the Dnieper and the Bug, the steppe between these rivers, the right of free navigation on the Black Sea, and free passage for its commercial vessels through the Bosporus and Dardanelles straits.

## 1777

*March.* The alliance with Prussia is renewed.

## 1779

*May 2 (13).* Prussia and Austria sign the Treaty of Teschen. With the mediation of Russia and France, the treaty resolves the conflict over Bavarian succession.

## 1780

*February 28 (March 11).* Amid the conflict between England and its American colonies, Catherine publishes a manifesto proclaiming the right of "armed neutrality" and calling for respect for the rules of maritime rights.

*May 27 (June 7).* Catherine II meets with Joseph II at Mogilev.

## 1781

Denmark, Holland, Sweden, Prussia and Austria accede to the notion of "armed neutrality."

Potemkin constructs a fortress, barracks and a shipbuilding facility at Kherson.

## 1782

*October.* Russia and Denmark sign a treaty of friendship and commerce.

## 1783

Georgia is made a Russian protectorate.

Gustavus III of Sweden and Catherine II hold talks at Fredrikshamn.

*March 28 (April 8).* Catherine II issues a manifesto, prepared by Potemkin, declaring the annexation of the Crimea. Potemkin is given the title Prince of Tauride.

## 1787

Ekaterinoslav (Dnepropetrovsk) is founded on the Dnieper.

*May.* Despite British opposition, Russia signs a commercial treaty with France.

*June.* Catherine II meets with Stanislaus II at Kanev. The Polish monarch is unable to secure any relaxation of Russian domination of his country, where patriots continue their efforts to effect a national restoration. (These efforts will lead to the adoption of the Constitution of May 1791.)

*August.* Turkey declares war on Russia.

## 1788

*June.* Taking advantage of Russo-Turkish hostilities, Gustavus III declares war on Russia. A Swedish squadron menaces Kronstadt, and Swedish troops take Nyslott and march on St. Petersburg.

*December.* Suvorov takes Ochakov, on the Black Sea, with the help of Potemkin.

## 1789

*August.* The Swedes are defeated at sea by Admiral Samuel Greig, and on land by Admiral P. Chichagov and the prince of Nassau-Siegen.

Suvorov and the prince of Coburg defeat the Turks at Focsani, at the same time as the Austrians are conquering Belgrade. Potemkin takes Bendery and Gadzhibei (the future Odessa).

*August 30 (September 10).* Catherine II and Joseph II of Austria prepare a memorandum of agreement on the partition of the Ottoman Empire and on the formation of Dacia, which will consist of Moldavia, Wallachia and Bessarabia and have a Greek Orthodox sovereign at its head. Bosnia and Serbia are returned to Austrian control.

## 1790

*March.* The Russians suffer reversals in Finland.

*August.* The Swedes defeat the Russian fleet at Svensksund.

*August 3 (14).* Russia and Sweden sign the Peace of Wereloe, which preserves the territorial status quo.

## 1791

*December 29 (January 9, 1792).* Russia and Turkey sign a peace treaty at Jassy. The Treaty of Kuchuk Kainarji is reaffirmed, and Turkey recognizes the Russian annexation of the Crimea and cedes the steppes of Ochakov.

## 1792

*April.* In Poland, supporters of Russia form the Confederation of Targovica. The Constitution of May 3, 1791, is revoked, and preparations for war against Russia are interrupted.

*May 7 (18).* Russia intervenes militarily in Poland.

## 1793

*January 1 (12).* Russia and Prussia enter into an agreement on the second partition of Poland.

*January 12 (23).* The second partition of Poland is effected. Russia obtains the territory southwest of the Dvina River (western Belorussia, including Minsk and part of Volynia) and Podolia.

*January 28 (February 8).* Following the execution of Louis XVI, Catherine II annuls all treaties signed with France.

*March 14 (25).* Russia signs a treaty of alliance and financial assistance with England.

*September.* Catherine II recognizes the count of Provence, the brother of the executed Louis XVI, as regent of the Kingdom of France. All Frenchmen sojourning in Russia are required to swear an oath of nonadherence to the principles of the French Revolution.

## 1794

*March.* The Polish insurrection against the Russian occupiers begins.

*March 24 (April 4).* Tadeusz Kosciuszko defeats Russian forces at Raclawice. Russian garrisons in Warsaw come under attack.

*April 11 (22).* An insurrection erupts at Vilnius (Vilna).

*September 29 (October 10).* Russian and Prussian troops crush Kosciuszko's patriotic forces at Maciejowice.

*October 24 (November 4).* Suvorov seizes Praga, a suburb of Warsaw, which is forced to capitulate. The Polish insurrection is defeated.

## 1795

*October 13 (24).* The third partition of Poland takes place: Russia obtains Courland, Samogitia and the remainder of Lithuania, Belorussia and Volynia.

*November 14 (25).* Stanislaus II abdicates.

# Economy and Society

## 1762

*January.* Peter III reduces taxes on salt and lowers customs duties.

*February.* A state bank is created. It places in circulation 5 million rubles worth of assignats (paper rubles).

*August.* The Senate decrees the abolition of all monopolies.

## 1763

A Finance Commission is created; it is charged with the casting and the regularization of money, as well as with the creation of paper currency backed by gold.

A home for abandoned infants is established.

*August.* Catherine II awards the domains situated between Tsaritsyn and Astrakhan to the Moravian Brothers, a religious community. She grants the Brothers a substantial advance of funds, the right to freely exercise their religion, their own courts, and a 30-year dispensation from taxes and military service.

## 1764

A general regulation on the education of children is issued; it is inspired by Catherine II and based on the Rousseauist principle of segregated education according to sex. An institute dedicated to

the education of young noble girls (the future Smolny Institute) is established.

*October.* In order to set an example for her subjects, Catherine II has herself inoculated with the smallpox vaccine.

*December.* Ivan Betsky is given the task of formulating a plan for pedagogical institutions. An appeal is issued for foreign teachers.

A register of noble domains and of ecclesiastical and state properties is created.

## 1766

Catherine II suggests to the Free Society of Political Economy, which she founded, that it sponsor an essay competition on the abolition of serfdom and its consequences. The Society receives 120 submissions.

## 1769–1796

Russia puts into circulation 264 million rubles in the form of bank notes. The government borrows 47 million rubles from foreign sources and 82 million rubles from domestic sources.

## 1770

A plague epidemic strikes Moscow and rioting breaks out.

## 1772

A society to aid widows and orphans is established.

## 1773

The Institute of Mines is created.

## 1780

State controls over industry, imposed by Peter the Great, are abolished. A school of commerce is established.

## 1782

A protectionist tariff is put into effect. The number of factories in the country increases by a factor of four (to more than

3,000). Russia becomes the world's largest producer of iron, cast iron and copper.

Agricultural production is greatly increased. For the first time, Russia becomes an exporter of wheat.

## 1783

Schools for teachers are created (10 are established in St. Petersburg). The schools are based on the Austrian *Trivial-schulen* model, which was inspired by the Austrian pedagogue F. I. Yankovich.

## 1786

The State Assignat Bank is established.

The "Schools Statute" is published.

## 1791

Catherine II decrees the Pale of Settlement, 25 western provinces where Jews are permitted permanent residence.

## 1794

Property of the imperial family worth 1.5 million rubles is remitted to the State Treasury to remedy the deficit.

# Civilization and Culture

## 1763

Voltaire and Catherine II begin their correspondence.

## 1764

The construction of the first Hermitage, designed by Vallin de la Mothe, is begun in St. Petersburg.

The Academy of Fine Arts is reorganized, and Ivan Betsky becomes its president.

## 1765

The French encyclopedist Diderot sells his library to Catherine II for the sum of 16,000 pounds. He retains the use of the library until his death, and is given a yearly pension of 1,000 pounds.

The Physiocrat Mercier de la Rivière travels in Russia. Catherine II will later ridicule his reform projects in one of her plays.

## 1766

Denis Fonvizin stages his play *The Brigadier*, a satire of the mores of the nobility, in particular their francophilia.

## 1767

August Ludwig Schlözer, who, on orders of the empress, assembled the ancient sources for Russian history and published an anthology of laws and customs (which was used in the compilation of the *Nakaz*), publishes in Prussia a history of the reign of Catherine II entitled *The New Russia Transformed*.

Moscow University publishes a selection of articles from the *Encyclopedia*.

## 1768

Catherine II buys the collection of Count Brühl for 180,000 rubles. She collaborates on a translation of *Bélisaire*, a work by Jean-François Marmontel that is banned in France.

The first works by the editor and historian Nikolai Novikov appear.

## 1769

A periodical published by Novikov, the *Drone*, criticizes high society, courtly life and serfdom. It also engages in a polemic with the official review *All Sorts of Things* (the *Drone* will shortly be prohibited).

## 1770

Gardens designed by Vallin de la Mothe are constructed at the Hermitage.

The empress underwrites a trip to Siberia by Abbot Chappe d'Auteroche, a French geographer. Upon his return, the abbot will publish a book that is very critical of Russia, to which Catherine II will respond in her tract *The Antidote.*

## 1772

With Diderot acting as an intermediary, Catherine II acquires a collection of paintings of the French financier Antoine Crozat.

Novikov launches a new review, the *Painter.*

## 1773

*September 29 (October 10).* Diderot arrives in St. Petersburg, where he will remain until 1774. At the request of Catherine II, with whom he has frequent conversations, he prepares a plan for the education of Grand Duke Paul and a reform program for Russia.

## 1774

Novikov establishes a printing works, where he publishes *The Ancient Russian Library.*

## 1782

The equestrian statue of Peter the Great, by the French sculptor Etienne Falconet, is unveiled in St. Petersburg.

Frédéric César de la Harpe, a Swiss scholar, is appointed tutor to Grand Duke Alexander.

Fonvizin completes his play *The Hobbledehoy.*

## 1783

*January 13 (24).* Princess Catherine Dashkova is named director of the Russian Academy, which is modeled after the French Academy. She seeks to establish uniform rules of Russian spelling and grammar, to begin work on a dictionary and to "encourage the study of national history."

## 1786

Catherine II writes a series of plays in Russian and French that satirize freema-

sonry (*The Deceiver, The Deluded, The Siberian Shaman*).

## 1787

Freemasonry spreads throughout Russia (there are 145 lodges in Russia and an additional 75 in the portion of Poland annexed by Russia).

## 1790

Alexander Radishchev publishes his *Journey from St. Petersburg to Moscow,* a violent critique of serfdom and autocracy. Although it was initially authorized, the book is confiscated and its author is arrested and condemned to death but later sent into Siberian exile.

## 1791

Nikolai Karamzin founds *Moscow Journal,* in which he publishes his own works as well as literary criticism and translations.

## 1796

Catherine II orders the dissolution of all Masonic lodges. Novikov, a founding member of the first Russian Masonic lodge, is arrested and imprisoned in Schlüsselburg; Prince Trubetskoi is exiled.

---

### SERFDOM IN 1762

| Number of Serfs | Percentage of Proprietors |
|---|---|
| Less than 20 | 51 |
| 21 to 100 | 31 |
| 101 to 500 | 15 |
| 501 to 1,000 | 2 |
| More than 1,000 | 1 |

# Chapter 11                                    1796–1801

# Paul I and "Military Despotism"

Paul I did not ascend the throne until he was 42 years old. Confined to his domain at Gatchina, where Catherine II kept him out of the way, and threatened with being deprived of his rights to the throne in favor of his eldest son, Grand Duke Alexander, Paul waited for his mother's death with ill-concealed impatience. Marked for life by the coup d'état of 1762 and by the assassination of his father that had followed shortly thereafter, he devoted himself to the nurturing of a cult to the memory of Peter III.

Finally coming to power in 1796, Paul I was obsessed by a passionate desire to avenge his father and to erase the work of Catherine II. Reflecting his anxious nature and unstable character, Paul's policies were erratic and incoherent: He issued 500 decrees, many of them contradictory and each following the other at a frenetic pace, during the course of a reign that lasted less than five years. He provoked discontent amongst all classes of society and, very quickly, a nearly unanimous opposition formed against him. Paul's assassination was viewed by people throughout the country as a deliverance.

Liberal at first in reaction to the policies of his mother, Paul I freed Alexander Radishchev, Nikolai Novikov and Tadeusz Kosciuszko. But soon he set himself up as the champion of counterrevolution: He rooted out imaginary Jacobin plots, strengthened censorship and closed the borders. Paul also sought to bully the nobility. Angered by what he saw as its loyalty to the late empress and by the benefits it received from her favors, he attacked the nobility's privileges and abolished the Charter of 1785. Yet despite taking some halfway measures, Paul failed to effect any real improvement in the living conditions of the peasantry.

Paul's foreign policy was also full of contradictions. A pacifist when he took the throne, he ended up declaring war on France and Spain after the former occupied Malta. Joining the Second Coalition, Paul sent General Alexander Suvorov and Admiral Fedor Ushakov to fight in Italy and the Mediterranean. Yet shortly thereafter, believing that he had been betrayed by his allies, Paul formed a league of neutral countries with Prussia, Sweden and Denmark. On the eve of his assassination, he was planning an alliance with Napoleon Bonaparte.

# Politics and Institutions

## 1796

*November 6 (17).* Paul I becomes czar. In the days that follow, all individuals detained by the Secret Chancellery are freed and a general amnesty is declared for all officials facing prosecution. Nikolai Novikov is freed from the fortress at Schlüsselburg, and Alexander Radishchev is called back from exile. The 12,000 Poles who were detained in St. Petersburg after the insurrection of 1795 are given their freedom.

The former states of Livonia and Estonia, which had been abolished by Catherine II, are reestablished.

A decree is issued authorizing judicial recourse for "persons demanding their freedom."

*November 8 (19).* A decree is issued declaring that nobles serving in the regiments of the Guards will be subject to punishment for absenteeism.

*November 19 (30).* A decree is issued reestablishing all of the colleges that were abolished by Catherine II. Paul I places directors-general at the head of the colleges; these de facto ministers are to report directly to him.

*November 23 (December 4).* Three new military regulations (one governing the infantry and two governing the cavalry), all copied from Prussian regulations, are promulgated.

A Treasury Ministry is established.

*December.* Princess Catherine Dashkova is exiled to her estate at Troitskoe, where she will "ponder her memories of 1762."

*December 22 (January 2, 1797).* Article 15 of the Charter of 1785, which exempted the nobility from corporal punishment, is abolished.

## 1797

*February 5 (16).* Paul I confirms one of Catherine II's last decrees, which ordered the closing of all printing houses not authorized by the government and the establishment of various secular and ecclesiastical censorship offices.

*April 5 (16).* The coronation of Paul I is held in Moscow.

Paul issues a new law of succession, which provides for succession to the throne according to primogeniture in the male line, and the Statute on the Imperial Family, which institutes a system of appanages (*udels*).

*April 23 (May 4).* The right of the nobility to present its collective grievances to the sovereign, to the Senate, and to the provincial governors is abrogated.

## 1798

The 50 provincial governments created by Catherine II are reduced to 41. As an economizing measure, the fighting forces of the army are reduced; 45,440 troops are demobilized.

## 1799

A Department of Appanages is established. It is endowed with sufficient domains to provide for the needs of the imperial family, in order to save the Treasury the great expense necessary to maintain the Court.

Noble assemblies in the provincial governments are abolished.

*September.* Count Fedor Rostopchin and Nikita Panin are put in charge of the College of Foreign Affairs and then of the Chancellery.

*November 1 (12).* A decree is issued concerning the status of corporations.

## 1800

A Ministry of Commerce is established.

*March.* A military reform establishes administrative autonomy for the artillery.

*May 2 (14).* Elected members of noble tribunals are replaced by state officials.

*August 23 (September 4).* A new regulation is issued covering all municipal governments: Elected town councils are replaced by state administrators.

## 1801

*February.* Count Rostopchin is disgraced and exiled.

*March 11–12 (23–24).* A plot to force the abdication of Paul I is hatched by Count Peter Pahlen (the military governor of St. Petersburg), Plato Zubov and Count Leonti Bennigsen, with the assent of Grand Duke Alexander. The emperor, however, is strangled at St. Michael's Castle, which he had constructed to insure his security.

# Foreign Affairs

## 1796

*November.* The forces sent to Persia by Catherine II are recalled, and the military recruitment ordered in August is suspended.

## 1797

*October.* After the signing of the Treaty of Campo Formio, which ended the War of the First Coalition against France, Paul agrees to accept into his service regiments of the Prince of Condé that Austria is unable to maintain.

*December.* Louis XVIII takes refuge at Mitava. The Russian government grants him a pension of 200,000 rubles.

## 1798

The entry of all French nationals into Russia is prohibited.

*April–May.* Prince Nikolai Repnin attends the Congress of Berlin and proposes a quadruple defensive alliance between Russia, Austria, Prussia and England.

*September.* Following Napoleon Bonaparte's seizure of Malta in June, Paul I issues a manifesto declaring that he is placing the Knights of Malta under his protection.

The Russian fleet, under the command of Admiral Fedor Ushakov, wins its first victories in the Mediterranean, taking Cerigo and Zante.

*November 17 (28).* Paul is proclaimed grand master of the Knights of Malta.

## 1799

*April 16 (27).* Russian forces under General Alexander Suvorov, together with Austrian forces, defeat General Jean Moreau at Cassano d' Adda, opening the way to Milan.

*May 14 (25).* Turin is seized.

*June.* Paul I declares war on Spain.

*June 6–8 (17–19).* Suvorov defeats General Jacques Macdonald on the Trebbia River.

*July 17 (28).* Mantua is taken.

*August 4 (15).* Suvorov defeats General Barthélemy Joubert at Novi.

*August 6 (17).* Austro-Russian forces, commanded by General Alexander Korsakov, are driven back behind the Rhine by Marshal André Masséna.

*September 8 (19).* A Russian flotilla is defeated at Bergen.

*September 16 (27).* Masséna inflicts a severe defeat on Korsakov at Zurich before Suvorov's forces (who, in a superhuman effort, had battled their way through the St. Gotthard Pass) could arrive to assist their compatriots.

*October 7 (18).* Paul I, unhappy with his allies, breaks with England and Austria.

*October 18 (29).* Paul I signs a treaty of alliance with Sweden at Gatchina.

*November.* Following Bonaparte's coup d'état (the 18th of Brumaire), Paul ponders a rapprochement with the French leader.

## 1800

*July.* France frees and repatriates its Russian prisoners.

*October.* With an eye toward dividing the Ottoman Empire, Rostopchin proposes an alliance with France against England.

*December.* A series of treaties is entered into by Russia, Prussia, Sweden and Denmark, reaffirming the system of "armed neutrality" established in 1780.

*December 9 (21).* Bonaparte appeals to Paul I for a rapprochement between France and Russia.

*December 31 (January 12, 1801).* Paul I orders General Orlov, hetman of the cossacks, to march on British India with 22,500 troops.

## 1801

*January 2 (14).* Paul I demands that Louis XVIII leave Mitava and move to Kiel, and withdraws his pension.

# Economy and Society

## 1796

*November 29 (December 10).* At the behest of the peasants, the tax-in-kind on wheat is replaced by cash assessments.

## 1797

*January.* The Treasury contracts for a loan of 88 million florins from the Amsterdam market.

*February.* An uprising in the government of Orel is put down by Repnin. The provinces of Tula and Kaluga also experience unrest. (During the reign of Paul I, 278 peasant revolts will occur.)

*April.* A manifesto is issued limiting peasants' unpaid-labor obligation to three days per week; work is prohibited on Sundays and holidays.

*December 7 (18).* A special "assistance bank" is established for the nobility; it will make 25-year loans at 6 percent interest.

## 1798

*April 8 (19).* The Protestant University of Dorpat, which serves the nobility of Courland, Livonia and Estonia, is reorganized.

*July 23 (August 3).* The Russian-American Company, founded in 1784, is granted a 20-year monopoly on commerce with the new Russian Pacific colonies, the Kuril and Aleutian Islands, and Alaska.

*December.* A medical school is established, and orphanages are founded.

## 1799

*November 1 (12).* A decree on the status of corporations is issued.

# Religious and Cultural Life

## 1797

*March 7 (18).* A decree is issued proclaiming freedom of religion (with the sole exception of Catholic propaganda in Poland).

## 1798

*March 1 (12).* A decree is issued authorizing the Old Believers to build churches in all dioceses.

*April.* The importation of French books is prohibited.

## 1799

*April.* With the support of his close associate the czar, Father Gabriel Gruber seeks to obtain the official reestablishment by the Pope of the Jesuit order in Russia. Rumors spread that Paul I has converted to Catholicism.

## 1800

*April.* A decree is issued prohibiting the importation of all foreign books.

*October.* With the assent of the metropolitan of Moscow, the decree of 1798, which instituted a policy of tolerance toward Old Believers, is extended to the former capital, where Old Believers may henceforth settle.

*November.* Paul I meets with the Duke of Serra Capriola, the ambassador of the Two Sicilies. The czar declares himself in favor of a reunion of the Roman Catholic and Eastern Orthodox Churches.

# Chapter 12                   1801–1815

# The Reforms of Alexander I and the European Wars

The incoherence that characterized Russian policy under Paul I ended with the accession of Alexander I. From the very beginning of his reign, Alexander displayed his intention to reform the country. Several measures were quickly adopted: The public realm was liberalized; new governmental entities were created, including various ministries; and the groundwork was laid for a national system of education. Postponed because of Russia's participation in the anti-Napoleonic coalition (1805–1807), reform was taken up again following the reversal of alliances at Tilsit.

Count Mikhail Speransky looked toward the gradual transformation of autocracy into a constitutional monarchy. This prospect threatened the position of a nobility that was already alarmed by the possibility—albeit a very limited one—of the reopening of the question of serfdom. The strength of the nobility's opposition, the disastrous consequences for the Russian economy of the continental blockade, and the menace represented by the creation of the Grand Duchy of Warsaw led Alexander I to sanction a new confrontation with Napoleonic forces and to dismiss Speransky in March of 1812.

The Russian campaign, after the disaster of the invasion of the country and the occupation of Moscow by the French, sparked a burst of national pride that led to the liberation of Russian territory and projected the country into active participation in the defeat of the Napoleonic Empire and the reorganization of Europe at the Congress of Vienna. By 1815, Russia had joined the ranks of the great European powers. It controlled Finland, a major portion of Polish territory, and Bessarabia, which it had seized from the Turks. The patriotic and nationalist spirit that emerged from these victories would be sustained by confrontations with the West in the coming years.

## Politics and Institutions

### 1801

*March 11–12 (23–24).* Paul I is assassinated during the night. His son Alexander I succeeds him.

*March–April.* Initial reform measures are adopted: An amnesty is declared, political prisoners are freed, borders are reopened and restrictions are ended on the importation of foreign books.

*March 30 (April 11).* A permanent council with 12 members is established and charged with the study and preparation of laws.

*April 2 (14).* The Charter of the Nobility and the Municipal Regulations are reaffirmed.

The Secret (or Unofficial) Committee meets for the first time. Its members are Nicholas Novosiltsev, Paul Stroganov, Victor Kochubei and Adam Czartoryski. The committee will continue to meet until 1803.

## 1802

*September 8 (20).* A ukase is issued concerning the rights and duties of the Senate, which becomes the supreme institution of judicial and administrative control. A manifesto is also issued creating eight ministries: War, Navy, Foreign Affairs, Justice, Interior, Finance, Education, Commerce. These ministries replace the colleges established by Peter the Great.

## 1804

*July.* A moderate censorship law is adopted.

## 1807

*January.* A committee charged with the preservation of public security is formed. Mikhail Speransky becomes Alexander I's principal advisor on administrative issues.

## 1808

Count Aleksei Arakcheev is appointed minister of war (he will serve until 1810).

Speransky is charged with organizing the work of the commission on the codification of laws.

## 1809

Speransky presents the czar with his "Plan for State Reform," which looks toward the gradual establishment of a constitutional monarchy.

## 1810

*January 1 (13).* Marking a very partial implementation of Speransky's proposals, a State Council is established to replace the Permanent Council. Speransky is appointed secretary of state. Arakcheev becomes head of the Department of Military Affairs of the State Council.

## 1811

The state ministries are thoroughly restructured and their number is increased to 11.

Alexander I reads Nicholas Karamzin's *Memoir on Ancient and Modern Russia*, a pamphlet opposing Speransky's reform program.

## 1812

*March 17 (29).* Speransky is dismissed, accused of treason, and exiled to Nizhni Novgorod.

## 1815

Alexander I meets with Julie de Krüdener, "the Mystic Baroness," at Heilbronn.

# Foreign Affairs and Colonial Policy

## 1801

*June 5 (17).* An Anglo-Russian agreement is signed at St. Petersburg, reflecting the rapprochement between the two powers.

*September.* The annexation of eastern Georgia is confirmed.

*September 26 (October 8).* The Franco-Russian Treaty of Paris is signed. It includes a secret agreement dealing with the indemnification of dispossessed German princes and with matters relating to Italy.

## 1803

Russia conquers Mingrelia in the Caucasus.

## 1803–1806

Ivan Kruzenshtern leads an around-the-world naval expedition, during which the northern Pacific Ocean is explored.

## 1804

Russian domination of the Caucasus is extended to Imeritia, Guria and the Gandzha khanate. As a result of Russian annexations in Georgia, a war breaks out between Russia and Persia. The war will last until 1813.

Novo Arkhangelsk (Sitka) becomes the center of Russian power in Alaska.

## 1805

In the Caucasus, Russia conquers Karabakh and Shirvan.

Russia breaks with France and joins the Third Coalition.

*March 30 (April 11).* An Anglo-Russian alliance is established.

*July 28 (August 9).* Austria joins the Anglo-Russian alliance.

*September 11 (23).* The Russian alliance with Turkey is renewed.

*October 30 (November 11).* Prince Mikhail Kutuzov scores a victory over the French at Krems.

*November 20 (December 2).* Russian and Austrian forces are defeated by Napoleon's army at Austerlitz.

## 1806

In the Caucasus, Russia conquers Baku and Derbent.

Russia participates in the Fourth Coalition, along with England, Prussia and Sweden.

*November 9 (21).* At Berlin, Napoleon declares a continental blockade.

*November 15 (27).* The French army occupies Warsaw, displacing Prussian forces.

*November (December).* The Russo-Turkish conflict erupts again: Turkey declares war on Russia after the latter occupies the Danubian principalities.

## 1807

*January 27 (February 8).* A battle between allied Russian and Prussian forces and those of Napoleon occurs at Eylau; there is no clear victor.

*June 2 (14).* The Russians are defeated by Napoleon at Friedland.

*June 13–14 (25–26).* A meeting is held between Napoleon and Alexander I at Tilsit, on the Niemen River.

*June 25 (July 7).* The Treaty of Tilsit is entered into by France and Russia, which agree to an alliance. Russia recognizes the creation of the Grand Duchy of Warsaw and receives the region surrounding Bialystok.

*August 12 (24).* Russia and Turkey declare an armistice.

*October 26 (November 7).* Diplomatic relations between Russia and England are broken.

## 1808

Russia establishes diplomatic relations with the United States.

*September 15 (27)–October 20 (November 1).* Napoleon and Alexander I meet at Erfurt.

*September 30 (October 12).* The Treaty of Erfurt renews the Franco-Russian alliance. Nonetheless, relations between the two countries cool because of Alexander I's reticence to fight a war against Austria.

## 1808–1809

Russia and Sweden are at war with one another. Russia occupies Finland and issues an imperial manifesto, in March 1808, announcing the incorporation of Finnish territory into Russia.

## 1809

*March.* Alexander I presides over a Finnish Diet at Borgå and announces the creation of the Grand Duchy of Finland, whose grand duke is the Russian emperor.

War with Turkey erupts again.

*June–July.* Russia is formally an ally of France in the latter's war with Austria.

*September 5 (17).* The Peace of Fredrikshamn ends the Russo-Swedish War. The Swedes recognize the Russian annexation of Finland and the Åland Islands.

*October 2 (14).* The Treaty of Vienna establishes peace with Austria. Most of Galicia is given to the Grand Duchy of Warsaw, while Russia receives Tarnopol.

## 1810

In the Caucasus, Russia conquers Abkhazia.

*February.* Efforts to bring about the marriage of Napoleon and Grand Duchess Anne collapse. Franco-Russian relations rapidly deteriorate.

## 1811

*April.* Russia protests France's annexation of the Duchy of Oldenburg; the Franco-Russian alliance is ruptured.

*December 7 (19).* Kutuzov overcomes Turkish forces near Rushchuk.

## 1812

Fort Ross is founded by the Russians in California. This marks the farthest extent of Russian expansion in North America.

Diplomatic and military preparations are made for a Franco-Russian conflict.

*February 12 (24).* A Franco-Prussian alliance is formed.

*March 2 (14).* A Franco-Austrian alliance is formed.

*March 24 (April 5).* A Russo-Swedish alliance is formed.

*May.* Napoleon is at Dresden; Czar Alexander is at Vilna.

*May 16 (28).* The Peace of Bucharest is signed, ending hostilities between Russia and Turkey. Russia retains Bessarabia.

*May 21 (June 2).* A secret Austro-Russian accord is signed.

*June 12 (24).* The French Grand Army crosses the Niemen, beginning the invasion of Russia.

*June 16 (28).* Napoleon reaches Vilna.

*July 6 (18).* The raising of a militia to complement Russian fighting forces is announced.

*July 16 (28).* Vitebsk is lost.

*August 6 (18).* Smolensk is lost.

*August 8 (20).* Kutuzov takes command of Russian forces, replacing Prince Mikhail Barclay de Tolly, who is accused of having opened the way for the enemy to move on Moscow.

*August 26 (September 7).* The Russians are defeated by Napoleon in the bloody Battle of Borodino, 60 miles west of Moscow.

*September 2 (14).* The first elements of Napoleon's Grand Army enter Moscow, which has been evacuated by Russian forces and by a portion of the city's population. Fires break out, destroying more than two-thirds of the city.

*October 7 (19).* The Grand Army's retreat begins.

*October 12 (24).* The Battle of Maloyaroslavets forces the Grand Army to retake the route it devastated on its way into Russia.

*November 15–17 (27–29)*. The remnants of the Grand Army cross the Berezina River.

*December 11 (23)*. Alexander I enters Vilna.

*December 18 (30)*. A neutrality agreement is signed by Russia and Prussia.

## 1813

*January 28 (February 9)*. Russian forces occupy Warsaw.

*February 16 (28)*. The Treaty of Kalisz seals the alliance between Russia and Prussia.

*March–May*. A Russo-Prussian offensive in Germany is halted at the Battles of Lützen, on April 20 (May 2), and of Bautzen, on May 8–9 (20–21).

*May–July (June–August)*. An armistice prevails, during which time the anti-French alliance is enlarged to include Russia, Prussia, Sweden, England and Austria.

*August*. The conflict is renewed.

*October 4–7 (16–19)*. Russian, Prussian and Austrian forces defeat Napoleon's army in the "Battle of the Nations" at Leipzig.

*October 12 (24)*. The Russo-Persian War ends with the signing of the Treaty of Gulistan. Persia recognizes Russian sovereignty over Georgia.

## 1814

*January–February*. Russian forces participate in the allied invasion of France.

*February 25 (March 9)*. Austria, Prussia, England and Russia agree to a 20-year alliance in the Treaty of Chaumont.

*March 18–19 (30–31)*. Paris surrenders. Allied forces enter the city, with Alexander I at the head of Russian troops.

*May 18 (30)*. The First Treaty of Paris is signed. The borders of France are reestablished at their approximate location as of January 1, 1792.

*September*. Alexander I personally participates in the opening of the Congress of Vienna.

## 1815

*May 28 (June 9)*. The Congress of Vienna closes. Russia obtains most of the Grand Duchy of Warsaw, which it fashions into the Kingdom of Poland. Austria acquires Galicia, and Prussia gains Poznania.

*June 6–8 (18–20)*. The Battle of Waterloo takes place without the participation of Russia.

*June 24 (July 6)*. Allied forces again occupy Paris.

*September 14 (26)*. At the initiative of Alexander I, Russia, Prussia and Austria create the Holy Alliance. Invoking the Holy Trinity, the powers promise one another fraternity and mutual assistance.

*November 8 (20)*. The Second Treaty of Paris is signed. (The treaty envisages a five-year allied occupation of France; 30,000 Russian troops are to participate, out of a total allied force of 150,000. The Congress of Aix-la-Chapelle, which will meet in 1818, will approve an early evacuation of French territory by allied forces.) The Quadruple Alliance (England, Austria, Prussia and Russia) is formed.

# Economy and Society

## 1801

Following the accession of Alexander I, distributions of populated lands to the nobility are ended.

*May 28 (June 9).* Offers to sell serfs that do not also involve the sale of land are banned from the newspapers.

*December 12 (24).* The monopoly of the state and of the nobility over landed property is abolished. Henceforth, commoners will be permitted to acquire land without serfs.

## 1802

Production of sugar from beets is begun in the central provinces (it will expand rapidly in the Ukraine after 1835).

The first threshing machines to be produced in Russia are manufactured in the Moscow factory of an Englishman named Wilson.

*April 21 (May 3).* The University of Dorpat (Tartu) is reestablished.

## 1803

The Duke of Richelieu, a French emigré, becomes governor of Odessa.

*January 24 (February 5).* Education is reorganized in Russia. The country is divided into six educational districts, each led by a trustee, and a hierarchy of institutions is established, running from parish schools to universities. The University of Vilnius will soon be reestablished (in April), and the Demidov Gymnasium (secondary school) is opened in Iaroslavl (it will later become the Demidov Law School).

*February 20 (March 4).* A ukase concerning free agriculture is issued. It provides for the voluntary emancipation of serfs and assures that freed serfs receive some land. This law has little effect (only 47,000 serfs are freed during the reign of Alexander I).

## 1804

Measures instituted on behalf of serfs in Livonia fix their exact obligations to their masters while guaranteeing serfs hereditary tenure.

The Free Economic Society extols a report that demonstrates the superiority of paid labor over forced labor.

The Oginsky Canal, connecting the Niemen and the Dnieper, is constructed.

*November 5 (17).* A statute is issued granting autonomy to the universities. The Pedagogical Institute of St. Petersburg is founded (it will become a university in 1819). Preparations are made for the establishment of the Universities of Kharkov (opened in 1805) and of Kazan (opened in 1814).

*December 9 (21).* A law is issued concerning the Jews: Freedom of religion is guaranteed, but Jews must remain in the residence zone in the western provinces called the Pale of Settlement.

## 1805

A steam engine is first put to use in the cotton mill at Alexandrovsk, a state factory near St. Petersburg.

A Polish gymnasium is opened in Krzemieniec, in Volynia.

## 1807

Serfdom is abolished in the Grand Duchy of Warsaw.

Russia participates in the continental blockade after signing the Treaty of Tilsit.

*March 15 (27).* The registration of peasants (whereby certain state peasants had been forced to work in factories and mines) is abolished in the Urals.

## 1808

The sale of serfs at markets and fairs is forbidden.

The first privately owned cotton mill is opened in St. Petersburg.

## 1808–1811

The Mariinsk Canal System and the Tikhvin Canal System are built, connecting the Baltic Sea to the Volga, and thence to the Caspian Sea.

## 1809

*August 6 (18).* A ukase makes obligatory either a secondary education or the passage of an examination for individuals seeking to enter the high echelons of the civil service.

The right of landowners to deport serfs to Siberia is abolished. (This right will be reestablished in 1822.)

## 1810

The continental blockade has a catastrophic effect on Russian commerce and industry.

The ruble bank note is worth 33 silver kopecks. Speransky puts forward a plan to reform state finances. The plan includes government borrowing, taxation and limits on the money supply.

The first Russian military colony (populated by peasant-soldiers) is established in the government of Mogilev.

The Imperial Lycée is established at Tsarskoe Selo. Alexander Pushkin will study there from 1811–1817.

*December 19 (31).* A new customs tariff is instituted; it is favorable to English goods transported by neutral ships and unfavorable to French products imported overland.

## 1812

*December.* Believing that the elimination of serfdom is imminent, peasants riot in Penza.

## 1814

The ruble bank note is worth 25 silver kopecks.

## 1815

Peasant unrest erupts in the provinces of Poltava, Kursk and Orenburg.

The first Russian steamship is constructed at the Baird Foundry in St. Petersburg. The ship makes a celebrated voyage from Petersburg to Kronstadt.

# Civilization and Culture

## 1801

Construction begins on the Cathedral of Our Lady of Kazan in St. Petersburg; Andrei Voronikhin is the architect. Mikhail Kozlovsky designs a monument to Alexander Suvorov.

## 1802

The *Messenger of Europe* is founded by Nikolai Karamzin. Vasili Zhukovsky translates Gray's *Elegy*.

## 1803

Alexander Shishkov publishes his *Treatise on the Old and the New Styles of the Russian Language*.

## 1804

Ivan Pnin publishes *An Essay on Enlightenment with Reference to Russia*, which recommends an educational plan as part of a larger program of moderate reforms.

## 1805

Construction begins on the St. Petersburg Stock Exchange; Thomas de Thomon is the architect.

## 1806

Work begins on the reconstruction of the Admiralty in St. Petersburg; Adrian Zakharov is the architect. Construction begins on the Institute of Mines (designed by Andrei Voronikhin) and the Smolny Institute (designed by Giacomo Quarenghi).

### RUSSIAN FOREIGN TRADE AND THE CONTINENTAL BLOCKADE, 1801–1812
#### (in millions of silver rubles)

| Year | 1801 | 1802 | 1803 | 1804 | 1805 | 1806 | Average |
|------|------|------|------|------|------|------|---------|
| Exports | 44.5 | 49.4 | 59.0 | 51.7 | 60.7 | 49.6 | 52.5 |
| Imports | 34.6 | 40.3 | 44.4 | 39.2 | 42.7 | 37.6 | 39.8 |
| Total | 79.1 | 89.7 | 103.4 | 90.9 | 103.4 | 87.2 | 92.3 |

| Year | 1807 | 1808 | 1809 | 1810 | 1811 | 1812 | Average |
|------|------|------|------|------|------|------|---------|
| Exports | 40.4 | 28.3 | 34.5 | 34.2 | 34.7 | 38.8 | 35.2 |
| Imports | 27.2 | 16.2 | 19.8 | 20.6 | 23.1 | 23.2 | 21.7 |
| Total | 67.6 | 44.5 | 54.3 | 54.8 | 57.8 | 62.0 | 56.8 |

## 1808
The *Russian Messenger* is founded by S. Glinka. V. Zhukovsky publishes *Liudmila*.

## 1809
The first volume of Ivan Krylov's *Fables* is published. The School for Dramatic Arts is established in Moscow.

## 1812
*Son of the Fatherland* is founded by N. Grech. V. Zhukovsky publishes his patriotic poem "The Bard in the Camp of the Russian Warriors." I. Terebenev's anti-French caricatures, in the tradition of Russian popular woodcuts (*lubok*), are published.

*December.* The Bible Society of Russia is founded, with Alexander Golitsyn as president.

## 1814
Alexander Pushkin publishes his first poems in the *Messenger of Europe.* Konstantin Batiushkov publishes his poem "In the Shadow of a Friend."

# The Holy Alliance and the End of the Spirit of Reform

From 1815 onward, the ambiguous nature of the policies pursued by Alexander I became increasingly apparent, as did the frequent gulf between his proclaimed intentions and his actions. In foreign relations, the great principles that underlay the Holy Alliance counted for little when it came to solving actual problems. In reality, Russian national interests were pursued without fail, as can be seen in the development of Russian policy toward Greece and the Balkans. In domestic affairs, the granting of a constitution to the Kingdom of Poland appeared to signal a new burst of reforms, but those that were put forward were limited to confidential matters and were not long-lived.

At the same time, Alexander I was unable to gain the support of his country's most conservative elements. These reactionaries, who were shocked by his religious ideas and by his "cosmopolitanism," were nonetheless able to win numerous victories. This reactionary trend is associated with Alexis Arakcheev, Alexander's chief assistant during the second half of his reign. In the 1820s, under Arakcheev's tenure, despotism reached its zenith with the intensification of censorship, the purges in the universities, the dissolution of Masonic lodges, and the creation on a grand scale (and despite numerous revolts) of the disastrous military colonies.

Faced with a czar who had exiled Alexander Pushkin, the opposition was very limited and took the form of secret societies whose members were drawn from the ranks of the younger nobility and the military. Often influenced by Western liberalism, this opposition would eventually become public in the Decembrist Rebellion of 1825.

## Politics and Institutions

### 1815

Count Alexis Arakcheev is given a major role in governing the country. Although he does not have an official portfolio, he is charged with supervising all of the activities of the Committee of Ministers and becomes the czar's right-hand man.

*November 15 (27).* A constitutional charter is granted to the Kingdom of Poland by the Russian emperor, who sits on its throne. The charter provides for an elected Diet, a government and an army.

## 1816

Prince Alexander Golitsyn, chief procurator of the Holy Synod, is named minister of public instruction; this ministry will become the Ministry of Religious Affairs and Public Instruction in 1817.

Count Karl Nesselrode is named minister of foreign affairs (he will hold the position until 1856).

*February.* The Union of Salvation, a secret society, is founded in St. Petersburg. Its members drawn from the ranks of army officers, the society seeks a constitution for Russia. Members include Alexander and Nikita Muraviev, Sergei Trubetskoi and Paul Pestel.

## 1817

Secret societies are formed among young Polish university students (including the Panta Koïna in Warsaw, and the Society of Philomats, led by Adam Mickiewicz, in Vilnius).

## 1818

Secret reform programs, including Nikolai Novosiltsev's constitutional project and Arakcheev's plan for freeing the serfs, are put forward to no effect.

The Union of Salvation renames itself the Union of Welfare.

*March 15 (27).* Alexander I inaugurates the first Polish Diet. This is believed to foreshadow the extension of a constitutional regime to the whole empire.

## 1819

A constitution is developed for Finland but not put into effect.

The Ministries of the Interior and of the Police are combined and placed under the direction of Viktor Kochubei.

*March.* Count Mikhail Speransky becomes governor general of Siberia.

## 1820

The Jesuits are expelled from Russia.

Alexander Pushkin is exiled to southern Russia.

*June.* A special committee charged with drafting new censorship regulations is formed. The committee includes Mikhail Magnitsky and Admiral Alexander Shishkov.

*October 17 (29).* The elite Semenovsky Guards regiment stages a mutiny in St. Petersburg to protest against the brutality of its commanding officer, Colonel Fedor Schwartz.

## 1821

The Union of Welfare dissolves itself. It is replaced by two more-radical secret societies: the Southern Society (led by Pestel, whose program of action is called *Russian Justice*) in the Ukraine, and the Northern Society (led by Nikita Muraviev, whose program is called Constitution) in St. Petersburg.

The Patriotic Society is founded in Warsaw by Lukasinski.

## 1822

Despite the arrest of the leadership of the Patriotic Society, the group's activities continue.

*January.* Constantine, the brother of Alexander I, secretly renounces his right to the throne (this will be officially confirmed by Alexander in August 1823).

*January 26 (February 7).* Speransky's reforms of the Siberian administration are instituted.

*August 1 (13).* All secret societies and Masonic lodges are banned.

## 1823

Egor Kankrin is named minister of finance (a post he will hold until 1844).

The secret societies of students in Vilnius are repressed (Adam Mickiewicz will be exiled in Russia in 1824).

The Society of United Slavs, which espouses a federalist program, is formed in Volynia; it will reunite with the Southern Society in 1825.

The Polish Patriotic Society's activities continue.

**1824**

*May 15 (27).* Alexander Golitsyn, the minister of religious affairs and public instruction, is disgraced. He is replaced by Admiral Shishkov, who pursues a nationalist and reactionary program.

**1824–25**

Meetings take place between the Southern Society and the Patriotic Society. The societies disagree over the location of Poland's historic borders.

**1825**

*November 19 (December 1).* Alexander I dies at Taganrog.

# Foreign Affairs and Colonial Policy

**1818**

*September–November.* Alexander participates in the Congress of Aix-la-Chapelle, which approves an early evacuation of allied forces from France.

**1819–1821**

A Russian expedition led by Thaddeus Bellingshausen and Mikhail Lazarev explores Antarctica.

**1820**

*October–December.* Russia prepares for the Congress of Troppau, at which Alexander I will propose an intervention against the revolution in Naples.

**1821**

*January–May.* Alexander participates in the Congress of Laibach.

*March.* The Greek uprising against Ottoman domination begins. Alexander refuses to assist Ypsilanti in raising the Danubian principalities to rebellion against the Turks.

*June 16 (28).* The Russian position on Greek affairs takes shape: The Russian ambassador to Constantinople, Stroganov, demands that the Turks evacuate the Danubian principalities and stop massacring Greeks.

*September 4 (16).* Russia claims exclusive rights in Alaska north of the 51st parallel.

**1822**

*September–December.* Russia participates in the Congress of Verona, which approves a French military intervention in Spain.

**1824**

*April 5 (17).* Russia and the United States sign a treaty concerning Alaska. Freedom of navigation and of fishing are restored, and Russian colonization is limited to the territory north of the 54th parallel. This treaty marks the start of the Russian retreat from the Pacific Northwest.

**1825**

England and Russia sign an agreement dealing with Alaska.

# Economy and Society

**1816**

The serfs in Estonia are freed, but they are not provided with land.

Businessmen are forbidden to purchase serfs to work in their factories.

A moderate customs tariff that abolishes several trade barriers is adopted. The University of Warsaw is founded.

## 1816–1821

At the initiative of Alexander I, the number of military colonies is increased. Arakcheev organizes the new colonies.

## 1817

The serfs of Courland are given their freedom.

A state commercial bank is founded. (It will not be a success, and a portion of its deposits will be yielded to the State Land Bank.)

Finance Minister D. Gurev launches a program of borrowing in order to reduce the money supply.

A state monopoly on the sale of alcohol is declared.

The Makarev fair is transferred to Nizhni Novgorod.

The construction of paved roads begins (approximately 235 miles will be in service by 1825, and 2,000 miles by 1850).

The Lycée Richelieu is founded in Odessa.

## 1818

An agronomic society is founded in Moscow.

A teaching society is approved.

## 1819

The serfs are freed in Livonia. Rebellions break out in the military colonies (in particular at Chuguev, in the Ukraine).

A new liberal customs tariff is instituted, removing various barriers. It is violently opposed by industrialists.

The Pedagogical Institute of St. Petersburg becomes a university.

Mikhail Magnitsky conducts a purge at the University of Kazan. The following year he will become trustee of the district.

## 1820

The Bezborodko Gymnasium is founded at Nezhin. (Nikolai Gogol will study there between 1821 and 1828.)

A massive peasant uprising occurs in the Don region.

## 1822

Another new customs tariff is adopted, marking a return to a system of high trade barriers that will last until 1857 (there will be some relaxations in 1841 and 1850). Protection is accorded to the textile industry in particular, resulting in rapid development of weaving and of chintz printing: Textile factories are established at Ivanovo, and the Morozov works opens at Ore-khovo-Zuevo. Printed calico will be produced in the Zindel works, which will open near Moscow in 1823.

## 1824

Regulations governing guilds are adopted that strictly limit industrial and commercial activities by peasants and the simple "bourgeois."

*December 20 (January 1, 1825).* A law is passed authorizing manufacturers to free their serfs with the permission of the Committee of Ministers.

## 1825

A state foundry is established at Alexandrovsk. (The first rolling mill will be introduced there in 1826.)

The *Review of Manufacturing and Commerce* is founded.

# Civilization and Culture

## 1815

The Arzamas literary group is formed in St. Petersburg (it will meet until 1818). The group includes Vasili Zhukovsky,

## WAGE WORKERS IN RUSSIAN ENTERPRISES, 1804–1825
(forced labor still prevailed in the wool, metallurgy and paper industries)

| Industry | Number of Enterprises 1804 | 1825 | Percentage of Wage Workers 1804 | 1825 |
|---|---|---|---|---|
| Wool | 157 | 324 | 10 | 18 |
| Linen | 285 | 196 | 60 | 71 |
| Cotton | 196 | 484 | 83 | 95 |
| Silk | 328 | 184 | 73 | 83 |
| Paper | 64 | 87 | 22 | 24 |
| Iron and steel | 28 | 170 | 28 | 22 |
| Leather | 843 | 1,784 | 97 | 93 |
| Ropemaking | 58 | 98 | 85 | 92 |

Alexa nder Pushkin, Konstantin Batiushkov and Prince Peter Viazemsky.

**1816**
The first volume of the *History of the Russian State* is published by Nikolai Karamzin (twelve volumes will appear between 1816 and 1829).

**1817**
The Frenchman Auguste Ricard de Montferrand is charged with the design and construction of the Cathedral of St. Isaac in St. Petersburg (completed in 1858). The reconstruction of the University of Moscow (designed by D. Gilardi) is begun. K. Batiushkov publishes his poem "Dying Tass."

**1818**
The first architectural project of Carlo Rossi is begun in St. Petersburg; his works will eventually include the Elagin

Island ensemble (1818–1822), the Mikhailovsky Palace (1819–1825) and the General Staff Headquarters (1819–1829). The monument to Kuzma Minin and Dmitri Pozharsky, designed by Ivan Martos, is inaugurated in Red Square in Moscow. The first issue of the *Annals of the Fatherland* appears.

**1820**
Pushkin's *Ruslan and Liudmila* is published. A society for the encouragement of academic artists is founded. The painter Alexei Venetsianov begins to depict scenes from peasant life; his work will include *The Grange* (1821–1823).

**1821**
As a result of a national subscription, the actor Mikhail Shchepkin is emancipated and begins a brilliant career in Moscow. Pushkin completes *The Prisoner of the*

*Caucasus*, which will be published in 1822.

## 1822

Pushkin completes *The Fountain of Bakhchisarai*, which will be published in 1824.

## 1823

Pushkin begins *Eugene Onegin*, which will be published in 1831.

"The Lovers of Wisdom," a literary group, is formed in Moscow. Its members include Dmitri Venevitinov, Vladimir Odoevsky, Ivan Kireevsky and William Kukhelbeker. The group publishes a journal, *Mnemosyne*.

The journal *Polar Star* is founded by Kondrat Ryleev and Alexander Bestuzhev.

## 1824

Alexander Griboedov completes *Woe from Wit*, which will not be performed until 1831. Pushkin completes *The Gypsies*, which will be published in 1827. The Bolshoi Theater and the Maly Theater, designed by Osip Bove, are completed in Moscow.

## 1825

The *Moscow Telegraph* is founded by N. Polevoi. The *Northern Bee* is founded; the editors, Faddey Bulgarin and later Nikolai Grech, are merely servile spokesmen for the regime.

Pushkin begins *Boris Godunov*, which will be published in 1831. Baron A. Delvig completes his poem "The Bathing Women." Ivan Kozlov completes *The Monk*. K. Ryleev completes *Voinarovsky*.

# Chapter 14                    1825–1855

# Nicholas I and Conservative Modernization

The reign of Nicholas I began with the Decembrist uprising, which was quickly suppressed. Nicholas's refusal to countenance any concession to liberal aspirations characterized the period 1825–1855. During his reign, the Polish insurrection of 1831 was crushed, and Russia assisted Austria in putting down the Hungarian revolt of 1849. The period also saw an enormous increase in the means of repression, including the establishment of the Corps of Gendarmes, the strengthening of censorship, and the use of repressive measures to bring the universities into line with the new conservatism. All of these actions reflected the spirit of the official ideology of autocracy, orthodoxy and nationalism that had been put forward by Count Serge Uvarov.

Nicholas's reign was also characterized by a continuation of the process of modernization begun under Alexander I. Laws were codified by Count Mikhail Speransky, technical education was developed, and a modern bureaucracy with specially skilled functionaries was established. Although the creation of the Ministry of State Domains opened the way for the gradual transformation of the condition of state peasants, the ministry did not fundamentally challenge the social order, the stability of which seemed to be a condition for the continuance of autocracy. Industrial development, already behind that of the West, accelerated, thanks to strict protectionism in certain sectors, notably in weaving and in cotton milling. The textile industry began to employ increasing numbers of wageworkers, unlike the metallurgical industry of the Urals, which continued to rely primarily on forced labor.

During Nicholas I's reign, an intelligentsia also began to form in opposition to the bureaucracy, the landed nobility and the new industrial entrepreneurs. "Slavophiles" and "Westernizers" began to question their relationship to the "people" as well as to Russia's past and future. At the same time, Russian literature enjoyed a veritable "golden age" despite the government's rigorous censorship. But the nation's actual strength did not measure up to Nicholas I's ambitions abroad. He led the country into an ever more adventurous foreign policy vis-à-vis Turkey that culminated in the Crimean War, which revealed the weakness and inflexibility of the Russian Empire at this stage in its history.

# Politics and Institutions

## 1825

Alexander I's death creates a power vacuum. Nicholas, Paul I's third son, is hesitant to ascend the throne. Before agreeing to become emperor, Nicholas makes his brother Constantine swear allegiance to him.

*December 14 (26).* The Decembrist military uprising is prematurely launched by conspirators in the Northern Society. The insurrection is put down on Senate Square in St. Petersburg.

## 1826

The trials of the Decembrists result in five death sentences (including those of Paul Pestel and Kondrat Ryleev) and more than 100 deportations to Siberia.

*January.* An uprising by the Chernigov Regiment, led by Sergei Muraviev-Apostol, is put down in the Ukraine.

*January 31 (February 12).* The czar's Private Chancellery is developed. The Second Section, charged with the codification of laws, is established under the direction of Mikhail Speransky.

*June 10 (22).* Censorship is strengthened (it will be softened somewhat in 1828).

*July 3 (15).* The Third Section of the Chancellery is created. Directed by Count Alexander Benckendorff, it oversees the political police and the Corps of Gendarmes, which is responsible for safeguarding state security.

*July 13 (25).* The five leaders of the Decembrists are executed.

*December 6 (18).* The Secret Committee of the Sixth of December is established. Presided over by Victor Kochubei, it is charged with administrative reform. The Secret Committee will remain in existence, without making any noteworthy achievements, until 1832.

## 1828

The Fourth Section of the Chancellery, responsible for women's education and public assistance, is created.

*December.* In Warsaw, Under-Lieutenant Piotr Wysocki forms a secret society whose recruits are drawn from students at the officers' school.

## 1830

The *Complete Collection of Laws of the Russian Empire*, the first result of Speransky's efforts, is published. It is a 45-volume compilation of Russian laws issued since the Code of 1649.

*November 17 (29).* The Polish revolt begins in Warsaw. The Belvedere Palace is seized, and Grand Duke Constantine, commander of the army, is forced to flee.

## 1831

*January 13 (25).* Nicholas I is deposed as ruler of Poland by the Polish Diet.

*January 18 (30).* A national government led by Adam Czartoryski is formed in Poland.

*January 24 (February 6.)* Commanded by Marshal Hans von Diebitsch-Zabalkansky, 115,000 Russian troops march into Poland.

*February 13 (25).* Diebitsch-Zabalkansky is halted outside Warsaw in the Battle of Grochow.

*May 14 (26).* The Poles suffer a crushing defeat at Ostrolenka.

*Spring.* An insurrection in the empire's western provinces is put down.

*August 25–26 (September 6–7).* The Battle of Warsaw takes place. The city capitulates.

*August 27 (September 8)*. General Ivan Paskievich restores order to Warsaw.

*December*. A new regulation is issued concerning the participation of the nobility in local elections. Only those nobles who possess more than 100 souls or 3,000 *desyatinas* of arable land may enjoy direct suffrage.

## 1831–1832

The first meetings of the Nikolai Stankevich Circle are held in Moscow. Members will include Vissarion Belinsky, Timofei Granovsky and Mikhail Bakunin.

## 1831–1833

The Universities of Warsaw and of Vilna are closed, as is the Krzemieniec Lycée.

## 1832

A severe repression, including confiscations and deportations, is carried out in Poland and in the western provinces of the empire.

*February 14 (26)*. The Constitution of the Kingdom of Poland is replaced by an organic law: Poland is integrated into the Russian empire, and the army and the Diet are suppressed. Poland retains autonomy only for administrative matters.

## 1833

The *Code of Laws* (15 volumes) is published, reflecting a vigorous effort to systematize the law in Russia.

Celebrated for his formula "autocracy, orthodoxy, nationalism," Count Serge Uvarov becomes minister of public instruction (he will serve until 1849).

## 1834

Members of a circle founded in Moscow by Alexander Herzen and Nikolai

Ogarev are arrested. Herzen is banished to the province of Viatka.

The duration of visits to other countries is limited to five years for nobles and three years for commoners. (In 1851 these limitations will be tightened to three years and two years, respectively.)

N. Polevoi's *Moscow Telegraph* is banned.

## 1836

The Fifth Section of the Chancellery, charged with supervising the administration of state peasants, is created.

Nikolai Nadezhdin's *Telescope* is banned for having published the first of Peter Chaadaev's *Philosophical Letters*.

## 1837

*December 27 (January 7, 1838)*. The Fifth Section of the Chancellery is transformed into the Ministry of State Domains and put under the direction of Paul Kiselev. The local administration of state peasants is fundamentally reformed by the development of a program for self-administration.

## 1840

The Lithuanian Statute is abrogated, and Russian law is imposed on the western provinces of the empire.

## 1842

*April 15 (27)*. A new statute diminishes the powers of the State Council.

## 1843

The Sixth Section of the Chancellery, charged with the administration of the Caucasus, is created.

## 1845

A criminal code is promulgated.

The Petrashevsky Circle begins to meet in St. Petersburg. Led by Mikhail Petrashevsky, a disciple of the French socialist Charles Fourier, the circle is frequented by the writers Mikhail Saltykov-Shchedrin and Feodor Dostoyevsky.

**1846**

A Slavophile manuscript, "Letters from Riga," is circulated by Yuri Samarin; it denounces the preponderance of Germans in the administration.

*January.* The Brotherhood of Cyril and Methodius is founded in Kiev by the historian Nikolai Kostomarov and the poet Taras Shevchenko. They recommend the abolition of serfdom and propose a Slavic federation that would include the Ukraine. (The members of the Brotherhood will be arrested in 1847.)

*February 13 (25).* Nikolai Milyutin issues a new statute concerning the towns, but its application will be very limited.

**1847**

A criminal code based on the Russian code of 1845 is introduced into Poland.

*January.* Herzen leaves Russia.

**1848**

*February.* In Paris, Herzen participates in France's Revolution of 1848.

*March 14 (26).* An imperial manifesto is issued declaring that Russia, the bulwark of Europe, will not be lost to revolution.

*April 2 (14).* A secret committee is established to supervise censorship.

*June.* Bakunin participates in the Slavic Congress at Prague.

**1849**

*April 23 (May 5).* The members of the Petrashevsky Circle are arrested; 21 are condemned to death, including Dostoyevsky.

*December 22 (January 3, 1850).* After a simulated execution, the death senten-

ces of the members of the Petrashevsky Circle are commuted; those who were condemned are deported.

**1852**

Censors attack the *Muscovite*, a Slavophile journal.

**1853**

Herzen establishes a Russian publishing house in London.

**1855**

*February 18 (March 2).* Nicholas I dies.

# Foreign Affairs

**1826**

*March 23 (April 4).* An Anglo-Russian protocol proposes a mediation between the Turks and the Greeks.

*July.* The Russian Caucasus region is attacked by the armies of the shah of Persia, resulting in a new Russo-Persian War that will continue until 1828.

*September 25 (October 7).* A Russo-Turkish convention is signed at Akkerman. It provides for freedom of movement for merchant ships in the Bosporus and Dardanelles straits, and for autonomy for Serbia, Moldavia and Wallachia.

**1827**

*June 24 (July 6).* A convention is signed in London by England, France and Russia: The countries will send naval forces to separate Greek and Turkish fighting forces.

*October 1 (13).* Yerevan is seized by the Russians in the course of the Russo-Persian War.

*October 8 (20).* A Turkish-Egyptian fleet is destroyed in the Bay of Navarino by English, French and Russian squadrons.

## 1828

*February 10 (22).* The Peace of Turkmanchai is signed by Russia and Persia. Under its terms, Russia annexes Yerevan and Nakhichevan, merchant ships have the right to travel freely on the Caspian Sea, and Russia receives reparations.

*April 14 (26).* Russia declares war on Turkey and launches military operations in the Caucasus.

*June 23 (July 5).* Kars is taken from the Turks.

*September 29 (October 11).* In the Balkans, Varna is captured from the Turks.

## 1829

*June 27 (July 9).* The Russians take Erzerum.

*August 20.* Russian forces seize Adrianople.

*September 2 (14).* A Russo-Turkish treaty is signed at Adrianople. Under its terms, Russia annexes the mouth of the Danube, the towns of Anapa and Poti on the eastern coast of the Black Sea, and the districts of Akhalkalaki and Akhaltsikhe in the Caucasus. Additional terms mandate free passage of commercial ships through the Straits and declare Serbia, Moldavia and Wallachia to be autonomous countries under the protection of Russia. Greece remains a vassal state of Turkey.

## 1830

*January 22 (February 3).* England, France and Russia sign the Protocol of London, which guarantees the complete independence of Greece.

## 1832

*May 28 (June 9).* Pope Gregory XVI condemns the Polish uprising in his encyclical *Cum primum.*

## 1833

*April.* At the request of Sultan Mahmud II, Russia intervenes in the First Turko-Egyptian War. Ten thousand Russian troops disembark on the Asian shore of the Bosporus strait.

*June 26 (July 8).* Russia and Turkey sign the Treaty of Unkiar Skelessi. It provides for an eight-year alliance and contains a secret clause mandating the closing of the Dardanelles strait to any foreign warships upon Russia's demand.

*September 7 (19).* An agreement signed by Russia and Austria at Münchengrätz provides mutual guarantees concerning their respective Polish territories.

*October 3 (15).* A secret pact of mutual assistance is signed at Berlin by Prussia, Austria and Russia.

## 1834

In the Caucasus, Khamil (the third imam of Dagestan) leads an uprising that will continue until his capture in 1859.

## 1836

Russian, Austrian and Prussian troops temporarily occupy the free city of Cracow (they will evacuate the city in 1841).

## 1838

*July.* An Austro-Russian declaration made at Teplitz pushes Turkey into another conflict with Egypt.

## 1839

The European powers continue to intervene in the Turko-Egyptian conflict. Russia seeks a rapprochement with England.

A Russian campaign against Khiva departs from Orenburg (it will end in failure).

## 1840

*July 3 (15).* A convention on the Bosporus and Dardanelles straits is signed in London by England, Russia, Austria and Prussia. The countries agree that no foreign warships are to enter the Straits in times of peace.

## 1841

*July 1 (13).* Another convention on the Straits is signed by England, Russia, Austria, Prussia and France. The agreement reaffirms that the Bosporus and the Dardanelles are to be closed to all foreign warships in times of peace. Russia loses the privileged position it had gained in the Treaty of Unkiar Skelessi (1833).

## 1842

*August 17 (29).* The Nanking Treaty is signed by England and China. The English compete with the Russians for the Chinese trade. (For example, Chinese tea carried to Europe by English ships is cheaper than tea transported overland via Irkutsk.)

## 1844

*June.* Nicholas I travels to London.

## 1846

Russian control is extended over most of Kazakh territory.

*March.* Russian troops participate in the repression of the Cracow uprising.

*November 4 (16).* Austria annexes Cracow.

## 1847

*July 22 (August 3).* A concordat is reached between Russia and the Holy See. It defines the position of the Catholic Church in Russia, but it is unable to resolve all outstanding disputes.

## 1848

*July.* Russian troops intervene to restore order in the Danubian principalities.

## 1849

*April 19 (May 1).* The Agreement of Balta Liman is signed by Russia and Turkey. It provides for the joint occupation of the Danubian principalities. (The agreement will be rescinded in 1851.)

*June.* Russia assists Austria in putting down the Hungarian insurrection. Paskievich commands 170,000 troops in this action.

*August 1 (13).* The Hungarians, defeated at Vilagos, capitulate.

## 1849–1855

Led by Captain Gennadi Nevelskoi, an expedition to the Far East explores the mouth of the Amur River, surveys Sakhalin Island and establishes the first Russian settlement at Nikolaevsk (August 1850).

## 1850

A dispute arises between France and Russia over the Holy Sites (in the Holy Land).

*November 17 (29).* "The Retreat of Olmütz" takes place: Russia assists Austria in blocking the formation of a German federal state under the aegis of the Hohenzollerns.

## 1852

The Franco-Russian dispute over the Holy Sites intensifies. Catholics, backed by France, and Orthodox, supported by Russia, dispute the custody of the sites. Both powers put pressure on Turkey, which decides the issue in France's favor in December.

# 1853

Sakhalin Island is occupied temporarily by the Russians.

The fortress of Ak Mechet (Simferopol), in the Kokand territory, is conquered.

*January.* Nicholas discusses the possibility of dismembering Turkey, the "Sick Man of Europe," with the English ambassador Lord Seymour. The English government does not favor the proposal.

*February 23 (March 7).* Russia sends a special envoy, Prince Alexander Menshikov, to Constantinople. He demands absolute protection for the Orthodox Church in the Ottoman Empire. With the encouragement of England, Turkey rejects the Russian demand.

*May 9 (21).* Russia and Turkey break diplomatic relations.

*Early June.* An Anglo-French naval force arrives at the entrance to the Dardanelles.

*June 21 (July 3).* Russian troops under the command of Prince Mikhail Gorchakov invade the Danubian principalities.

*September 14 (26).* Nicholas I meets with Emperor Franz Joseph of Austria at Olmütz. Attempts at a reconciliation with England and France are rebuffed.

*October 4 (16).* Turkey declares war on Russia. Military operations begin in the Balkans.

*November 18 (30).* A Turkish squadron is destroyed by Admiral Paul Nakhimov at Sinop.

*December 23 (January 4, 1854).* The Anglo-French squadron arrives at the Bosporus.

# 1854

Vernyri (Alma Ata) is founded.

*February 15 (27).* The French and English issue an ultimatum to Russia

that its troops evacuate the Danubian principalities.

*February 28 (March 12).* France, England and Turkey enter into an alliance.

*March 15–16 (27–28).* England and France declare war on Russia. The Crimean War begins.

*March 28 (April 9).* England, France, Prussia and Austria declare their respect for the territorial integrity of the Ottoman Empire. Russia is isolated.

*April–September.* Austria pressures Russia to leave the Danubian principalities.

*April 8 (20).* Austria and Prussia enter into an alliance.

*June 2 (14).* Austria and Turkey sign an accord.

*July–August.* The French and English join forces at Varna, on the Black Sea.

*July–September.* The Russian armies retreat, and the Austrians occupy the Danubian principalities.

*July 27 (August 8).* The Conference of Vienna is held. Austria, England and France propose a four-point agreement that would include a collective guarantee of the independence of the Danubian principalities and of Serbia, international protection of Christians in the Ottoman Empire, free navigation on the Danube, and revisions to the 1841 agreement on the Straits that are unfavorable to Russian interests. Russia refuses to concede.

*September 2 (14).* French, English and Turkish troops disembark in the Crimea.

*September 8 (20).* The Russians are defeated at Alma, opening the way to Sevastopol for the allies.

*September 14 (26).* The siege of Sevastopol begins. The city has been fortified by the engineer Frants

Todleben, and its defense will be led by Admiral Nakhimov.

*October (October–November).* The Russians launch two attempts to break their encirclement: the Battle of Balaklava on October 13 (25) and the Battle of Inkerman on October 24 (November 5). Both end in the defeat of Russian forces.

*November 20 (December 2).* Austria declares that it will enter the war if Russia does not accept the demands formulated in Vienna in July.

## 1855

*January 14 (26).* Sardinia enters the war against Russia. The war will be continued by Czar Alexander II until it is ended by the Treaty of Paris, March 18 (30), 1856.

*January 26 (February 7).* Russia and Japan sign a treaty that provides for a division of the Kuril Islands by the two countries, and for their joint possession of Sakhalin Island.

# Economy and Society

## 1826

In his entry in an essay competition organized by the Academy of Sciences on the fall of wheat prices, the economist A. Fomin establishes a connection between the wheat crisis and the social system in Russia.

Peasant uprisings increase in number.

The Bible Society of Russia is disbanded.

## 1827

The University of Helsingfors (Helsinki) is founded.

The state monopoly on the sale of liquor is abolished.

The farm system is reestablished.

The first joint-stock insurance company is established.

*August.* Access to universities, institutes and gymnasiums is limited to free persons.

*August 26 (September 7).* An obligation of military service (with the possibility of conscription at 12 years of age) is imposed on Jews.

## 1828

The Technological Institute of St. Petersburg is founded.

A manufacturing council is created.

*December 8 (20).* A new statute for primary and secondary schools is promulgated.

## 1830–1831

An epidemic of cholera breaks out; it is accompanied by "cholera riots" in St. Petersburg and the provinces.

## 1831

The sending of youths under the age of 18 to study abroad is prohibited.

The Butenapov brothers establish an agricultural machinery factory in Moscow.

## 1832

An academy for civil engineers is founded.

A commercial treaty is signed with the United States.

A customs barrier is established between Poland and the rest of the Russian empire.

*February 10 (22).* A new individual or hereditary status is created, the "burgher of distinction." Endowed with certain privileges, the status does not lead to eventual entry into the nobility.

## 1832–1834

Russia suffers bad harvests and resultant famine.

**1833**

Prohibitions are imposed on the selling of serfs without land at auction in order to pay off private debts, and also on sales that would result in the separation of family members.

**1834**

The *Review of the Ministry for Public Instruction* is founded.

The University of Kiev is founded.

**1835**

A "Statute Concerning the Jews" redefines the Pale of Settlement (provinces where Jews are permitted permanent residence) in 15 western and southern provinces.

A textile mill is established in St. Petersburg by an Englishman named Wilson. It is one of the first joint-stock companies in Russia.

The first law regulating relations between owners and workers is promulgated.

*March.* A secret committee is created to examine the peasant question, but it fails to achieve any practical results.

*July 26 (August 7).* A new statute on universities reduces their autonomy and strengthens the powers of trustees.

**1836**

Metallurgical establishments in the Urals begin using the puddling process for producing iron. By 1845, this procedure will account for 45 percent of the region's iron production.

**1837**

The first passenger railway is built; it runs for approximately 16 miles from St. Petersburg to Tsarskoe Selo.

Prince Anatoly Demidov, the owner of a foundry in the Urals, asks the French engineer Le Paly to study the mining of coal in the Donets River region. (Total

production will increase from 15,000 tons in 1839 to 250,000 tons in 1871, and to 25 million tons in 1913.)

**1839**

Construction begins on a railway from Warsaw to Vienna (it will be completed in 1848).

Employing a steam engine imported from Belgium, the Geyer cotton mills in Lodz are mechanized.

*March 1 (13).* The Uniates of the western provinces of the empire are forced to reunite with the Orthodox Church.

*July 1 (13).* Finance Minister Count Igor Kankrin puts through a monetary reform resulting in the silver ruble becoming the official monetary unit; the paper ruble is given an exchange rate of 3.5 to the silver ruble. (In 1843 paper notes will have to be exchanged for credit rubles, which will circulate at par with silver rubles. Monetary stability will persist until the Crimean War.)

**1840**

*June 18 (30).* A law is promulgated authorizing the liberation of factory serfs. This will result in a large-scale shift to wage labor in the textile industry. A high level of forced labor will be maintained, however, in the metallurgical industry.

*August.* The government institutes measures intended to increase the farming of potatoes. Strong peasant resistance will emerge (including "the potato riots," an uprising of state peasants in the middle Volga region in 1842).

**1841**

Customs duties are relaxed.

Members of the Dukhobors sect are deported to the Caucasus.

A peasant uprising takes place in Guria.

## 1842

Construction begins on a railway between Moscow and St. Petersburg (it will be completed in 1851).

With the end of England's prohibition on the exportation of weaving machines, the 1840s will be a period of rapid growth in the Russian textile industry; the importation of raw cotton will greatly increase.

*April 2 (14).* A decree on "indebted peasants" is issued. It calls for contracts between owners and peasants, under which each peasant would receive for life a sufficient parcel of land in exchange for certain definite obligations. This law meets with little success.

## 1843

The first telegraph line connects St. Petersburg and Tsarskoe Selo.

*April 8 (20).* A ukase is promulgated to promote migration to the east. This will spark the development of Siberia (more than 50,000 persons will officially migrate between 1844 and 1861).

## 1844

*June 12 (24).* Landowners are authorized to liberate their house serfs without land by means of bilateral contracts.

*December 19 (31).* The Kahal, the autonomous organization of Jewish communities, is abolished.

## 1844–1848

"Inventories" are gradually introduced into the western provinces. They strictly establish the obligations of serfs and limit the power of Polish landowners.

## 1845

*June 11 (23).* A manifesto limits the access of civil servants to noble status. Hereditary nobility will now be bestowed only on those occupying the fifth rank instead of the eighth, as had previously been the case.

*August.* Children younger than 12 years of age are prohibited from night work.

## 1846

The "Corn Laws" are abolished in England, and, as a result, the export of Russian grain increases.

The Hübner Calico Manufacturing Company is established in Moscow.

## 1847

*October 27 (November 8).* Serfs are authorized to buy their freedom from their masters, in the event that the estate is put up for sale to cover debts. The effect of this measure will be very limited.

## 1847–1848

Cholera epidemics rage.

## 1848

*March 3 (15).* Serfs are granted the right to acquire unpopulated land and buildings, with the consent of their masters.

## 1849

Prince P. Shirinsky-Shikhmatov takes over the administration of universities and institutes, and he establishes new restrictions. The size of the student body is limited to 300 paying students at each university, and instruction in certain fields (including philosophy and constitutional law) is suspended.

A shipbuilding factory is established at Sormovo.

## 1850

A list of noble families in Georgia is published. Since 1831, however, a large portion of the Polish nobility in the Ukraine had been gradually stripped of its status.

## 1851

Customs barriers between Poland and the rest of the empire are abolished.

## 1852

The Southern Railway Society is established. The length of the Russian rail network will be 650 miles in 1855.

## 1854

The ruble depreciates during the Crimean War, and its convertibility will be abandoned until the adoption of the gold standard in 1897.

Encouraged by the ukase of April 3 (15), which called for volunteers for the Baltic Fleet, serfs migrate in huge numbers from the central provinces toward Moscow. They are forcibly repressed.

# Civilization and Culture

## 1826

Vasili Zhukovsky becomes the tutor of the czarevitch Alexander. Nikolai Lobachevsky elaborates a non-Euclidean geometry.

## 1827

The *Moscow Herald* is founded by Mikhail Pogodin. Construction of the Narva Gates, designed by Vasili Stasov, begins in St. Petersburg (it will not be completed until 1834). Portrait of Alexander Pushkin, by Orest Kiprensky.

## 1828

Pushkin writes *Poltava* (published in 1829) and begins *The Slave of Peter the Great*. Alexander Polezhaev: *The Song of the Shipwrecked Sailor*.

## 1829

Nikolai Gnedich publishes a translation of *The Iliad*. Mikhail Lermontov begins *The Demon* (completed in 1839). Mikhail

Zagoskin launches the genre of the Russian historical novel with *Iuri Miloslavsky or the Russians in 1612*. Nikolai Polevoi: *History of the Russian People* (6 volumes, published 1829–1833). In St. Petersburg, construction begins on the Senate and the Synod, both designed by Carlo Rossi.

## 1830

The *Literary Gazette* is founded by Baron A. Delvig. Pushkin writes *Tales of Ivan Belkin* and begins work on *The Stone Guest*. A school of architecture is founded.

## 1831

Premiere of *Woe from Wit*, by Alexander Griboedov. Pushkin completes *Eugene Onegin* and begins *The Tale of the Golden Cockerel* and *The Tale of the Czar Saltan;* he responds to the European partisans of Poland in *To Russia's Detractors*. Nikolai Gogol: *Evenings on a Farm near Dikanka*. The *Telescope* is founded by Nikolai Nadezhdin. In St. Petersburg, the collection of the Rumyantsev Museum is opened to the public (it will be transported to Moscow in 1861).

## 1832

Alexander Bestuzhev: *Ammalat Bek*. M. Lermontov: *The Angel*. Mikhail Glinka: *Trio pathétique*. The Institute of Painting and Sculpture is founded in Moscow; it is a more progressive institution than the old Academy. Completion of the Alexander Theater in St. Petersburg (C. Rossi).

## 1833

Emelyan Lenz discovers the law of the direction of inductive currents. Pushkin writes *The Bronze Horseman*. Karl Briulov completes his painting *The Last Day of Pompeii*. Nicholas I commissions

A. Lvov to write a national anthem, "God Save the Czar."

**1834**

The *Reading Library* is founded by Josip Senkovsky. Vissarion Belinsky: *Literary Reveries.* Pushkin: *The Queen of Spades, History of Pugachev.* In St. Petersburg, construction of the Alexander Column (Ricard de Montferrand).

**1835**

The chair of Russian history is inaugurated at Moscow University by Mikhail Pogodin. First volume of verse by Alexei Koltsov. Gogol: *Mirgorod* (with "Taras Bulba"), *Arabesques* (with "Nevsky Prospect," "Diary of a Madman," and "Portrait") and *The Nose.* Nikolai Pavlov: *Three Tales.* A. Vierstovsky: *Askold's Tomb,* an opera.

**1836**

Pushkin completes *The Captain's Daughter* and *The Stone Guest,* and he founds the *Contemporary,* which publishes the poetry of Fedor Tiutchev. Gogol: *The Inspector General.* Opera by M. Glinka: *Ivan Susanin (A Life for the Czar).*

**1837**

M. Lermontov: *Death of the Poet,* on the death of Pushkin, who was killed in a duel on January 29 (February 10). Peter Chaadaev: *Apology of a Madman.* Alexander Ivanov begins his monumental painting *The Appearance of Christ before the People* (1837–1857). In Moscow, construction begins on the Church of Christ the Savior (Konstantin Ton), which will be completed in 1883.

**1838**

M. Lermontov: *The Song about the Czar Vassilevich.* Construction begins on the Grand Palace in the Kremlin in Moscow (K. Ton), which will be completed in 1849.

**1839**

Creation of the Observatory of Pulkovo, near St. Petersburg (Vasili Struve). Development of Slavophile ideas: Alexei Khomiakov, *On the Old and the New;* Ivan Kireevsky, *An Answer to A.S. Khomiakov.* Founding of the Westernizer journal *Annals of the Fatherland,* edited by A. Kraevsky; Vissarion Belinsky is the journal's literary critic. Timofei Granovsky holds the chair of world history at Moscow University.

**1840**

M. Lermontov publishes *A Hero of Our Time* and *The Novice.* Nikolai Nekrasov: *Dreams and Sounds.* Sergei Aksakov begins *The Family Chronicle.* Publication of *Kobzar,* the first collection of verse by the Ukrainian poet Taras Shevchenko.

**1841**

M. Lermontov is killed in a duel. The *Muscovite,* a Slavophile organ, is founded by M. Pogodin. Alexis Tolstoy: *The Vampire.* The Russo-Byzantine style of K. Ton is officially adopted for the construction of churches and public buildings.

**1842**

Nikolai Zinin synthesizes aniline dye. Gogol: the first part of *Dead Souls* (he will burn the second part), *The Overcoat, The Marriage.* Evgeni Baratynsky, *The Gypsy.* Glinka's opera *Ruslan and Liudmila.*

**1843**

Alexander Herzen: *Dilettantism in Science.* The Marquis Astolphe de Custine publishes *Russia in 1839 (Journey for Our Time)* in Paris.

**1844**

Vladimir Odoevsky: *Russian Nights.*

## 1845

The Russian Geographical Society is founded. Mikhail Petrashevsky collaborates on the *Pocket Dictionary of Foreign Words in the Russian Language* (1845–1846), which covertly examines the ideas of pre-Marxist socialists.

## 1846

Feodor Dostoyevsky: *The Double, Poor Folk*. Alexander Herzen completes *Who Is to Blame?*

## 1847

N. Nekrasov takes over the *Contemporary*, which begins publishing Ivan Turgenev's *Sketches from a Hunter's Album*. Gogol: *Selected Passages from Correspondence with Friends*. Dostoyevsky: *The Landlady*. Ivan Goncharov: *A Common Story*. Sergei Soloviev holds the chair in Russian history at Moscow University. Publication of the Prussian baron Agustus von Haxthausen's *Studies on the Interior of Russia*. The French ballet master Marius Petipa arrives in St. Petersburg.

## 1848

Dostoyevsky: *White Nights*. M. Glinka: *Kamarinskaia*. Painting by Pavel Fedotov: *Matchmaking for the Major*.

## 1849

Translation of *The Odyssey* by V. Zhukovsky. Construction begins on the Armory in the Kremlin in Moscow (K. Ton); it will be completed in 1851.

## 1850

Turgenev: *Diary of a Superfluous Man, A Month in the Country*. Alexander Ostrovsky: *It's a Family Affair, We'll Settle It among Ourselves*. A. Herzen: *From the Other Shore* and *On the Development of Revolutionary Ideas in Russia* (in German).

## 1851

S. Soloviev publishes the first volume of *The History of Russia from Most Ancient Times* (29 volumes will be published between 1851 and 1879).

## 1852

Turgenev completes his *Sketches from a Hunter's Album*. A. Herzen undertakes *My Past and Thoughts*. Leo Tolstoy: *Childhood*. The Hermitage Museum is inaugurated in St. Petersburg.

## 1854

The first collection of poetry by F. Tiutchev appears. A. Ostrovsky: *Poverty is Not a Crime*. Leo Tolstoy: *Boyhood*. Turgenev: *Two Friends, A Quiet Spot*.

# Chapter 15    1855–1881

# Alexander II: The "Czar-Liberator"?

Alexander II came to power in the midst of the Crimean War. As soon as the conflict had ended, the czar launched a program of thorough-going reforms: first and foremost, the emancipation of the serfs, but also a whole series of measures that transformed local administration, justice, education and, later, the army. These changes were real, even if they did not envisage the abolition of the autocratic system but only its modernization. The application of reforms remained dependent on the will of the czar, who, depending upon the circumstances, could curb them or modify their range as he pleased. This spirit of reform, however, did not preclude the ruthless crushing of the Polish rebellion in 1863. Moreover, the limited nature of Alexander's reforms led to a break with the radical-ized segment of the intelligentsia and to a revolt of the younger genera-tion. This was evident in the nihilism of the 1860s, the populism of the 1870s, and the drift toward terrorism that culminated in the assassination of the czar in 1881.

Alexander's uncompleted drive for modernization kept the peasants under the heavy yoke of the rural commune, which gave them plots of land that were not sufficient to support them in the face of accelerated demo-graphic growth. At the same time, however, Alexander's reforms did help to put into place the economic infrastructure that would set the stage for future industrial development: a large increase in the railway network (which developed into the principal commercial route for European Russia); the slow development of a banking system; and the appearance of pioneering facilities for the production of carbon and steel in the Ukraine, and of petroleum in Baku.

An active and often brilliant foreign policy allowed Alexander II to overcome the humiliation of the Treaty of Paris, which ended the Crimean War. He used to advantage, when he deemed it necessary, the powerful Pan-Slavic sentiment to which a segment of Russian society adhered: Russia posed as the liberator of Bulgaria and as the protector of Orthodox Balkan peoples. In addition, the country maintained its position in the Caucasus even as it expanded farther into Central Asia and the Far East. But Russia's expansion also caused anxiety on the part of England and Japan, the other colonial powers in these regions.

# Domestic Events and Reforms

## 1855

*February 18 (March 2).* Upon the death of Nicholas I, his son Alexander II ascends the throne.

## 1856

Peasant uprisings increase in number (80 will occur each year, on average, between 1855 and 1861).

The debate over serfdom intensifies. There is a growing number of proposals for emancipation (including those of Konstantin Kavelin, Alexander Koshelev and Yuri Samarin), and discussions of the issue appear in the press (the *Contemporary*) and in the publications of Alexander Herzen from London.

*March 30 (April 11).* In an address to the nobility of Moscow, the czar states that it will be better to begin to abolish serfdom from above than to wait until it begins to abolish itself from below.

*May.* In an address to the Polish nobility at Warsaw, the czar cautions against idle dreams about nationalism. Nevertheless, an amnesty permits the repatriation of several thousand Poles who had been deported to Siberia.

## 1857

An agricultural society led by Count A. Zamoyski is established in Warsaw.

In London, Alexander Herzen and Nikolai Ogarev begin publishing the periodical *Kolokol* (the "Bell"). The chief voice of the opposition, this publication will be read even at the Russian Court itself.

*January.* A secret committee is created to study the possible emancipation of the serfs.

*November 20 (December 2).* An imperial decree mandates that provincial committees of the nobility be created to work out proposals for the emancipation of the serfs.

## 1858

The secret committee examining the emancipation question is transformed into the Main Committee for Peasant Affairs. In the provincial committees, a fierce disagreement arises over the shape of the reform: A majority of the nobility from the north, where the farmland is relatively infertile, supports providing emancipated serfs with land, whereas the nobility from the "black earth" regions opposes giving land to freed serfs.

Peasants who till the appanages (the domains of the imperial family) are emancipated.

The Slavic Committee of Moscow is formed with the approval of the government.

## 1859

*March.* Drafting commissions are established to review the work of the provincial committees. The majority of the commissions' members (including Nikolai Miliutin) are reformers.

## 1860

*October 10 (22).* The drafting commissions reviewing proposals for emancipating the serfs complete their work. An emancipation statute is submitted to an oversight committee.

## 1861

*February.* Patriotic demonstrations take place in Poland. Troubles persist despite the efforts of the czarist government to rally to its side a segment of the Polish aristocracy.

*February 19 (March 3).* A statute abolishing serfdom is enacted. Despite numerous restrictions, 20 million serfs on private domains (one-half of the country's peasants) are emancipated. A "temporary dependence" period of 49 years is established, during which the former serfs are obligated to reimburse the state for the compensation it extends to the landowners for land transferred to the peasants. The peasants are also subject to the tight control of a new system of rural communes (an outgrowth of the old mir), in which communal possession of the land and periodic redistribution of plots is maintained. The land received by the peasants quickly proves insufficient to support them.

*April.* A peasant uprising in Bezdna, in the province of Kazan, is repressed; the peasants had called for their immediate freedom and for land. The months that follow bring more denunciations of the incomplete nature of the reform, including those of Herzen and Ogarev in *Kolokol,* and of Nikolai Chernyshevsky in the *Contemporary.* In addition, the "nihilist" movement emerges among the younger generation, as evidenced in the works of Dmitri Pisarev and Nikolai Dobroliubov, and in the calls for revolt issued by Nikolai Shelgunov, Mikhail Mikhailov (*To the Younger Generation*) and Peter Zaichnevsky (*Young Russia,* 1862).

*September–October.* Student agitation occurs in Kazan, St. Petersburg and Moscow.

*October 2 (14).* A state of siege is proclaimed in Poland.

*Late 1861.* The secret society *Zemlia i Volia* (Land and Freedom), made up of various revolutionary circles in St. Petersburg and the provinces, is organized by Alexander and Nikolai Serno-Solovievich.

## 1862

In Poland, the "Reds" (the revolutionaries, as opposed to the moderates, or

"Whites") disseminate propaganda and prepare to lead an insurrection.

*February.* The liberal nobility of the province of Tver calls for the reconvening of the *Zemskii Sobor.*

*May.* Huge fires break out in St. Petersburg; the authorities use them as an opportunity to denounce the "nihilist" agitation. Numerous arrests will be made in the months that follow, including those of Pisarev and Chernyshevsky (the latter will write *What Is to Be Done?* while in prison). The secret society Land and Freedom begins to break apart (it will disband completely in 1864).

*September 24 (October 6).* A new procedure for conscription is instituted in Poland. Hereafter, conscription will be effected not by the drawing of lots but by lists drawn up by the administration.

## 1863

*January 10 (22).* The Polish rebellion erupts prematurely. Even though it spreads to a few western provinces of the empire (particularly Lithuania), the uprising is weakened by the division between "Reds" and "Whites" and by the inertia of the peasantry. Greeted with hostility by most Russians (with the exception of certain individuals like Herzen and Mikhail Bakunin), the rebellion is brutally put down by the czar's troops. Extremely violent repressive measures are taken in Lithuania and in the Kingdom of Poland. All areas of autonomous Polish authority are eliminated, and confiscations, deportations and Russification occur on a massive scale. In the northwestern and southwestern provinces the terms of the peasants' reimbursement for land are made more advantageous to the peasantry than is the case in the rest of the empire, a measure clearly directed against the Polish landed gentry.

*June 18 (30).* A liberal statute on universities becomes law under the auspices of Education Minister Alexander Golovnin. The statute provides universities with greater autonomy; permits the election of rectors, deans and professors; and limits the power of curators.

*June 26 (July 8).* A statute is enacted granting peasants on the appanages significant plots of land and making redemption payments obligatory.

## 1864

*January 1 (13).* Local administration is reformed by the creation of the zemstvo system. District assemblies are to be elected for three-year terms by three electoral constituencies: large landed proprietors, town dwellers and peasants. In turn, the district assemblies will elect provincial assemblies. Under the tutelage of the administration, the zemstvos are responsible for public health, local instruction, regional transportation and economic development. The zemstvo system is confined to the 34 central provinces of the empire.

*February 19 (March 2).* An agrarian reform advantageous to the peasantry is instituted in Poland: Peasants receive land without any redemption requirement.

*July 14 (26).* A statute on public primary education is enacted. The authority to create and to manage primary schools is conferred on the zemstvos; a scholarly council representing the state, the Church and the zemstvos is charged with supervising education.

*November 19 (December 1).* A statute on education is enacted. Hereafter, "classical" gymnasiums will be the sole route to a university education, while "modern" gymnasiums (modeled on the German *Realschulen*) will lead to higher technical training.

*November 20 (December 2).* The judiciary is reformed, based on a plan by Sergei Zarudni. The reform provides for equality before the law, the independence and irremovability of judges, and the use of juries in criminal trials. The office of justice of the peace (elected by the district zemstvos) is created, as are district courts and courts of appeal.

## 1865

A new code of military justice is promulgated. It is one of a series of reforms instituted by Dmitri Miliutin, minister of war from 1861 to 1881.

*January.* The assembly of the Moscow nobility calls for the convocation of an Assembly of the Russian Land. The czar rejects this request.

*April 6 (18).* A new, fairly liberal censorship statute is enacted.

## 1866

*April 4 (16).* Dimitri Karakozov makes an unsuccessful attempt on the life of Alexander II. Although this is the isolated act of a young member of the small Ishutin circle, a wave of repression will follow. The *Contemporary* and the *Russian Word* are suppressed, and conservatives hostile to reform assume positions of power (among them is Count Dmitri Tolstoy, the chief procurator of the Holy Synod since 1856, who becomes minister of education).

*November 24 (December 6).* A new statute on state peasants is enacted. Their right to the perpetual use of their plots is confirmed, along with the theoretical possibility of ownership in the future.

## 1867

A Slavic congress is organized in Moscow without Polish participation.

## 1868

A Slavic committee is formed in St. Petersburg (others will be formed in Kiev and Odessa in 1869 and 1870).

## 1869

Mikhail Bakunin and Sergei Nechaev meet in Geneva and draft the *Revolutionary Catechism*. In Moscow, Nechaev founds a secret society, "People's Retribution," which executes one of its members, a student named Ivanov, for treason. (Dostoyevsky will write about this incident in *The Demons*.)

Peter Lavrov's *Historical Letters* (1868–1869) is published.

Nikolai Danilevsky's *Russia and Europe* is published. Panslavist sentiment grows rapidly.

## 1870

*January 9 (21)*. Alexander Herzen dies.

*June 16 (28)*. Municipal reform is instituted. Municipal dumas are to be elected, with suffrage based on property qualifications. These bodies will, in turn, elect local mayors. Under the control of the higher administration, these municipal bodies are charged with the management of local transportation, education, health, lighting and provisioning.

## 1870–1873

The populist Chaikovsky circle forms in St. Petersburg. The circle includes Nikolai Chaikovsky, Mark Natanson, Sophia Perovskaia, Peter Kropotkin and Sergei Kravchinsky.

## 1871–1872

Laws of July 30 (August 11), 1871, and of May 15 (27), 1872, which are enacted at the initiative of Minister of Education Dmitri Tolstoy, strengthen the teaching of classical languages in the classical gymnasiums and transform the modern gymnasiums into "modern schools"; the latter's program of study is reduced to six years.

## 1872

The interior minister is granted the power to ban any publication he deems to be injurious.

## 1873

Populist groups multiply.

Bakunin publishes *The State and Anarchy*.

In Zurich, Lavrov publishes the first issue of the review *Vpered* ("Onward").

## 1874

*January 1 (13)*. Dmitri Miliutin introduces military reforms. They make military service obligatory for all (commitments are reduced to six years from 25), require that a portion of recruits be called up by lot, and reduce the duration of service in accordance with a person's educational attainment.

*Spring–Summer*. The "movement to the people," launched by the populists, reaches its apogee. Thousands of students agitate in the countryside (especially in the Volga and Don regions and in the Ukraine, where insurrections have occurred in the past). The peasants do not respond, and many students are arrested.

## 1875

In Odessa, the nobleman Evgeni Zaslavsky founds the short-lived South Russian Workers' Union.

In Geneva, Peter Tkachev founds the review *Nabat* (the "Alarm").

## 1876

A new *Zemlia i Volia* (Land and Freedom) society is formed by populists, including George Plekhanov, Alexander Mikhailov, M. Natanson and Vera Figner. The society's members wish to put forward a plan of action that is firmly grounded in popular aspirations. The circle is based in St. Petersburg and has relations with numerous local groups. Various factions emerge, including the "rioters," who are influenced by Bakunin (who dies on June 19 [July 1]), the "propagandists," who follow Lavrov, and the "conspirators," who follow Tkachev.

A budding Ukrainian nationalist movement is repressed. A ukase bars the use of the Ukrainian language in any publication that is not of a historical or philological character.

The historian Mikhail Dragomanov emigrates to Geneva.

*December 6 (18)*. *Zemlia i Volia* organizes a demonstration in front of Our Lady of Kazan Cathedral in St. Petersburg. The gathering of more than 200 persons is addressed by Plekhanov.

## 1877

Using a falsified imperial manifesto, the populist Iakiv Stefanovich fails in his attempt to launch a peasant uprising at Chigirin, in the Ukraine.

## 1877–1878

Mass trials of populists are held (50 populists are tried in March 1877; 193 are tried from October 1877 to January 1878).

## 1878

*January 24 (February 5)*. Vera Zasulich makes an attempt on the life of General Fedor Trepov, the police chief of St. Petersburg. She is acquitted by a jury on March 31 (April 12), and, with the complicity of the crowd, she is able to escape the police, who are waiting to rearrest her.

*August 4 (16)*. S. Kravchinsky assassinates General N. Mezentsev, chief of the political police in St. Petersburg. Faced with an increase in assassination attempts, the government steps up its repressive measures, which include the creation of military tribunals and the passing of sentences by administrative fiat.

*Late 1878*. The Northern Union of Russian Workers is formed in St. Petersburg by Stephen Khalturin. The organization establishes relations with *Zemlia i Volia*.

## 1879

Certain members of *Zemlia i Volia* systematically develop a strategy of terrorism.

*February 9 (21)*. Prince D. Kropotkin, governor general of Kharkov, is assassinated.

*April 2 (14)*. Alexander Solovev fails in his attempt on the life of Alexander II.

*June–July*. *Zemlia i Volia* holds congresses in Lipetsk and Voronezh at which differences among members over terrorism come into the open. As a result of these differences, the society splits into two groups: One group, *Narodnaia Volia* (Will of the People), whose members include A. Mikhailov, Andrei Zheliabov, S. Kravchinsky and Sophia Perovskaia, favors terrorist methods; whereas the other, *Chernyi Peredel* (Black Repartition), whose members include George Plekhanov, Vera Zasulich and Pavel Axelrod, favors propaganda. In the end, the latter group will evolve toward Marxism.

*August 26 (September 7)*. The executive committee of *Narodnaia Volia* condemns the czar to death.

*November 19 (December 1)*. An attempt against the imperial train is unsuccessful.

## 1880

Konstantin Pobedonostsev is named chief procurator of the Holy Synod (he will hold the post until 1905).

*February 5 (17).* An unsuccessful attempt on the life of the czar destroys the imperial dining room at the Winter Palace in St. Petersburg.

*February 12 (24).* A Supreme Executive Commission, directed by General Mikhail Loris-Melikov, is created and given broad powers. A policy described as being a "dictatorship of the heart" guides the work of the commission, which seeks to make overtures to liberal moderates while waging an unyielding struggle against revolutionary movements.

*August 6 (18).* The Supreme Executive Commission and the Third Section of the chancellery (the secret police) are disbanded. Their former duties are taken up by the Interior Ministry, of which Loris-Melikov is placed in charge.

## 1881

*January 28 (February 9).* Loris-Melikov advances a reform program calling for limited participation by representatives elected by the zemstvos and the dumas in the consideration of proposed laws.

*March 1 (13).* Alexander II is assassinated in St. Petersburg by members of *Narodnaia Volia.* The murdered czar had just given his approval in principle to Loris-Melikov's reform program.

# Foreign Affairs

## 1855

The Crimean War continues following the accession of Alexander II to the throne.

*March–June.* Because of the nature of its opponents' demands, Russia breaks off negotiations in Vienna.

*August 27 (September 8).* The French general Marie de MacMahon takes the Malakhov Tower at Sevastopol. The allies make a final assault on the city, which is evacuated by Russian troops on August 29 (September 10).

*November 16 (28).* The Russians capture Kars, in the Caucasus.

*December.* Austria pressures Russia to negotiate a peace.

## 1856

*January.* Russia agrees to enter peace negotiations.

*February 13 (25).* The opening of the Congress of Paris is attended by delegations from Russia, France, England, Turkey, Sardinia, Prussia and Austria.

*March 18 (30).* The Treaty of Paris is signed, ending the Crimean War. Russia gives up southern Bessarabia, Kars is returned to Turkey, and the Black Sea and its shores are neutralized. The integrity of the Ottoman Empire and the independence of the Danubian principalities are guaranteed by all parties.

## 1857

*September.* Alexander II and Louis Napoleon meet in Stuttgart. They inaugurate a Franco-Russian rapprochement against Austria that will last until 1862.

## 1858

Russia achieves diplomatic success in the Balkans: Milos Obrenovic is restored in Serbia; the empire intervenes on the side of the Montenegrins, who are fighting against the Turks, and it assists in bringing about the union of Moldavia and Wallachia.

*May 16 (28)*. Russia and China sign the Aigun Treaty, which permits Russia to annex the territory north of the Amur River.

## 1859

*August 26 (September 7)*. Imam Khamil surrenders in the Caucasus. To the west, the Russians engage in a pacification campaign in Circassia. The campaign will last until 1864, by which time 400,000 Circassians will have emigrated to Turkey.

## 1860

*November 2 (14)*. China and Russia sign the Treaty of Peking, under the terms of which Russia annexes the territory east of the Ussuri River. A Russian maritime province is created, and Vladivostok is founded.

## 1863

Following the Polish rebellion, Russia enters into a rapprochement with Prussia but suffers a rupture in its relations with France.

*January 27 (February 8)*. Count Constantine Alvenslaben, a Prussian diplomat, agrees on behalf of his country to permit Russia to pursue Polish insurgents onto Prussian territory.

## 1864

The Russians advance in Turkestan and take Chimkent.

## 1865

Diplomatic relations between Russia and the Holy See are broken on account of the repressive measures taken against Catholics in Poland and in the western provinces of the empire following the Polish insurrection.

*June*. General Mikhail Cherniaev takes Tashkent.

## 1867

*March 18 (30)*. Russia sells Alaska and the Aleutian Islands to the United States for $7.2 million.

*July*. A general government is formed in Turkestan, with the capital at Tashkent. General Konstantin Kaufmann is placed in charge.

## 1868

*May 2 (14)*. Samarkand is conquered by Russian forces.

*June*. The Emirate of Bukhara becomes a Russian protectorate.

## 1870

Nikolai Przhevalsky begins his expeditions in Central Asia.

*October 19 (31)*. Foreign Minister Alexander Gorchakov, using the Franco-Prussian War to Russia's advantage, announces that Russia no longer considers itself bound by the provision of the Treaty of Paris that guarantees the neutrality of the Black Sea.

## 1871

*January–March*. Russia achieves a diplomatic success at the London Conference. By agreement of the participants (including England and Prussia) on March 1 (13), the neutrality of the Black Sea is ended.

## 1873

The League of Three Emperors, an alliance between Germany, Austria-Hungary and Russia, is formed.

## 1875

*April–May*. Russia intervenes diplomatically on France's behalf during the Franco-German crisis.

*April 25 (May 7)*. Russia and Japan sign the Treaty of St. Petersburg: Russia regains control of all of Sakhalin Island, while the Kuril Islands revert to Japanese control.

*July–August.* Uprisings take place in Herzegovina, then in Bosnia, against Ottoman domination. Austria and Russia decline to become involved.

## 1876

*February 19 (March 3).* Russia annexes the Khanate of Kokand.

*April.* An uprising in Bulgaria is savagely repressed by the Turks.

*July.* Serbia and Montenegro declare war on Turkey. Despite an influx of Russian volunteers, the Serbs and Montenegrins are defeated.

*November.* The Russian army engages in a partial mobilization against the Turks.

## 1877

*January 3 (15).* An Austro-Russian accord on the Balkans is reached.

*April 4 (16).* An agreement with Romania permits the free passage of Russian troops over its territory.

*April 12 (24).* Russia declares war on Turkey.

*July 7 (19).* Russian troops take the Shipka Pass, in the Balkans.

*November 6 (18).* Kars, in the Caucasus, is taken.

*November 28 (December 10).* After a lengthy resistance, Plevna, in the Balkans, surrenders to the Russians.

## 1878

*January 8 (20).* Russia conquers Adrianople.

*January 19 (31).* A Russo-Turkish armistice begins.

*February 19 (March 3).* The Treaty of San Stefano is signed by Russia and Turkey, creating an autonomous Great Bulgaria. Although it will exist within the framework of the Ottoman Empire,

Great Bulgaria will be subject to the direct influence of Russia.

*June–July.* Chancellor Otto von Bismarck of Germany mediates between England, Austria-Hungary and Russia at the Congress of Berlin.

*July 1 (13).* The Treaty of Berlin is signed. Under its terms Great Bulgaria is divided into the autonomous principality of Bulgaria and the province of Eastern Rumelia, which is to be subject to Turkish rule. In addition, Austria-Hungary obtains the right to administer Bosnia-Herzegovina, and Serbia, Montenegro and Romania obtain their independence. Russia maintains control over southern Bessarabia, Kars and Batum.

## 1881

*January.* Russia advances into Turkmenia and occupies Geok Tepe.

# Economy and Society

## 1855

Provoked by military call-ups for the Crimean War, peasant agitation breaks out in the Ukraine.

The credit ruble is depreciated.

## 1856

A slight softening of anti-Jewish measures takes place: First, the military mobilization of Jewish children is abolished, then dispensations are permitted from the requirement that Jews reside in the Pale of Settlement.

## 1857

The Society of Russian Railways is created. The first wave of railroad construction occurs, supported by private capital.

A liberal customs tariff is instituted.

## 1858

The tenth "revision of souls" is completed. The estimated population of the empire is 75 million (60 million live in European Russia, and 55 million of these reside in rural areas). The population of St. Petersburg is 500,000; that of Moscow, 450,000.

The first deliveries of regular mail take place.

## 1859

"Temperance campaigns" are launched, provoking peasant unrest.

## 1860

The State Bank is created, replacing the former state credit establishments (it will have 40 branches by 1870).

## 1862

The Finance Ministry is reformed by Count Mikhail Reutern. A unified state budget will be published for the first time.

A planned monetary reform does not take place.

## 1863

The direct taxation of alcohol production is replaced by an indirect excise tax.

In urban areas, the head tax is replaced by a property tax.

## 1864

Private banks multiply: The first commercial credit bank opens in St. Petersburg, and the first land bank is established by the zemstvo of Chersonese.

## 1865

The Lycée Richelieu in Odessa is transformed into a university.

## 1868

A moderate customs tariff is instituted.

Nikolai Putilov purchases the State Foundry, which had been opened in St. Petersburg in 1801.

## 1869

The Russian University of Warsaw opens its doors.

A corps of inspectors charged with surveying primary schools is created.

Vasili Bervi, under the pseudonym N. Flerovsky, publishes *The Condition of the Working Class in Russia.*

## 1870

The first major strike in Russian history occurs in St. Petersburg at the Neva Cotton-spinning Mill.

A Russian section of the First International is created in Geneva.

## 1872

The first volume of Karl Marx's *Das Kapital* is published in Russia (the work is translated by N. Danielson and approved by the censor).

The augmentation of levies on the peasantry continues: From 1861 to 1872, the head tax has increased by 80 percent.

## 1873

Russia feels the effects of the European industrial crisis.

A metallurgical factory is established at Bryansk.

## 1874

The first congress of southern Russian mine owners is held at Taganrog.

## 1875

Petroleum production in Baku reaches 82,000 tons (in 1885 it will reach 1,902,400 tons).

In the Kholm region, the last remaining Polish Uniates are forced to convert to Orthodoxy.

## 1878

As a result of the Russo-Turkish War, the value of the paper ruble declines to 66 percent of the value of the metal ruble.

The Bestuzhev courses, which provide higher education to women, are established in St. Petersburg.

**1878–1879**

A wave of strikes occurs in St. Petersburg.

**1879**

Electric lighting is installed in St. Petersburg.

**1880**

During the period 1860–1880, the volume of Russian grain exports has increased from 12 million to 40 million centners (one centner equals approximately 220 pounds).

The length of the Russian rail network has also increased dramatically, from 930 miles in 1865, to 12,400 miles in 1880.

# Civilization and Culture

**1855**

Leo Tolstoy: *Sevastopol Tales* (1855–1856). Nikolai Chernyshevsky: *The Aesthetic Relation of Art to Reality*. A. Afanasev: *Russian Popular Fairy Tales* (1855–1863). *Roussalka*, an opera by Alexander Dargomyzhsky.

**1856**

Ivan Turgenev: *Rudin*. Mikhail Saltykov-Shchedrin: *Provincial Sketches* (1856–1857).

**1857**

L. Tolstoy: *Youth*.

**1858**

Alexei Pisemski: *A Thousand Souls*.

**1859**

Ivan Goncharov: *Oblomov*. I. Turgenev: *A Nest of the Gentry*. The Russian Musical Society is founded under the direction of Anton Rubenstein.

**1860**

Alexander Ostrovsky: *The Thunderstorm*. I. Turgenev: *On the Eve*.

**1861**

Feodor Dostoyevsky: *Notes from the House of the Dead* (1861–1862). *The Eastern Procession*, a painting by Vasili Perov.

**1862**

I. Turgenev: *Fathers and Sons* (the hero, Bazarov, is the embodiment of the new "nihilist" generation).

The St. Petersburg Conservatory of Music is founded. At the same time, a group of composers known as the "Five" (Mili Balakirev, César Cui, Modest Mussorgsky, Alexander Borodin and Nikolai Rimsky-Korsakov) is formed in reaction to the prevailing academicism, which looks to Western rather than to Russian culture for inspiration.

**1863**

Vladimir Dal begins publishing his *Explanatory Dictionary of the Living Russian Language* (1863–1866). Nikolai Chernyshevsky: *What Is to Be Done?* N. Nekrasov begins *Who Can Be Happy in Russia?* (1863–1877). A. Pisemsky: *A Troubled Sea*. Thirteen students, led by the painter Ivan Kramskoi, resign from the School of Fine Arts to protest against what they consider to be an overly academic subject for an art competition; they found the "artists' artel." Ivan Sechenov: *Reflexes of the Brain* (this lays the foundation for Ivan Pavlov's work).

**1864**

F. Dostoyevsky: *Notes from the Underground*.

**1865**

L. Tolstoy: *War and Peace* (1865–1869). *The Funeral*, a painting by V. Perov.

## 1866

F. Dostoyevsky: *Crime and Punishment.* The Moscow Conservatory and the Russian Historical Society are founded; the latter will publish 148 volumes between 1867 and 1916.

## 1867

I. Turgenev: *Smoke.* N. Rimsky-Korsakov: *Sadko* (opera).

## 1868

F. Dostoyevsky: *The Idiot.* M. Mussorgsky: *Boris Godunov* (1868–1872). The *Annals of the Fatherland*, edited by Nikolai Nekrasov and M. Saltykov-Shchedrin, reappears.

## 1869

I. Goncharov: *The Precipice.* A. Borodin begins the opera *Prince Igor* (it will be completed by Rimsky-Korsakov). Dmitri Mendeleev publishes *The Fundamentals of Chemistry*, which includes the Periodic Table of Elements.

## 1870

M. Saltykov-Shchedrin: *The History of a City.* I. Kramskoi founds *Peredvizhniki* (the Society of Wandering Art Exhibitions), which is dedicated to bringing art directly to the people. The wealthy patron Savva Mamontov purchases the Abramtsevo estate, where artists and intellectuals will come together and elaborate the elements of the "neonationalist" style.

## 1871

N. Nekrasov: *Russian Women* (1871–1872). F. Dostoyevsky: *The Demons* (1871–1872). A. Ostrovsky: *The Forest. Apotheosis of War*, a painting by Vasili Vereshchagin (1871–1872).

## 1872

Nikolai Leskov: *Cathedral Folk.* V. Perov paints a portrait of Dostoyevsky. M.

Mussorgsky begins *Khovanshchina* (it will be completed by Rimsky-Korsakov).

## 1873

N. Leskov: *The Enchanted Wanderer.* L. Tolstoy: *Anna Karenina* (1873–1877). I. Kramskoi paints a portrait of L. Tolstoy. Ilya Repin: *The Volga Boatmen.*

## 1874

Pavel Melnikov completes *In the Woods. Repair Work on the Railroad*, a painting by Konstantin Savitsky. An archaeological congress meets in Kiev.

## 1875

Vladimir Soloviev: *The Crisis of Western Philosophy.*

## 1876

*Swan Lake*, a ballet by Peter Tchaikovsky. The electric arc lamp (the "Russian light") is invented by Pavel Iablochkov. The first complete translation of the Bible into modern Russian.

## 1877

I. Turgenev: *Virgin Soil.* N. Rimsky-Korsakov: *100 Russian Folk Songs.*

## 1878

N. Rimsky-Korsakov: *May Night.* P. Tchaikovsky: *Eugene Onegin. All Quiet at the Shipka Pass*, a triptych by V. Vereshchagin.

## 1879

*The Trial of Pugachev*, a painting by V. Perov.

## 1880

M. Saltykov-Shchedrin completes *The Golovlevs.* F. Dostoyevsky: *The Brothers Karamazov* (1879–1880). The liberal monthly journal *Russian Thought* is founded in Moscow. P. Tchaikovsky: *The 1812 Overture.* A. Borodin: *In the Steppes of Central Asia.*

## 1881

Paintings: I. Repin, *Portrait of Mussorgsky*; Vasili Surikov, *The Morning of the Streltsy Execution*; Vladimir Makovsky, *Bank Failure.*

N. Rimsky-Korsakov: *Snegurochka.*

# Chapter 16 1881–1894

# Alexander III and the "Counter Reforms"

The assassination of Alexander II ushered in a period of violent reaction. Alexander III began his reign by issuing a manifesto reaffirming autocracy. He surrounded himself with ultraconservative ministers, and he used a new arsenal of repressive measures to wage a merciless struggle against "revolution." In addition, he almost completely neutralized the reforms carried out by his predecessor in state administration, education and law. At the same time, his regime launched a new campaign of Russification. This was accompanied by anti-Semitic measures that echoed the first large-scale pogroms of 1881.

The 1880s saw a pause in Russia's industrial growth. During that decade, however, certain policies—the return to protectionism, the encouragement of French investment, and the start of construction on the Trans-Siberian railroad—prepared the way for the accelerated development that would be engineered by Sergei Witte, the minister of finance, beginning in 1892. The burden placed on the peasantry was increased, however, and the peasants were tied even more firmly to the rural commune. In 1891, a terrible famine called into question the government's policies and created a breach between the autocracy and the nobility. The zemstvos were likewise frustrated in their attempts to increase their authority and resources.

Populism reappeared under a "legal" guise, and populists continued their propaganda in favor of rural socialism. After Marxism had taken root among the Russians living abroad, the first Marxist circles began to appear within Russia itself. At the same time, Russia experienced the slow formation of a small working class that was still closely linked to rural society.

In foreign affairs, Russia remained isolated despite its membership in the League of Three Emperors. Russia clashed with Austria in the Balkans and with England on the borders of Afghanistan, and its policy of protectionism led to a veritable trade war with Germany. Only an alliance with France, progressively established from 1891 to 1894, allowed Russia to break out of its isolation and obtain some of the necessary capital for industrial development.

# Politics and Institutions

## 1881

The Department for Safeguarding Public Security and Public Order (*Okhrana*), a new secret police organization within the Ministry of the Interior, is established in St. Petersburg, Moscow and Warsaw; later, it will be expanded throughout the empire.

*April 3 (15).* The five individuals responsible for the assassination of Alexander II are hanged, including Andrei Zheliabov and Sofia Perovskaia.

*April 29 (May 11).* An imperial manifesto is issued at Konstantin Pobedonostsev's instigation. The new czar, Alexander III (son of Alexander II), reaffirms his commitment to autocracy. The liberal ministers Mikhail Loris-Melikov and Dmitri Miliutin resign.

*August 14 (26).* The "Temporary Regulations" are issued, placing Russia under the rule of martial law. These regulations, which will remain in effect until 1917, will be enforced frequently, particularly in 1904–1905.

## 1882

The Proletariat Party, a socialist group, is founded in Warsaw by L. Warynski; it is quickly decimated by arrests.

The *Communist Manifesto*, by Karl Marx and Friedrich Engels, is translated into Russian by George Plekhanov and Vera Zasulich (it was first published in London in 1848).

*May 30 (June 11).* Dmitri Tolstoy becomes minister of the interior. A long period of reaction begins, dominated by the personalities of Tolstoy, Konstantin Pobedonostsev (chief procurator of the Holy Synod) and Mikhail Katkov (editor of the *Moscow News*).

*August 27 (September 8).* New regulations on censorship are issued: Periodicals that receive three warnings will be subject to preliminary censorship. Most of the liberal periodicals will disappear in the years that follow, with the exception of the *Messenger of Europe*.

## 1883

*September.* A group calling itself the Emancipation of Labor is founded in Geneva; its leaders include Plekhanov, Zasulich and Pavel Axelrod. This event is generally viewed as the point of departure for Russian Marxism. Plekhanov publishes his article "Socialism and Political Struggle."

The first Marxist circles are formed in Russia, and they are quickly broken up by the police. Among them is a group formed by the Bulgarian student Dmitri Blagoev in St. Petersburg.

## 1884

The *Annals of the Fatherland* is suppressed.

The Holy Synod is given control over all primary schools. Parochial schools increase in number, and they are systematically granted advantages over secular schools.

*August 23 (September 4).* A new statute on universities is issued: The autonomy previously enjoyed by universities is eliminated, the trustees' powers are strengthened, and higher education for women is restricted.

## 1885

Russification is intensified in Poland: Russian becomes the language of instruction in primary schools (Polish language courses and those teaching religion are exempt).

Plekhanov writes *Our Differences,* marking the break between the Marxists and the Populists.

**1887**

The Polish National League and an Armenian social democratic group are founded in Geneva.

*May 8 (20)*  Five students arrested for plotting to assassinate Alexander III are executed, including Alexander Ulyanov, brother of Vladimir (the future Lenin).

*June 18 (30).*  Ivan Delianov, the minister of public instruction, issues a circular limiting access to gymnasiums (excluded are the sons of "coachmen, servants, laundresses and cooks"). The number of students will decline from 65,750 in 1882 to 63,860 in 1895. University fees increase fivefold.

**1889**

*July 12 (24).*  Justices of the peace are eliminated, except in large cities. Rural districts are to be governed by a *zemskii nachalnik,* or land captain, who holds all administrative and judicial powers. This nobleman, appointed by the government, reports to the minister of the interior.

**1890**

*Dashnaktsutuin,* an Armenian socialist party, is founded in Tiflis.

*June 12 (24).*  A "counter reform" of the zemstvos results in changes to the electoral system: The nobility gains in representation, the peasant vote is restricted, and administrative control is increased.

**1892**

The Polish Socialist Party is founded in Paris.

"Legal populism" is developed. This ideology seeks to promote a socialism based on the peasant mir and on groupings of small producers. Leaders of this movement include Nikolai Mikhailovsky (editor of *Russian Wealth*), V. Vorontsov (who will write *The Peasant Commune*) and N. Danielson (author of *Studies of Our Post-Reform National Economy,* which will be published in 1893).

*June 11 (23).*  Municipal "counter reforms" are adopted: A new statute on the cities increases the poll tax, thereby reducing by two-thirds the number of people eligible to vote; the statute also strengthens the powers of municipal administrations. Jews lose their right to vote for duma representatives.

**1893**

Vladimir Ulyanov (who will adopt the name Lenin in 1901) moves to St. Petersburg and becomes active in the circles of Marxist intellectuals.

In Poland, the *Liga Narodowa* and the Social Democratic Party of the Kingdom of Poland are founded.

In Georgia, the *Mesame Dasi,* a social-democratic organization, is founded.

**1894**

*October 20 (November 1).*  Alexander III dies at Livadia, the imperial palace in the Crimea.

# Foreign Affairs

**1881**

*June 6 (18).*  The League of Three Emperors, an alliance created in 1873 between Russia, Germany and Austria-Hungary, is renewed.

**1884**

The League of Three Emperors is renewed for the last time.

Merv, an important oasis in Turkistan (near the borders with Afghanistan and Persia), is annexed.

## 1885

The Bulgarian crisis begins: Russia denounces the unification of Eastern Rumelia and Bulgaria.

*March.* A crisis with England is provoked by Russian encroachments in Afghanistan, including the occupation of Pendjeh and the Russo-Afghan battle of Ak Tepe.

*August 29 (September 10).* An Anglo-Russian accord is signed establishing the borders of Afghanistan.

## 1886–1887

*August 1886.* The Bulgarian crisis intensifies: Alexander of Battenberg, the Bulgarian prince, is overthrown by Russophile officers.

*June 25 (July 7), 1887.* Despite Russian intrigues, Ferdinand of Saxe-Coburg, the candidate favored by Austria, ascends the Bulgarian throne.

## 1887

The League of Three Emperors is not renewed because of the tension between Russia and Austria over the Balkans.

*June 6 (18).* The Reinsurance Treaty is negotiated by German Chancellor Otto von Bismarck and Russian Foreign Minister Nikolai Giers. The treaty will fail to halt the rapid deterioration in Russo-German relations caused by Russia's protectionist policies.

## 1891

*July.* The French fleet visits Kronstadt, the Russian naval base outside St. Petersburg.

*August 15 (27).* The first diplomatic understanding between France and Russia is reached by an exchange of letters concerning mutual aid in the event that either country's security is threatened.

## 1892

*August 5 (17).* A military agreement between France and Russia is signed by their chiefs of staff in St. Petersburg.

## 1893

*October.* The Russian fleet visits the French naval base at Toulon.

## 1893–1894

*December–January.* The Franco-Russian military agreement is ratified by an exchange of letters between Foreign Minister Giers and the French ambassador in St. Petersburg.

## 1894

Diplomatic relations with the Holy See are reestablished.

# Economy and Society

## 1881

A short industrial crisis begins; although it is triggered by a larger world economic crisis, it is aggravated by Russia's lack of railways.

*Spring–Summer.* The first wave of pogroms against the Jews occurs in Elisavetgrad, Kiev and Odessa.

*December 28 (January 9, 1882).* A law is promulgated making the redemption of land obligatory for all former serfs, including those peasants still under "temporary obligation."

## 1882

A Peasant Bank is created to facilitate the purchase of land by individuals or collectives. It primarily benefits rich peasants.

A government bureau to oversee working conditions in factories is created. The employment of children under 12 years of age is prohibited, and the workday is limited to eight hours for those between the ages of 12 and 15.

A new "Statute Concerning the Jews" requires them to live in the cities and towns of the Pale of Settlement (25 western provinces) and bars them from owning land.

Telephone lines are installed in St. Petersburg, Moscow, Odessa and Riga.

## 1883

A law gives various non-Orthodox religious groups the freedom to worship but strictly limits their activities. The ban on conversions from Orthodoxy is strengthened.

*Terdjüman* (the "Interpreter"), a Pan-Turkish publication, is founded in the Crimean town of Bakhchisarai by I. Gasprinsky.

The Transcaucasus railway from Baku to Batum is completed.

## 1885

A law is enacted abolishing the poll tax throughout the empire, as of January 1, 1887.

The Land Bank for the Nobility is created. Despite the availability of loans at reduced interest, the bank does not bring a halt to the sale of noble lands. Noble landholdings will decline from 73 million *desyatinas* in 1877 to 65 million *desyatinas* in 1887, and to 55 million *desyatinas* in 1904. (A *desyatina* equals approximately 2.7 acres.)

The Catherine Railway, which connects the coal mines of the Donets region to the iron mines of Krivoi Rog, is opened, facilitating an enormous growth in Ukrainian metallurgy.

*January.* A massive strike by textile workers occurs at the Morozov Factory near Moscow. Out of a total of 11,000 employees, 8,000 go out on strike.

*June.* Nighttime labor is prohibited for women and adolescents.

## 1886

*May 18 (30).* A law requires the mir to approve any division of peasant family plots; the law is intended to counter the reduction in the size of plots.

*June 3 (15).* A law increases the prison terms for strikers (four months for participants, eight months for organizers) and limits the fines to one-third of a striker's salary.

*June 12 (24).* A law is enacted obligating state peasants to purchase their land parcels.

## 1887

Customs duties are increased by Finance Minister Ivan Vyshnegradsky. This provokes a clash with Germany, which raises its duties on wheat and closes its financial markets to Russian borrowers.

Quotas are placed on the number of Jews permitted to attend universities (10 percent of students at universities in the Pale, 3 percent at universities in Moscow and St. Petersburg, and 5 percent at universities in the rest of the empire).

The Congress of Iron Manufacturers is created.

## 1888

The Russian government is obliged to borrow from French financial markets for the first time.

The University of Tomsk is opened.

A rail connection from the Caspian Sea to Samarkand is established.

## 1889

*July 1 (13).* A law restricting internal migrations is enacted. It requires those seeking to migrate to obtain permission from the Ministry of the Interior and the Ministry of Imperial Domains.

## 1891

A catastrophic famine strikes the eastern "blacklands," affecting 20 provinces and 40 million peasants. It will be followed by a cholera epidemic in 1892.

A short economic recession occurs, a consequence of the world-wide recession of 1891–1892.

A protectionist tariff on all imports is established. This will lead to a commercial war with Germany in 1892–1894. Bilateral trade agreements will establish preferential tariffs.

More than twenty thousand Jews are expelled from Moscow.

*March 17 (29).* An imperial rescript announces the construction of the Trans-Siberian railroad, which will be largely completed by 1902. "Railway fever" strikes Russia, with the state taking the lead from private companies.

## 1892

*August 30 (September 11).* Sergei Witte becomes finance minister and establishes a policy of accelerated industrialization that will last until 1903. Indirect taxes are raised: The tax on matches increases 100 percent, while the taxes on beer, tobacco and oil increase 50 percent.

## 1893

The University of Dorpat (Yurev, the future Tartu) undergoes "Russification."

*June 8 (20).* Partial redistributions of land within the mir are prohibited, and the mir must observe a 12-year interval between general redistributions.

*December 14 (26).* Transfers of communal land to nonpeasant owners are prohibited. Withdrawal from the mir is made subject to a two-thirds vote of the communal assembly.

---

### THE PROTECTIONIST TARIFF OF 1891

(compared with the tariff of 1868)
in gold kopeks per pood
(the pood is roughly equivalent to 16.4 kg)

|  | 1868 | 1891 |
| --- | --- | --- |
| Charcoal | n/a | 2–3 |
| Iron ore | n/a | 10.5 |
| Rough cast iron | 5 | 45–52.5 |
| Wrought cast iron | 50–250 | 112.5–255 |
| Iron | 20–50 | 90–150 |
| Rails | 20 | 90 |
| Locomotives | 75 | 300 |
| Agricultural machines | n/a | 70–140 |
| Rough cotton | n/a | 120–135 |
| Spun, bleached cotton | 325 | 420–540 |

## 1894

A state monopoly on the sale of liquor is introduced, which will provide one-quarter of the regular budget revenue during the period 1894–1899.

A tax on rented lodgings is established. Grain prices, which have been declining since about 1875, reach their lowest point. Repressive measures are carried out against the Stundists (Ukrainian Baptists). *January 29 (February 10)*. A commercial treaty is signed with Germany.

# Civilization and Culture

## 1882

Leo Tolstoy completes *A Confession.* Gleb Uspensky: *The Power of the Soil.* The premier of Alexander Glazunov's First Symphony is held, with Mili Balakirev conducting. Construction begins on the Church of the Resurrection in St. Petersburg; it is designed in the neonationalist style (Alexander Parland, 1882–1907).

## 1883

Afanasi Fet: *Evening Lights.*

## 1884

*They Were Not Expecting Him*, a painting by Ilya Repin. The mathematician Sofia Kovalevskaia departs for the University of Stockholm.

## 1885

Vladimir Korolenko: *Makar's Dream.* K. Leontiev: *The East, Russia and Slavdom* (1885–1886). Paintings by I. Repin: *Ivan VI at the Death of His Son* and *Refusal to Take Confession.* A private opera is founded in Moscow under the patronage of Savva Mamontov.

## 1886

L. Tolstoy: *The Power of Darkness.* Classification of soils and the founding of pedology by Vasili Dokuchaev.

## 1887

Paintings: *The Boyarina Morozova*, by Vasili Surikov; *Girl with Peaches*, by Valentin Serov.

## 1888

Anton Chekhov: "The Steppe." Nikolai Rimsky-Korsakov: *Scheherazade* and *Russian Easter Festival.*

## 1889

Vladimir Soloviev: *Russia and the Universal Church.* Construction begins in Moscow on the Merchant Galleries (later the GUM department store); it is designed in the neonationalist style (A.N. Pomerantsev, 1889–1893).

## 1890

L. Tolstoy: *The Kreutzer Sonata.* Vasili Rozanov: *The Legend of the Grand Inquisitor.* Peter Tchaikovsky: *The Queen of Spades. Prince Igor*, an opera begun by Alexander Borodin, is completed by Rimsky-Korsakov. *Demon*, a painting by Mikhail Vrubel. Chekhov travels to Sakhalin Island (he will denounce the conditions in penal colonies in *The Island of Sakhalin*).

## 1891

I. Repin completes *The Cossacks of Zaporozhe Writing a Letter to the Turkish Sultan.*

## 1892

A. Chekhov: *Ward No. 6.* Fedor Sologub: *The Little Demon* (1892–1902). Paintings by Isaak Levitan (*The Road to Vladimir*) and by Repin (*The Arrest of a Propagandist*). The merchant Pavel

Tretyakov donates his collection of paintings to the city of Moscow.

**1893**

Dmitri Merezhkovsky: *On the Causes of the Decline of, and on the New Trends in, Contemporary Russian Literature.*

**1894**

Publication of the collection *Russian Symbolists* (including poems by Valeri Briusov). Konstantin Balmont: *Under Northern Skies.*

# Chapter 17                    1894–1903

# Nicholas II and the Continuing Aristocratic Reaction

The reign of Nicholas II up to the beginning of the 20th century was marked by a drive for accelerated economic growth. Leading this campaign was Finance Minister Sergei Witte, who succeeded in 1897 in pushing through monetary reform, including the adoption of the gold standard. Between 1890 and 1900 production doubled and the railroad network was extended into Asia. A new industrial landscape emerged, on which Ukrainian mining and metallurgy held a prominent position. But industrialization had a detrimental impact on the peasantry. Despite the onset of the first organized colonization in Siberia, rural overpopulation remained a serious problem, and the constraints of the rural commune system hindered peasant mobility.

Russia's political life began to restructure itself during this period. The still small bourgeoisie, whose members had achieved a limited political role in the zemstvos, gave rise to the liberals, who began to agitate for real participation in governing the country. In 1903, the most progressive individuals from among this element formed the Union of Liberation. Meanwhile, Socialist Revolutionaries for the most part borrowed from the populist tradition of rural agitation, but there were some individuals within their ranks who were also attracted to terrorism. The Marxists, encouraged by the rapid development of capitalism in Russia and by the appearance of the first large-scale workers' movements, remained nonetheless divided over the proper organization for the Social Democratic Party, which they founded in 1898. Between 1900 and 1903, the conjunction of various crises—an industrial crisis, agrarian unrest, endemic student agitation—accelerated political development by demonstrating the urgency of the need to find a solution to the problems gripping Russian society.

The autocracy's response to political and social unrest was to stiffen repressive measures, to alienate itself from the zemstvos by its continued refusal to sanction any form of national representation, to seek to channel worker unrest by organizing "police unions" that proved difficult to control, and to resort to extreme forms of nationalist and anti-Semitic diversions. In the end, the blindness of the regime pushed it into an increasingly adventurous Far Eastern policy that culminated, in 1904, in the Russo-Japanese War.

# Politics and Institutions

## 1894

Upon the death of Alexander III, his son Nicholas II becomes czar.

The controversy over the proper route to Russian economic development continues to rage. Marxist critiques of populism appear: *Who Are the "Friends of the People" and How Do They Fight the Social Democrats?* by Lenin; and *Critical Remarks on the Economic Development of Russia*, by Peter Struve.

## 1895

*January 17 (29).* Responding to an appeal of the deputies of the provincial zemstvo of Tver, Nicholas II condemns the "insane dream" of an elected assembly.

*November.* Following a meeting with George Plekhanov in Geneva, Vladimir Ulyanov (Lenin) brings together several Marxist circles in St. Petersburg to form the Union of Struggle for the Liberation of the Working Class.

*December 9 (21).* Most of the members of the Union are arrested, including Lenin and Julius Martov. Lenin will spend 15 months in prison and then three years in exile in Siberia.

## 1896

*August.* At the initiative of Dmitri Shipov, president of the Moscow zemstvo, the presidents of all the zemstvos hold a meeting at the fair in Nizhni Novgorod. Another meeting, planned for the following year, is forbidden by the authorities.

## 1897

New political groups reflecting the populist tradition are formed, particularly in Saratov, Minsk and Kharkov. Proclaim-ing themselves "Socialist Revolutionaries" (SRs), these groups intend to renew agitation amongst the peasantry.

Roman Dmowski founds the National Democratic Party of Poland.

*September 25–27 (October 7–9).* In Vilnius, the Union of Jewish Workers in Lithuania, Russia and Poland (the "Bund") is founded.

## 1898

*March 1–3 (13–15).* In Minsk, the Russian Social Democratic Labor Party (RSDLP) is founded by a congress of nine delegates representing Marxist committees and the Bund. A manifesto is drafted by Struve.

## 1899

New currents in Russian Marxism appear: the "economism" of the Union of Struggle in St. Petersburg, which gives priority to the everyday demands of workers (its review is called *Workers' Thought*); the economism of the Union of Russian Social Democrats Abroad (*Workers' Cause* and Ekaterina Kuskova's manifesto, *Credo*); and "legal" Marxism, influenced by the German Edward Bernstein, which will evolve toward liberalism under the influence of Struve.

*February.* Student demonstrations and strikes occur in St. Petersburg and then at universities throughout the empire.

*February 3 (15).* An imperial manifesto declares that the laws of the Russian Empire take priority over the laws of Finland. A vast Russification program, directed by the new governor general, Nicholas Bobrikov, is launched in Finland.

*July 29 (August 10).* Provisional regulations are issued by Minister of Public Instruction Nikolai Bogolepov permitting the drafting into the military (as privates) of student agitators.

## 1900

The Social Democratic Party of Poland becomes the Social Democratic Party of Poland and Lithuania.

The first issue of *Revolutionary Russia*, the journal of the Socialist Revolutionaries, is published in Finland.

*June.* Russian is made the official language of government in Finland.

*July.* Lenin leaves Russia to live abroad.

*December 11 (24).* The first issue of *Iskra* (the "Spark"), a journal expressing the views of the group made up of Lenin, Martov, Alexander Potresov, Plekhanov, Pavel Axelrod and Vera Zasulich, is published in Leipzig. In bringing out this review, which will be sold clandestinely in Russia, its organizers have two objectives: to combat economism and to spur the establishment of clandestine Marxist committees.

## 1901

The Socialist Revolutionary Party (SR) is founded in Berlin at a meeting of the Russian Socialist Revolutionaries, the Union of Socialist Revolutionaries living abroad, and the Agrarian Socialist League, which maintains its autonomous existence. The party, whose members include Viktor Chernov, Ekaterina Breshkovskaia, Grigori Gershuni and Abraham Gotz, advocates agitation amongst the peasantry (rural socialism), a federalist political program, and, for certain members, recourse to terrorism. A terrorist combat organization will be led by Gershuni and, later, by the double agent Yevno Azev.

The chief procurator of the Holy Synod, Konstantin Pobedonostsev, excommunicates Leo Tolstoy.

*February.* N. Bogolepov, the minister of public instruction, is assassinated by the Socialist Revolutionary Peter Karpovich.

*March.* Student agitation erupts again: Street demonstrations are violently repressed.

*August 23 (September 5).* Direct relations between zemstvos are prohibited.

## 1902

In *What Is to Be Done?*, Lenin spells out his views on building a strongly centralized revolutionary party. Most social democratic groups rally to the *Iskra* line.

*April 2 (15).* The interior minister, Dmitri Sipiagin, is assassinated by the Socialist Revolutionary S. Balmashev. Sipiagin is replaced by Viacheslav Plehve, who conducts a systematic policy of repression.

*June 23–26 (July 6–9).* An informal meeting of zemstvo presidents in Moscow, initiated by D. Shipov, produces a moderate liberal program.

*July.* The first issue of the journal *Osvobozhdenie* ("Liberation") appears in Stuttgart. This marks the birth of a more radical liberalism, one that is constitutional and democratic. It draws support from the more advanced elements of the zemstvos (Ivan Petrunkevich) as well as from the urban bourgeoisie, the liberal professions and intellectuals (Professor Pavel Miliukov, the lawyer Vasili Maklakov), and some former Marxists (Struve) and former populists.

## 1903

The Union of Liberation is founded in Schaffhausen. It is made up of diverse liberals who have coalesced around the journal *Liberation*.

*June.* The property of the Armenian clergy is confiscated, and the policy of

Russification is intensified in Armenia, particularly in the area of education.

*July 17 (30)–August 10 (23).* The Second Congress of the Russian Social Democratic Labor Party meets in Brussels and then in London. The delegates disagree on the purpose and objectives of the party and split into two factions: the Bolsheviks (led by Lenin) and the Mensheviks (led by Martov). The Bund withdraws, having been refused autonomy within the party.

*August.* Witte falls into disgrace and is forced to leave the Finance Ministry.

# Foreign Affairs

## 1895

The Sino-Japanese War ends. Russia acts as the protector of China. The Russo-Chinese Bank is founded, and an appeal is issued for foreign capital.

An Anglo-Russian accord is signed on the division of Pamir, a region in Central Asia bordering Russia, China and Afghanistan.

## 1896

*May 22 (June 3).* Russia and China sign a mutual defense treaty against Japan. The Russo-Chinese Bank is accorded the right to construct and to hold an 80-year lease on the Chinese Eastern Railway, which will provide a direct connection between Chita and Vladivostok through Manchuria.

*September 23–27 (October 5–9).* Nicholas II makes an official visit to France.

## 1897

*April–May.* Austria and Russia agree to maintain the status quo in the Balkans.

*August.* Félix Faure, the president of the French republic, makes a visit to St. Petersburg.

## 1898

*March 15 (27).* A Sino-Russian treaty is signed: China leases the Liaotung Peninsula, including Port Arthur, to Russia for 25 years. The Chinese Eastern Railway Company is granted a concession to construct a southern Manchurian rail line from Harbin to Port Arthur.

*April 13 (25).* Russia and Japan sign an accord that recognizes Japan's special interests in Korea.

## 1899

*May 6 (18).* At Russia's initiative, representatives from 26 countries attend the opening of the First Hague Peace Conference.

*August.* French Foreign Minister Théophile Delcassé visits St. Petersburg. The Franco-Russian alliance is strengthened.

## 1900

The Boxer Rebellion erupts in China. Russia establishes a military occupation in Manchuria.

## 1902

*January 17 (30).* An Anglo-Japanese alliance is signed. England recognizes Japan's special interests in Korea.

*March 26 (April 8).* Russia and China reach an accord on the gradual withdrawal of Russian troops from Manchuria.

## 1903

Russo-Japanese relations deteriorate, due in large part to the actions of certain Russian government officials: the intrigues of Alexander Bezobrazov's Korean "lobby," the nomination of Admiral Evgeni Alexeyev as viceroy of the Far East, and the maintenance of Russian occupation troops in Manchuria.

*September 19 (October 2).* Nicholas II and Franz Joseph, meet at Mürzsteg and reach an accord on Macedonia.

# Economy and Society

## 1895

The first electric tramway goes into operation in Moscow.

## 1896

The First All-Russian Congress of Industry and Commerce (including an industrial exposition) takes place at Nizhni Novgorod.

As a result of A. Kulomzin's mission, a Bureau of Migration is established to encourage settlement in Siberia. Facilities to promote travel to the region and habitation are set up, but freedom of departure for potential settlers is incomplete. Nine hundred thousand persons will migrate to Siberia between 1896 and 1900, compared with 165,000 for the years 1885–1896. In 1897 the total population of Siberia will reach 5.7 million.

*May.* A tragic stampede occurs among the crowds attending the coronation festivities for Nicholas II in Moscow. More than 1,000 people die.

*May–June.* A strike by 35,000 textile workers in St. Petersburg is the culmination of the intensification of labor unrest that began in 1894 and coincided with the rise in industrial activity.

## 1897

The first complete census of the population of the Russian Empire is undertaken. The total population of the country is set at 129 million, of which only 13 percent live in urban areas. The population is increasing by 1.6 million each year.

Witte puts through a monetary reform: The ruble is devalued to one-third of its former value, the gold standard is adopted, and the existence of large reserves allows the paper ruble to become convertible.

*June 2 (14).* The workday is limited to 11 hours and 30 minutes, and Sunday is made a day of rest.

## 1898

Taxes on commerce and industry are reformed.

The legal Marxist Mikhail Tugan-Baranovsky publishes *The Russian Factory, Past and Present.*

An uprising occurs in Andizhan in Central Asia.

## 1899

A report prepared by Dmitri Mendeleev ("The Sleeping Urals") reveals that the backwardness of metallurgy in the Urals can be attributed to the use of charcoal for smelting and to a scarcity of foreign capital. By contrast, the Ukraine produces 65 percent of Russia's coal, 50 percent of its cast iron and 45 percent of its steel.

Lenin's *The Development of Capitalism in Russia,* a critique of populism written during his Siberian exile, is published.

## 1900

Russia begins to experience a short but severe economic crisis that is caused in part by a world economic crisis (1900–1903). Especially hard hit is metallurgy, and the crisis marks the end of the great wave of Russian railroad construction. Bankruptcies, layoffs and salary reductions are widespread.

Russia participates in the Universal Exposition in Paris.

## 1901

Bad harvests occur, demonstrating once again the urgent need for agrarian reform.

## INDUSTRIAL PROGRESS FROM 1890 TO 1900
(in millions of poods; 1 pood is equal to 16.4 kg)

| Production | 1890 | 1900 |
|---|---|---|
| Cast iron | 56.6 | 179.1 |
| Charcoal | 367.2 | 986.3 |
| Cotton (for necessities) | 8.3 | 16.0 |
| Iron and steel | 48.3 | 163.0 |
| Petroleum | 226.0 | 631.0 |
| Sugar | 24.6 | 48.5 |
| | | |
| Size of the railway system (in miles) | 18,000 | 33,000 |
| Foreign investments in industrial works and banking (in gold kopeks) | 214,000,000 | 911,000,000 |

In an effort to channel labor movements toward ends the regime deems desirable, the *Okhrana* begins to organize "police unions." These unions are controlled by Sergei Zubatov, a member of the secret police.

## 1902

The Trans-Siberian Railway opens with the completion of the Trans-Manchurian line, although there remains a gap in service at Lake Baikal. A trip from Moscow to Vladivostok takes 15 days.

Worker agitation continues: A huge demonstration takes place in May in Sormovo (this will inspire Maxim Gorky to write his novel *Mother*), and a general strike occurs in November in Rostov.

*January 22 (February 4)*. A Special Commission on the Needs of the Agricultural Industry is created by Witte. The commission launches a broad inquiry and establishes 618 local committees to carry out investigations throughout the country.

Opposition to the new interior minister, Vyacheslav Plehve, grows.

*March–April*. A strong wave of agrarian unrest sweeps the provinces of Kharkov and Poltava; large domains are attacked and pillaged. The unrest is violently repressed. The entire affair is a reflection of the near catastrophic problems facing rural Russia: overpopulation, the meager size of peasant plots, and the heavy burden of taxes and other payments. The SRs increase their presence in the countryside.

*July*. In response to the industrial crisis, a large cartel (Prodamet) is formed to sell Russian metallurgical products. By 1908, the cartel will be responsible for the sale of 90 percent of the metallurgical production of southern Russia, and of 45 percent of the national's total production. Similar cartels are formed for other industries as well, including coal (Produgol), railroads and petroleum.

## 1903

Labor strikes increase in number (200,000 workers walk off their jobs in 1903). In Odessa and southern Russia, labor unrest exposes the weakness of the *Zubatovshchina* (police unions).

*February 26 (March 11)*. An imperial manifesto proclaims the immutability of the communal plot as well as the right of peasants to obtain land outside the commune.

*March 12 (25)*. The responsibility of the peasant commune for redemption payments owed by its members is ended.

*April 6 (19)*. A huge pogrom begins in Kishinev. It will continue for two days with the complicity of local authorities (the anti-Semitic acts are encouraged by Interior Minister Plehve). Several hundred Jews are killed or injured, and the incident has strong international repercussions.

*June 2 (15)*. A law makes employers responsible for compensating workers who are injured in work accidents.

*June 10 (23)*. The position of worker-representative (*starosta*) is created in factories and other workplaces.

# Civilization and Culture

## 1895

A paper by Alexander Popov describing the principles behind the wireless transmission of Morse code is presented to the Physical Chemistry Society. Dmitri Merezhkovsky begins his trilogy *Christ and Antichrist* with *Julian the Apostate*. A large-circulation daily newspaper, the *Russian Word*, is founded in Moscow (by 1916 the paper will have a circulation of 700,000).

## RUSSIA'S PRINCIPAL COMMERCIAL PARTNERS IN 1901

**Exports (in gold rubles)**

| | |
|---|---|
| Germany | 178,855,000 |
| Great Britain | 156,751,000 |
| Holland | 84,689,000 |
| France | 61,222,000 |
| Austria | 30,217,000 |
| United States | 4,000,000 |
| Total Russian exports: | 761,683,000 |

**Imports (in gold rubles)**

| | |
|---|---|
| Germany | 210,954,000 |
| Great Britain | 102,954,000 |
| United States | 34,921,000 |
| France | 27,792,000 |
| Austria | 24,901,000 |
| Total Russian imports: | 593,425,000 |

## 1896

Anton Chekhov: *The Seagull*. Fedor Chaliapin makes his debut with the Moscow Private Russian Opera. The first cinematic presentation takes place in St. Petersburg.

## 1897

A. Chekhov: *Uncle Vanya* and *The Muzhiks*.

## 1898

Vladimir Soloviev: *A Justification of the Good*. The painter Viktor Vasnetsov completes *The Bogatyrs*. The Moscow Art Theater is founded by Konstantin Stanislavsky and Vladimir Nemirovich-Danchenko. Chekhov's play *The Seagull* is successful.

The first issue of the review *The World of Art* appears, published by Sergei Diaghilev, Alexander Benois, Lev Bakst and Mikhail Vrubel. The review, which will be published until 1904, will play a crucial role in the diffusion of artistic culture and in the establishment of modern art in Russia.

## 1899

Maxim Gorky: *Foma Gordeev*. Leo Tolstoy completes *Resurrection*, which marks his break with the Church.

## 1900

*The Swan Princess*, a painting by M. Vrubel. Nikolai Rimsky-Korsakov: *The Tale of the Czar Saltan*.

## 1901

Lev Shestov: *Dostoyevsky and Nietzsche: The Philosophy of Tragedy*. A. Chekhov's *Three Sisters* is performed for the first time.

## 1902

M. Gorky writes *The Lower Depths* and becomes the director of the publishing company *Znanie* ("Knowledge"), which produces inexpensive books. *Problems of Idealism*, a collection of essays edited by Nikolai Berdiaev and Sergei Bulgakov, is published. The "modern style" of architecture is developed with the Moscow Art Theater designed by F. Shekhtel. A. Chekhov and Vladimir Korolenko resign from the Academy of Sciences to protest the exclusion of Gorky.

## 1903

Philosophical-religious gatherings are convened by D. Merezhkovsky, Zinaida Gippius and Dmitri Filosofov, who also found the review *New Path*. S. Bulgakov: *From Marxism to Idealism*. Alexander Bogdanov: *Empiriomonism*. Vasili Rozanov: *The Family Question in Russia*. The Iaroslavl train station is designed by F. Shekhtel (1903–1904). Konstantin Tsiolkovsky publishes his paper "Investigation of Interplanetary Space by Means of Rocket Devices," in which he sets down the physical principles of rocket propulsion.

Chapter 18                                    1904–1907

# The First Russian Revolution and Its Failure

The military reversals suffered by Russia in 1904–1905 in its war with Japan were accompanied by a new wave of agitation that included strikes, terrorist activity and campaigns by the zemstvos to obtain national representation. The crisis took a decisive turn in January 1905 in St. Petersburg, when the events of Bloody Sunday shattered the traditional image of the czar as the protector of the nation. A veritable revolution began, during which the first "soviets" came into being. The revolution even drew support from the military, as evidenced by the mutiny on the battleship *Potemkin.*

Faced with a general strike, the regime responded with the October Manifesto, which guaranteed civil liberties and created the Duma, a legislature elected through universal suffrage. Although this new arrangement satisfied the more conservative and moderate forces who had sought change, it did not hinder the radicalization of the more advanced elements of society, who continued to press for even greater changes until the crushing of the Moscow Soviet in December 1905. Very quickly, the new constitutional regime found itself circumscribed by authoritarian practices, as evidenced by the dismissal of Sergei Witte as head of the Council of Ministers and by the dissolution of the First Duma in 1906.

Reaction increased under the ministry of Peter Stolypin. In an action resembling a coup d'état, in June 1907 he had the Second Duma dissolved and a new electoral law imposed. Outwardly, it appeared that the czarist regime had weathered the storm. Worker and peasant movements were violently repressed, and the dismissal of the Duma demonstrated the sharp limits on the political activity of liberal and constitutional elements. In fact, however, Russia was profoundly transformed by the ordeal: Political parties asserted themselves, the autocratic system was overtly contested, and the Duma, although shorn of its powers, could serve as a forum for the opposition. Meanwhile, the Social Democrats, in full retreat, sought to garner lessons from the events of 1905. They focused in particular on the experience of the soviets, which suggested a new revolutionary strategy, one that Lenin would seek to put into practice in 1917.

# Politics and Institutions

## 1904

*January 3–5 (16–18)*. The Union of Liberation holds a congress in St. Petersburg.

*May*. Lenin publishes *One Step Forward, Two Steps Back*.

*June 3 (16)*. Nicholas Bobrikov, the governor general of Finland, is assassinated by a young employee of the Finnish Senate.

*July 15 (28)*. Interior Minister Viacheslav Plehve is assassinated by Yegor Sazonov, a member of the Socialist Revolutionary Party (SR).

*August 11 (24)*. The infliction of corporal punishment by cantonal tribunals is abolished.

The czarevitch Alexis is born.

*August 26 (September 8)*. Prince Peter Sviatopolk-Mirsky is appointed interior minister.

*November 6–9 (19–22)*. A congress of representatives of the zemstvos is held in St. Petersburg. It adopts an 11-point program that will be popularized by liberals in a "banquet campaign."

*December*. A large strike by petroleum workers takes place in Baku.

*December 12 (25)*. An imperial ukase promises limited reforms.

*December 22 (January 4, 1905)*. The first issue of Lenin's new journal *Vpered* ("Forward") appears following his break with *Iskra*.

## 1905

*January 3 (16)*. A strike breaks out at the Putilov factories in St. Petersburg.

*January 9 (22)*. The events of "Bloody Sunday" take place in St. Petersburg. Led by the priest George Gapon, 100,000 persons who had marched to the Winter Palace to present a petition to the czar are fired upon by police.

*January 14 (27)*. A general strike begins in Warsaw. A demonstration there will be violently repressed on the 16th (29th).

*January 20 (February 2)*. Alexsander Bulygin replaces Sviatopolk-Mirsky as minister of the interior.

*January 29 (February 11)*. The short-lived "Shidlovsky Commission" is established to look into the situation of workers.

*February 4 (17)*. Grand Duke Sergei, an uncle of the czar, is assassinated.

*February 6–9 (19–22)*. Violent confrontations between Armenians and Tatars erupt in Baku.

*February 18 (March 3)*. A manifesto is issued calling for a struggle against sedition. A rescript ("the Bulygin Rescript") promises that elected representatives will participate in legislative activity. A ukase recognizes the right of petition.

*February (March)*. In the first flare-up of agrarian unrest of the revolution, manors are pillaged and burned.

*March (April)*. The first "professional unions" are established (including an academicians' union and a lawyers' union).

*April 12–17 (April 25–May 30)*. A Bolshevik congress is held in London, and a Menshevik congress is held in Geneva.

*April 17 (30)*. A ukase is issued permitting freedom of religion. It will never be implemented.

*April 18 (May 1)*. Strikes and demonstrations occur in Warsaw and Lodz.

*April 22–26 (May 5–9)*. The first regular congress of the zemstvos meets in Moscow.

*May 8–9 (21–22)*. A Union of Unions is established at Moscow under the direction of Pavel Miliukov.
*May 12 (25)*. A strike by textile workers begins in Ivanovo-Voznesensk.
*May 15 (28)*. The first "soviet" (council) is formed in Ivanovo. It will sit for 65 days.
*May 24–26 (June 6–8)*. The second regular congress of the zemstvos meets in Moscow. It issues an address to the czar and a Manifesto of the Nation.
*June 9–11 (22–24)*. Insurrectionary strikes occur in Lodz. Agitation of a decidedly nationalistic character sweeps Poland.
*June 14–24 (June 27–July 7)*. A mutiny takes place on the battleship *Potemkin*, and rioting occurs in Odessa.
*June (July)*. Agrarian unrest worsens.
In Geneva, Lenin publishes *Two Tactics of Social Democracy in the Democratic Revolution*.
*July 6–8 (19–21)*. A congress of the zemstvos and of the dumas meets in Moscow.
*July 31–August 1 (August 13–14)*. The All-Russian Peasant Union is established at a congress in Moscow.
*August*. An All-Russian Moslem League is formed at Nizhni Novgorod.
*August 6 (19)*. A manifesto is issued announcing the creation of the "Bulygin Duma," which is intended to be a purely consultative body. The electoral system that will be used to choose its members combines suffrage based on property qualifications and suffrage by class.
*August 27 (September 9)*. The universities reopen and are given back their autonomy.
*September 19–October 5 (October 2–18)*. Typographers go on strike in Moscow.

*October 8 (21)*. A railway strike begins and is quickly transformed into a general strike of a clearly political character.
*October 12–18 (25–31)*. A congress meeting in Moscow establishes the Constitutional Democratic Party ("Cadets"). The party is an outgrowth of the Union of Liberation.
*October 13 (26)*. The St. Petersburg Soviet is established. It will publish a journal called *Izvestia*.
*Mid-October (Late October)*. Approximately 1.5 million workers are on strike in Russia, including 700,000 railroad workers.
*October 17 (30)*. The October Manifesto is issued. Prepared by Witte, the manifesto guarantees civil liberties, foresees the implementation of universal suffrage, and calls for the creation of a representative Duma with true legislative power.
*October 18–21 (October 31–November 3)*. A pogrom occurs in Odessa. Anti-Semitic violence, instigated by militant nationalists known as the "Black Hundreds," increases in the western provinces.
*October 19 (November 1)*. Konstantin Pobedonostsev, chief procurator of the Holy Synod, is dismissed.
A Council of Ministers is established, presided over by Witte.
*October 22 (November 4)*. A partial amnesty is declared. Finnish autonomy is restored. The Union of the Russian People, an extreme-right organization, is formed.
*October 26–28 (November 8–10)*. A mutiny occurs at the naval base at Kronstadt.
*October 29 (November 11)*. The St. Petersburg Soviet supports a strike for an eight-hour workday.

*November 3 (16).* Redemption payments are abolished for former serfs.

*November 6–10 (19–23).* The Second Congress of the Peasants' Union meets in Moscow. The organization is dominated by SRs. Peasant unrest continues to increase.

*November 8 (21).* Lenin returns to Russia.

*November 10 (23).* The Union of the 17th of October, which will become the Octobrist Party, is organized.

*November 10–15 (23–28).* Riots occur on ships of the Russian fleet in the Black Sea.

*November 11–15 (24–28).* An insurrection breaks out in Sevastopol.

*November 22 (December 5).* The Moscow Soviet is formed.

*November 26 (December 9).* The authorities arrest George Nosar-Khrustalev, the leader of the St. Petersburg Soviet. He is replaced by a three-person triumvirate, which includes Leon Trotsky.

*December.* The regime embarks on a pacification campaign in the Baltic provinces, Poland, the Ukraine, the Caucasus and Siberia.

*December 2 (15).* A "Financial Manifesto" is issued by the St. Petersburg Soviet, calling for a fiscal and financial strike.

*December 3 (16).* The members of the St. Petersburg Soviet are arrested.

*December 8–18 (21–31).* An insurrection breaks out in Moscow following an appeal by the Moscow Soviet, the majority of whose members now identify with the Bolshevik line. The movement is defeated in street battles in the Presnia district of the city.

*December 11 (24).* A new electoral law is announced. Instead of providing for universal suffrage, the law puts into

effect a system of indirect voting by district, based on property qualifications: One elector is to be chosen for every 2,000 landed proprietors, for every 7,000 city dwellers, for every 30,000 peasants, and for every 90,000 workers.

*December 12–17 (25–30).* A Social Democratic Party conference is held at Tammerfors (Tampere), Finland.

*December 31 (January 13, 1906).* The First Congress of the Socialist Revolutionary Party is held in Finland.

## 1906

A commission is appointed to make preparations for a council of the Orthodox Church. The council will never take place.

*February 8–12 (21–25).* The founding congress of the Octobrist Party is held.

*February 20 (March 5).* The State Council is transformed into an upper legislative chamber; half of its members will be appointed by the czar, and the other half will be elected by very limited suffrage.

*March 4 (17).* Political associations and professional organizations are legalized, but numerous restrictions are placed on their activities.

*April 3 (16).* Russia negotiates an international loan of 2.25 billion francs, half of which it receives from the French government. The loan is needed to reestablish the country's finances on a firm footing following the Russo-Japanese War.

*April 10–25 (April 23–May 8).* The Fourth Congress of the Russian Social Democratic Labor Party is held in Stockholm. The congress seeks to reunite the Bolsheviks and the Mensheviks.

*April 16 (29).* Sergei Witte is dismissed as head of the Council of Ministers; he is replaced by Ivan Goremykin.

## POPULAR MOVEMENTS IN 1905

| Month | Number of peasant uprisings | Number of striking workers |
|---|---|---|
| January | 17 | 443,929 |
| February | 109 | 293,152 |
| March | 103 | 73,081 |
| April | 144 | 104,646 |
| May | 299 | 220,523 |
| June | 492 | 155,741 |
| July | 248 | 152,474 |
| August | 155 | 104,133 |
| September | 71 | 37,851 |
| October | 219 | 518,752 |
| November | 796 | 325,534 |
| December | 575 | 433,357 |
| Total | 3,228 | 2,863,173 |

*April 23 (May 6).* Nicholas II promulgates the Fundamental Laws: The Duma is given very limited powers, and government ministers will not be responsible to that body.

*April 27 (May 10).* The First Duma meets. The majority of its members are from the opposition: 37 percent are Cadets, and 20 percent are Labor deputies who represent a moderate wing of SR and were elected despite the party's decision to boycott the elections.

*May 5 (18).* In an address to the czar, the Duma calls for a genuine constitutional regime.

*June.* Agrarian unrest breaks out again.

*June 1–3 (14–16).* A pogrom takes place in Bialystok.

*July 8 (21).* Peter Stolypin replaces Goremykin as president of the Council of Ministers.

*July 9 (22).* The First Duma is dissolved by the czar.

*July 10 (23).* The Vyborg Manifesto is signed by 182 opposition deputies of the defunct Duma. It calls on the populace to boycott taxes and military service.

*July 17–20 (July 30–August 2).* Short-lived mutinies break out in Sevastopol, Kronstadt and Reval (Tallin).

*August 12 (25).* An assassination attempt is made on Stolypin.

*August 19 (September 1).* Military courts-martial are established. One thousand persons will be condemned to death over an eight-month period.

*November.* The Polish Socialist Party splits into a left faction and a revolutionary faction led by Jozef Pilsudski. The workday is limited to 10 hours (a measure infrequently complied with). An oil pipeline from Baku to Batum, on the Black Sea, is completed.

*November 9 (22).* Stolypin puts forward an agrarian reform program: A ukase gives peasants the right to leave the commune and encourages the consolidation of allotted strips of communal land into individually owned plots. The key objective of the reform is to create a large class of independent proprietors among the peasantry. According to estimates, the total number of privately owned peasant plots (as opposed to communal lots) will rise from 2.8 million in 1905 to 5.5 million in 1914, the latter figure representing approximately 44 percent of total farmland exploited by Russian peasants. The Stolypin reform will be strengthened by additional laws adopted in 1910 and 1911.

## 1907

*February 20 (March 5).* The Second Duma (also known as the "Red Duma" and the "Duma of Extremes") meets. The Social Democrats gain more seats (the party has abandoned its electoral boycott), as do representatives of the extreme right. Cadet representation is considerably smaller than it was in the First Duma.

*April 30–May 19 (May 13–June 1).* The Fifth Congress of the Russian Social Democratic Labor Party is held in London. The Bolsheviks are in the majority.

*May–June.* Terrorist activity increases.

*June 1 (14).* Stolypin demands that the Second Duma expel 55 Social Democratic deputies and lift the legislative immunity enjoyed by 16 of them.

*June 3 (16).* In what amounts to a coup d'état, the Second Duma is dissolved and the electoral law is modified. Under a new law, each vote of a large-landed proprietor will be the equivalent of the votes of 7 city dwellers, of 30 peasants, or of 60 workers.

# Foreign Affairs: War Chronology

## 1904

*January 26–27 (February 8–9).* The Japanese fleet launches a surprise attack on Port Arthur. The Russo-Japanese War begins.

*March 31 (April 13).* The Russian navy is defeated at Port Arthur. Vice Admiral Stepan Makarov is killed.

*July 17 (30).* The Japanese beseige Port Arthur.

*July 28 (August 10).* The Port Arthur Fleet suffers another defeat at the hands of the Japanese and attempts to reach Vladivostok.

*August 13–21 (August 26–September 3).* The Battle of Liaoyang takes place. Russian forces retreat to Mukden.

*December 20 (January 2, 1905).* Russian forces capitulate at Port Arthur.

## 1905

*February 25 (March 10).* The Japanese defeat the Russians at Mukden.

*May 14–15 (27–28).* After a voyage of more than seven months around the Cape of Good Hope, the Russian Baltic Fleet, commanded by Admiral Zinovi Rozhdestvensky, is destroyed in the Tsushima Strait.

*July 11 (24).* Kaiser Wilhelm II of Germany and Nicholas II sign the Treaty of Björkö, a secret defensive alliance.

*August 23 (September 5).* The Treaty of Portsmouth, negotiated with the mediation of President Theodore Roosevelt, is signed by Russia and Japan. Russia cedes to Japan Port Arthur, the southern portion of the Manchurian Railway, and the southern half of Sakhalin Island.

# Civilization and Culture

## 1904

Anton Chekhov: *The Cherry Orchard.* Alexander Blok: *Verses about the Beautiful Lady.* Publication of the first volume of the *Course in Russian History*, by Vasili Kliuchevsky, professor of history at the University of Moscow. Valentin Serov: portrait of Maxim Gorky. Nikolai Rimsky-Korsakov: *The Tale of the Town of Kitezh.* Ivan Pavlov is awarded the Nobel Prize in physiology and medicine for his neurophysiological research.

## 1905

Alexander Kuprin: *The Duel.* Sonia Terk (Delaunay) settles in Paris. The press expands rapidly (from 1,000 periodicals in 1900, to almost 1,500 in 1905, to 2,400 in 1913) thanks to a relative liberalization of censorship laws.

## 1906

Valeri Briusov: *Stephanos.* Vladimir Korolenko begins work on *The History of My Contemporary.*

## 1907

Maxim Gorky: *Mother.* Dmitri Merezhkovsky, Zinaida Gippius and Dmitri Filosofov: *The Czar and the Revolution* (published in Paris). N. Rimsky-Korsakov: *The Golden Cockerel.* Alexander Scriabin: *Poem of Ecstasy.* The Blue Rose exhibition of Symbolist Art is held in Moscow, with the assistance of the patron Nikolai Riabushinsky.

# Political Blockage and Economic Growth

From the dissolution of the Second Duma to his assassination in 1911, Peter Stolypin, the last great reformer of the czarist epoch, dominated the political life of the empire. Stolypin was convinced that Russia's modernization could be achieved by fundamental agrarian reform. Indeed, he believed that reforming agriculture alone could create the necessary conditions for transforming Russia into a modern state based on the rule of law. He moved first against the peasant communes, assuming that their dismantlement would lead to the establishment of a new class of peasant-proprietors that would guarantee the stability of the czarist regime. Stolypin found it difficult, however, to secure the support of the deputies in the Duma; his frequent clashes with that body were as much a consequence of his authoritarian manner as of his policies themselves. The Third Duma, with its conservative majority, and then the Fourth, in which the power of the right and of a virulent extreme right were further strengthened, met in an atmosphere of latent crisis that provoked a portion of the Octobrists to rejoin the opposition and diverted from power a good percentage of deputies of moderate opinion.

Although it was still quite small, the new business bourgeoisie aspired to play a role in politics that was commensurate with the one it had begun to play in the economic development of the country. It sought to accelerate the pace of development by promoting the interests of industrial cartels and banking monopolies. Meanwhile, the urban working class, perhaps 3 million-strong at this time, was becoming more and more alienated from the countryside. As was the case with the impoverished peasants, however, the workers were increasingly swayed by the propaganda of the revolutionary parties (the Social Democrats in the cities, the Socialist Revolutionaries, or SRs, in the countryside).

Even though the rupture between the Bolsheviks and the Mensheviks became irreversible in 1912, the revolutionary parties soon found new sources of strength in the increasing agrarian and student unrest and labor strikes that shook the country. In addition, the non-Russian nationalities stepped up their resistance to the government's program of Russification. Yet the country's economic and social transformations were also accompanied by an intellectual revival, one in which the materialism and positivism of the preceding generation gave way to new aesthetic, philosophical and religious ideas.

# Politics and Institutions

## 1907

*June.* Semyon Ter-Petrosyan (Kamo), a Social Democrat, carries out a spectacular "expropriation" by stealing 250,000 rubles that were being transferred to the State Bank of Tiflis.

*November 1 (14).* The Third Duma (also known as the "Duma of the Lords") meets. One-third of the deputies are from parties of the right or extreme right; one-third are from the Octobrists; and the remainder are from the Constitutional Democrats (Cadets), non-Russian nationalities or small left-wing groups.

*December.* Lenin emigrates once again; he will not return to Russia for nearly 10 years.

## 1908

Yevno Azev, the leader of the terrorist wing of the Socialist Revolutionaries (SRs), is revealed to be a double agent.

## 1909

A latent crisis develops in the Duma: A faction of the Octobrists headed by Alexander Guchkov attempts to defend the prerogatives of the deputies against the increasing intolerance of the czar's ministers.

The Bolsheviks split into factions: The "conciliators" favor a rapprochement with the Mensheviks; the "otzoviki" insist on a recall of the Social Democratic deputies in the Duma; and the "god builders," led by V. A. Bazarov and Alexander Bogdanov, challenge the materialism of orthodox Marxism. Lenin responds to this factionalism in his book *Materialism and Empirio Criticism* (in 1911, he will organize a training school for Bolsheviks at Longjumeau, near Paris, in response to the organization of a similar school at Capri by Maxim Gorky).

*May 31 (June 13).* The Duma approves a law that strengthens the Russification program in Finland.

## 1910

*November 7 (20).* Leo Tolstoy dies; demonstrations occur at his funeral.

## 1911

The Musawat (Equality) Party is founded in Baku. Initially a socialist party, Musawat will eventually espouse Azerbaijani nationalism.

*March 14 (27).* Zemstvos are introduced in the western provinces of the empire.

*September 5 (18).* Peter Stolypin is assassinated by a double agent. Vladimir Kokovtsov becomes prime minister.

## 1912

Kholm, a part of Poland considered to be Russian and Orthodox, is reunited with Russia.

*January 5–17 (18–30).* The Sixth Congress of the Russian Social Democratic Labor Party is held in Prague. The break between the Bolsheviks and the Mensheviks becomes irreversible.

*March.* In the Duma, Guchkov raises the issue of Grigori Rasputin's role in the imperial entourage. (Rasputin, a self-proclaimed *starets*, or "holy man," gained considerable influence over Empress Alexandra and a portion of the imperial entourage because of his apparent power to cure the czarevitch Alexis's hemophilia.)

*April 22 (May 5).* The first issue of *Pravda* ("Truth"), the Bolshevik's daily newspaper, appears in St. Petersburg (in 1913, the paper's average circulation will reach 40,000). Joseph Stalin is a member of the paper's editorial board.

*June.* Lenin leaves Paris to settle in Austrian Galicia.

*June 9 (22).* The term of office of the Third Duma ends.

*June 15 (28).* The office of justice of the peace, which had been abolished in 1889, is reestablished. Jews are barred from this office.

*August.* In an unsuccessful attempt to reunify the Social Democratic Labor Party, Leon Trotsky forms the "August Bloc" in Vienna.

*November 15 (28).* The Fourth Duma goes into session. The position of the right is stronger than in the previous Duma, while the center, represented by the Octobrists, has lost ground.

## 1913

The tricentennial of the Romanov dynasty is celebrated.

At Lenin's instigation, Stalin writes *Marxism and the National Question.* The work is critical of federalism and of the Austro-Marxist concept of "national-cultural autonomy," but it affirms the right of oppressed nations to independence.

## 1914

*January 30 (February 12).* Ivan Goremykin replaces Kokovtsov as prime minister.

# Foreign Affairs

## 1907

*June 2 (15)–October 5 (18).* Russia participates in the Second Conference of The Hague.

*July 17 (30).* Russia and Japan sign an accord that establishes their respective spheres of influence in Asia and the Far East. Russia's sphere encompasses

northern Manchuria and Outer Mongolia; Japan's encompasses southern Manchuria and Korea.

*August 18 (31).* An Anglo-Russian accord on spheres of influence in Asia clears the way for the formation of the Triple Entente between France, England and Russia.

## 1908

*April 10 (23).* Russia signs an accord with Germany, Denmark and Sweden concerning the Åland Islands.

*July.* Poles and Russians attend a "neo-Slavic" Congress in Prague. A short-lived rapprochement is effected.

*September 24 (October 7).* Austria announces its annexation of Bosnia and Herzegovina. A Balkan crisis erupts, and Russo-Austrian tension mounts.

## 1909

*March.* After Germany pressures Russia into abandoning support for Serbia, the latter is obliged to accept Austria-Hungary's annexation of Bosnia and Herzegovina.

*October.* A Russo-Italian accord recognizes Russia's interests in the Bosporus and Dardanelles straits and Italy's interests in Libya.

## 1910

*October 22 (November 4).* Nicholas II and his cousin Kaiser Wilhelm II of Germany meet in Potsdam.

## 1911

*August 6 (19).* A Russo-German accord is reached concerning Persia.

*December.* With Russia's support, Outer Mongolia proclaims its autonomy vis-à-vis China.

## 1912

*March–May.* Russian diplomats assist in the creation of the Balkan League between Bulgaria, Serbia, Montenegro and Greece. The League grants Russia the power to arbitrate disputes between its members.

*October.* The First Balkan War breaks out, pitting Serbia, Montenegro, Greece and Bulgaria against Turkey.

*October 21 (November 3).* Russia and Mongolia sign a Treaty of Friendship.

## 1913

A plan for increasing the size of the Russian army is announced: The fighting force is projected to rise from 1.2 million to 1.42 million in 1914, and to 1.8 million in 1917.

*May 17 (30).* The Treaty of London ends the First Balkan War. Having been defeated, Turkey is forced to give up most of its European territories. Disagreements immediately break out among the victors.

*June 16 (29).* The Second Balkan War erupts, pitting Bulgaria against its former allies (Serbia, Montenegro and Greece), who are now joined by Romania and Turkey.

*July 28 (August 10).* The Treaty of Bucharest formalizes the defeat of Bulgaria in the Second Balkan War. In the war's aftermath, Russia experiences diplomatic reversals in the Balkans, including Bulgaria's tilt toward Austria-Hungary.

*October 23 (November 5).* A Sino-Russian accord recognizes the autonomy of Mongolia.

## 1913–1914

*December–January.* A crisis erupts between Russia and Germany when the latter sends General Liman von Sanders to Constantinople to modernize the Turkish army.

# Economy and Society

## 1907

The concentration of Russian industry continues. Cartels are formed in the metallurgy industry in the Urals (*Krovlya*) as well as in the industries producing copper (*Med*), ores (*Prodarug*), rubber and cement.

With the encouragement of the state, the pace of colonization in Siberia accelerates. From 1906 to 1914, 4 million persons will migrate to Siberia (more than 15 percent of them, however, will elect to return to their former homes).

## 1908

*May 3 (16).* A law makes 10 years of primary education obligatory. The number of enrolled primary-school students will increase from 4 million in 1900 to 7.2 million (including 2.3 million girls) in 1914.

## 1909

Russia enjoys an exceptional harvest and becomes the world's largest grain exporter (30 percent of its total harvest is exported).

The University of Saratov is founded. Women's access to universities is restricted, and the enrollment of Jews is subject to rigid quotas.

The State Council refuses to legalize the formation of congregations of Old Believers.

## 1910

The Russo-Asiatic Bank is created by the merger of the Russo-Chinese Bank and the Northern Bank; 60 percent of the new bank's capital is from France.

The creation of finance monopolies intensifies, and these entities acquire control over entire sectors of the economy.

## EVOLUTION OF THE POPULATION

|      | Total population | Percentage rural population | Percentage urban population |
|------|------------------|-----------------------------|-----------------------------|
| 1897 | 129,000,000      | 87.0                        | 13.0                        |
| 1913 | 172,000,000      | 84.5                        | 15.5                        |

## POPULATION GROWTH IN MAJOR CITIES
(in millions of residents)

|                | 1863 | 1897  | 1914  |
|----------------|------|-------|-------|
| St. Petersburg | 539  | 1,265 | 2,119 |
| Moscow         | 462  | 1,039 | 1,763 |
| Riga           | 77   | 282   | 588   |
| Kiev           | 68   | 248   | 520   |
| Odessa         | 119  | 404   | 500   |

## POPULATION GROWTH IN BURGEONING INDUSTRIAL CITIES
(in millions of residents)

|              | 1863 | 1897 | 1917 |
|--------------|------|------|------|
| Baku         | 14.0 | 112  | 232  |
| Ekaterinberg | 20.0 | 118  | 211  |
| Ivanovo      | 1.5  | 54   | 146  |

A new period of accelerated industrial development begins.

Measures are taken to promote the creation of Russian colonies in Turkestan; Russians already account for 40 percent of the total population of this region.

The first Russian automobiles and airplanes are built.

*June 14 (27).* A law institutionalizes the ukase of November 9 (22), 1906, that expanded the opportunity of peasants to leave the communes.

## 1911

*January (February).* Student unrest breaks out. The minister of public education, Lev Kasso, bars all meetings on university property and limits the autonomy of universities.

*May 29 (June 11).* Another law is enacted to facilitate the dissolution of peasant communes.

## 1912

*April 4 (17).* The "Lena Massacre" takes place: Two hundred and seventy persons are killed when a demonstration by Siberian mine workers is brutally repressed.

*June 23 (July 6).* A statute concerning accident and health insurance is enacted.

## 1913

The population of the empire is set at 170 million.

The Russian government purchases the Warsaw-Vienna Railroad Company. By 1914 Russia will have more than 43,000 miles of railroad track.

A new wave of strikes begins: From June 1913 to July 1914, 1.75 million workers will participate in strikes.

*October 28 (November 10)*. The Beilis trial, in which a Jew is accused of ritual murder, ends in Kiev with the acquittal of the defendant by a jury.

## 1914

An agreement is reached on a new French loan to Russia: Five hundred million francs are to be made available each year for the next five years for the development of strategic railroads in western Russia.

Loans to, or guaranteed by, the Russian state now total 8–9 billion rubles, one half of which is from France. Foreign private investment in Russia now totals 2 billion rubles, one third of which is of French origin.

*February (March)*. Demonstrations occur in the Ukraine on the centennial of the birth of the poet Taras Shevchenko.

*June–July*. Massive strikes occur in Baku and in St. Petersburg.

# Civilization and Culture

## 1908

The second volume of verses by Alexander Blok appears. Leo Tolstoy: "I Cannot Be Silent." Maxim Gorky: *A Confession. Stenka Razin*, the first great Russian motion picture, is directed by V. Romashkov. The first exhibition of paintings by the group known as the

Golden Fleece is held in Moscow; post-impressionist French art is strongly represented. Ilya Mechnikov wins the Nobel Prize for medicine for his embryological and immunological research.

## 1909

A collection of essays entitled *Vekhi* ("Signposts") is published; it contains articles by, among others, Nikolai Berdiaev, Sergei Bulgakov and Peter Struve. The collection is intended to be an indictment of positivist and materialist tendencies among the socialist-leaning intelligentsia.

Andrei Bely: *The Silver Dove, Ashes, The Urn*. Igor Grabar begins publishing his *History of Russian Art* (1909–1916).

## 1910

In Paris Sergei Diaghilev presents Igor Stravinsky's *The Firebird*. Russian ballet begins to receive huge acclaim, thanks to the choreography of Mikhail Fokin, the set designs of Lev Bakst and Alexander Benois, and the dancing of Anna Pavlova and Vaslav Nijinsky.

Marc Chagall settles in Paris (he will return to Russia in 1914). In Moscow the group of painters known as the "Jack of Diamonds" forms around Mikhail Larionov; the group's exhibitions help to increase the renown of the Russian avant-garde.

## 1911

N. Berdiaev: *The Philosophy of Freedom*. Anatoli Lunacharsky: *Religion and Socialism*. In Munich a group called "Der Blaue Reiter" is formed; one of its members is Vasili Kandinsky, who publishes *On the Spiritual in Art*. I. Stravinsky: *Petrushka*.

## 1912

The "Poets' Atelier" is founded by Anna Akhmatova, Nikolai Gumilev and Osip Mandelstam. This marks the birth of the

## PEASANT MIGRATION TO/FROM SIBERIA
## MIGRANT FAMILIES FROM 1901 TO 1913

| | Total number of families migrating to Siberia | Number of families leaving Siberia | Percentage of families leaving |
|---|---|---|---|
| 1901 | 83,326 | 26,530 | 31.8 |
| 1902 | 77,272 | 19,997 | 25.8 |
| 1903 | 88,072 | 14,153 | 16.1 |
| 1904 | 37,063 | 6,428 | 17.6 |
| 1905 | 37,168 | 5,535 | 14.6 |
| 1906 | 135,274 | 8,940 | 6.6 |
| 1907 | 421,335 | 20,176 | 4.8 |
| 1908 | 649,866 | 30,318 | 5.6 |
| 1909 | 593,806 | 56,775 | 9.6 |
| 1910 | 285,878 | 76,118 | 26.6 |
| 1911 | 161,519 | 74,717 | 46.3 |
| 1912 | 176,528 | 34,783 | 19.6 |
| 1913 | 219,976 | 23,506 | 10.7 |

"acmeist" movement, which is formed in reaction to symbolism.

Sergei Prokofiev: First Piano Concerto. The futurist manifesto *A Slap in the Face of Public Taste* is issued by Vladimir Mayakovsky and Velimir Khlebnikov. The Donkey's Tail Exhibition, organized in Moscow by M. Larionov, includes paintings by Kasimir Malevich and Vladimir Tatlin.

**1913**

M. Gorky: *My Childhood*. A. Bely: *Petersburg* (1913–1916). Vasili Rozanov: *Fallen*

*Leaves* (1913–1915). O. Mandelstam: *Peter*. The principles of rayonism are formulated by M. Larionov and Natalia Goncharova. *Black Square on a White Background*, a painting by K. Malevich. In Paris the Russian Ballet creates a dance rendition of I. Stravinsky's *Rite of Spring*.

**1914**

A. Akhmatova: *The Rosary. Bottle*, a relief by V. Tatlin. Russia participates in the Leipzig Book Fair; 106 million volumes were published in Russia in 1913.

# Chapter 20                    1914–1916

# Russia During the First World War

When Russia accepted the risk of war by announcing a general mobilization on July 18 (31) 1914, the authorities sought to project an image of
a state certain of its strength and faithful to its mission of protecting its "little
brother" Serbia. When the war did come in August 1914, it was not unpopular
with the public; in the Duma all but a few socialist groupings joined together
to form a "Sacred Union" of political parties. On the field of battle, however,
ominous signs were quick to appear. Only with great difficulty was Russia able
to compensate for its defeats in East Prussia by occupying a portion of Austrian
Galicia and by achieving victories over the Turks in the Caucasus. Moreover,
a war that had been expected to be short lingered on. Military defeats suffered
by Russia during the summer of 1915 were soon accompanied by a loss of
confidence in the ability of the country's leaders to conduct a prolonged war.
The Duma deputies of the center and of the moderate left coalesced in a
"Progressive Bloc" that called in vain for the appointment of a new government
that would command the country's confidence.

While industrial and commercial organizations and various assistance committees were bonding together to supplement the government's insufficient
war effort, the regime was gradually cutting itself off from all of its potential
supporters. With Nicholas II choosing to take personal command of Russia's
military forces, it began to appear as if a political void existed at the heart of the
country's power structure. A series of ministerial changes and scandals contributed to an extremely troubled atmosphere, as did the assassination of Grigori
Rasputin in December 1916.

From 1915 onward, Russia's mounting economic problems were aggravated
by the loss of portions of its territory and by a rupture of direct trade links with
its allies. A disorganized transport system made the restocking of the front lines,
as well as areas behind the lines, increasingly difficult. Particularly hard hit were
those cities experiencing an influx of refugees; the rising demand for food and
other necessities resulted in price increases that far outstripped any increases
in wages. Strikes, the incidence of which had fallen to an insignificant level at
the outbreak of the war, soon became widespread once again (in 1916 more
than 1 million workers walked off their jobs). At the same time, unrest began
to sweep through the army, and the opposition of the socialists to the "imperialist war" grew. It was a discredited and weakened regime that would be
caught by surprise by the events of February (March) 1917.

## World War I in Eastern Europe

Central powers

Neutral

Allied and associated powers    (1914)  Date entered war

## Politics and Institutions

### 1914

*July 7–10 (20–23).* President Raymond Poincaré and Prime Minister René Viviani of France visit St. Petersburg.

*July 16 (29).* A law makes military authority superior to civil authority in war zones.

*July 26 (August 8).* An extraordinary session of the Duma convenes. A "Sacred Union" of political parties is declared, and financial credits for the conduct of the war are approved (Trudovik [Labor] and Social Democratic deputies abstain from voting on both questions). Following the declaration of war, Russian socialists divide into factions: Some, led by George Plekhanov, rally to the Sacred Union; others, led by Julius Martov, pursue an internationalist line; a third group, led by Lenin, opts for defeatism (Lenin writes his article "The War and Russian Social Democracy").

*July (August).* An All-Russian Union of Towns and an All-Russian Union of Zemstvos are established, the latter under the direction of Prince Lvov, to care for the sick and wounded.

*August 14 (27).* Grand Duke Nicholas, the commander-in-chief of Russian forces, issues a proclamation to the Poles setting out a plan for the reunification of Polish lands under the leadership of the czar. At the same time, the Austrians form Polish legions under the direction of Jozef Pilsudski.

*August 18 (31).* St. Petersburg is renamed Petrograd.

*September.* A. Szeptycki, the Uniate metropolitan of Lvov, is arrested and deported, first to Kiev, then to Suzdal. The Ukrainians of Galicia undergo Russification.

*November.* Five Bolshevik members of the Duma are arrested. In 1915 they will be sentenced to be deported to Siberia.

## 1915

*January 27–29 (February 9–11).* The Duma meets for three days and approves a budget. Outside of these sessions, the government rules by decree.

*March.* Colonel Sergei Miasoedov is executed for treason. Minister of War Vladimir Sukhomlinov is discredited because of Russia's unpreparedness for the war. He will be forced to resign and will be indicted for treason.

*July 19 (August 1).* A new session of the Duma is convened. Deputies call in vain for the appointment of a government that can command the confidence of the country.

*August.* The political crisis worsens. In the Duma a "Progressive Bloc" encompassing two-thirds of the Octobrist and Cadet deputies is formed.

*August 23 (September 5).* Nicholas II arrives at the headquarters of the General Staff at Mogilev and takes personal command of Russian forces.

*August 23–26 (September 5–8).* The Bolsheviks and the Mensheviks participate in the First International Socialist Conference, which is held in Zimmerwald, Switzerland. Finding the conference's *Manifesto for Peace* inadequate, Lenin and Grigori Zinoviev form the "Zimmerwaldian Left," a group that hopes to transform the "imperialist war" into a "revolutionary civil war."

*August 26 (September 8).* The Duma's Progressive Bloc publishes a program calling for political and administrative reforms.

*September 3 (16).* The Duma session ends without a date being fixed for the convening of the next session.

## 1916

*January 20 (February 2).* Ivan Goremykin is replaced as prime minister by Boris Stürmer, a creature of Grigori Rasputin with a reputation of being a Germanophile.

*April 11–17 (24–30).* The Second International Socialist Conference is held in Kienthal, Switzerland. The position of the "Zimmerwaldian Left" is strengthened. Lenin writes *Imperialism, the Highest Stage of Capitalism,* which will be published in 1917.

*June.* Stürmer takes over the Foreign Ministry while continuing to serve as prime minister.

*November 1 (14).* At the opening meeting of the autumn session of the Duma, the leader of the Cadets, Pavel Miliukov, delivers a celebrated speech that concludes with the words, "What is this? Imbecility or treason?" The address, a broad critique of the government and of the imperial entourage, is seconded by a leader of the nationalist right-wing deputies.

*November 10 (23).* Stürmer is dismissed. He is replaced as prime minister by Alexander Trepov.

*Night of December 16–17 (29–30).* Rasputin is assassinated by Prince Felix Yusupov, the nationalist deputy Vladimir Purishkevich and Grand Duke Dmitri.

*December 17 (30).* The Duma adjourns.

*December 27 (January 9, 1917).* Trepov is dismissed as prime minister and replaced by Nikolai Golitsyn. There are rumors of pressure being brought to bear on the czar to abdicate the throne.

# War Chronology

## 1914

*June 15 (28).* Austrian Archduke Franz Ferdinand is assassinated at Sarajevo.

*July 15 (28).* Austria-Hungary declares war on Serbia.

*July 16–17 (29–30).* A partial mobilization of Russian troops is announced. On July 18 (31), a general mobilization will be ordered.

*July 18 (31).* Germany issues an ultimatum to Russia.

*July 19 (August 1).* Germany declares war on Russia.

*July 24 (August 6).* Austria-Hungary declares war on Russia.

*August 4 (17).* A Russian offensive in East Prussia begins. Although General Pavel Rennenkampf will score an initial victory at Gumbinnen on August 7 (20), Russian troops will suffer a crushing defeat in the Battle of Tannenberg on August 13–17 (26–30). This reversal will lead General Alexander Samsonov to commit suicide, and retreating Russian troops will suffer yet another defeat at the Masurian Lakes on August 27–September 1 (September 9–14).

*August 5 (18).* Russia launches an offensive against Austria in eastern Galicia. Lvov is taken on August 21 (September 3). Przemysl is besieged, and eastern Galicia (up to the San River) is occupied by Russian forces. Russia controls the foothills of the Carpathian Mountains.

*October 16–17 (29–30).* The Turks bombard the Russian coast of the Black Sea. The war with Turkey opens a new front in the Caucasus.

*November–December.* A German offensive in Russian Poland results in the capture of Lodz on November 23 (December 6); the offensive is stopped at Warsaw.

*December.* The number of troops mobilized by Russia reaches 6.5 million. By 1917 this figure will have risen to 15 million, of which 55 percent will have been captured, wounded or killed.

## 1915

*January.* The Turkish offensive in the Caucasus that was launched at the end of 1914 is defeated.

*February 27 (March 12).* The British government agrees in principle to Russia's annexation of Constantinople. A similar accord will be reached with the French government on March 28 (April 10).

*March 9 (22).* The Austrian garrison at Przemysl capitulates.

*April 19 (May 2).* A major Austro-German offensive begins. The Russian lines are broken at the Görlitz Gap in Galicia.

*May 21 (June 3).* The Russian army is forced to abandon Przemysl.

*June 9 (22).* Lvov is lost.

*July 1 (14).* A German offensive is launched along the eastern front.

*July 22–23 (August 4–5).* Russian forces abandon Warsaw.

*August 12 (25).* Brest-Litovsk is lost.

*September.* Vilnius is lost.

*October.* Russian forces succeed in stabilizing the front along a line running through Riga, Pinsk and Tarnopol.

*November 23–25 (December 6–8).* The Allies (Russia, England and France) meet at Chantilly, near Paris, to coordinate their plans for an offensive in 1916.

## 1916

*February 3 (16).* The Russians take Erzerum from the Turks.

*April 5 (18).* The Russians capture Trebizond from the Turks.

*May 22 (June 4).* The victorious offensive of General Alexei Brusilov in Galicia and Bukovina begins. It will last until July 31 (August 13).

*August 14 (27).* Romania enters the war on the side of the Allies. The invasion of Romania by German troops places Russia's southern front in jeopardy.

*October.* Sailors of the Baltic Fleet who had mutinied are brought to trial.

Desertions increase in number, and fraternization with the enemy occurs on occasion.

*October 23 (November 5).* In the "Act of the Two Emperors," the monarchs of Germany and Austria-Hungary promise to create a Polish state governed by a hereditary constitutional monarch out of territory conquered from Russia.

# Economy and Society

## 1914

Social unrest declines with the start of the war (70 strikes with 35,000 partici-

pants occur during the last five months of 1914).

The western borders of the empire from the Baltic to the Black Sea are closed because of the conflict. Trade with the Allies must pass through Archangel or Vladivostok (Murmansk will also be used when a railway line to that city is completed in 1916).

The sale of alcohol is forbidden for the duration of the war.

## 1915

*May 28–29 (June 10–11).* Xenophobic riots and demonstrations occur in Moscow.

*June 7 (20).* A central committee of war industries is created under pressure from business interests who wish to participate in the management of the war economy; they denounce the negligence of the government.

*July.* The Union of Towns and the Union of Zemstvos create *Zemgor*, a body charged with centralizing the resupply of the troops.

*August.* In response to the demands of the Duma, new technical bodies are created and given responsibility for national defense, transportation, provisions, fuel and, later, refugees.

The incidence of strikes increases; bloody clashes occur at Ivanovo.

## 1916

The economic and social situation begins to deteriorate rapidly: Commerce breaks down, shortages of industrial products and foodstuffs become widespread, and price increases greatly outpace wage increases.

Approximately 1,400 strikes, involving a total of more than 1 million workers, take place during 1916. The strikes take on an increasingly political character.

*January.* The value of the paper ruble is 56 kopecks (it will fall to 27 kopecks by February 1917). From 1914 to 1917, there is a three-fold increase in public debt, a four-fold increase in budgetary expenditures, and a six-fold increase in paper money in circulation.

*May.* There are 3.3 million refugees in Russia; many of them have been ordered to leave their homes because of military retreats along the front.

*June 25 (July 8).* A ukase decrees the mobilization for forced labor of nearly 400,000 inhabitants of Turkestan and of the region of the steppes. A massive insurrection of Kazakh tribes is violently repressed.

# Civilization and Culture

## 1915

Vladimir Mayakovsky: *The Cloud in Pants.* Ivan Bunin: *The Gentleman from San Francisco.* Maxim Gorky: *Among the People.* At Petrograd, the Futurist exhibitions *Tramway V* and *0.10* are held. The *Suprematist Manifesto* is issued by Ivan Puni and Kasimir Malevich, who also publish *From Cubism to Suprematism.*

## 1916

Sergei Prokofiev: *Scythian Suite.*

# The Revolution of February 1917 And the Fall of the Romanovs

Since the very beginning of 1917, shortages of bread and fuel had been feeding an escalating series of riots and strikes in Petrograd. These disturbances would culminate in the decisive days of the "February Revolution" (March 8–11).

Once the czarist regime had fallen, a Provisional Government was formed. Made up of members of the Duma drawn from the Progressive Bloc, the new government was quickly recognized by several western countries. The Provisional Government immediately declared a general amnesty, proclaimed the freedom to unionize and the right to strike, and promised autonomy to the non-Russian nationalities. But it was also forced to take note of the growing power of the Soviet of Workers' and Soldiers' Deputies, which had installed itself in the Tauride Palace. Filled with constant pressures and negotiations, relations between these two power centers were difficult.

A succession of crises gradually stripped the new government of its credibility. Because it was a provisional regime charged with administering the Russian state until a Constituent Assembly could be elected, the government postponed any serious reforms. Such delays, however, merely served to rekindle the impatience of the workers and the peasants. Moreover, the Provisional Government's fidelity to the war aims and to the anti-German alliance of the previous regime clashed with the desire for peace of an army less and less capable of conducting military operations. Notwithstanding its tentative attempts to form a coalition with moderate elements in the Petrograd Soviet, the Provisional Government continually displayed an inability to gauge the mood of the people. Its lack of understanding and initiative left it vulnerable to attacks from extremists, especially from the Bolsheviks, who knew all too well how to use simple and effective slogans to gain popular support.

## Politics and Institutions

### 1917

*January 9 (22).* A strike by 50,000 workers and a demonstration in Petrograd commemorate the events of Bloody Sunday that sparked the Revolution of 1905.

*February 5 (18).* To put down any revolts, the government creates a special military administration for Petrograd

# Russian Revolution (1917) and Russian Civil War (1918–1922)

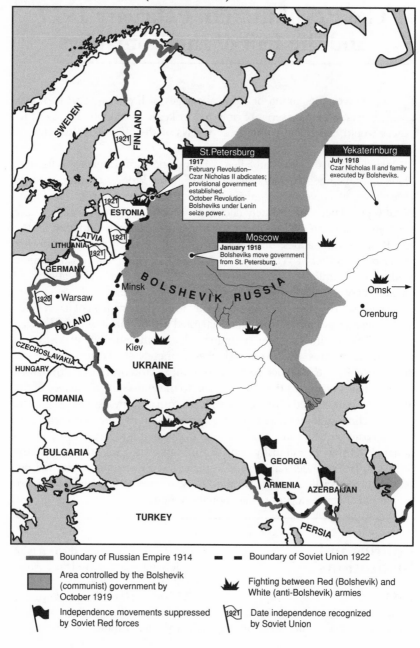

**St.Petersburg**
**1917**
February Revolution–
Czar Nicholas II abdicates;
provisional government
established.
October Revolution-
Bolsheviks under Lenin
seize power.

**Yekaterinburg**
**July 1918**
Czar Nicholas II and family
executed by Bolsheviks.

**Moscow**
**January 1918**
Bolsheviks move government
from St. Petersburg.

SWEDEN

FINLAND

1921

ESTONIA

LATVIA 1921
LITHUANIA 1921

GERMANY

Minsk

BOLSHEVIK RUSSIA

Omsk

Orenburg

1920 ●Warsaw

POLAND

CZECHOSLAVAKIA
HUNGARY

Kiev

UKRAINE

ROMANIA

BULGARIA

GEORGIA

ARMENIA  AZERBAIJAN

TURKEY

PERSIA

━━━━ Boundary of Russian Empire 1914 ▬ ▬ Boundary of Soviet Union 1922

Area controlled by the Bolshevik
(communist) government by
October 1919

Fighting between Red (Bolshevik) and
White (anti-Bolshevik) armies

Independence movements suppressed
by Soviet Red forces

1921 Date independence recognized
by Soviet Union

under the command of General Sergei Khabalov, who had played a role in the repression of 1905.

*February 14 (27).* The Duma convenes. Some deputies demand the recall of incompetent ministers. Approximately 80,000 workers go on strike in Petrograd.

*February 18 (March 3).* Workers go on strike at the Putilov factories.

*February 22 (March 7).* A lockout occurs at the Putilov factories.

*February 23 (March 8).* On International Women's Day, an enormous demonstration takes place in Petrograd to protest the scarcity of food.

*February 24 (March 9).* Demonstrations grow in Petrograd; antiwar and antiautocracy slogans are prominent. The first clashes with the police take place.

*February 25 (March 10).* A quasi-general strike occurs in Petrograd. The police intervene, but the cossacks refuse to shoot at the demonstrators. That evening Nicholas II sends a telegram from the General Staff's headquarters in Mogilev, ordering an end to the disorder in the capital.

*February 26 (March 11).* Violent clashes occur between demonstrators and the army. Officers order soldiers to fire on the crowds, resulting in 150 casualties. Despite the appeals of its president, Mikhail Rodzianko, for a government that enjoys the country's confidence, the Duma is dismissed.

*February 27 (March 12).* Soldiers mutiny in Petrograd. They fraternize with workers, seize the Arsenal and occupy some public buildings as well as the Winter Palace.

Two rival centers of power emerge: a provisional committee of the Duma that is made up of centrist and leftist deputies;

and the Petrograd Soviet of Workers' Deputies, which is joined by many soldiers. The Soviet, with the Menshevik Nikolai Chkheidze as president and the Trudovik Alexander Kerensky as vice president, installs itself in the Tauride Palace.

*February 28 (March 13).* The first issue of *Izvestia*, the organ of the Petrograd Soviet, appears. In the weeks that follow, the number of soviets in the provinces will multiply.

*March 1 (14).* In its first *prikaz*, or Order Number 1, the Petrograd Soviet invites soldiers to elect committees in every military unit, thereby bringing the army under its control. The Soviet also agrees to support the government formed by the Duma if certain conditions are met.

*March 2 (15).* A Provisional Government succeeds the provisional committee of the Duma. Its leadership includes the following: Prince Georgi Lvov, president; Pavel Miliukov (Cadet), foreign minister; Alexander Guchkov (Octobrist), minister of war and the navy; and Kerensky (Trudovik), justice minister.

In Pskov, Nicholas II abdicates—both for himself and for his son—in favor of his brother, Grand Duke Michael.

*March 3 (16).* Grand Duke Michael, whose safety cannot be guaranteed by the Provisional Government should he ascend the throne, refuses to become czar.

*March 4 (17).* In Kiev, a *Rada* (Ukrainian Central Council) presided over by the historian Mikhail Grushevsky is formed.

*March 5 (18).* *Pravda*, the Bolshevik organ, resumes publication.

*March 6 (19).* The Provisional Government announces its program: political amnesty, the convocation of a

Constituent Assembly elected by universal suffrage, guarantees of political liberty and of civil equality, and the continuation of the war to a victorious conclusion.

*March 7 (20).* The Constitution of Finland is reinstated.

*March 7–12 (20–25).* In Zurich, Lenin writes his *Letters from Afar.* He calls on the Petrograd Soviet to break with the Provisional Government and to inaugurate a new phase of the revolution.

*March 8 (21).* The imperial family is arrested.

*March 12 (25).* The Bolsheviks Joseph Stalin and Lev Kamenev return to Petrograd from exile.

The death penalty is abolished.

*March 17 (30).* The Provisional Government recognizes Poland's right to independence.

*March 23 (April 5).* In Petrograd, solemn funerals are held for those who died during the February Revolution.

*March 29–April 3 (April 11–16).* The first All-Russian Conference of Soviets of Workers' and Soldiers' Deputies takes place. The Conference elects a Central Committee, the majority of whose members are Mensheviks and Socialist Revolutionaries (SRs).

*April 3 (16).* Lenin returns to Petrograd.

*April 4 (17).* Lenin reads his "April Theses" to the Bolsheviks. In addition to calling for a struggle against the continuation of the war and for the denial of any support to the Provisional Government, Lenin advocates the creation of a republic of soviets, the transfer of all land to the peasants' soviets, the nationalization of banks and the creation of a revolutionary International.

*April 7 (20).* The "April Theses" are published in *Pravda.*

*April 12 (25).* A law is passed granting freedom of assembly and association.

*April 18 (May 1).* In Petrograd, a large antiwar demonstration takes place on the occasion of May Day.

*April 20–21 (May 3–4).* The "April Crisis" occurs. The Petrograd Soviet issues a strong protest against Foreign Minister Miliukov's note to the Allies confirming Russia's commitment to the war. Workers and soldiers demonstrate against the Provisional Government's foreign policy. The Bolsheviks attempt to rally the demonstrators behind their party's slogans. Violent clashes with nationalist elements occur. Following the "April Crisis," the Bolsheviks will support the formation of "Red Guards" (armed units of proletarians).

*April 24–29 (May 7–12).* The Seventh Bolshevik Party Conference is held. Despite strong opposition from within its ranks, the party adopts the main points of Lenin's "April Theses."

*April 29 (May 12).* The minister of war, Alexander Guchkov, resigns, citing his lack of authority over the army.

*May 1 (14).* After negotiating with the Provisional Government, the Petrograd Soviet authorizes its representatives to participate in a coalition government.

*May 2 (15).* Foreign Minister Miliukov resigns.

*May 4 (17).* Leon Trotsky returns from exile and attempts to reconcile his followers, the "Mezhraiontsy," with the Bolsheviks.

*May 5 (18).* A new Provisional Government is formed with the participation of representatives of the Petrograd Soviet. Known as the First Coalition Government, it includes Prince Georgi Lvov as president, the Trudovik Alexander Kerensky as minister of war, the Socialist

174

Revolutionary (SR) Viktor Chernov as minister of agriculture and the Menshevik Irakli Tsereteli as minister of posts and telegraphs.

*May 7–12 (20–25).* An All-Russian Conference of Mensheviks is held.

*May 25–June 4 (June 7–17).* A congress of SRs is held in Moscow; the Left SRs present their own platform.

*June 3–24 (June 16–July 7).* The first All-Russian Congress of Soviets of Workers' and Soldiers' Deputies takes place in Petrograd; 285 SRs, 248 Mensheviks and 105 Bolsheviks are among the 822 delegates. Despite the fact that the majority of delegates to the congress supports the coalition government, Lenin announces that the Bolsheviks are ready to take power.

*June 10 (23).* The First Universal (a fundamental law) of the Ukrainian *Rada* proclaims the autonomy of the Ukraine.

*June 18 (July 1).* On the same day that a Russian offensive is launched in Galicia, the Bolsheviks, using their anti-war slogans, seize control of a demonstration that had been organized by the Petrograd Soviet to show support for the Provisional Government.

*July 1 (14).* A compromise is reached between the Provisional Government and the Ukrainian *Rada* on the question of Ukrainian autonomy.

Zemstvos are created in the western and southern provinces.

*July 2 (15).* A new ministerial crisis occurs: The Cadet ministers resign in protest against the Provisional Government's policy toward the Ukraine.

*July 3–4 (16–17).* The "July Days" take place in Petrograd: Workers, soldiers and Kronstadt sailors stage violent demonstrations against the Provisional Government and the Soviet. After some

hesitation, the Bolsheviks support the demonstrations, which are suppressed by loyal troops. Severe measures are taken against the Bolsheviks, who are accused of being agents in the pay of Germany. Lenin leaves clandestinely for Finland.

*July 8 (21).* Following the resignation of Prince Lvov, Kerensky forms a transitional cabinet.

*July 18 (31).* The Provisional Government dissolves the Finnish Diet, which had proclaimed autonomy for Finland.

*July 24 (August 6).* With the consent of the Soviet, Kerensky forms a second coalition government with a socialist majority.

*July 26–August 3 (August 8–16).* The Seventh Bolshevik Party Congress is held. The Congress declares that the power of the state can be won only by a carefully planned armed insurrection. The Congress recognizes the adherence of Trotsky's Mezhraiontsy group and elects a Central Committee that includes, among others, Lenin, Kamenev, Grigori Zinoviev, Stalin and Trotsky.

*August 12–15 (25–28).* The Provisional Government convenes a consultative conference in Moscow. The conference, attended by almost 2,500 delegates chosen by the government from all walks of life, hears General Lavr Kornilov call for a strengthening of discipline within the army.

*August 25 (September 7).* The "Kornilov Affair" begins. Under the pretense of preventing a possible Bolshevik insurrection, Kornilov sends the Third Corps of the Cavalry, led by General Alexander Krymov, and the infamous "Savage Division" to Petrograd and demands the resignation of the ministers.

*August 27 (September 9).* The Cadet ministers resign. After a period of hesitation, Kerensky dismisses General Kornilov from his post as commander-in-chief and makes an appeal to the Soviets. Factory workers, railway workers and soldiers take up the defense of the capital and block the advance of Krymov's troops.

*August 30 (September 12).* Kerensky assumes command of the army. The attempted coup d'état ends.

*August 31 (September 13).* General Krymov commits suicide.

*September 1 (14).* Kerensky proclaims a republic and forms a directorate of five members who are charged with governing until a new administration can be formed. General Kornilov is arrested.

*September 4 (17).* Trotsky is released on bail.

*September 6–15 (19–28).* A Congress of Russian Peoples meets in Kiev and calls for the creation of a democratic, federal state.

*September 9 (22).* The Bolsheviks take control of the management of the Petrograd Soviet. Trotsky will be elected president.

*September 13 (26).* In his "Historical Letters," which he composes in Finland and addresses to the Bolshevik Central Committee, Lenin proclaims his support for insurrection.

*September 14–22 (September 27–October 5).* In Petrograd, a "democratic conference" is convened to establish the principles that will guide the government until the election of the Constituent Assembly. Its only action is to appoint a "Council of the Republic," a kind of pre-Parliament.

*September 25 (October 8).* Kerensky forms a third coalition government.

# World War I and Foreign Affairs

## 1917

*March 6 (19).* The Provisional Government affirms its desire to respect the accords that the czarist regime had concluded with the Allies and to continue the war until victory.

*March 9 (22).* The Provisional Government is recognized by the United States.

*March 11 (24).* The Provisional Government is recognized by France, Great Britain and Italy.

*March 14 (27).* The Petrograd Soviet issues an appeal to the people of the world for a peace without annexations.

*March 27 (April 9).* Under pressure from the Soviet, Foreign Minister Pavel Miliukov appeals to the citizens of Russia for an equitable and durable peace without annexations.

*April.* The Allies send delegations of socialists to Russia (the Thomas-Henderson and the Cachin-Moutet-Sanders missions) in an effort to keep Russia in the war.

*April 18 (May 1).* In a note to the Allies, Miliukov reaffirms Russia's commitment to see the war through to a final victory, and he confirms the necessity of insuring the peace with "guarantees and sanctions."

*May 5 (18).* The prime minister of the coalition government declares that he is in favor of a peace "without annexations or indemnities, based on a people's right to self-determination."

*May 22 (June 4).* General Aleksei Brusilov is named commander-in-chief of Russian forces, replacing General Mikhail Alekseev.

*June 18 (July 1).* A Russian offensive in Galicia, ordered by Kerensky on June 16 (29) and commanded by Brusilov, begins. It will be halted in the middle of July after having had some success. An Austro-German counteroffensive will be launched, and Tarnopol will be occupied on July 11 (24). Desertions increase in the Russian army.

*July 12 (25).* The death penalty is reinstated at the front.

*July 18 (31).* General Kornilov is named commander-in-chief of Russian forces, replacing Brusilov.

*August 19 (September 1).* A German offensive is launched on the Baltic front.

*August 21 (September 3).* The Germans occupy Riga and threaten Petrograd.

*August 30 (September 12).* Kerensky dismisses Kornilov and proclaims himself commander-in-chief.

## Economy and Society

### 1917

*February.* A bread shortage occurs in Petrograd.

*March 10 (23).* Under pressure from the Soviet, the workday is limited to eight hours in Petrograd.

*March 12–16 (25–29).* The crown properties are transferred to the state.

*March 15 (28).* A Central Bureau of Syndicates is established in Moscow and Petrograd.

*March 20 (April 2).* All restrictions relating to nationality and religion are abolished.

*March 25 (April 7).* A state monopoly on grains is established. Price controls and bread rationing are instituted in Petrograd. Local supply committees are created.

*March 26 (April 8).* A campaign is launched to borrow funds for the war effort.

*April 21 (May 4).* Regulations are issued concerning agrarian committees: Local committees and a Central Agrarian Committee are established to prepare an agrarian reform. Faced with a multitude of peasant initiatives, the Provisional Government decides to wait until a Constituent Assembly is elected before making any fundamental reforms.

*April 23 (May 6).* A law is issued on the formation of factory committees, which control the hiring and firing of workers.

*May 1 (14).* The first All-Muslim Conference opens in Moscow.

*May 4–28 (May 17–June 10).* The first All-Russian Congress of Peasants' Deputies meets in Petrograd. The Congress, the majority of whose deputies are SRs, calls for the transfer of large estates to the peasantry without compensation to owners.

*May 5 (18).* A Ministry of Labor, headed by Matvei Skobelev, is created by the first coalition government.

*May 19 (June 1).* The first meeting of the Central Agrarian Committee is held.

*May 30–June 3 (June 12–16).* The first conference of Petrograd factory committees takes place. The conference adopts the Bolsheviks' "Theses."

*June 12 (25).* An emergency tax on income is established.

*June 21 (July 4).* An Economic Council and a Central Economic Committee are created in order to coordinate the country's economy.

*June 21–28 (July 4–11).* An All-Russian Conference of Trade Unions convenes in Petrograd.

*July.* The economic and social situation of the country deteriorates. Output declines (metallurgical production drops by 40 percent and textile production drops by 20 percent from February to July). Russia experiences inflation, unemployment is aggravated by lockouts, and violence and pillaging increase in the countryside.

*August 15 (28).* A council of the Russian Orthodox Church convenes in Moscow.

# Civilization and Culture

## 1917

Andrei Bely, *Revolution and Culture.* Simeon Frank: *The Soul of Man: An Introduction to Philosophical Psychology.* The first issue of the philosophical review *Thought and Speech,* edited by the neo-Kantian G. Shpet, is published.

# Chapter 22                                          1917

# Lenin and the October Revolution

Unlike the February Revolution, the October Revolution was the result of a careful plan by the Bolsheviks. The planning was guided by Lenin, who, after encountering some strong resistance, succeeded in winning his comrades over to his views. On October 24 and 25 (November 6 and 7) several thousand Red Guards, as well as soldiers and sailors won over by the Bolsheviks, surrounded the capital and occupied strategic points within it (train stations, arsenals, warehouses, the Central Telegraph Office, the State Bank headquarters). The Military Revolutionary Committee, the guiding force behind the Bolshevik insurrection, proclaimed the overthrow of the Provisional Government on October 25 (November 7).

In the predawn hours of October 26 (November 8), following the firing of a warning cannonade by the cruiser *Aurora*, the insurgents stormed the Winter Palace, to which the ministers of the Provisional Government had withdrawn. The insurgents easily overcame the resistance of the young military cadets and the "women's battalion" that constituted the sole defense of a government that had lost its authority. While this was taking place, the Second Congress of Soviets was being presented with the fait accompli. Dominated by the Bolsheviks, the Congress of Soviets ratified the insurrection and, as its final acts, authorized the creation of a new Council of People's Commissars and approved decrees on peace and land.

Within a few days it became clear that the "Great October Revolution," which had succeeded almost without a shot having been fired, represented a total break with the past. For the Bolsheviks, however, several years of unremitting struggle would be required before they were finally able to establish their absolute power.

## Politics and Institutions

### 1917

*September 29 (October 12).* In the Bolshevik newspaper *Rabochii put'*, Lenin publishes an article entitled "The Crisis Has Matured." His appeal for an immediate insurrection clashes with the view of the majority of Bolsheviks.

*October 7 (20).* The "Pre-Parliament" convenes. The Bolsheviks walk out of the opening session.

Lenin secretly returns to Petrograd from Finland.

*October 10 (23).* A secret meeting of the Bolshevik Central Committee is

179

held. With the help of Yakov Sverdlov, who reports that a military plot is being hatched in Minsk, Lenin secures a vote favoring an insurrection (10 members of the Central Committee are in favor, and 2—Lev Kamenev and Grigori Zinoviev—are against). A Political Bureau that includes Lenin, Zinoviev, Kamenev, Leon Trotsky, Grigori Sokolnikov and Andrei Bubnov is established.

*October 12 (25).* The Petrograd Soviet establishes a Military Revolutionary Committee in order to defend the city against the Germans. The Bolsheviks, led in this effort by Trotsky, transform the Military Revolutionary Committee into the instrument of the armed uprising. The Committee calls on the army regiments in the capital, the Red Guards and the Kronstadt sailors to rally to it.

*October 16 (29).* A meeting of an enlarged Bolshevik Central Committee approves Lenin's call for an insurrection. Advance preparation for the uprising is assigned to the Bolshevik Military Organization, which will act in the name of the Party in coordination with the Military Revolutionary Committee of the Petrograd Soviet.

*October 18 (31).* An article by Kamenev that is hostile to the premature unleashing of an insurrection is published in Maxim Gorky's newspaper *Novaya Zhizn* ("New Life").

*October 22 (November 4).* The Military Revolutionary Committee of the Soviet declares that only orders from the General Staff that have been countersigned by the Committee will be considered valid.

*October 24 (November 6).* The Soviet breaks openly with the Provisional Government, which had attempted to bar the printing of Bolshevik newspapers and

had called for reinforcements to defend Petrograd. Bolshevik forces smash the government seals on the Party's press and, during the day, they prevent government troops from raising the city's bridges.

The insurrection begins. During the night of October 24–25 (November 6–7) the Red Guards, together with soldiers and sailors who have rallied to the Bolshevik cause, take control of the capital without serious difficulty. Lenin arrives at the Smolny Institute, the headquarters of the insurrection, where the Second Congress of Soviets is meeting. Meanwhile, the ministers of the Provisional Government withdraw to the Winter Palace, and Alexander Kerensky flees in search of reinforcements.

*October 25 (November 7).* Petrograd (with the exception of the Winter Palace) is in the hands of the insurgents. The Soviet's Military Revolutionary Committee proclaims the overthrow of the Provisional Government and takes power.

*Night of October 25–26 (November 7–8).* With the support of the cruiser *Aurora*, the insurgents attack the Winter Palace, which falls into their hands at 2:30 in the morning.

The Second Congress of Soviets convenes at the Smolny Institute (there are approximately 390 Bolsheviks and 150 Left SRs [Socialist Revolutionaries] among the 650 deputies). A new Presidium with a Bolshevik majority is elected. Mensheviks and Right SRs hostile to the seizure of power walk out of the Congress. The Congress approves the insurrection and issues the manifesto "To All Workers, Soldiers and Peasants."

*October 26 (November 8).* The Bolshevik insurrection begins in Moscow.

After violent combat, the insurgents will take the Kremlin on November 3 (16).

The City Duma of Petrograd establishes an All-Russian Committee for the Salvation of the Country and of the Revolution, made up of Mensheviks and Right SRs hostile to the Bolsheviks.

*Night of October 26–27 (November 8–9).* The last meeting of the Second Congress of Soviets is held. The Congress approves the formation of the Council of People's Commissars (*Sovnarkom*), a new, all-Bolshevik government. Presided over by Lenin, the government also includes Trotsky (people's commissar for foreign affairs), Stalin (people's commissar for nationalities), Aleksei Rykov (people's commissar for the interior) and Anatoli Lunacharsky (people's commissar for public instruction). A new Central Executive Committee of the Soviets (VTsIK), with a majority of Bolsheviks and Left SRs, is established. Decrees on peace and on land, drafted by Lenin, are adopted.

*October 27 (November 9).* An offensive is launched against Petrograd by Kerensky and General Peter Krasnov. It will be halted at Pulkovo Heights on October 30 (November 12).

*October 28 (November 10).* A decree on the press is published. Counterrevolutionary newspapers are banned.

*October 29 (November 11).* An uprising of cadets from military schools in Petrograd is put down.

The All-Russian Committee of Railway Workers (*Vikzhel*) issues an ultimatum demanding the formation of a socialist coalition government.

*October 31 (November 13).* The Soviet in Baku takes power.

*November 1 (14).* A resolution of the Bolshevik Central Committee formalizes the collapse of talks with other socialists on the formation of a coalition government.

At Gatchina, Bolshevik representatives succeed in rallying the troops assembled by Kerensky and Krasnov to the cause of the revolution. Kerensky eludes capture. Although Krasnov is arrested, he will soon be released and will join the counterrevolutionary forces in the Don region.

The Soviet in Tashkent takes power. Thus far, Soviet authority has been secured in Iaroslavl, Tver, Smolensk, Nizhni Novgorod, Kazan, Samara, Saratov, Rostov and Ufa.

*November 2 (15).* The "Declaration of Rights of the Peoples of Russia" is issued. It proclaims the principles of equality and popular sovereignty, along with the right of self-determination, including secession.

*November 4 (17).* In an act of protest against the Party's refusal to form a coalition government, several Bolsheviks (including Kamenev, Zinoviev and Rykov) quit the Central Committee of the Party and the Council of People's Commissars. They will shortly retake their positions on these bodies.

*November 7 (20).* The Ukrainian *Rada* issues its Third Universal. Although the law proclaims a Ukrainian People's Republic, it does not formally break with the Russian republic; instead, it calls on Russia to transform itself into a federation.

*November 8 (21).* Yakov Sverdlov is elected to head the Central Executive Committee of the Soviets (VTsIK).

*November 10–25 (November 23–December 8).* An emergency Congress of Peasants' Soviets meets in Petrograd. Dominated by SR delegates, it approves a decree on land tenure and sends 108 of its members to the Central Executive Committee of the Soviets.

*November 12 (25).* Elections for a Constituent Assembly begin. The vote will be 58 percent for the SRs, 25 percent for the Bolsheviks (who nonetheless dominate the voting in Petrograd and Moscow as well as among the troops in the west and north), and 13 percent for the Constitutional Democrats (Cadets) and assorted "bourgeois" groupings.

*November 15 (28).* A Transcaucasian Commissariat is established in Tiflis. It will organize resistance to the Bolsheviks in Georgia, Armenia and Azerbaijan.

*November 19–28 (December 2–11).* In Petrograd, the First Congress of Left Socialist Revolutionaries meets and transforms itself into an independent party.

*November 20 (December 3).* Lenin and Joseph Stalin call on the Moslems of Russia and of the East to liberate themselves from all forms of oppression. In Ufa, a Moslem National Assembly meets to prepare for national cultural autonomy for Russia's Moslems.

*November 24 (December 7).* Finland declares its independence from Russia.

*November 26–December 10 (December 9–23).* The Second Congress of Peasants' Soviets meets in Petrograd. It is dominated by Left SRs who support the Bolsheviks' policies.

*November 28 (December 11).* A decree is issued calling for the arrest of the leaders of the Cadet party, who are accused of organizing a civil war.

*November–December.* The first counterrevolutionary armies are formed. Generals Mikhail Alekseev and Lavr Kornilov create a "volunteer army" in Novocherkassk; in December they will form a "triumvirate" with General Al-

exei Kaledin, the hetman of the Don Cossacks.

*December 2 (15).* The Cadets are barred from the Constituent Assembly. Rostov is seized by the volunteer army.

*December 4 (17).* An ultimatum to the Ukrainian *Rada* demands that it recognize Soviet power in the Ukraine.

*December 7 (20).* The Cheka (the All-Russian Extraordinary Commission for Struggle against Counterrevolution, Sabotage and Speculation) is created and placed under the direction of Felix Dzerzhinsky.

*December 9 (22).* An accord between the Bolsheviks and the Left SRs permits members of the latter party to enter the government. The Left SRs are given the Agriculture, Justice, and Post and Telegraph Commissariats.

*December 11 (24).* The First Pan-Ukrainian Congress of Soviets opens at Kharkov. Dominated by the Bolsheviks, it will proclaim the Ukrainian Soviet Republic the next day.

*December 13 (26).* Lenin's "Theses on the Constituent Assembly" is published in *Pravda*. He declares that the body must submit itself entirely to the authority of the soviets.

*December 18 (31).* The Council of People's Commissars recognizes the independence of Finland.

# World War I and Foreign Affairs

## 1917

*October 26 (November 8).* A decree on peace is issued. It calls on all belligerents to begin immediate talks aimed at arriving at a just and democratic peace without annexations or reparations.

*November 1 (14).* Following the flight of Kerensky, General Nikolai Dukhonin becomes commander-in-chief of Russian forces.

*November 8 (21).* In a note to all belligerents, Trotsky, the people's commissar for foreign affairs, proposes that they begin negotiations to end the war.

*November 9 (22).* General Dukhonin is dismissed for refusing to engage in armistice talks with the Germans. He is replaced by Ensign Nikolai Krylenko, the people's commissar for war. The Bolsheviks announce their intention to publish the secret treaties relating to the war.

*November 14 (27).* Germany accepts Russian's offer of armistice negotiations.

*November 20 (December 3).* Armistice negotiations between Russia and the Central Powers (Germany, Austria-Hungary, Bulgaria and Turkey) are convened at Brest-Litovsk.

Krylenko assumes control of the General Staff headquarters in Mogilev. General Dukhonin is murdered by soldiers and sailors.

*December 2 (15).* A 28-day armistice is agreed to at Brest-Litovsk.

*December 9 (22).* Peace talks open at Brest-Litovsk. Germany is represented by Minister of Foreign Affairs Richard von Kühlmann and General Max von Hoffmann, Austria by Minister of Foreign Affairs Ottakar Czernin. The Soviet delegation, led by Adolf Ioffe, calls for a peace treaty that does not include annexations or reparations but that respects the right of self-determination.

*December 27 (January 9).* Following a 10-day interruption negotiations resume at Brest-Litovsk. (The Soviets had insisted on the interruption in order to allow the Entente Powers—principally England, France, Italy and the United States—the opportunity to join the talks; they refused to so.) The Soviet delegation is now led by Trotsky.

# Economy and Society

## 1917

*October 16–19 (October 29–November 1).* A conference of proletarian educational and cultural organizations meets in Petrograd under the leadership of Anatoli Lunacharsky. In November, the group will adopt "Proletkult" as its official name.

*October 26 (November 8).* A decree on land is issued: Large estates are expropriated without compensation, and land is placed under the control of agrarian committees and peasants' soviets. In many cases, the decree merely legalizes the de facto situation in the countryside. On average, the land expropriation adds one desyatina (2.7 acres) of land to each peasant family plot.

*October 29 (November 11).* A decree is issued establishing an eight-hour work day.

*November 5 (18).* Metropolitan Tikhon is elected patriarch of Moscow (the patriarchate had just been reestablished by a council of the Orthodox Church).

*November 7 (20).* The bread ration in Petrograd is reduced to 150 grams.

*November 9 (22).* A decree on accident insurance is issued.

*November 10 (23).* Grades and inequalities of rank within the civil administration are abolished.

*November 14 (27).* A decree establishes worker control in all industrial enterprises with more than five employees. Control will be exercised through elected committees under the authority of a national council.

*November 22 (December 5).* The judicial system is reorganized: Judges are to be elected, and revolutionary tribunals will be established.

*December 2 (15).* The Supreme Council of National Economy (VSNKh) is established. It is given overall control of the national economy and supervisory power over provincial councils (*sovnarkhozes*).

*December 11 (24).* A decree on unemployment insurance is issued.

*December 14 (27).* Banks are nationalized.

*December 15 (28).* The Russian-Belgian Metallurgical Society is nationalized.

*December 18 (31).* Civil marriages are instituted; the state is secularized. A decree on divorce is issued.

*December 22 (January 4).* A decree on health insurance is issued.

*December 27 (January 9).* The Putilov factories are nationalized.

Chapter 23        1918–1920

# The Civil War and War Communism

Although the seizure of power in Petrograd had been accomplished with relative ease, the new Soviet regime would face widespread opposition for more than three years.

The Treaty of Brest-Litovsk, signed in March 1918, ended Russia's participation in World War I, but the conditions imposed by Germany were quite burdensome to the fledgling Soviet state. On the domestic scene, outbreaks of resistance to the new regime, while at first localized, soon engulfed the country in a long civil war between the "Whites" and the partisans of Soviet authority.

Two factors made the prosecution of the Civil War more difficult: the growth of nationalist unrest on the part of the non-Russian peoples of the former empire, and the military intervention of Russia's former Allies on the side of the Whites. The scale of the Allied intervention would increase following Russia's separate peace at Brest-Litovsk, and then further intensify after the Allies concluded a general armistice with the Central Powers in November 1918. The White forces, however, were poorly coordinated along immense fronts, divided over the future of Russia, and heavily dependent on the Allies. Although the Whites were largely defeated by 1920, the Polish-Soviet War and Peter Wrangel's last offensives in the south would prolong the Civil War for several months.

In order to mobilize all of their power for this merciless struggle, the Bolsheviks chose to establish a regime of political and economic dictatorship that brooked no concessions. They created their own secret police (the Cheka) in December 1917, dissolved the Constituent Assembly (in which they were a minority) in January 1918, and methodically eliminated all of their opponents (including the Socialist Revolutionaries, or SRs). While they legitimized the "Red Terror" as necessary to defend the Revolution, the Bolsheviks also consolidated their monopoly on power by writing a constitution for the Russian Socialist Federal Soviet Republic (RSFSR) that guaranteed them a leading role.

In the economic sphere, "War Communism" entailed an intensification of the Bolshevik's economic policies of 1917, the primary objective of which had been to supply provisions to the military and the citizenry. In pursuit of that end, nationalization of industry was expanded and labor became obligatory. The brutal actions taken to requisition provisions in the countryside soon pitted the new central government against a peasantry that sought to defend the gains it had made in 1917.

# Politics and Institutions

## 1918

*January 5 (18).* The Constituent Assembly is convened in Petrograd. The Bolsheviks, who are in the minority (they have approximately 175 representatives, whereas the SRs have 410), leave the Assembly.

*January 6 (19).* The Constituent Assembly is dissolved by a decree of the Central Executive Committee of the Soviets.

*January 10–18 (23–31).* The Third Congress of Soviets meets. It adopts the "Declaration of the Rights of the Toiling and Exploited People" and proclaims the establishment of the Russian Socialist Federal Soviet Republic (RSFSR).

*March 6–8.* The Seventh Bolshevik Party Congress is held. The party changes its name to the Russian Communist Party (Bolshevik). It adopts Lenin's theses against the "Left Communists" and, at Nikolai Bukharin's initiative, supports the continuation of the revolutionary war.

*March 12.* Moscow becomes the capital of the Soviet state.

*March 14–16.* The Fourth Congress of Soviets ratifies the Treaty of Brest-Litovsk. The Left SRs quit the government in protest against this decision.

*April.* In *The Immediate Tasks of the Soviet Government,* Lenin reiterates the need for a strong state.

*April 11–12.* The Cheka conducts operations against anarchists in Moscow.

*June 14.* The Central Executive Committee of the Soviets excludes the Right SRs and the Mensheviks from all soviets in retaliation for their counter-revolutionary activities.

*July 4–10.* The Fifth Congress of Soviets is convened in Moscow.

*July 6.* While the Congress of Soviets is in session, the Left SRs launch a revolt in Moscow: Yakov Blymkin assassinates the German ambassador, Baron Wilhelm von Mirbach; Felix Dzerzhinsky, the head of the Cheka, is arrested; the Central Post Office is occupied.

*July 7.* The government reestablishes control with the assistance of Latvian sharpshooters under the command of General Ioakim Vatsétis. Many Left SRs are arrested. In the provinces, the SR terrorist Boris Savinkov leads an uprising in Yaroslavl that will last until July 21.

*July 10.* The Fifth Congress of Soviets ratifies the first Constitution of the RSFSR. Local soviets will be elected by "universal suffrage" (which is, in fact, limited to those citizens whose income is earned by their labor). The local soviets will elect deputies to the Congress of Soviets, which will delegate its governing authority to the Central Executive Committee (VTsIK). The president of the VTsIK, Yakov Sverdlov, will function as head of state. The members of the government (*Sovnarkom*) will be chosen by the VTsIK.

*Night of July 16–17.* The imperial family is executed in Ekaterinburg.

*August 4.* All "bourgeois" journals are prohibited.

*August 30.* Moisei Uritsky, chairman of the Petrograd Cheka, is assassinated by an SR student, Leonid Kanegisser. On the same day, Fanny Kaplan, an SR, seriously wounds Lenin. The Soviet government announces that it will respond to this "White" terror with a "Red" terror.

*October.* In the face of the White threat and foreign intervention, the Mensheviks offer their support to the government. Their exclusion from the soviets will be lifted on November 30.

## 1919

*March 16.* Yakov Sverdlov dies. Mikhail Kalinin will succeed him as president of the VTsIK on March 30.

*March 18–23.* The Eighth Congress of the Communist Party is held in Moscow. A new program is adopted. The Congress creates a Political Bureau (Politburo) made up of five members (Lenin, Lev Kamenev, Leon Trotsky, Joseph Stalin and Nikolai Krestinsky), an Organizational Bureau (Orgburo) and a Secretariat of the Central Committee.

*December 2–4.* The Eighth Communist Party Conference is held. New bylaws are adopted and an effort is made to rigorously control recruitment.

## 1920

*February 7.* The People's Commissariat of State Control becomes the Commissariat of Workers' and Peasants' Inspection (*Rabkrin*), headed by Stalin.

*March 29–April 5.* The Ninth Communist Party Congress is held. A faction known as the "Democratic Centralists" denounces excessive centralization and abuses of authority.

*June.* Lenin publishes *Left-Wing Communism: An Infantile Disorder.*

*September 22–25.* The Ninth Communist Party Conference meets. A "Control Commission" is set up to receive complaints against the Party.

*December 22–29.* The Eighth Congress of Soviets is held in Moscow. This will be the last governing forum at which the Mensheviks and SRs will be permitted to express their views.

# Economy and Society

## 1918

*January 7–14 (20–27).* The First All-Russian Congress of Trade Unions is held is Petrograd. The Bolsheviks advocate the subordination of the factory committees to the trade unions.

*January 21 (February 3).* All domestic and foreign debts of the Russian state are canceled.

*January 23 (February 5).* The merchant fleet is nationalized.

Church and state are separated. The Orthodox Church will no longer be permitted a role in education.

*February 1 (14).* The Bolshevik government adopts the Gregorian calendar.

*February 19.* A law is issued reaffirming the principle of socialization of land.

*April 2.* The People's Commissariat of Food Supply is given broad powers in the rationing of foodstuffs.

*April 3.* Labor discipline is strengthened and piecework is introduced.

*April 22.* Foreign trade is nationalized.

*May 13.* The Commissariat of Food Supply is granted emergency powers for use against peasants who refuse to deliver their produce.

*June 11.* In the countryside, committees of poor peasants (*Kombedy*) are formed to conduct the struggle against the wealthy peasants (kulaks). By November, the committees will number more than 100,000, but they will eventually be dissolved because of their excesses in carrying out their mission.

*June 28.* All major industrial sectors are nationalized.

*August 2.* Higher education is made available unconditionally to all young people over 16 years of age.

*August 20.* Urban dwellings are socialized.

*September 14.* The metric system is introduced.

*September 16.* The first Soviet legal code on the family is issued.

*October 10.* Orthography (spelling) is reformed by decree.

*October 29–November 4.* In Moscow, the First Congress of Workers' and Peasants' Youth Organizations is held. The Communist Union of Youth (Komsomol) is founded.

*November 21.* Domestic trade is nationalized.

*December 10.* A Labor Code is published.

**1919**

*January 11.* A general system of requisitioning is put into place. It permits the confiscation of agricultural surpluses.

*February 14.* A decree proclaims all land to be the property of the state; henceforth, land is only to be used collectively.

*March 20.* Consumer cooperatives are given control over the entire system of distribution.

*April 12.* The first "Communist Saturday" (unpaid, voluntary labor) is organized by railway workers on the Kazan-Moscow line.

*October 10.* Russia is subjected to an economic blockade by the Allies; it will remain in effect until January 1920.

*December.* Trotsky declares the necessity of "militarizing labor."

*December 26.* A decree establishes the goal of abolishing illiteracy.

**1920**

*January 29.* Labor is made obligatory.

*February 21.* A commission is set up to plan the electrification of Russia (GOELRO). It envisions the construction of approximately 30 electric power stations within 10 to 15 years.

*September 17.* A decree is issued on "workers' schools" (*Rabfak*).

*November–December.* A controversy over trade unions erupts. Some workers violently criticize Trotsky for attempting to put into practice in the transportation sector his views on the necessity for state control of all trade unions.

*November 29.* All small enterprises employing more than ten workers (or even 5, if the enterprise is mechanized) are nationalized.

*December.* The paper ruble is worth 13,000 times less than it was in 1913. The use of barter and other forms of payment-in-kind spreads.

# World War I, the Civil War and the Foreign Intervention

## 1918

*January 5 (18).* At Brest-Litovsk, General Max von Hoffmann of Germany puts forward, in the form of an ultimatum, the Central Powers' conditions for peace. Among the conditions is that Russia cede its western territories.

*January 11 (24).* Three positions on the Brest-Litovsk negotiations emerge within the Bolshevik Central Committee. Lenin wants to accept the Central Powers' conditions for peace in order to consolidate the revolution at home. The Left Communists, led by Bukharin, want to continue the war in order to transform it into a worldwide revolutionary war. Trotsky puts forth an intermediate position that would have Russia withdraw from the war without signing a peace.

Trotsky's position is supported by a majority in the Central Committee.

The Fourth Universal of the Ukrainian *Rada* proclaims independence for the Ukraine.

*January 15 (28)*. A decree establishes the Workers' and Peasants' Red Army. In the effort to strengthen the military capacity of the new regime, military service will be made obligatory, former officers of the czarist army will be actively recruited, the election of officers will be abolished and political commissars will be placed amongst the troops. Organized by Trotsky, the Red Army will become a powerful and disciplined fighting force.

*January 26 (February 8)*. The Bolsheviks take power in Kiev.

*January 27 (February 9)*. At Brest-Litovsk, the Central Powers conclude a separate peace with the Ukrainian *Rada*.

*January 28 (February 10)*. Applying his formula "neither war nor peace," Trotsky declares that the state of war between Russia and the Central Powers is at an end.

*January 29 (February 11)*. A decree establishes a Red Navy. The ataman Alexei Kaledin, having failed in his attempt to lead an uprising of the Don Cossacks, commits suicide.

*February*. Having been defeated on the Don River (at Rostov and Novocherkassk), the anti-Soviet Volunteer Army is forced to retreat to the Kuban under difficult circumstances (this will be known as the "Icy March"). After Kokand is seized by troops sent by the Soviet of Tashkent, the independent government of Turkistan is dissolved.

*February 18*. After issuing an ultimatum, the Austrians and Germans launch an offensive against Russia. Despite the Soviet acceptance of the conditions for peace on the night of February 18, the armies of the Central Powers continue their offensive.

*February 23*. A new ultimatum with even harsher conditions for peace is issued by the Germans. A majority in the Central Committee sides with Lenin in favoring an immediate peace; the vote is seven in favor and four (including Bukharin) opposed, with four members (including Trotsky) abstaining. The "socialist homeland" is declared to be in danger. The enemy will be halted at Narva and Pskov.

*March 1*. With German support, the Ukrainian *Rada* returns to Kiev.

*March 3*. Russia signs a peace treaty with the Central Powers (Germany, Austria-Hungary, Bulgaria and Turkey) at Brest-Litovsk. Russia loses Poland, Finland, the former Baltic provinces, the Ukraine and part of Belorussia. Russia also cedes Kars, Ardahan and Batum to Turkey. In all, Russia loses one-quarter of its population, one-quarter of its arable land, and nearly three-quarters of its iron, steel and coal industries. After the conclusion of the treaty, Trotsky resigns as commissar of foreign affairs; he will become the commissar of war on April 8.

*March 9*. British forces land at Murmansk. Their original mission had been to repulse the attacks of the Germans and the Finns in the north.

*April 5*. Japanese troops land at Vladivostok. The Japanese will be followed by the Americans, the British and the French.

*April 13*. General Lavr Kornilov is killed in a battle at Ekaterinodar. General Anton Denikin succeeds him as head of the Volunteer Army.

*April 22*. With the encouragement of Turkey, a Transcaucasian Federal Republic, independent of Russia, is established.

*April 29.* In the Ukraine, the *Rada* is dissolved and the hetman Paul Skoropadsky takes power with the support of Germany.

*May 11.* General Peter Krasnov is elected ataman of the Don Cossacks.

*May 25.* The Czech Legion (made up of approximately 50,000 former prisoners of war), which was supposed to have been evacuated through Vladivostok, joins up with adversaries of the Soviet regime.

*May 26.* The Transcaucasian Federal Republic is dissolved and replaced by three autonomous republics (Georgia, Armenia and Azerbaijan).

*May 29.* A general mobilization of the Red Army is declared.

*May 30.* Georgi Chicherin becomes commissar of foreign affairs.

*June 8.* In Samara, Right SRs and Mensheviks form a "Committee of Members of the Constituent Assembly."

*June 23.* A "Siberian Government" made up of conservatives and monarchists is formed in Omsk.

*July.* Attacks by the Whites on Tsaritsyn begin.

*August 2.* Allied troops land in Archangel. The Supreme Administration of the Northern Oblast is established; it is led by the former Populist Nikolai Chaikovsky.

*August 4.* British forces arriving from Persia occupy Baku.

*August 6.* White armies take Kazan.

*September 8–23.* The Ufa Conference is held in an effort to provide leadership for anti-Bolshevik organizations and parties in the east. A directorate presided over by the SR Nikolai Avksentiev is established.

*September 10.* In its first major victory, the Red Army retakes Kazan.

*September 15.* The British abandon Baku to the Turks.

*November 13.* After the signing of the Armistice between the Allies and Germany, the Soviet government declares the Treaty of Brest-Litovsk to be null and void.

*November 14.* In the Ukraine, a directorate led by Simon Petlyura is formed. It will overthrow the hetman Paul Skoropadsky and take power in Kiev on December 14.

*November 18.* In Omsk, Admiral Alexander Kolchak (former commander of the Black Sea Fleet) overthrows the Ufa directorate with the support of the Allies and proclaims himself "supreme ruler of Russia."

*November 23.* The French and British intervention in the Black Sea begins.

*November 30.* A Council of Workers' and Peasants' Defense is created and presided over by Lenin.

## 1918–1919

*November 1918–January 1919.* The Red Army conducts an offensive in the Baltic countries. With the support of the RSFSR, the short-lived Soviet regimes in Estonia, Latvia and Lithuania are established.

## 1919

*January 1.* The Soviet Republic of Belorussia is established.

*January 8.* General Denikin, the head of the Volunteer Army, brings Don and Kuban forces under his command.

*January 22.* President Woodrow Wilson proposes that all of the parties to the Russian conflict meet at a conference on Prinkipo Island (in the Sea of

Marmara). The Whites refuse to participate.

*February 5.* Kiev is taken by the Red Army. The Ukrainian directorate of Simon Petlyura places itself under French protection.

*March 2–6.* In Moscow, the First Congress of the Comintern (also called the Third International or the Communist International) is attended by 52 delegates from 30 countries. Grigori Zinoviev is elected its president.

*March 4.* Admiral Kolchak launches an offensive in the direction of Simbirsk and Samara.

*April 6.* The Bolsheviks occupy Odessa. The city is evacuated by the French, who retreat to the Crimea.

*April 28.* The Red Army launches a counteroffensive against Kolchak's forces.

*May.* The White general Nikolai Yudenich launches an offensive against Petrograd. The offensive will be turned back at the end of June.

*May 19.* General Denikin launches an offensive against the Ukraine and the Volga region.

*May 26.* The Allies' Supreme Council agrees to support Admiral Kolchak in exchange for promises of a democratic regime and respect for the rights of nationalities.

*June 9.* The Red Army retakes Ufa from Kolchak. Forced to battle in retreat, he will lose the Urals during July and August.

*June 24.* Kharkov is taken by Denikin's troops.

*June 30.* The Whites, led by Denikin, take Tsaritsyn.

*August 31.* The White armies occupy Kiev.

*September 12.* A new offensive against Moscow is launched by Denikin.

Kursk will be seized (September 20), followed by Orel (October 13). Tula will be threatened.

*September 28.* Yudenich launches a new offensive against Petrograd. It will reach the outskirts of the city on October 20.

*October 11.* The Red Army begins a counteroffensive against Denikin.

*Late October.* The Red Army launches a successful counteroffensive against Yudenich, who retreats in disorder into the Baltic region.

*November 14.* The Red Army retakes Omsk from Kolchak.

*November 17.* The Red Army retakes Kursk from Denikin.

*December.* The Red Army retakes Kharkov (December 12) and Kiev (December 16).

*December 8.* The Allies' Supreme Council provisionally establishes the eastern border of Poland at the Curzon Line, which generally follows the Bug River. (Poland finds this border unsatisfactory.)

# 1920

*January.* The Red Army retakes Tsaritsyn (January 3), Krasnoyarsk (January 7) and Rostov (January 10).

*January 4.* Admiral Kolchak renounces his title of supreme ruler of Russia in favor of Denikin.

*February 2.* In Dorpat, a peace treaty is signed by the RSFSR and Estonia.

*February 7.* Abandoned by the Czech Legion, Kolchak is executed in Irkutsk.

*February–March.* The Bolsheviks retake control of Archangel and Murmansk.

*March 27.* Novorossisk is retaken by the Red Army. Denikin retreats to the Crimea, where he cedes power to General Peter Wrangel.

*April 6.* A Far Eastern Republic is established in eastern Siberia.

*April 25.* A war between Russia and Poland begins. The offensive is led by General Jozef Pilsudski, who is allied with the Ukrainian Simon Petlyura, and has as its goals the establishment of Poland's eastern borders and the creation of a Polish-Ukrainian federation.

*April 26.* The Soviet People's Republic of Khoresm is proclaimed.

*April 28.* Soviet power is installed in Azerbaijan.

*May 7.* Kiev is occupied by Polish troops.

A peace treaty is signed between Russia and independent Georgia.

*June.* Taking advantage of the Soviet-Polish conflict, the White armies under Wrangel launch an offensive into the Ukraine from the Crimea.

*June 5.* In the conflict between Russia and Poland, a counteroffensive is launched by Soviet troops on the southwestern front. They reach Zhitomir and retake Kiev.

*July 4.* Soviet troops commanded by Mikhail Tukhachevsky launch an offensive on the western front. They will arrive on the outskirts of Warsaw at the beginning of August. Lenin believes that the invasion of Poland will lead to the establishment of Soviet power there and spark a socialist revolution in Germany.

*July 12.* A treaty between the RSFSR and Lithuania is signed. Under its terms, the Soviets recognize Lithuania's right to Vilnius against the claim of Poland.

*July 19–August 7.* The Comintern holds its Second Congress and adopts Lenin's "21 Points," which outline the requirements for membership in the Third International. The key requirement is a rejection of the Social Democratic model and an embrace of the Bolshevik model.

*August 11.* A peace treaty between the RSFSR and Latvia is signed in Riga.

*August 16.* The "Miracle on the Vistula" occurs: The Poles, with the support of a Franco-British force led by General Maxime Weygand, liberate Warsaw and take the offensive. This puts an end to Soviet hopes of a wider European revolution.

*September 1–8.* The First Congress of Peoples of the East is held in Baku.

*October 8.* The Soviet People's Republic of Bukhara is established.

*October 12.* The Poles and the Soviets declare an armistice and begin peace negotiations in Riga.

*October 14.* In Dorpat, the RSFSR and Finland sign a peace treaty that permits the RSFSR to retain eastern Karelia.

*October 28.* The Red Army begins its offensive against Wrangel's forces. It will take the Isthmus of Perekop (November 7–11) and occupy the entire Crimea (November 17). Allied naval forces evacuate almost 140,000 White troops and civilians to Constantinople.

*November 29.* The Soviet Republic of Armenia is proclaimed.

# Civilization and Culture

## 1918

The Bolshevik Revolution occupies a central place in literary and dramatic works: *The Twelve*, by Alexander Blok; *Christ Is Risen*, by Andrei Bely; *Mystery-Bouffe*, by Vladimir Mayakovsky, directed by Vsevolod Meyerhold.

Alexandra Kollontai: *The Family and the Communist State; The New Morality and the Working Class.* Marc Chagall is named commissar of fine arts in Vitebsk. Art education is reorganized with the establishment of the State Free National Art Studios, which in 1920 will become the Supreme Studios of Art and Technique (*Vkhutemas*).

*February.* Proletkult, now led by Alexander Bogdanov, holds a conference in Moscow and affirms its autonomy from the state.

## 1919

Artistic expression in the cause of the revolution finds new outlets in agitprop (agitation and propaganda) trains and ROSTA (Windows of the Russian Telegraphic Agency).

*January.* The literary group "Imaginists" issues a manifesto. A representative work of the group is *Maria's Keys*, by Sergei Esenin (1920).

*May.* The State Publishing House (*Gosizdat*) is founded.

*August 26.* Theaters are nationalized.

*August 27.* The film industry is nationalized.

## 1920

*October.* The All-Russian Association of Proletarian Writers (VAPP) is formed by a group of dissident *Proletkult* members known as *Kuznitsa* (Forge).

*November.* A "Celebration of the Masses" is held in Petrograd on the third anniversary of the October Revolution.

*December 10.* A letter from the Central Committee to *Proletkult* informs the organization that it is being made subordinate to the Communist Party; A. Bogdanov is expelled.

Chapter 24                                    1921–1924

# The Tactical Retreat: The Beginning of the New Economic Policy

Following six consecutive years of war and devastation, the young Soviet state had to contend with new disasters. In addition to suffering vast human losses due to famine and epidemics, the state was confronted by an utter disintegration of the national economy. Not only had industrial and agricultural output fallen sharply from their prewar levels, but popular discontent soon expressed itself in peasant revolts, workers' strikes and the rebellion of sailors at Kronstadt in February and March 1921. While the authorities were ruthlessly repressing these uprisings, the Tenth Communist Party Congress sought to reinforce the discipline and cohesion of Party members.

The Tenth Party Congress also marked the beginning of the New Economic Policy (NEP). Intended to open the way for the renewal of the country, the NEP's first objective was to rally the peasantry to the regime and to restore the peasants' confidence. The policy of requisitioning crops and livestock was replaced first by a tax-in-kind and then by a cash assessment, and producers were permitted to sell surplus crops. In the realms of commerce and industry, a private sector was allowed to reappear, while the state retained exclusive control of the economy's "commanding heights." Beginning in 1924–1925, increases in production and in productivity resulted in a marked economic upturn that benefitted the entire population.

The early 1920s also saw an overhaul of the country's institutional structures: The Union of Soviet Socialist Republics (USSR) was created in 1922, and a federal constitution was ratified in 1924.

These economic and institutional reforms were accompanied by a hardening of the struggle against the regime's opponents, by an intensification of the pressure for ideological conformity, and, within the Communist Party itself, by a reinforcement of centralization and control. But with the onset of Lenin's illness (he suffered his first stroke in May of 1922), a power struggle developed within the Party. Joseph Stalin, who became general secretary of the Party in 1922, would use a debate over the NEP to gradually impose his absolute authority.

194

# Politics and Institutions

## 1921

Autonomous Soviet Socialist Republics are created in Dagestan, Abkhazia, Adzhar and the Crimea.

*January–February.* Dissension breaks out within the ranks of the Party over the social crisis gripping the country. This marks the beginning of a serious political crisis.

*February 8.* Peter Kropotkin dies. The last anarchist demonstration in Moscow occurs at his funeral.

*February 25.* The Red Army and Georgian Bolsheviks take Tiflis. The government of the Menshevik Noi Jordania is ousted, and the Soviet Socialist Republic of Georgia is proclaimed.

*February 28–March 18.* The Kronstadt Rebellion occurs when 14,000 sailors of the Baltic Fleet and workers at the naval base at Kronstadt rise up against the Communist regime. On February 28 the rebels issue a petition calling for the return of civil liberties, the recognition of the right to form independent political parties, and the election of new soviets. On March 2 the rebels form a Provisional Revolutionary Committee and call for a new revolution; it is clear that anarchist ideas are influencing the rebellion. A bloody repression of the rebellion begins on March 7. Led by Mikhail Tukhachevsky, the repression proceeds according to plans drawn up by Leon Trotsky. On March 18 the rebellion is ended. The repression of the Kronstadt Rebellion also marks the end of the activity of other political parties in the country.

*March 6–18.* The Tenth Congress of the Communist Party meets in Moscow. At the same time that he is launching the New Economic Policy (NEP), Lenin affirms the necessity of maintaining party unity. Under his leadership, the Congress condemns factions (the "Workers' Opposition" and "Democratic Centralism") and adopts an extreme (and secret) measure that allows the Central Committee to exclude those individuals who are responsible for factional activity. A purge of the Party ensues.

## 1922

*February 6.* The GPU (the State Political Administration) replaces the Cheka; in 1923 the GPU will be renamed the OGPU.

*March 12.* The Soviet Republics of Georgia, Armenia and Azerbaijan form a Federation of Soviet Socialist Republics of Transcaucasia.

*April 3.* Joseph Stalin is elected general secretary of the Party's Central Committee.

*April 27.* The Autonomous Soviet Socialist Republic of Yakutsk is established.

*May 26.* Lenin suffers his first stroke. He will be forced to withdraw from political life until the beginning of October.

*June 9–August 9.* A trial of a group of Socialist Revolutionaries (SRs) takes place.

*September 23–24.* Stalin presents his plan for the "autonomization" of the soviet republics; in reality, the plan would absorb the republics into the Russian Socialist Federal Soviet Republic (RSFSR). Lenin forces Stalin to modify his views and to prepare the way for a voluntary union of all of the republics within the context of a new state structure.

*October 6.* The Central Committee ratifies a new plan that guarantees the equality of the republics within a federal union. Stalin and Sergo Ordzhonikidze,

# Union of Soviet Socialist Republics (1922–1991)

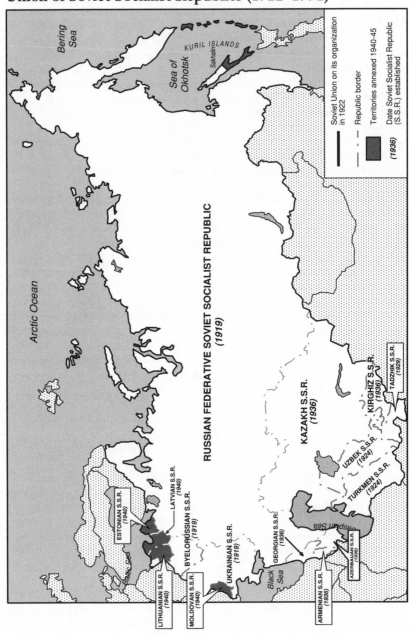

however, refuse to permit the direct entry of Georgia into the union, and a Trancaucasian Socialist Federal Soviet Republic will be created on December 13.

*October 25.* Vladivostok is retaken by Russian forces following its evacuation by the Japanese.

*November 15.* The Far Eastern Republic is annexed to the RSFSR.

*December 16.* Lenin suffers another stroke.

*December 23–26.* In his "Letter to the Congress" (also known as his "Testament"), Lenin expresses his concerns about the evolution of the Party and gives his appraisal of the other leaders of the revolutionary struggle.

*December 30.* The First Congress of the Soviets of the Union meets in Moscow. It approves a Declaration and a Treaty of Union between the Soviet Republics of Russia, the Ukraine, Belorussia and Transcaucasia, thereby establishing the Union of Soviet Socialist Republics (USSR). A Central Executive Committee of the Union, led by Mikhail Kalinin, is elected by the Congress.

## 1923

*January 4.* In a postscript to his "Testament," Lenin recommends the dismissal of Stalin as general secretary.

*March 5.* Lenin appoints Trotsky to defend the Georgian Communists before the Central Committee against charges brought by Stalin and Felix Dzerzhinsky.

*March 9.* Lenin suffers another stroke. This ends his participation in political affairs.

*April 17–25.* The Twelfth Party Congress convenes without Lenin. Superficial unanimity masks a power struggle. His authority increasing, Stalin

forms a troika with Grigori Zinoviev and Lev Kamenev.

*May 30.* The Buryat-Mongol Autonomous Soviet Socialist Republic is created.

*July 6.* The Central Executive Committee of the USSR approves a Constitution: The USSR is constituted as a federal state that guarantees the equality of its people and their right of secession. The Central Executive Committee (VTsIK), which consists of a Council of the Union (elected by the Congress of Soviets) and a Council of Nationalities, delegates its powers to its Presidium and to the Council of People's Commissars (*Sovnarkom*). Restrictions on universal suffrage are maintained.

*July 25.* The Autonomous Soviet Socialist Republic of Karelia is established.

*October 8.* In a letter to the Central Committee, Trotsky warns of the danger of the degeneration of the Party and of the growing power of the general secretary, Stalin.

*October 15.* In a declaration addressed to the Politburo, 46 "Old Bolsheviks" (including Evgeni Preobrazhensky, Grigori Piatakov and Leonid Serebriakov) criticize the Party's economic policies and the "dictatorship" exercised by certain Party members.

## 1923–1924

*December 1923–January 1924.* Public discussion takes place on the "New Course" proposed by Trotsky. On December 15, Stalin attacks "Trotskyism" in *Pravda.*

## 1924

*January 16–18.* The Thirteenth Party Congress is held. Stalin makes public the secret clause adopted at the Tenth Congress concerning the exclusion of members for factional activity, and he condemns the "errors" of Trotsky.

*January 21.* Lenin dies. He immediately becomes the object of a veritable cult. Aleksei Rykov succeeds him as president of the Council of People's Commissars.

# Foreign Affairs

## 1921

*February 26.* A friendship treaty is signed with Persia.

*February 28.* A friendship treaty is signed with Afghanistan.

*March 16.* A friendship treaty is signed with Turkey.

A commercial accord negotiated by Leonid Krasin is entered into with Great Britain. This marks the first major breach in the diplomatic isolation of Soviet Russia.

*March 18.* The Treaty of Riga is signed with Poland. By setting the Polish-Soviet border to the east of the Curzon Line, the treaty allows Poland to regain territories populated by Ukrainians and Belorussians.

*May 6.* A provisional commercial accord is entered into with Germany.

*June 22–July 12.* The Third Congress of the Comintern meets in Moscow. Taking account of a renewed revolutionary surge in Europe, the Congress advocates the consolidation of Communist parties.

*July 3–19.* The founding congress of the Red Trade Union International (Profintern) is held in Moscow.

*November 5.* A treaty of friendship and cooperation is signed with Mongolia.

## 1922

*April 10–May 19.* A Soviet delegation participates in an international eco-

nomic conference in Genoa. No solution is reached on the problem of the loans to the former Russian regime.

*April 16.* The Treaty of Rapallo, completed during the Genoa Conference, is signed by Soviet Russia and Germany. The two countries reestablish diplomatic ties and pledge to develop their economic and commercial relations. Secret negotiations will result in military cooperation.

*June 15–July 20.* A conference held at The Hague fails to solve the problem of the debts incurred by czarist Russia.

## 1923

*January 27.* An accord is reached between the USSR and Sun Yat-sen in southern China. The Soviets send military advisors to Canton and push for a "united front" between the Chinese Communist Party and the Kuomintang.

*May.* Tensions rise in the relations of the USSR with Western Europe: Great Britain denounces "anti-British propaganda" in India, Persia and Afghanistan, and on May 10 the Soviet diplomat Vatslav Vorovsky is assassinated in Lausanne by a White émigré.

*August 1.* A convention on the Bosporus and Dardanelles straits, negotiated at a conference in Lausanne (November 1922–July 1923), is signed by representatives of the USSR (the convention will never be ratified by the Soviet government). The agreement calls for the demilitarization of the Straits and for freedom of navigation by warships and commercial shipping.

# Economy and Society

## 1921

*January–February.* Social unrest breaks out in urban areas and in the countryside.

*February 22.* The State Economic Planning Commission (Gosplan) is established.

*March 8–16.* At the Tenth Party Congress, Lenin pushes through his policies with respect to trade unions ("schools of communism"). This Congress marks the end of War Communism and the advent of the New Economic Policy (NEP). The objectives of this new policy are to restore the confidence of the peasantry in the regime, in part by permitting them to sell excess produce on the free market, and to help facilitate industrial expansion by restoring commercial relations between urban areas and the countryside. The policy involves accepting the return of certain forms of private enterprise and the assistance of foreign specialists in rebuilding the national economy. The state, however, maintains control over banking, transportation, large industrial enterprises and foreign trade.

*March 21.* A decree replaces the requisitioning of agricultural products by the state with a tax-in-kind, which in turn will be gradually replaced by a cash assessment.

*March 28.* A decree is issued authorizing the free exchange of agricultural products.

*April 7.* A decree is issued restoring the independence of consumer cooperatives.

*May 17.* The decree of November 1920 that nationalized small industrial enterprises is revoked.

*July 5.* A decree is issued authorizing the leasing of state enterprises to private parties.

*July 7.* A decree authorizes the creation of small private craft and industrial enterprises employing up to 20 workers (10 workers if production is mechanized).

*Summer.* The harvest is a disaster. Famine affects 30 million persons and results in 5 million deaths, despite a national and international humanitarian relief effort (an agreement will be signed with the American Relief Administration in August).

*August 9.* The Council of People's Commissars issues instructions on the principles of the NEP.

*August 12.* The Council of Labor and Defense (STO) releases new guidelines for the operations of large industrial enterprises: State enterprises are granted complete management autonomy and are encouraged to operate in accordance with commercial principles. State enterprises are also encouraged to join huge trusts that are established in most industries.

*September 2.* A new law on universities is adopted.

*October 4.* A decree is issued reopening the State Bank (Gosbank).

*December 10.* All enterprises employing up to 10 workers are reprivatized.

## 1922

New Civil, Penal and Labor Codes are promulgated.

*February 26.* A decree is issued authorizing the confiscation of Church valuables to aid the starving. The resistance of Patriarch Tikhon provides the pretext for a violent antireligious campaign.

*May 1.* The Kashira State Regional Electrical Power Plant, near Moscow, goes into operation.

*May 19.* The "Pioneers," a Communist youth organization intended to inculcate schoolchildren with Communist values, is established.

*October 11.* A decree is issued concerning the circulation by the State Bank of a new paper currency, the *chervonetz* ruble. Each unit of the new currency is the equivalent of the former 10-ruble piece; although it is backed by gold and foreign currency reserves, it is not convertible. Initially, the *chervonetz* is issued only in large denominations. At the time of its issue, prices are approximately 200,000 times higher than what they were in 1913.

*December 1.* An Agricultural Code takes effect. It permits peasants to choose between individual or collective exploitation of their land, and authorizes the hiring of agricultural workers.

## 1923

The first Soviet airline opens.

A plan is created to eliminate illiteracy among the 18- to 35-year-old segment of the population before 1927.

*January.* A state alcohol monopoly is established.

*April 10.* A decree is issued clarifying the law on state trusts.

*April 17–25.* At the Twelfth Party Congress, Trotsky analyzes the "scissors crisis" (the rise of industrial prices coupled with the fall of agricultural prices), which will come to a head in the autumn. The crisis will be resolved in 1924 with the intervention of the state, which will push down industrial prices and encourage a rise in agricultural prices.

*June 16.* Patriarch Tikhon recognizes his past "mistakes" and declares his loyalty to the regime. He will shortly be freed from house arrest.

*August 19.* The first Agricultural Exposition opens in Moscow.

# Civilization and Culture

## 1921

The Marx-Engels Institute and the Institute of Red Professors are established

in Moscow. In Petrograd, the "Serapion Brotherhood," a literary group, is formed. The Bolshevik Alexander Voronsky founds the review *Krasnaia Nov* ("Red Virgin Soil"), which welcomes contributions from non-Communist "fellow travelers" who support the regime. The "formalist school," whose adherents include Yuri Tynyanov, Boris Eikhenbaum and Viktor Shklovsky, is founded. A collection of essays by Russian émigrés entitled *Smena Vekh* ("Changing Landmarks") is published in Prague; the essays advocate collaboration with the new regime from a nationalist standpoint. The FEKS (Factory of the Eccentric Actor) is founded by Grigori Kozintsev, Leonid Trauberg and Sergei Yutkevich. *The Way of the Proletariat of Petrograd* is painted by Pavel Filonov (1920–1921).

*August 7.* The poet Alexander Blok dies.

*August 24.* The acmeist poet Nikolai Gumilev, accused of plotting against the regime, is executed.

*October.* Maxim Gorky, ill and in disagreement with the policies pursued by the Party, leaves Russia.

## 1922

The Left Front of the Arts (LEF) is founded by Vladimir Mayakovsky and Osip Brik. *The Naked Year*, a novel, is published by Boris Pilnyak. "Armored Train 14-69," a short story, is published by Vsevolod Ivanov. *Kotik Letaev*, an autobiographical narrative, is published by Andrei Bely. The poems of Marina Tsvetaeva (*Verstes*) and of Anna Akhmatova (*Anno Domini MCMXXI*) are published. Liubov Popova designs a constructivist set for *The Splendid Cuckold*, a play by F. Crommelynck and directed by Vsevolod Meyerhold. Massive expulsions from the country of literary, scientific and religious figures (including, among others, the philosophers Nikolai Berdiaev and Sergei Bulgakov) occur.

*May 1.* The first exhibition of the paintings of the Association of Artists of Revolutionary Russia (AKhRR) opens in Moscow.

## 1923

The journal *Na Postu* ("Standing Guard") is published by proletarian writers of the October Group. These writers will take control of the Russian Asso-

ciation of Proletarian Writers (RAPP) and will systematically attack the "fellow travelers." These latter writers will establish a new literary group, *Pereval* (the Pass).

*Chapaev*, a historical novel by Dmitri Furmanov about the heroes of the Civil War, is published. The Association of Proletarian Musicians is founded. The Association of New Architects is established by N. Ladovsky and N. Dokuchaev.

# Chapter 25                    1924–1929

# The Rise of Stalin

The struggle for succession began before the death of Lenin, who had started to express his concerns about the evolution of the Party in 1922. Stalin's rise to absolute power would be accomplished in stages. Among his great strengths was his shrewd ability to pose as a humble spokesman for Leninism. Eager to convey the impression that the interests of the Party were his main concern, Stalin would often avoid direct involvement in the great controversies of the day before assuming the role of mediator. At the same time, however, Stalin used the office of general secretary to strengthen his grip on the Party's bureaucracy, which was undergoing a profound change due to a huge influx of new cadres who had less political experience and were more pliant than the veterans of the Revolution and the Civil War. Although Stalin was not as intelligent as many of his adversaries, he gained complete control over a power base that he was able to mobilize to great advantage. In the struggle against new "enemies," Stalin never hesitated to use repressive measures developed during earlier years. Now, however, the enemies were no longer external; they were within the Party itself.

Personal rivalries were coupled with political and economic controversies during this period. Momentous choices had to be made regarding the future of the USSR. Whether to continue or abandon the New Economic Policy (NEP), whether it was possible to build socialism in one country, and what role the Comintern should play were just some of the major issues that confronted Party authorities. Debates were often marked by confusion and ambiguity, and alliances and counteralliances were quickly formed and then re-formed in a merciless struggle for power.

At the beginning of this period (1924–1925), Stalin was aligned with Grigori Zinoviev and Lev Kamenev in a ruling "troika" opposed to Leon Trotsky. In 1925, however, Stalin forced out the opponents of the NEP (including Zinoviev and Kamenev), who then joined Trotsky and Alexander Shliapnikov's "Workers' Opposition" to form the "United Opposition," which itself collapsed at the end of 1927. Then in 1928 Stalin made an about-face by abandoning his alliance with the peasantry, and the following year he succeeded in eliminating the "Right Deviation" (led by Nikolai Bukharin, Alexei Rykov and Mikhail Tomsky), which supported the NEP. These maneuvers allowed Stalin to set the country on the road to accelerated industrialization, central planning and collectivization. Stalin was now master of the Party, and he proceeded to subject the entire country to the ordeal of a new battle.

# Politics and Institutions

## 1924

*January 26.* Petrograd is renamed Leningrad.

*January 26–February 2.* The Second All-Union Congress of Soviets is convened. Stalin puts himself forward as a faithful heir of Leninism. The Constitution of the Union of Soviet Socialist Republics (USSR) is ratified.

*Late January.* The Party launches a massive recruitment campaign among the working class.

*February 9.* The Nakhichevan Autonomous Soviet Socialist Republic is created.

*April 1.* The first issue of the *Bolshevik*, the organ of the Central Committee of the Communist Party, appears.

*May 23–31.* The Eighth Party Congress is held. Lenin's "Testament" is not made public. Stalin is confirmed in the post of general secretary.

*August–September.* An anti-Communist uprising in Georgia is quickly crushed by Soviet troops.

*October.* In the preface to the third volume of his works (*The Lessons of October*), Trotsky attacks Zinoviev and Kamenev. They will launch a vigorous counterattack in November–December and receive guarded support from Stalin, who begins to elaborate the theory of "socialism in one country."

*October 12.* The Autonomous Soviet Socialist Republic of Moldavia is established.

*October 14.* The Tadzhik Autonomous Soviet Socialist Republic is established.

*October 27.* The Uzbek and Turkmen Soviet Socialist Republics are created.

## 1925

*January 15.* Trotsky resigns as people's commissar of war. He will be replaced on January 26 by Mikhail Frunze, who himself will be replaced within a year by Kliment Voroshilov.

*April 10.* Tsaritsyn is renamed Stalingrad in honor of its defender during the Civil War.

*April 21.* The Chuvash Autonomous Soviet Socialist Republic is created.

*April 27–29.* The Fourteenth Party Conference is held. It confirms the fall of Trotsky and approves Stalin's theory of the "construction of socialism in one country." The ruling troika dissolves when Stalin opposes Zinoviev and Kamenev and throws his support to the "Right" (led by Bukharin), which favors the continuation of the NEP.

*December 18–31.* The Fourteenth Congress of the Russian Communist Party (Bolshevik) is held. The Party, which now has a total of nearly 1.1 million members and candidate members, renames itself the Communist Party (Bolshevik) of the USSR. Kamenev and Zinoviev fail in their attack against Stalin. Kamenev is demoted to the rank of deputy member of the Politburo. Zinoviev loses control of the Leningrad Party organization, which is purged under the direction of Sergei Kirov.

## 1926

*February 1.* The Kirghiz Autonomous Soviet Socialist Republic is established.

*April.* The "United Opposition" is formed when Trotsky allies himself with Kamenev and Zinoviev, his former adversaries. They call for the development of heavy industry, a struggle against the kulaks and assistance to revolutionary movements throughout the world.

*July 14–23.* A fierce controversy breaks out at a plenum of the Central Committee (Felix Dzerzhinsky dies of a heart attack during the session). The plenum condemns the "illegal" methods of the United Opposition, which had published its program, the "Declaration of the Thirteen." Zinoviev is ousted from the Politburo.

*October 16.* The United Opposition issues a "self-criticism" disavowing its "secessionist maneuvers."

*October 18.* The *New York Times* publishes Lenin's "Testament." Stalin accuses Trotsky of duplicity.

*October 23–26.* A plenum of the Central Committee ousts Trotsky and Kamenev from the Politburo and removes Zinoviev from the chairmanship of the Communist International.

*October 26–November 3.* The Fifteenth Party Conference confirms Stalin's victory over the United Opposition.

## 1927

*Spring.* Under attack from Trotsky for his China policy, Stalin uses reversals in foreign affairs suffered by the USSR (including the break in diplomatic relations with Great Britain) to emphasize the necessity of Party unity in the face of the "danger of war."

*September 3.* In a platform addressed to the Central Committee, opposition leaders renew their criticism of Stalin.

*October 21–23.* A plenum convenes and ousts Trotsky and Zinoviev from the Central Committee.

*November 7.* The leaders of the United Opposition organize street demonstrations in Moscow and Leningrad on the tenth anniversary of the Revolution.

*November 12–14.* At a plenum of the Central Committee, Trotsky and Zinoviev are ousted from the Party, and Kamenev and Christian Rakovsky are ousted from the Central Committee.

*December 2–19.* Stalin's opponents suffer a total defeat at the Fifteenth Party Congress. Seventy-five "Trotskyites-Zinovievites" (including Kamenev, Grigori Piatakov, Karl Radek and Rakovsky) are ousted from the Party, as are the partisans of the "Democratic Centralism" group. Some of those who are removed, including Kamenev and Zinoviev, will issue "self-criticisms" and be reintegrated into the Party in 1928.

## 1928

*January 17.* Trotsky leaves Moscow for a forced exile in Alma Ata. Arrests of Stalin's opponents increase.

*Spring–Summer.* Differences within the Party over major economic policies increase. Stalin affirms the necessity of accelerated development of heavy industry and the collectivization of agriculture. The Right, led by Bukharin, Rykov and Tomsky, favors the continuation of the NEP and an alliance with the peasantry.

*May 18–July 6.* The Shakhty trial is held: Fifty-three engineers and technicians from the Donbas region are charged with industrial sabotage (11 are condemned to death, and 5 are actually executed).

*July 11.* Bukharin and Kamenev hold a secret meeting.

*September 30.* The conflict between the Right and Stalin becomes public knowledge when *Pravda* publishes Bukharin's "Notes of an Economist."

*November 16–24.* At Stalin's behest, a plenum of the Central Committee condemns "Right opportunism" without denouncing the rightist leaders (Bukharin, Rykov and Tomsky) by name.

## 1929

*January 22.* Trotsky is ordered expelled from the USSR; he leaves Alma Ata for Constantinople.

*April 16–23.* A plenum of the Central Committee condemns "Right deviation" and relieves Bukharin of his positions as editor of *Pravda* and chairman of the Comintern. A purge will be ordered by the Sixteenth Party Conference (April 23–26).

*November 10–17.* A plenum of the Central Committee ousts Bukharin from the Politburo and reiterates accusations against Bukharin, Rykov and Tomsky, the leaders of the Right. They will publish a complete self-criticism on November 26.

*December 5.* The Tadzhik Soviet Socialist Republic is established.

*December 21.* As the country celebrates the 50th birthday of Stalin, a cult of personality emerges.

# Foreign Affairs

## 1924

*February 2.* The USSR establishes diplomatic relations with Great Britain.

*February 7.* The USSR establishes diplomatic relations with Italy.

*May 31.* The USSR establishes diplomatic relations with China. The countries agree to a joint administration of the Chinese Eastern Railway.

*June 17–July 8.* The Fifth Congress of the Comintern is marked by an offensive against "Trotskyite" elements.

*August 8.* A new commercial accord is signed with Great Britain. British conservatives, however, will block the ratification of this agreement in October, following the publication of the "Zinoviev letter" (of questionable authenticity), in which the Comintern encouraged British Communists to promote an uprising in the armed forces.

*October 28.* The USSR establishes diplomatic relations with France.

## 1925

*January 20.* An accord is reached on the reestablishment of diplomatic relations between the USSR and Japan. (Japan will complete its evacuation of the northern portion of Sakhalin Island in May.)

*October 12.* A new commercial accord is signed with Germany.

## 1926

*March 20.* Chiang Kai-shek, the new leader of the Kuomintang, launches an armed attack against the Chinese Communists and their Soviet advisors.

*April 24.* The Treaty of Berlin (a neutrality treaty) is signed by the USSR and Germany.

*May.* Great Britain accuses the Soviet Union of supporting a general strike by British trade unions that began on May 4.

*September 28.* The USSR signs a nonaggression pact with Lithuania.

*October.* Zinoviev loses the chairmanship of the Comintern. He is replaced by Bukharin.

## 1927

*April 12.* Chinese Communist fighters are massacred in Shanghai by Chiang Kai-shek's forces. This is a serious defeat for Stalin's policy in China.

*May.* The USSR participates in the International Economic Conference in Geneva.

*May 27.* Following a search of the London office of Arcos, the Soviet trade delegation, Great Britain breaks diplomatic relations with the USSR.

*June 7.* Peter Voikov, the Soviet ambassador to Poland, is assassinated by a White émigré in Warsaw.

*November 10–12.* A worldwide Congress of Friends of the USSR is held in Moscow.

*November 30.* Maxim Litvinov, an assistant to Commissar of Foreign Affairs Georgi Chicherin, presents a four-year plan for the total abolition of armed forces to the League of Nations.

*December.* Relations between the USSR and China cool after the Kuomintang crushes a Communist insurrection in Canton.

## 1928

*July 17–September 1.* The Sixth Congress of the Comintern is held. A program is adopted, a break is effected with "rightist" elements, and an aggressive policy that targets social democratic parties for attack is reinstituted.

*September 6.* The USSR signs the Kellogg-Briand Pact, which renounces war, after having initially criticized it.

## 1929

*February 9.* The "Litvinov Protocol" is signed by the USSR, Poland, Romania, Latvia and Estonia. Under the terms of the protocol, the parties undertake to apply the Kellogg-Briand Pact on a regional basis.

*May 27.* The Chinese government raids the Soviet consulate at Harbin.

*July 10–11.* The Chinese seize the Chinese Eastern Railway. This act will lead to a break in diplomatic relations between the USSR and China on July 17.

*October 3.* Diplomatic relations are restored between the USSR and Great Britain.

*December 22.* The Protocol of Khabarovsk is signed by the USSR and China. After armed engagements on the Sino-Soviet border, and the intervention of Soviet troops in Manchuria, the status quo ante is restored; joint administration of the Chinese Eastern Railway resumes.

# Economy and Society

## 1924

There are 1.2 million persons unemployed in the Soviet Union.

The Order of the Red Banner is established.

*February 5–22.* A monetary reform is instituted. The *sovznaki* is withdrawn from circulation following an exchange of this currency for the new *chervonetz* ruble, at the rate of one new ruble for 50,000 *sovznaki*. Monetary stability is restored.

*April.* The League of the Godless is founded.

*April 7.* Patriarch Tikhon dies and is not replaced. In his "Testament" he appeals for loyalty to the Soviet regime.

## 1925

*April.* Bukharin declares: "We must tell the peasants, all the peasants, enrich yourselves." This conciliatory policy toward the peasantry is approved by the Fourteenth Party Conference (April 27–29).

*July 10.* The Telegraphic Agency of the Soviet Union (TASS) is established.

*September 23.* A law is enacted establishing compulsory military service of two years.

*December 6.* The Lenin Electrical Power Plant at Shatura, near Moscow, goes into service.

*December 18–31.* At the Fourteenth Party Congress, Stalin advocates rapid industrialization.

## 1926

The first census of the USSR is conducted. The total population of the country is set at 147 million. The rural population accounts for 82 percent of the total, the urban population for 18 percent.

*June 18.* A special tax is imposed on the profits of "Nepmen," a class of capitalists that came into existence with the advent of the NEP.

*July 6.* The first electrified railway is opened between Baku and Sabunchi.

*November 19.* A new Family Code, more liberal with respect to marriage and divorce than the 1918 code, is promulgated.

*December 19.* A hydroelectric station on the Volkhov River goes into service.

## 1927

The Shevchenko Sovkhoz (state farm) near Odessa establishes the practice of lending agricultural equipment. It will be the precursor to the Machine Tractor Stations (MTS) that will be organized on a wide scale in 1929.

Construction begins on the Lenin Hydroelectric Station (Dnieproges) on the Dnieper River. The construction project becomes a model of "worker heroism."

As a result of a bad harvest and the reduction of prices by the state, the supply of grain declines. There will be a scarcity of bread in the cities at the beginning of 1928.

*March 30.* Metropolitan Sergei, who was arrested in December 1926, is freed. He advocates the complete submission of the Orthodox Church to Soviet authorities in order to assure the Church's survival.

*April 18–26.* The Fourth Congress of the Soviets approves in principle a five-year economic plan that is being prepared by VSNKh (the Supreme Council of the National Economy, led by Valerian Kuibyshev) and Gosplan (led by Gleb Krzhizhanovsky).

*October 16.* A gradual shift to a seven-hour workday is announced.

*December 2–19.* The Fifteenth Party Congress approves the elimination of capitalist elements in the economy. The Congress gives priority to heavy industry and to a gradual, 10- to 15-year process of collectivization of agriculture.

## 1928

A direct attack on Islam is launched: Mosques are closed and pilgrimages to Mecca are barred.

*January.* During a tour of the Urals and Siberia, Stalin launches a violent campaign against peasants who refuse to deliver their wheat. A campaign of denunciation against the kulaks begins, the authorities reinstate the requisition of agricultural produce, and recalcitrant peasants are arrested. (The method of grain collection that was developed after Stalin's tour will come to be called the "Ural-Siberian method.")

*July 4–12.* At a plenum of the Central Committee, the Right, led by Bukharin, Tomsky and Rykov, attacks the economic policies of Stalin, who defends his desire to abandon the NEP.

*September 1.* The Order of the Red Banner of Labor is established.

*September 30.* *Pravda* publishes Bukharin's "Notes of an Economist," which stresses the necessity of avoiding a break with the peasantry.

*October 1.* The First Five-Year Plan officially begins. The Plan calls for the use of voluntaristic and authoritarian methods to achieve its arbitrarily established yet extremely ambitious objectives (which are denounced by the statistician Nikolai Kondratiev). Absolute priority is given to heavy industry (which accounts for 78 percent of all industrial investment). Although the Plan calls for collectivizing agriculture slowly (17.5 percent of cultivated land in five years), in practice collectivization will be achieved much more quickly.

*November 4.* An electrical equipment factory goes into operation in Moscow.

*December 10–24.* The Eighth Trade Union Congress is held. The policies of Tomsky (a leader of the Right) are called into question. Tomsky will be officially stripped of his position as head of the Central Council of Trade Unions in June 1929.

*December 15.* A new Agrarian Code limits the freedoms accorded to the peasantry in December 1922.

## 1929

The construction of the city of Magnitogorsk and its metallurgical complex begins.

Bread rationing is reintroduced in the cities.

*April 8.* A decree is issued regulating religious life. The control exercised by the authorities over parishes is reinforced. In May, an amendment to Article 13 of the Soviet Constitution will make "antireligious propaganda" legal.

*April 23–29.* The Sixteenth Party Conference approves the First Five-Year Plan but revises the objectives upward. The Conference appeals for the widespread application of "socialist emulation."

*May 20–28.* The Fifth Congress of Soviets approves the First Five-Year Plan.

*June 5.* As pressure builds for a more rapid collectivization of agriculture, a decree is issued establishing Machine Tractor Stations (state agricultural equipment depots). These entities will enter into contracts with individual kolkhozes (collective farms) for the completion of major tasks.

*August 27.* Continuous production is begun with the introduction of work-team rotations. The "five-day week" takes away from Sunday its character as a regular day of rest.

*September.* The authority of the directors of enterprises is increased.

*September 13.* Anatoli Lunacharsky is relieved of his duties as people's commissar of public instruction. In 1929–30, a major portion of technical education will come under the authority of the Supreme Council of the National Economy (VSNKh).

*November 7.* In *Pravda*, Stalin proclaims a "great change" in the policy of collectivization of agriculture. A plenum of the Central Committee (November 10–17) will approve an accelerated pace of collectivization as well as the creation of a People's Commissariat of Agriculture, which will be established in December under the direction of Y. Yakovlev.

*December 5–10.* The First Congress of the Shock Brigades is held in Moscow. As the year ends, the Party disseminates the slogan "The Five-Year Plan in Four Years!"

*December 27.* Stalin announces the general application of collectivization and the advent of "the liquidation of the kulaks as a class."

# Civilization and Culture

## 1924

The Literary Center of the Constructivists (LTsK) is founded. "V.I. Lenin," a poem by Vladimir Mayakovsky. *The Badgers*, a novel by Leonid Leonov. *Cities and Years*, a novel by Konstantin Fedin. "Homecoming," "Russia of the Soviets" and "Leaving Russia," poetry by Sergei Esenin. Sergei Eisenstein films his first great motion picture, *Strike. The Extraordinary Adventures of Mr. West in the Land of the Bolsheviks*, a film directed by Lev Kuleshov. The Association for Contemporary Music is founded by artists who reject the idea of a "proletarian music." The Ukrainian historian Mikhail Hrushevsky endorses the Soviet regime.

## 1925

*White Guard*, a novel by Mikhail Bulgakov. *Cement*, a novel by Fedor Gladkov. *The Battleship Potemkin*, a film by S. Eisenstein. The constructivists Alexander Vesnin and M. Ginzburg found the Association of Contemporary Architects (OSA).

*June 18.* The Central Committee adopts a resolution "on Party policy in the domain of literature." The resolution, which recommends tolerance toward "fellow travelers," is contrary to the position of the most virulent of the proletarian writers, who have organized themselves into the Association of Russian Proletarian Writers (RAPP).

*December 28.* The poet S. Esenin commits suicide.

## 1926

*Red Cavalry*, a collection of stories by Isaac Babel. *The Days of the Turbins*, a play by M. Bulgakov. *The Tale of the Unextinguished Moon*, by Boris Pilnyak. *Mother*, a film by Vsevolod Pudovkin, from the novel by Maxim Gorky. *The Foundry*, a symphony by Alexander Mosolov.

## 1927

*Envy*, a novel by Yuri Olesha. *The Rout*, a novel about the Civil War, by Alexander Fadeyev. "The Year 1905," a poem by Boris Pasternak. *The End of St. Petersburg*, a film by V. Pudovkin. *October*, a film by S. Eisenstein. *The October Symphony*, a symphony by Dmitri Shostakovich. *The Delegate*, a painting by Georgi Ryazhsky. *The Death of the Commissar*, a painting by Kuzma Petrov-Vodkin. The Izvestia Building is constructed in Moscow.

## 1928

Publication of *The Quiet Don*, a novel by Mikhail Sholokov, begins. *12 Chairs*, a satirical novel about the NEP, by Ilya Ilf and Evgeni Petrov. *The Bedbug*, a satirical play by V. Mayakovsky. *Sublieutenant Kizhe*, a novel by the formalist Yuri Tynyanov. Manifesto of OBERIU (the Association for Real Art). *The Heir to Genghis Khan* (*Storm Over Asia*), a film by V. Pudovkin. *The Defense of Petrograd*, a painting by Alexander Deineka. The French architect and painter Le Corbusier visits Moscow and collaborates on the design of the Tsentrosoyuz Building. M. Gorky visits the USSR; he will rally to the regime at the beginning of the 1930s.

## 1929

RAPP launches a campaign of intimidation against "fellow travelers." Attacked in the course of this campaign are Evgeni

Zamyatin, who will emigrate in 1931; and B. Pilnyak, who submits to his critics and writes *The Volga Flows to the Caspian Sea*, in which he concedes to the new spirit of the years of the "great change."

The publication of *Peter I*, a vast historical novel by Alexei Tolstoy, be-gins. *Old and New*, a film by S. Eisenstein. *The Man with the Movie Camera*, a film by Dziga Vertov. The Union of Proletarian Architects of Russia is formed and denounces "formalism" in architecture.

# Chapter 26 1930–1934

# The Formation of the Stalinist USSR

The First Five-Year Plan, officially launched on October 1, 1928, marked a decisive turning point in the history of the Soviet Union. The Plan accorded high priority to industrialization and set especially ambitious goals for heavy industry. Achieving these objectives required an enormous effort: The nation had to mobilize a large workforce (whose capabilities, of necessity, had to be improved), competent technicians and, at times, foreign expertise. To that end, the authorities created a veritable "mystique" about the Plan, offered material incentives to workers, and created a system of control that weighed ever heavier on the Soviet worker. At the beginning of 1933, it was announced that the First Five-Year Plan had been accomplished nine months ahead of schedule, and that exceptional results had been achieved in heavy industry (where production is said to have increased by 273 percent). A number of the Plan's objectives were not attained, however, and difficulties had arisen as a result of the rigidity of the planning process.

As for the countryside, the plan had initially called for a gradual shift to collectivization of agriculture. At the end of 1929, however, the pace of collectivization was accelerated, and a widespread application of the kolkhoz system became the order of the day. After the party decreed a "liquidation of the kulaks as a class," collectivization was carried out by force and by the increasing use of terror. By the end of the First Five-Year Plan, 210,000 kolkhozes (70 percent of cultivated land), 4,300 sovkhozes (10 percent of cultivated land) and 2,400 Machine Tractor Stations (MTS) were in existence. But the price of rapid collectivization—a decline in overall production and a traumatized peasantry—was to prove catastrophic.

The First Five-Year Plan also left its mark on the political life of the country. The Party appeared more united as opponents either rallied to the cause or were removed in purges of "bad Communists." Responsibility for economic failures was quickly assigned to "saboteurs" who were put on trial. Then in 1934, after the Seventeenth Party Congress, a relative calm seemed to settle on the country, and the USSR affirmed its return to the community of nations by gaining admission to the League of Nations.

# Politics and Institutions

## 1930

*April 7.* A new decree marks the expansion of the network of labor camps (until 1928 the camps had been confined to the area around the White Sea). The GULAG (Main Administration of Camps) is established under the direction of the OGPU (the secret police).

*June 26–July 13.* The Sixteenth Party Congress confirms the defeat of the Right (Mikhail Tomsky is forced out of the Politburo) and announces the accelerated passage to socialism. The members of the new Politburo are Stalin, Kliment Voroshilov, Lazar Kaganovich, Mikhail Kalinin, Sergei Kirov, Stanislav Kossior, Valerian Kuibyshev, Vyacheslav Molotov, Alexei Rykov and Ianis Rudzutak.

*November 25–December 7.* The trial of the "Industrial Party," which is accused of organizing a foreign intervention with Paris émigrés, takes place. The "Peasant Labor Party," led by Professors Nikolai Kondratiev and Alexander Chayanov, is also denounced and accused of sabotaging collectivization.

*December 19.* Molotov succeeds Rykov (who is removed from the Politburo) as chairman of the Council of People's Commissars.

## 1931

*March 1–9.* The trial of the Menshevik "Union Bureau" takes place.

## 1932

*February 20.* Leon Trotsky is deprived of his Soviet citizenship.

*March 20.* The Kara-Kalpak Autonomous Soviet Socialist Republic is created.

*Late Summer.* Mikhail Riutin, a former ally of Nikolai Bukharin, and A. Slepkov circulate a program (known as the "Riutin platform") favorable to the economic ideas of the Right. They call for the return of the Party to democracy and for the ouster of Stalin, "the evil genius of the Revolution." Led by Kirov, a majority of the Politburo refuses to acquiesce to Stalin's demand for the death sentence for Riutin, who is accused of terrorism and attempted assassination.

*October 9.* Militants accused of complicity with Riutin are ousted from the Party, including Lev Kamenev and Grigori Zinoviev, who are deported.

*November 8–9.* Stalin's second wife, Nadezhda Alliluyeva, commits suicide under mysterious circumstances.

## 1933

*January 12.* The Central Committee issues a resolution approving a purge of the Party (800,000 will be purged in 1933, 340,000 in 1934). Total Party membership (including candidate members) will drop from 3.5 million on January 1, 1933, to 2.35 million on January 1, 1935.

*April 12–18.* A trial of engineers accused of sabotage is held.

*May 8.* A secret decree from Stalin and Molotov puts an end to the massive and disorderly character of arrests.

*July 7.* The old Ukrainian Bolshevik Nikolai Skrypnik commits suicide. Native Party cadres are purged in the Ukraine.

## 1934

*January 26–February 10.* The Seventeenth Party Congress (the "Congress of the Victors") is held. Stalin compromises with moderate members of the Politburo. Former opponents engage in self-criticism (Nikolai Bukharin is elected a deputy member of the Central Committee). The new Secretariat consists of Stalin, Kaganovich, Andrei Zhdanov and Kirov (who plays a prominent role at the Congress). The Politburo includes Stalin, Molotov, Kaganovich, Voroshilov, Kalinin, Sergo Ordzhonikidze, Kuibyshev, Kirov, Andrei Andreyev and Kossior (members); and Anastas Mikoyan, Vlas Chubar, Grigori Petrovski, Pavel Postyshev and Rudzutak (deputy members). The Commissariat of Workers' and Peasants' Inspection (*Rabkrin*) is abolished.

*May 7.* The Jewish Autonomous Territory of Birobidzhan is created on the Amur River; the populating of this territory is intended to strengthen the defense of the Sino-Soviet border.

*May 27.* A partial amnesty restores some rights to the kulaks.

*June 8.* A law on "treason against the fatherland" establishes the death penalty and the collective responsibility of entire families for individual acts.

*June 24.* The headquarters of the Ukrainian government and Party are moved from Kharkov to Kiev.

*July 10.* The police and security functions of the OGPU are transferred to the People's Commissariat of Internal Affairs (NKVD), which is reorganized under the leadership of Genrikh Yagoda. The NKVD also takes over the administration of labor camps, which are now fully developed.

# Foreign Affairs

## 1930

*January 26.* The White general Alexander Kutepov is kidnapped in Paris by Soviet intelligence operatives.

*July 21.* Maxim Litvinov replaces Georgi Chicherin as commissar for foreign affairs.

## 1931

*May 6.* The Soviet-Lithuanian non-aggression pact of September 28, 1926, is renewed for five years.

*June 24.* The USSR and Afghanistan sign a treaty of neutrality and nonaggression in Kabul. This agreement replaces the treaty of August 31, 1926, and will itself be renewed on March 29, 1936.

The treaty of neutrality with Germany, (the "Treaty of Berlin"), signed in 1926, is renewed for three years. The protocol will be ratified on May 5, 1933, a few months after Adolf Hitler comes to power.

## 1932

*January 21.* A nonaggression pact is signed with Finland.

*February 2.* The Geneva Disarmament Conference opens. Litvinov reissues his proposal for complete and general disarmament.

*February 5.* A three-year nonaggression pact is signed with Latvia.

*May 4.* A three-year nonaggression pact is signed with Estonia.

*July 25.* A three-year nonaggression pact is signed with Poland.

*November 29.* France and Russia sign a two-year nonaggression pact. The agreement is intended to be a counterweight to increasing German militarism.

*December 12.* Diplomatic relations with China are reestablished in the face of the Japanese threat. (Japan had invaded Manchuria the previous year and established there the puppet state of Manchukuo in 1932.)

## 1933

*May 18.* The Franco-Soviet nonaggression pact is ratified unanimously by the French Chamber of Deputies.

*September 2.* A five-year nonaggression treaty with Italy is signed.

*November 16.* The United States establishes diplomatic relations with the USSR.

*December 29.* Molotov and Litvinov give speeches to the Central Committee expressing the view that Hitler's Germany constitutes a threat to the USSR. The deterioration in Soviet-German relations will lead to the termination of military cooperation between the two countries.

## 1934

French foreign minister Louis Barthou elaborates a proposal for an "Eastern Pact," which he will pursue until his assassination on October 9. The pact would establish a system of collective security in central and eastern Europe and include a mutual-assistance treaty between France and the Soviet Union.

*January 11.* The Soviet Union concludes a commercial treaty with France (it will be modified on January 6, 1936).

*February 4.* Diplomatic relations with Hungary are established.

*February 16.* A new commercial treaty is concluded with England (it envisages balanced bilateral trade by 1937).

*April–May.* Separate nonaggression pacts with Lithuania, Latvia and Estonia (April 4), Finland (April 7) and Poland (May 5) are renewed for 10 years.

*June 9.* Diplomatic relations are established with Romania and Czechoslovakia.

*July 11–23.* Diplomatic relations are established with Bulgaria.

*September 18.* The USSR is admitted to the League of Nations by a vote of 39 to 3 (Holland, Switzerland and Portugal voting against), with 7 abstentions. The USSR also becomes a member of the League's Council.

# Economy and Society

## 1930

*January 5.* A proclamation of the Central Committee "on the pace of collectivization and the measures taken by the state to aid the building of kolkhozes" distinguishes three stages in the "voluntary" process of collectivization. In practice, the forced establishment of kolkhozes will take place at an accelerated pace.

*January 30 and February 1.* The Central Committee, the Central Executive Committee and *Sovnarkom* (the Council of People's Commissars) issue resolutions on the struggle against the kulaks. In 1929–30, according to official figures, 240,000 kulak families prohibited from joining kolkhozes are deported. (According to unofficial estimates, however, the actual number of deportees during these years is between 5 million and 10 million.) Among the immediate consequences of forced collectivization and "dekulakization" are the utter disorganization of labor in the countryside and active and passive resistance on the part of the peasantry, including the slaughter of livestock on a massive scale.

*March 1.* A model statute is issued on the establishment of cooperative farms. These are to take the form of the artel, in which land, livestock and equipment are held in common. The statute would allow peasants to retain their homes, a plot of land and the right to keep one cow and small livestock.

*March 2.* Stalin publishes his article "Dizzy with Success" in *Pravda*. Placing responsibility for the catastrophic results of collectivization on the excesses of local authorities, he calls for a halt to coercive methods.

*March 14.* The Central Committee resolves to "struggle against deviations from the Party line in the drive for collectivization." The proportion of peasant households that have been collectivized will drop from 55 percent in March to 24 percent in July. This proportion, however, will climb steadily in the years that follow: 52 percent in 1931, 71 percent in 1934.

*April 6.* The Order of the Red Star and the Order of Lenin are created.

*May 1.* The Turksib, a rail link between Turkestan and Siberia, is completed.

*June 17.* The Felix Dzerzhinsky Tractor Factory, built with the help of American engineers, goes into operation in Stalingrad.

*June 26–July 13.* The Sixteenth Party Congress approves the slogan "The Five-Year Plan in Four Years." The Congress orders a redoubling of the collectivization effort and places an absolute priority on technical progress.

*August 14.* The Central Executive Committee and *Sovnarkom* pass resolutions on universal obligatory primary education. From 1927 to 1933, the number of pupils in schools for general education will rise from 11.6 million to 21.4 million.

*November.* Ordzhonikidze becomes director of the Supreme Council of National Economy (VSNKh).

## 1931

Approximately 5,000 foreign engineers and technicians are working in the USSR; of these, 2,000 are Americans.

*January 1.* The Rostov agricultural equipment factory, on the Don River, is put into service.

*February.* Workbooks are introduced for industrial workers. (These books record a worker's employment history and indicate the reasons for leaving his previous employment; they must be presented to management when entering into new employment.)

*March.* The Sixth Congress of Soviets approves a new method for remunerating kolkhozniks. Whereas members of a collective farm had previously been paid on a per capita basis, henceforth their compensation will be based on the amount of work performed, measured in "workday units" (*trudoden*).

*June 23.* At a Conference of Industrial Managers, Stalin gives a speech calling for the organized recruitment of workers and for the stabilization of the work force. He also mounts a campaign against "egalitarianism" in wages.

*August 2.* The Central Committee issues a resolution on the pace of collectivization and on the strengthening of the kolkhozes.

*October 1.* The Kharkov Tractor Factory and the rebuilt Moscow Automobile Factory (AMO) are put into operation. Soviet production of motor vehicles will increase from 4,000 heavy and passenger vehicles in 1931 to 136,500 in 1936.

*October 11.* The decision is made to liquidate what remains of private commerce.

## 1931–1933

The White Sea–Baltic Canal (also known as the Stalin Canal) is built by hundreds of thousands of prison laborers. The labor camps of the OGPU, and later the NKVD, will play an increasingly important role in the early five-year plans.

## 1932

Kolkhoznik markets are established. After they have fulfilled their obligations to the state, kolkhozes and individual kolkhozniks are authorized to sell their excess wheat and agricultural produce without taxation.

As construction begins on the new city of Komsomolsk, on the Amur River, measures are taken to encourage the colonization of the Far East.

The construction of the Moscow subway begins.

*January 1.* The Gorky Automobile Factory begins operation.

*January 5.* The responsibilities of the Supreme Council of National Economy (VSNKh) are parcelled out among three newly created People's Commissariats (for heavy industry, light industry and timber). This reflects a shift to the administration of industry by government ministries.

*January 30–February 4.* The Seventeenth Party Conference adopts a set of directives proposed by Kuibyshev and Molotov for the Second Five-Year Plan (1933–37). The goals of this Plan are less ambitious than those of the First Five-Year Plan. Priority is to be maintained for the energy, iron and steel, machine tool and transportation industries. The production of consumer goods is to be increased. The collectivization of agriculture is to continue.

*January 31.* The first blast furnace at Magnitogorsk is put into service. The plant uses iron from the Urals and coal from the Kuzbas region.

*April.* A metallurgical complex commences operation at Kuznetsk.

*April 20–29.* The Ninth Congress of Trade Unions is held. The Congress loses much of its power. The next Congress will not take place until 1949.

*August 7.* A law dealing with "the protection of the property of state enterprises, kolkhozes and cooperatives, and the strengthening of public property" is

enacted. Penalties are established for its contravention, including the death penalty for theft.

*August 25.* The authority of school directors is strengthened.

*October 4.* The first mines are opened in the coal-bearing Pechora River region.

*October 10.* Dnieproges, the hydroelectric station on the Dnieper River, goes into service. It supplies power to the metallurgical and chemical complexes at Dnepropetrovsk and Zaporozhe.

*November 15.* Work discipline is strengthened: One day of unjustified absence will result in the dismissal of the worker and the loss of the social advantages (housing and a ration card) connected with the position.

*December 27.* The internal passport, which had been abolished at the time of the Revolution, is reintroduced. This step permits authorities to control and to limit the movements of the urban population, especially workers. Kolkhozniks are not issued passports and are henceforth tied to the land.

*December 31.* The First Five-Year Plan is declared to have been achieved in four years and three months. Soviet propaganda contrasts this success with the economic crisis that has gripped the capitalist world since 1929. Heavy industrial production has increased 273 percent (110 percent of the Plan's goal), but the objectives for coal, cast iron and electricity production have not been attained. The production of consumer goods has risen more slowly than planned (84 percent of the goal). In the agricultural sector, 210,000 kolkhozes have been created (61 percent of cultivated land is collectivized), along with 4,300 sovkhozes and 2,400 Machine Tractor Stations. Agricultural production remains erratic, however, and livestock has declined by 40 percent or more, depending upon the region. The average annual rate of inflation was 9 percent during the period 1928–1932.

## 1932–1933

A terrible famine occurs. Largely caused by excessive requisitions, the famine is ignored by the authorities. Famine is particularly severe in the Ukraine, and it will be deliberately used to break the remaining resistance to collectivization on the part of the peasantry. Estimates of deaths range from 3 million to 6 million.

## 1933

The first Soviet liquid-fueled rocket is launched.

*January 7–12.* A plenum of the Central Committee decides to establish "political sections" in the Machine Tractor Stations in order to effect the political education of kolkhozniks.

*January 19.* A system requiring mandatory deliveries of grain by kolkhozes, according to rules and at prices fixed by the state, is restored.

*June.* The Commissariat of Labor is dissolved. Its responsibilities are given over to trade unions, which become de facto state administrative agencies.

*July 1.* The Chelyabinsk Tractor Factory begins operations.

*July 15.* The Urals Heavy Machine-Building Factory is opened at Sverdlovsk.

*November 15.* The first blast furnace at the ironworks at Zaporozhe is put into service.

## 1934

The rescue of the crew of the icebreaker *Cheliuskin*, which had sunk into the ice while attempting to travel from Mur-

mansk to Vladivostok, receives heavy publicity.

*January 23.* A factory for the construction of turbines is opened at Kharkov.

*January 26–February 10.* The Seventeenth Party Congress revises downward the targets for the Second Five-Year Plan because of difficulties encountered during 1933 (the first year of the Plan).

*April 16.* The honor "Hero of the Soviet Union" is created.

*September.* The aviator Mikhail Gromov breaks the world distance record.

# Civilization and Culture

## 1930

Political attacks on historians are stepped up: Eugene Tarlé is denounced by the official school (led by Mikhail Pokrovsky) and deported.

*Earth,* a film by Alexander Dovzhenko. The second Lenin Mausoleum, designed by Alexei Shchusev, is built in Moscow. *Lenin at Smolny,* a painting by Isaak Brodsky.

*January.* Viktor Shklovsky repudiates formalism in an article in *Literary Gazette.*

*April 14.* Vladimir Mayakovsky commits suicide. He had joined the Russian Association of Proletarian Writers in February.

## 1931

Accused of "nationalism," the Ukrainian historian Mikhail Hrushevsky is forced to leave Kiev and settle in Moscow. His followers are dismissed or arrested.

*The Golden Calf,* a satire by Ilya Ilf and Evgeni Petrov. *The Hydrocentral* a novel by Marietta Shaginian. *Road to Life*, a film by Nikolai Ekk about the "wild" children (groups of children who lost their families during the Civil War and famine).

*October.* *Proletarian Revolution* publishes an article by Stalin titled "On Some Questions about the History of Bolshevism." An ideological dictatorship comes into existence.

## 1932

Literary works exalt the new tasks of socialist construction: *Time, Forward!*, a novel by Valentin Kataev; *Power*, a novel by Fedor Gladkov (1932–1938); *Virgin Soil Upturned*, a novel by Mikhail Sholokhov; *How the Steel Was Tempered*, a novel by Nikolai Ostrovsky (1932–1934); *Skutarevsky*, a novel by Leonid Leonov.

*April 23.* The Central Committee passes a resolution on the "recasting of literary and artistic organizations." All existing movements are disbanded. New unions (the Union of Soviet Writers, the Union of Soviet Architects, the Union of Soviet Musicians) are formed and placed under stringent Party control. Conformity to the dogmas of socialist realism becomes obligatory. An institute for the training of young writers is established.

*November 15.* The Museum of the History of Religion and Atheism is opened in the Cathedral of Our Lady of Kazan in Leningrad.

## 1933

The All-Russian Academy of Arts is established in Leningrad. In 1947 it will become the Academy of Arts of the USSR and be moved to Moscow.

Ivan Bunin, an emigré living in Paris, receives the Nobel Prize for literature.

*The Kolkhoz Watchman*, a painting by Sergei Gerasimov. Publication begins of a new *Small Soviet Encyclopedia* (1933–1947); it corrects the first edition (1928–1931), which no longer conforms to the official ideology.

## 1934

The Academy of Sciences is moved from Leningrad to Moscow.

The poet Osip Mandelstam, who had read his anti-Stalin poem to his friends, is arrested. He is sentenced to three years of internal exile.

Films: *Three Songs of Lenin* (Dziga Vertov); *Chapaev* (Georgi and Sergei Vassiliev); *Jolly Fellows* (a musical comedy by Grigori Alexandrov).

*January 1.* The Academy of Architecture of the USSR is established.

*May 15.* The Central Committee and *Sovnarkom* pass a resolution concerning "the teaching of national history in the schools of the USSR." The new policy, a reaction to the historical school of Pokrovsky, will involve the rediscovery of prerevolutionary Russian national history and the rehabilitation of the czarist state. In August Stalin, Zhdanov and Kirov will prepare their "Critical Comments on the Prospectuses for History Textbooks in the USSR," which will be published in 1936.

*August 17–September 1.* The First Congress of the Union of Soviet Writers meets. Foreign writers participate, among them André Malraux and Louis Aragon. The bylaws of the Union are approved. Zhdanov reminds the writers of their obligation to follow the rules of socialist realism. "Fellow travelers" (including Vsevolod Ivanov) engage in self-criticism.

# Chapter 27                               1934–1938

# The Revolution on Trial

Following the assassination of Sergei Kirov in Leningrad on December 1, 1934 (undoubtedly at the instigation of Stalin), a long period of massive and brutal repression and terror began. The most spectacular component of this terror was a series of three "show trials," held from 1936 to 1938, that resulted in the elimination of the most notable representatives of the Bolshevik old guard. Confessions extracted from the accused incriminated them in all kinds of offenses, many of which were completely implausible (plotting against the leadership, maintaining relations with Leon Trotsky, committing treason on behalf of Germany or Japan, sabotaging industry and agriculture). During this same period, another series of secret trials resulted in the elimination of the highest echelons of the Red Army in 1937.

The Party was swept by massive purges at all levels: Anyone who, at one moment or another, had opposed Stalin's policies was ousted. Although the purges facilitated the promotion of new individuals, their own futures remained uncertain because of the climate of constant fear and suspicion in which they operated. Outside of the Party, meanwhile, Soviet society was subjected to a hellish "education." A constant, carefully prepared barrage of propaganda assigned responsibility for all societal problems to a variety of groups (engineers, peasants, writers). Virtually anyone might be swept into the vortex of arrests and speedy trials that almost invariably resulted in death or deportation to a prison camp for a period of forced labor.

Even as the daily practice of institutionalized terror reinforced Stalin's authority, the Constitution of 1936 provided the Soviet Union (the self-proclaimed first "socialist state") with a democratic facade. In addition to affirming the leading role of the Party in Soviet society, the new Constitution enshrined the concept of a centrally planned economy. In essence, the Second and Third Five-Year Plans continued the objectives and methods of the first by emphasizing industrialization and the collectivization of agriculture.

Confident of its economic success, which it loudly proclaimed, the Soviet Union aspired to play a major role in international affairs. Seeking allies against the Nazi threat in Europe and Japanese aggression in Asia, Soviet officials in 1935 had the Comintern adopt a new tactical policy that involved the formation of a "common front" with foreign leftist parties to combat the menace of fascism.

# Politics and Institutions

## 1934

*December 1.* Sergei Kirov is assassinated in Leningrad by the young Communist Leonid Nikolaev. The murder, which is actually committed at the instigation of Stalin, triggers the application of exceptional measures and terror, and sets the stage for an assault on the Party.

On the evening of December 1, a decree is issued accelerating judicial procedure and providing for the immediate imposition of the death penalty for terrorism. During the days that follow, expedited executions of supposed "White Guardists" and political prisoners take place in Leningrad, Moscow and Kiev.

*December 16.* Lev Kamenev and Grigori Zinoviev are arrested. Andrei Zhdanov replaces Kirov as head of the Leningrad Party organization.

*December 20.* The Mordovian Autonomous Soviet Socialist Republic is established.

*December 28.* The Udmurt Autonomous Soviet Socialist Republic is established.

*December 29.* The conviction and execution of Leonid Nikolaev and his "accomplices" is officially announced.

## 1935

*January 15–16.* A nonpublic trial of the "Moscow Center," which is accused of having encouraged the assassination of Kirov, is held. Zinoviev is sentenced to 10 years in prison, Kamenev to 5 years. A wave of arrests and deportations of the last "bourgeois" elements in Leningrad occurs.

*January 26.* The sudden death (officially the result of a heart attack) of Valerian Kuibyshev is announced. The director of Gosplan, he was considered to be a "moderate."

*January 28–February 6.* The Seventh Congress of Soviets meets and approves the drafting of a new constitution for the Soviet Union.

*February 1.* At a plenum of the Central Committee, Anastas Mikoyan and Vlas Chubar are elected full members of the Politburo; Zhdanov and Robert Eikhe are elected candidate members.

*February 23.* Nikolai Yezhov (who had replaced Kirov as secretary on the Central Committee) is named head of the Party's Control Commission.

*March 9.* *Pravda* announces the nomination of Nikita Khrushchev as first secretary of the Moscow Party organization.

*April 8.* Criminal responsibility is extended to children above the age of 12, who are now subject to the death penalty.

*May 25.* The Society of Old Bolsheviks is dissolved. It had criticized the death sentences imposed on "opponents" of the Party.

*June.* Andrei Vyshinsky becomes procurator general of the USSR.

*June 25.* The Society of Former Political Prisoners is dissolved.

*October 20.* The Kalmyk Autonomous Soviet Socialist Republic is established.

## 1936

The Mari, the Komi, the Chechen-Ingush, the North Ossetian and the Kabardino-Balkarian Autonomous Soviet Socialist Republics are established.

*January.* A new purge of the Party begins; an exchange of Party cards is mandated.

*June 12.* A draft of the new Soviet Constitution is published for public comment.

*August 19–24.* The first public show trial is held in Moscow. It is called the "trial of the sixteen," and among the defendants are Zinoviev, Kamenev, Evgeni Evdokimov and Ivan Smirnov. Accused of having formed a "Trotskyite-Zinovievite terrorist center," the 16 defendants confess to having had contact with Leon Trotsky, to participation in the murder of Kirov, and to plots against Stalin and other leaders. The defendants also implicate Nikolai Bukharin, Alexei Rykov and Mikhail Tomsky. Condemned to death, each of the 16 is executed the day after the close of the trial.

*August 23.* Tomsky, the former chairman of the Central Council of Trade Unions, commits suicide.

*September 10.* An investigation of Bukharin and Rykov is declared officially closed after finding "no justification in law" for legal proceedings against them.

*September 22.* Karl Radek is arrested.

*September 25.* In a telegram sent from Stalin's vacation retreat in Sochi, on the Black Sea, Stalin and Zhdanov order the replacement of Genrikh Yagoda as head of the People's Commissariat of Internal Affairs (NKVD) by Nikolai Yezhov. Yezhov's name will be associated with a two-year period of terror (the *Yezhovshchina*).

*November 25–December 5.* The Eighth Congress of Soviets, meeting in an extraordinary session, adopts the new Constitution on December 5. Key provisions of the document include the abolition of restrictions on universal suffrage, guarantees of individual liberties, the affirmation of the leading role of the Party in national life, and the enshrinement of central economic planning and collectivization. The Constitution also assures the equality of the federal republics, which increase in number from seven to 11 (two autonomous republics—Kazakhstan and Kirgizia—are made full federal republics, and Transcaucasia is divided into three separate federal republics—Armenia, Azerbaijan and Georgia). The Constitution also calls for the direct election (every four years) of a Supreme Soviet composed of two chambers: a Soviet of the Union and a Soviet of Nationalities. The president of the Presidium of the Supreme Soviet will be the head of state. Heavy publicity is given to the new Constitution, which Stalin declares to be "the most democratic in the world." The document was drafted under the direction of Bukharin.

## 1937

*January 23–30.* The second Moscow show trial (the "trial of the 17") takes place. The accused include Grigori Piatakov, Radek, Leonid Serebriakov and Grigori Sokolnikov. Charges brought against this "anti-Soviet Trotskyite center" include sabotage, espionage for Germany and Japan, and treason. Confessions secured from the defendants implicate Bukharin and Rykov. The trial results in 13 death sentences (including those of Piatakov and Serebriakov) and four prison terms (including 10 years each for Radek and Sokolnikov).

*February 18.* Sergo Ordzhonikidze dies. His death is officially attributed to a heart attack, but, in reality, he is either a suicide or a victim of murder.

*February 23–March 5.* A plenum of the Central Committee votes to oust Bukharin and Rykov from the Party; they are arrested on February 27. Stalin affirms the necessity of redoubling the struggle against the enemy.

*May.* The position of political commissar is restored in the army (the position had been abolished on March 15, 1934).

*May 31.* General Jan Gamarnik, chief of the Political Administration of the Red Army, commits suicide.

*June 11.* The arrest and conviction, in a secret trial, of eight military leaders accused of treason is announced. (The convictions are based on falsified documents prepared by the NKVD, acting in concert with the German Gestapo.) The condemned include Marshal Mikhail Tukhachevsky, Iona Yakir, Jeromin Uborevich, R. Eideman, August Kork and Vitovt Putna of the Red Army. Word of their execution is made public the next day. In the following months a massive purge of the Soviet armed forces will completely destroy its leadership: Among those executed will be 3 of 5 marshals, all 8 admirals, 14 of 16 army commanders, 90 percent of the corps commanders, and 35,000 out of 80,000 other officers.

*August 15.* The political commissars in the army are placed at the same rank as the military officers. Henceforth, orders are to be signed jointly.

*December 12.* The first elections for the Supreme Soviet are held. The Communist Party and its supporters garner 98.6 percent of the vote.

*December 20–21.* The 20th anniversary of the creation of the state security services is celebrated at the Bolshoi Theater.

*December 31.* A Commissariat of the Navy is established, underlining the new importance accorded to naval forces.

## 1937–1938

*January 1937.* Five million persons are detained in Soviet prisons and labor camps.

*January 1937–December 1938.* Seven million arrests take place and 3 million persons are executed or die in labor camps.

*Late 1938.* Between 5 million and 8 million persons are now detained in Soviet labor camps.

## 1938

*January.* Khrushchev becomes first secretary of the Communist Party of the Ukraine (replacing Stanislav Kossior), and he succeeds Pavel Postyshev as a candidate member of the Politburo.

*January 12–19.* The first session of the new Supreme Soviet is held. Mikhail Kalinin is confirmed as head of state.

*March 2–13.* The third show trial (the "trial of the twenty-one") takes place in Moscow. Among the accused are figures as diverse as the "Rightists" Bukharin and Rykov, the "Trotskyite" Christian Rakovsky and the former director of the NKVD, Genrikh Yagoda. Various charges are lodged against this "Anti-Soviet Bloc of Rightists and Trotskyites," including plotting against Lenin and Stalin, complicity in the murders of Sergei Kirov, Valerian Kuibyshev and Maxim Gorky, and sabotage and treason. All but three are condemned to death and executed (Rakovsky is spared, but he will be shot in October 1941).

*July 20.* Lavrenti Beria is named deputy to Nikolai Yezhov at the NKVD, where he introduces a limited moderation of the terror.

*End of July.* Ianis Rudzutak, a member of the Politburo, is shot following a secret trial.

*October 1.* The *History of the All-Union Communist Party: Short Course* is published. It enshrines the Stalinist dogmas.

*November 23.* A purge of the leadership of Komsomol is announced.

*December 8.* Beria succeeds Yezhov as head of the NKVD. A significant relaxation of the terror follows.

# Foreign Affairs

## 1935

*March 23.* An accord is signed by Japan and the USSR, which sells to Manchukuo its interest in the Chinese Eastern Railway.

*May 2.* A Franco-Soviet mutual assistance pact is signed in Paris. Because of the reservations of French Prime Minister Pierre Laval, the agreement is not accompanied by a military convention.

*May 16.* A Soviet-Czech mutual assistance treaty is signed in Prague. By the terms of the agreement, the obligation of assistance will not be effective unless France respects its own undertakings to assist the parties against aggression.

*July 12.* The USSR establishes diplomatic relations with Belgium.

*July 13.* A commercial accord is concluded with the United States (it will be renewed each year until 1941). The share of goods from the United States in overall Soviet imports will rise from 7.7 percent in 1934 to 28.5 percent in 1938.

*July 25–August 25.* The Seventh (and last) Congress of the Comintern is held. The Congress confirms the tactical policy of forming "popular fronts" that unite all forces of the left against fascism.

## 1936

*January 10.* Vyacheslav Molotov, the head of the Council of People's Commissars, issues a report noting certain passages from Hitler's *Mein Kampf* that advocate German expansion into Russian areas. Five days later, Marshal Tukhachevsky will issue a report warning of the German threat and advocating

the modernization of the Soviet armed forces.

*February–March.* Following a delay, the French Chamber of Deputies and Senate ratify the Franco-Soviet pact.

*March 12.* The USSR and the People's Republic of Mongolia sign a mutual assistance treaty against the Japanese threat.

*July 20.* A new Convention of the Straits is signed at Montreux. Under the terms of the agreement, Turkey is granted sovereignty over the Bosporus and the Dardanelles, the free passage of commercial vessels is guaranteed in peacetime, and limitations are placed on the tonnage of warships passing through the Straits.

*August.* The USSR officially adheres to the policy advocated by France of nonintervention in the Spanish Civil War.

*October 23.* Ivan Maisky, the Soviet ambassador to London, protests against the assistance being given by Germany and Italy to Francisco Franco's nationalist insurgents in Spain. Maisky declares that the USSR no longer considers itself bound by the policy of nonintervention. The Soviet Union will begin to send war matériel and military advisors to the forces supporting Spain's government. Soviet citizens will not participate in the International Brigades, however, and the aid to Republican forces will be accompanied by a merciless struggle against Trotskyites and anarchists in Spain.

*November 26.* An anti-Comintern agreement is signed by Germany and Japan. The agreement includes a secret protocol directed against the USSR.

The Soviet Union achieves a rapprochement with the Chiang Kai-shek government in China.

## 1937

Soviet intelligence services strike outside of the country's borders: The White general Evgeni Miller is abducted in Paris, and former NKVD agent Ignace Reiss is murdered in Switzerland.

*July.* The USSR calls on the Chinese Communists to join with the Kuomintang in resisting Japanese aggression.

*August 21.* The Soviet Union signs a five-year nonaggression pact with China. Under the terms of the pact, the USSR agrees to supply war matériel to the Chinese.

## 1938

The Polish Communist Party is dissolved by the Comintern. A number of that Party's leaders who had taken refuge in the USSR disappear in prisons or in labor camps.

*March 1.* The Soviet Union and Germany agree to extend their commercial accord of December 24, 1936.

*March 15.* The USSR protests against the *Anschluss* (the German takeover of Austria on March 11–13).

*July 29–August 11.* Armed conflict breaks out between the USSR and Japan at Lake Khanka, on the border between Manchukuo and Russia in the Far East.

*September.* In the course of the crisis over the Sudetenland, the USSR declares itself ready to fulfill its obligations with respect to Czechoslovakia. (Since May, however, Soviet authorities have been noting the problem posed by their troops having to pass through Polish or Romanian territory to reach Czechoslovakia.)

*September 29–30.* The Munich Conference is held (neither Czechoslovakia nor the Soviet Union is invited to participate). An accord is reached between Germany, Italy, France and Great Britain on the annexation of the Sudetenland

by Germany. On October 2 the USSR will protest against both France's failure to live up to its agreements and Poland's occupation of the Teschen (Cieszyn) region of Czechoslovakia.

# Economy and Society

## 1935

*January 1.* Ration cards for bread and flour are abolished. A large increase in the price of these items will occur.

*February 17.* A new statute on kolkhozes is adopted by the Second Congress of Kolkhoznik Shock Brigades. The statute establishes the following limits on the "small individual cultivation" permitted to kolkhozniks: one plot of land of 2,500 to 5,000 square meters, one cow, two calves, one sow and her young, 10 lambs and goats, and as many chickens and rabbits as desired.

*May 4.* Stalin puts forward the formula, "the cadres decide all."

*May 15.* The first line of the Moscow subway goes into service.

*July 10.* A resolution is adopted by the Central Committee and by *Sovnarkom* on the redevelopment of Moscow.

*Night of August 30–31.* At the Irmino mine in the Donets River region, Alexei Stakhanov mines 102 tons of coal (14 times the norm). This exploit will inspire the "Stakhanovite Movement," which is aimed at promoting the "rational" use of human and technical resources, and lead to the imposition of ever higher production goals. (Stakhanov's "exploit" will eventually be viewed with suspicion in the Soviet press.)

*September 3.* A new law on schools increases the authority of the schoolmaster and strengthens discipline.

*September 22.* Ranks are reestablished in the Red Army. (The five top marshals are Kliment Voroshilov, Mikhail Tukhachevsky, Alexander Egorov, Vassili Blücher and Semyon Budenny.)

*September 29.* Consumer cooperatives in the cities are abolished in favor of state stores.

*October 1.* Ration cards are abolished for meat, fat, fish, sugar and potatoes. The regulated prices of these items rise to the free-market level.

*November 14–17.* The First Congress of Stakhanovite Workers of the USSR opens in Moscow. On November 17 Stalin gives a speech in which he says, "Life today is better, comrades. Life has become more joyous."

*November 25.* A new order, the Insignia of Honor, is created.

*December 30.* Limitations on access to higher education based on social origin are ended.

## 1936

*April 1.* A devaluation of the ruble occurs. The value of the ruble is no longer fixed in relation to the dollar but in relation to the French franc (3 francs to the ruble). In 1937, the value of the ruble will once again be pegged to the dollar (5.30 rubles to the dollar).

*June 27.* In an effort to rehabilitate the role of the traditional family in Soviet life, abortions, which had been legalized by a decree of November 18, 1920, are now banned. Maternity aid is instituted, and divorce is discouraged.

## 1937

The rate of industrial growth declines sharply.

*January 6.* A census is taken. The results, which reveal a large-scale loss of population, are not made public.

*April 1.* The Second Five-Year Plan is declared to have been achieved

in four years and three months. Production has risen by 137 percent in heavy industry (but objectives have not been met with respect to coal and cast iron), and by 100 percent in consumer goods. The number of kolkhozes reaches 240,000 (93 percent of cultivated land); there are 4,000 sovkhozes and 5,000 Machine Tractor Stations (MTS). Grain production shows some improvement.

*April 28. Sovnarkom* adopts a resolution on the Third Five-Year Plan.

*June 18–20.* The Soviet aviator Valeri Chkalov flies nonstop from Moscow to Vancouver, Washington.

*July 15.* The Moscow-Volga Canal opens.

## 1938

*January 1.* The Third Five-Year Plan (1938–1942) officially begins. Among its objectives are a 92 percent increase in industrial production and a 52 percent rise in agricultural production. Emphasis is placed on the development of modern sectors of the economy (aluminum, chemicals, electronic equipment). Even before it is interrupted by the war in 1941, the Plan will be adversely affected by domestic crises (the purges and the terror) and by the foreign situation (which requires a growing emphasis on military preparedness).

*March 13.* A decree mandates the teaching of Russian in all of the schools of the non-Russian republics.

*September 5.* A new law on higher educational institutions is adopted.

*December 20.* The workbook requirement is made universal; this places even greater limitations on the freedom of movement of workers.

*December 27.* The honor "Hero of Socialist Labor" is created.

*December 28.* A decree is issued to strengthen work discipline: The mobility of workers is discouraged by the elimination of the social advantages (such as better housing) gained by changing jobs.

# Civilization and Culture

## 1934

*December 20.* The linguist Nikolai Marr dies. His theory, which views language as a class phenomenon, will dominate Soviet linguistics until 1950.

## 1935

Anna Akhmatova begins to write her poem *Requiem* (1935–1940).

*March 7.* A circular orders the removal of the works of Trotsky, Zinoviev and Kamenev from the shelves of all libraries. Some months later, the works of Evgeni Preobrazhensky, Alexander Shliapnikov, Anatoli Lunacharsky and several others are added to the list.

## 1936

*January–March.* Violent attacks are made against artists who fail to conform completely with official directives. Those attacked include Dmitri Shostakovich (for his opera *Katerina Izmailovna*) and Mikhail Bulgakov (for his play *Molière*, which is performed at the Moscow Art Theater but then quickly banned by the authorities).

*May 15.* The Central Lenin Museum opens in Moscow.

*June 18.* Maxim Gorky dies under circumstances that remain mysterious to this day. André Gide, on a visit to the Soviet Union, delivers a eulogy at Gorky's funeral in Red Square.

## 1937

A solemn celebration is held on the 125th anniversary of the Battle of Borodino. A new history textbook manifests the rehabilitation of "national history" by presenting czarist colonization in a more positive light.

The arts and the sciences are strongly affected by the Stalinist terror. The writer Boris Pilnyak is arrested and disappears. *Bread,* a novel glorifying Stalin, by Alexei Tolstoy. *Lenin in October,* a film by Mikhail Romm. *Worker and the Collective Farm Girl,* a monumental sculpture for the Soviet Pavilion at the Universal Exposition in Paris, by Vera Mukhina. The writer Alexander Kuprin returns to the Soviet Union (he had emigrated following the October Revolution).

## 1938

The theater of Vsevolod Meyerhold is closed following his denunciation of Stalinist policies on the arts. Arrested and accused of espionage in 1939, Meyerhold will be executed in 1940.

*Alexander Nevsky,* a film by Sergei Eisenstein, opens. The film illustrates the return to a positive appreciation of great figures from Russian history. The musical score is by Sergei Prokofiev, who returned to the USSR in 1932.

Mark Donskoi begins bringing a trilogy about Maxim Gorky to the screen (*Childhood of Gorky,* in 1938; *Among People,* in 1939; and *My Universities,* in 1940). *Stalin and Voroshilov at the Kremlin,* a painting by Alexander Gerasimov.

Libraries are purged of all books deemed harmful to the state and to Soviet society.

*May.* Osip Mandelstam is arrested again. He will die on December 27 in a transit camp in the Soviet Far East.

# Chapter 28    1939–1945

# The Second World War

After the Munich Agreement of 1938, Stalin broke with the policy of collective security promoted by his minister of foreign affairs, Maxim Litvinov. In May 1939 Stalin replaced Litvinov with Vyacheslav Molotov, and on August 23 Stalin concluded the German-Soviet Pact. This treaty of "nonaggression" was complemented by a secret protocol that divided eastern Europe into spheres of influence and allowed Russia to annex eastern Poland, Karelia, the Baltic states, Bessarabia and Northern Bukovina in the months that followed.

The German-Soviet Pact did provide the Soviet Union with a needed respite from conflict. During that period, however, efforts to reorganize the army (which had been decimated by the purges) and to build up Soviet military strength could not compensate for the shockingly poor state of the country's defenses. On June 22, 1941, the Soviet Union was invaded by German forces greatly superior in determination and matériel. Within a few months, the German Blitzkrieg had brought the enemy to the gates of Leningrad and Moscow as well as to the outskirts of Kiev, where it then stalled. In 1942 Germany resumed its offensive in the direction of the Caucasus and the Volga.

Despite the difficult situation, Soviet leaders eventually succeeded in mobilizing all of the country's spiritual, human and material resources in a great burst of national unity. Stalin, who helped lead this effort, took the title of supreme commander and, before long, that of marshal. The German attack also brought the USSR out of its international isolation. Although the British and the Americans supplied the Soviet Union with weapons and matériel, Stalin waited impatiently for the Allies to open a second front in Europe.

The Battle of Stalingrad, which lasted from July 1942 to February 1943, marked the end of the German advance. Taking the initiative, the Red Army advanced through eastern and central Europe and captured Berlin just prior to the German capitulation in May 1945. Confident of its strength, the USSR participated in international conferences that set the conditions for peace and postwar reconstruction. By war's end, the new lines dividing Europe had already been drawn.

# Politics and Institutions

## 1939

*February 23.* Red Army Day is celebrated. Soldiers take a new patriotic oath of loyalty.

*March 10–21.* The Eighteenth Party Congress is held. Only 59 delegates from the previous Congress participate (1,108 out of 1,966 had been arrested). Andrei Zhdanov calls for an end to the massive purification drive, and a new recruitment campaign is launched with great success (the Party's ranks will increase from 2,307,000 members and candidate members in January 1939, to 3.4 million in January 1940). New bylaws are adopted. Central planning and the Party's control of economic life is strengthened.

Zhdanov and Nikita Khrushchev become full members of the Politburo, while Nikolai Shvernik and Lavrenti Beria become candidate members. In the Secretariat, Zhdanov is placed in charge of agitprop, and Georgi Malenkov is charged with directing the administration of cadres.

*September 1.* A law mandating universal military service is promulgated. The draft age is lowered to 19 years (18 years for secondary-school graduates), and the length of service is extended to 3 years (5 years in the navy).

*December 21.* Extravagant celebrations occur on the 60th birthday of Stalin.

## 1940

*August 13.* Political commissars in the army are replaced by adjunct commanders for political affairs.

## 1941

*February 3.* The security functions of the NKVD are transferred to a new organ, the NKGB (People's Commissariat for State Security).

*February 15–20.* The Eighteenth Communist Party Conference convenes. Nikolai Voznesensky, Malenkov and Alexander Shcherbakov are made members of the Politburo.

*May 6.* Stalin becomes chairman of the Council of People's Commissars, replacing Molotov, who becomes vice chairman of the Council and commissar for foreign affairs. Stalin is now head of government as well as general secretary of the Party.

*June 30.* A State Committee for Defense (GKO) is created. It is presided over by Stalin and includes Molotov, Beria, Malenkov and Marshal Kliment Voroshilov. The Committee will exercise absolute authority over Party organizations, the government and the army.

*July 3.* Stalin makes his first radio broadcast since the German invasion on June 22 (when he dropped from public view). Adopting a different tone, he appeals to the patriotism of the population.

*July 16.* Political commissars are reintroduced into the army.

*July 19.* Stalin becomes people's commissar for defense.

*August 8.* Stalin becomes supreme commander of the armed forces.

*August 28.* The Volga Germans are ordered deported to the eastern USSR, and their Autonomous Republic is dissolved.

*October 19.* Faced with the German advance, authorities declare a state of siege in Moscow. The government and the diplomatic corps are evacuated to Kuibyshev. Stalin remains in the Kremlin.

# World War II in Eastern Europe

North Sea

Baltic Sea

Danzig (GERMANY)

SOVIET UNION (1941)

POLAND (1939)

GERMANY (1939)

FRANCE

SLOVAKIA (1939)

HUNGARY (1941)

ROMANIA (1941)

YUGOSLAVIA (1941)

Black Sea

ITALY

Adriatic Sea

BULGARIA (1941)

ALBANIA (1941)

GREECE

TURKEY

Mediterranean Sea

Allied countries

Axis countries that became Allied countries

Axis countries

(1939) Date entered war

*November 7.* Addressing a military procession on Red Square, Stalin makes an appeal to Russian nationalism.

## 1942

*August 26.* General Georgi Zhukov becomes assistant to the supreme commander.

*October 9.* Unity of command is restored in the army: Political commissars are again replaced by adjunct commanders for political affairs.

## 1943

*March 7.* Stalin is named marshal by the Supreme Soviet.

*November.* Stalin again stresses the role of the Party as the organizer of the armed struggle and the inspiration for a future victory.

*Late 1943–Early 1944.* Having been accused of collaborating with the enemy, the Karachai and the Kalmyks are deported. The Karachai Autonomous Region and the Kalmyk Autonomous Republic are dissolved.

## 1944

*January 28–February 1.* A session of the Supreme Soviet is held. In each republic, a People's Commissariat for Defense and a People's Commissariat for Foreign Affairs is created.

*February 23.* Accused of collaboration with the enemy, the Chechens and the Ingush are deported, and their Autonomous Republic is dissolved.

*March 8.* The collective deportation of the Balkars is carried out.

*May 17–18.* The Crimean Tatars, accused of collaboration with the enemy, are deported to Kazakhstan and Central Asia, and their Autonomous Republic is dissolved.

*November 15.* The collective deportation of the Meskhetians is carried out.

## 1945

*June 24.* A great victory parade is held in Moscow. Homage is paid to the Russian nation.

*June 28.* Stalin is named generalissimo by the Supreme Soviet.

# Economy and Society

## 1939

The Bolshoi (Great) Fergana Canal is constructed.

*January.* A census is taken. The total population of the Soviet Union is set at 170.6 million, of which 33 percent live in urban areas. The total, although probably inflated, still bears witness to a veritable demographic catastrophe.

*March 10–21.* The Third Five-Year Plan is adopted by the Eighteenth Party Congress. The Congress declares that the impending completion of the task of building a socialist society will permit the gradual passage from socialism to communism.

*August 1.* The All-Soviet Agricultural exhibition is opened in Moscow.

## 1940

*May 7.* Diplomatic titles and the military ranks of general and admiral are reestablished.

*June 26.* A decree extends the workday to eight hours, and the workweek to six days. Unjustifiable absences are punishable by two to four months of forced labor in a prison camp. Workers are denied the right to freely change their employment. A decline in the quality of production can result in a trial before a government tribunal.

*Early September.* Soviet authorities threaten to suspend delivery of raw materials to Germany if that country does not speed up its delivery of industrial goods to the USSR.

*October 2.* Tuition exemptions are abolished in institutions of higher learning.

## 1941

The antireligion campaign is softened.

*February 15–20.* The Eighteenth Party Conference modifies the Third Five-Year Plan in order to accelerate the development of military capability.

*June 22.* On the same day as the German invasion, Metropolitan Sergius addresses a patriotic message to all Orthodox parishes.

*June 24.* A Council of Evacuation is created. From July to November, more than 1,500 enterprises will be transferred from the western regions to the Urals, western Siberia, Central Asia and Kazakhstan. In 1942, the Ural region will produce 40 percent of Soviet armaments.

*July.* Ration cards are introduced in Moscow and Leningrad.

*August 16.* A plan for a war economy is drawn up, covering the last quarter of 1941 and the year 1942.

*November.* Industrial production stands at 52 percent of the level achieved in November 1940. Under the German occupation, several categories of production suffer sharp drops, including coal (63 percent), iron (68 percent), steel (58 percent), railroad track (41 percent) and grain (38 percent).

## 1942

*February 13.* The urban population is mobilized to assist in production and construction.

*April 13.* The nonagricultural population is mobilized for the harvest.

*June.* A Muslim congress in Ufa calls for a struggle against fascism.

## 1943

*February 6.* Construction of a metallurgical complex in Chelyabinsk is completed.

*May 26.* The State Committee for Defense calls for the reconstruction of the railroads in the liberated territories.

*June 5.* The Council of People's Commissars floats a loan of 12 billion rubles.

*September 4.* Stalin receives Metropolitan Sergius and approves a meeting of a Church council to elect Sergius to the vacant patriarchal seat. The Depart-

ment for the Affairs of the Russian Orthodox Church is created.

*December 22.* The Council of People's Commissars approves a new patriotic national anthem to replace the "Internationale."

## 1944

*May 5.* A new war loan of 25 billion rubles is announced.

*May 15.* Patriarch Sergius dies. Funeral services will be held nationwide on May 18.

*May 19.* The Department for the Affairs of Non-Orthodox Sects is created.

*July 8.* New family legislation is issued: Divorce is made more difficult and costly; the principle of illegitimate birth is reestablished; and family allowances are increased while a tax is placed on unmarried persons.

## 1945

Pilgrimages to Mecca are permitted to resume.

*February 2.* Metropolitan Alexis of Leningrad is elected patriarch. A church council approves the *Regulation for the Administration of the Church*, which was drawn up by the Department for the Affairs of the Russian Orthodox Church.

*June 23.* A law is promulgated on the demobilization of the older members of the armed forces.

*August.* Churches are authorized to acquire buildings and sacred objects.

*August 19.* Gosplan is charged with the development of the Fourth Five-Year Plan for the recovery of the national economy (1946–1950).

The costs of the war: The death toll in the Soviet Union is set at 20 million persons; nearly half of these are civilians. (The official figure was recently revised to 27 million.) A large part of the country's economic infrastructure is destroyed. All indexes of production show a sharp decline at the end of the war (1940=100): agriculture (60), oil (62), iron ore (52), cast iron (59), cement (31). The number of homeless is estimated to be 25 million.

# Foreign Affairs and War Chronology

## 1939

*March 10.* Stalin declares at the Eighteenth Party Congress that the USSR will not allow itself to be drawn into a conflict that will benefit the big capitalist powers.

*April 17.* The USSR proposes a pact of mutual assistance to France and England; the agreement would include assurances with respect to the eastern European states that border on the USSR. Negotiations will continue until August.

*May 3.* The people's commissar for foreign affairs, Maxim Litvinov, is replaced by Vyacheslav Molotov. The attempt to work out a collective security arrangement is abandoned.

*May 11–September 16.* The Soviets and the Japanese clash in Mongolia. Zhukov scores a victory on the Khalka-Gol River in Mongolia on August 20.

*May 20.* Molotov meets with the German ambassador Friedrich von Schulenburg and conveys to him the Soviet desire for an improvement in relations between the two countries.

*July 24.* The British and the French agree to discuss a military convention with the USSR. At the same time, German-Soviet commercial negotiations are proceeding in Berlin.

*August 12–23.* French and British military delegations hold talks with Soviet officials in Moscow. The negotia-

tions break down when the USSR insists on the right of passage through Poland for the Red Army if conflict breaks out.

*August 19.* A commercial and credit agreement between the USSR and Germany is signed in Berlin.

*August 22.* The French government makes known its assent to the passage of the Red Army through Poland, despite Polish objections. The commissar for defense, Kliment Voroshilov, refuses to consider the new French position.

*August 23.* German Foreign Minister Joachim von Ribbentrop arrives in Moscow with full power to enter into an agreement. In the early hours of August 24, Molotov and Ribbentrop sign a Nazi-Soviet nonaggression pact. The agreement, which is published the next day and takes effect immediately is to remain in force for 10 years. It is accompanied by a secret protocol, the existence of which the USSR will deny for 50 years. The protocol divides eastern Europe into spheres of influence: Western Poland and Lithuania are accorded to Germany, while Finland, Estonia, Latvia and eastern Poland go to the USSR. The Soviet Union also gains confirmation of its interests in Bessarabia.

*September 3.* Following Germany's invasion of Poland, France and Great Britain declare war on Germany. The USSR, despite its promise of neutrality, will provide logistical support to Germany during the succeeding months.

*September 15.* An armistice is signed between the USSR, Japan and Mongolia.

*September 17.* The Red Army invades eastern Poland.

*September 28.* Molotov and Ribbentrop sign a treaty in Moscow on the demarcation of borders and on friendship. Secret protocols are also signed:

The line of demarcation between the Soviet and German spheres of influence is moved eastward toward the Bug River, Lithuania is transferred to the Soviet sphere, and Germany and the USSR coordinate their repression of the Polish resistance.

Under Soviet pressure, Estonia agrees to an "assistance pact" and cedes military bases to the USSR. Similar pacts will be signed with Latvia (October 5) and Lithuania (October 10).

*October 12.* The Soviet Union makes its demands known to Finland: The border is to be pushed back 42 miles from Leningrad, and the military base at Hangö (which controls entry into the Gulf of Finland), as well as the territories in the extreme north around Petsamo, are to be transferred to the Soviet Union.

*October 24.* The USSR agrees to provide grain, oil and other raw materials to Germany.

*October 27.* The Soviets cede Vilna to the Lithuanians.

*November 1.* The Supreme Soviet approves the annexation of the western Ukraine (and western Belorussia on November 2.) Soviet authorities organize a systematic deportation of Polish elites (as well as of many Ukrainians and Belorussians) to the eastern USSR. In addition to the 230,000 Polish prisoners of war, the Soviets will deport more than 1 million civilians between October 1939 and June 1941.

*November 30.* The "Winter War" begins: The USSR launches a military campaign against Finland, which refused to give in to the Soviet demands made in October. The Soviets profess support for a "People's Republic of Finland" led by the Finnish Communist Otto Kuusinen.

*December 14.* The USSR is expelled from the League of Nations for its aggression against Finland. Soviet forces bomb Helsinki.

## 1940

*February 11.* A German-Soviet commercial treaty is signed. From 1939 to 1940, the value of Soviet exports to the Third Reich will increase from 61.6 million rubles to 736.5 million rubles.

*March 12.* A treaty between the USSR and Finland is signed in Moscow. Finland cedes the Isthmus of Karelia and the city of Vyborg, and leases the Hangö base to the Soviets for 30 years. On March 31, the Autonomous Republic of Karelia will become the Karelian-Finnish Soviet Socialist Republic.

*May 10.* On the announcement of Hitler's attack on Holland, Belgium and Luxembourg, Molotov proclaims his confidence in the Germans' success.

*June 14–16.* The USSR issues an ultimatum to the three Baltic states. It reinforces its military presence in the Baltic states and moves to establish pro-Soviet governments, which will shortly be imposed by Soviet troops and commissars (June 17–21).

*June 24.* Diplomatic relations are established with Yugoslavia.

*June 26.* A Soviet ultimatum to Romania calls on that country to abandon Bessarabia and Northern Bukovina. These territories will be occupied by the Red Army on June 28.

*July 21.* The Baltic states become the Soviet Socialist Republics of Latvia, Lithuania and Estonia.

*July 31.* Having decided to attack the USSR, Hitler asks that an invasion plan be drawn up.

*August 2.* The Autonomous Soviet Socialist Republic of Moldavia annexes a

large part of Bessarabia, creating the Soviet Socialist Republic of Moldavia.

*August 3–6.* The USSR annexes the
Soviet Socialist Republics of Lithuania
(August 3), Latvia (August 5) and Estonia
(August 6).

The annexations of 1939–1940 increase the Soviet population by more
than 23 million.

*August 20.* Leon Trotsky is mortally
wounded in Mexico by Stalin's agent,
Ramon Mercader. Trotsky will die the
next day.

*September 27.* Molotov declares that
the Tripartite Pact, a military assistance
treaty signed by Germany, Italy and
Japan the previous day, does not affect
their relations with the USSR.

*November 12–13.* Molotov and Hitler hold talks in Berlin. Ribbentrop proposes that the USSR join the Tripartite
Pact.

*November 25.* The Soviet government sends a note to the German government stating its conditions for
joining the Tripartite Pact.

*December 18.* Hitler's "Directive No.
21" fixes May 15, 1941, as the date for
the launching of Operation Barbarossa,
a surprise attack on the USSR.

## 1941

*January 10.* A major agreement on
economic cooperation is signed by the
USSR and Germany.

*February 3.* The German High
Command finalizes plans for a massive
war effort directed toward the east.

*April 5.* A treaty of nonaggression
and friendship is signed by the USSR
and Yugoslavia. (Yugoslavia will be attacked by Germany the next day.)

*April 13.* A treaty of neutrality
signed with Japan guarantees borders in
the Far East.

*April 30.* With his forces engaged in
Yugoslavia and in Greece, Hitler must
postpone his planned offensive against
the Soviet Union by five weeks.

*May–June.* Reports of German plans
for an imminent attack multiply.

*June 6.* In preparation for their invasion of the Soviet Union, German authorities issue the "Decree of the
Commissars," which provides for the
immediate execution of political commissars who are captured.

Soviet authorities begin deporting a
large number of Lithuanian elites to the
east. Similar deportations from Latvia
and Estonia will begin on June 14.

*June 14.* TASS issues a statement denouncing the "rumors" of a possible
German attack against the USSR.

*June 21.* The Soviet ambassador in
Berlin protests 180 German violations of
Soviet airspace.

*June 22.* Just after 3:00 A.M., Operation Barbarossa, the invasion of the Soviet Union by the German *Wehrmacht*,
begins. Benefiting from the element of
surprise and from their superiority in
men and matériel, the Germans and
their allies will quickly occupy Latvia,
Lithuania, Belorussia and the western
Ukraine to Zhitomir, and take hundreds
of thousands of prisoners.

Prime Minister Winston Churchill of
Great Britain makes a radio speech offering aid to the USSR.

*June 22–27.* Romania, Italy,
Slovakia, Finland and Hungary enter the
war against the Soviet Union.

*June 24.* President Franklin Roosevelt hints at the possibility of American
aid to the Soviets.

*June 30.* Diplomatic relations between the USSR and Vichy France are
broken off.

234

*July 12.* The Soviets and the British sign a treaty of cooperation that prohibits either side from concluding a separate peace or armistice.

*July 16.* The Germans reach Smolensk.

*July 17.* The Germans create a Reich Ministry for the Eastern Occupied Territories and place it under the control of Alfred Rosenberg. The territories are organized into two commissariats (Ostland and the Ukraine). The occupation forces subject the civilian populace to arrests, executions, destruction of villages, forced labor and deportations.

Diplomatic relations are reestablished between the USSR and the Yugoslav government in exile in London.

*July 18.* A treaty of mutual assistance is signed by the Soviet Union and the Czech government in exile in London.

*July 30.* The Soviet Union establishes diplomatic relations with the Polish government in exile in London. A treaty of cooperation and a military agreement (signed on August 14) clear the way for the Poles to organize an army (the "Anders army," named after General Wladyslaw Anders) made up of former prisoners of war on Soviet territory.

*Early August.* German forces begin to push north toward Leningrad, east toward Moscow and southeast toward the Crimea and the Donets basin.

*August 10.* German operations against Odessa begin. The city will be evacuated by the Red Army on October 16.

*August 16.* A commerce and credit accord is signed with England.

*August 25.* Soviet and British troops enter Iran; in September, it will be divided into two occupation zones.

*September 8.* The Red Army loses Schlüsselburg.

The siege of Leningrad begins; it will last until January 1944.

*September 19.* Kiev falls.

*September 24.* The USSR accepts the principles of the Atlantic Charter.

*September 29–30.* German *Einsatzgruppen* massacre more than 33,000 Jews at Babi Yar, near Kiev.

*September 29–October 1.* A conference is held between the USSR, Great Britain and the United States in Moscow. A tripartite accord is reached on the war matériel to be delivered to the USSR up to June 30, 1942. The United States grants the Soviet Union a $1 billion credit for the year 1942.

*September 30.* The Battle of Moscow begins. The German offensive (Operation Typhoon), launched on October 2, will threaten the city but then stall.

*October 24.* Kharkov falls.

*October 30.* The siege of Sevastopol begins. The city will fall on July 4, 1942.

*November 15.* The second German offensive against Moscow begins.

*November 17–21.* Rostov-on-Don falls. The city will be retaken by the Red Army on November 29; this will temporarily close off German access to the Caucasus.

*December 5–6.* The Soviet counteroffensive at Moscow begins.

*December 16–17.* Soviet-British talks are held in Moscow (the "Eden mission," named after Foreign Minister Anthony Eden).

*Late December.* By the end of 1941, more than 2 million Soviets are held as prisoners of war.

## 1942

*January.* A Soviet counteroffensive liberates the Moscow region.

*January 1.* In Washington, the USSR signs a declaration affirming the principles of the Atlantic Charter.

*January 29.* An alliance is entered into by Great Britain, the Soviet Union and Iran.

*April 5.* Hitler issues a directive on the summer offensives for 1942. His primary objective is the oilfields of the Caucasus.

*May 8.* A German offensive in the Crimea is launched.

*May 9–28.* A Soviet offensive to retake Kharkov is repulsed.

*May 26.* Molotov is in London, where a 20-year treaty of alliance and friendship is signed with Great Britain. The USSR issues a strong appeal for the early opening of a second front.

*May 30.* A central staff for partisan forces is formed. The resistance movement, which has been particularly active in Belorussia since the autumn of 1941, in 1942–1944 will spread through a large portion of occupied territory.

*June 11.* An accord is signed in Washington by the Soviet Union and the United States. The agreement provides for mutual aid during the war and for cooperation in the postwar period.

*June 28.* A major summer offensive is launched by the Germans. Its key objectives are the Volga region (where the Battle of Stalingrad will take place from July 17, 1942, to February 2, 1943) and the oil wells of the Caucasus.

*July 28.* The Soviet High Command issues an order declaring "Not a single step backward."

*August 21.* The Swastika flies over Mount Elbrus, the highest point in the Caucasus.

*August 25.* A state of siege is proclaimed in Stalingrad. After vicious street fighting, the German Sixth Army under General Friedrich von Paulus will gain control of a large part of the city by mid-November, without, however, succeeding in conquering the Volga region.

*November 19.* The Soviet counteroffensive at Stalingrad begins. Moving in from the north, the forces of General Konstantin Rokossovsky and General Nikolai Vatutin converge on the Don with the forces of General Andrei Yeremenko from the south. On November 22, Soviet forces encircle the German Sixth Army.

*December.* A German counteroffensive led by Field Marshal Erich von Manstein is thrown back at Stalingrad.

## 1943

*January.* German forces retreat from the Caucasus. Hitler forbids the army of General von Paulus in Stalingrad to surrender, even though the army is being slowly decimated by Soviet attacks and by famine.

*January 12–18.* The blockade of Leningrad is eased somewhat when the Soviets retake Schlüsselburg on January 18.

*January 31–February 2.* General von Paulus capitulates at Stalingrad. Germans taken prisoner include 91,000 soldiers, 24 generals and 2,500 other officers. The episode is greeted with enormous elation abroad.

*February 9.* Churchill informs Stalin that the opening of a second front in Europe has been postponed to the summer of 1944. Relations between the USSR and its western allies enter a period of crisis.

*February–March.* The Soviets take Kursk (February 8), Rostov (February 14) and Kharkov (February 16); a German counteroffensive will retake Kharkov on March 14.

*April 13.* Germany announces the discovery at Katyn, near Smolensk, of the buried corpses of 4,000 Polish officers executed by the NKVD in 1940. The USSR accuses Germany of the massacre and uses the occasion to break diplomatic relations with the Polish government in exile.

*May 15.* The Communist International (Comintern) is dissolved to reassure the Allies of the USSR's new policy of not fomenting revolutions abroad. Moscow continues, however, to support Communists in central and eastern Europe.

*July 5–13.* The Battle of Kursk (Operation Citadel) takes place.

*July–December.* A series of offensives takes the Red Army to the banks of the Dnieper.

*August 26.* The USSR recognizes General Charles de Gaulle's French Committee of National Liberation.

*October 19–30.* In Moscow, the foreign ministers of the Soviet Union, Great Britain and the United States (Molotov, Anthony Eden and Cordell Hull, respectively) agree to continue the war until the capitulation of Germany.

*November 28–December 1.* The Teheran Conference is held. Roosevelt, Churchill and Stalin attend. The decision to open a second front in France in May 1944 is confirmed. Discussions are held on the creation of a United Nations Organization, on the future of Germany, and on moving Polish borders westward.

*December 12.* In Moscow, the Soviets sign a treaty of mutual assistance and cooperation with the Czechs.

*December 15.* The USSR breaks off relations with the Yugoslav government in exile and recognizes Josif Tito's Committee of National Liberation.

## 1944

*January 4.* The Red Army reaches the former (1939) Polish border at Sarny.

*January 15.* Russian forces begin to break out of Leningrad.

*January 20.* Novgorod is retaken.

*January 27–February 1.* The siege of Leningrad ends.

*February–March.* A Soviet spring offensive is launched. The Red Army liberates the Ukraine west of the Dnieper, the Dniester and the Pruth rivers are crossed, and Chernovtsy is taken on March 30.

*April 7–May 12.* The Crimea is retaken.

*April 10.* Odessa is liberated.

*June 9.* A Soviet offensive is launched in Karelia. Vyborg will be retaken on June 20.

*June 22.* A Soviet offensive is launched in Belorussia; Minsk will be retaken on July 3.

*July.* Vilna is taken on July 13, Bialystok on July 18, and Lublin (where a Polish National Liberation Committee is set up with support from Moscow) on July 22–24. In the liberated Polish territories, adherents of the Home Army are systematically arrested, deported or incorporated into General Zygmunt Berling's army, which is under Soviet control.

*August 1–October 2.* An insurrection in Warsaw is launched. The uprising, directed by the Polish non-Communist resistance, is crushed by the Germans. Soviet forces arrive in mid-September on the eastern banks of the Vistula, on the outskirts of the city, but do not come to the aid of the insurgents.

*August 20.* The Soviets launch an offensive against Romania. On August 23 King Michael will have the dictator Ion Antonescu arrested. A coalition government will be formed and will enter the war against Germany. The Red Army will arrive in Bucharest on August 31.

*August 21–September 28.* In Washington, the USSR participates in the talks at Dumbarton Oaks that lay the groundwork for the future United Nations.

*September 5.* The USSR declares war on Bulgaria.

*September 12.* Romania signs an armistice with the USSR, England and the United States.

*September 16.* Soviet troops enter Sofia, Bulgaria's capital.

*September 19.* Finland signs an armistice with the USSR and England. The Finns agree to cede Petsamo to the USSR and to pay war reparations.

*October 9–18.* Stalin and Churchill meet in Moscow, where they carve out spheres of influence in the Danube and Balkan regions. The USSR is accorded influence in 90 percent of Romania, 75 percent of Bulgaria, 50 percent of Hungary and of Yugoslavia, and 10 percent of Greece.

*October 11–13.* The USSR annexes the Tuva region in Asia.

*October 13.* Riga is retaken.

*October 20.* Belgrade is liberated by Tito's partisans and by Soviet troops.

*October 23.* The USSR, the United States, and England recognize the provisional government of the French republic.

*October 25.* Diplomatic relations are reestablished with Italy.

*October 28.* Bulgaria signs an armistice with the USSR, the United States and Great Britain.

*November 14.* In Czechoslovakia, the Soviet general Andrei Vlasov, who was captured by the Germans in 1942, agrees to cooperate with the Nazis. He issues an appeal (the "Prague Manifesto.") for a struggle against "Stalinist tyranny."

Vlasov also organizes a Russian Liberation Army.

*December.* A Soviet offensive is launched in Hungary; Budapest is encircled.

*December 10.* In Moscow, France and the Soviet Union sign a 20-year treaty of alliance and cooperation.

## 1945

*January 4.* The USSR recognizes the provisional government of the Polish republic, which is dominated by Communists and is hostile to the government in exile in London.

*January 12.* A new, large-scale Soviet winter offensive is launched in the direction of eastern Prussia, western Poland and Silesia.

*January 17.* Warsaw is taken.

*January 20.* An armistice is signed with Hungary.

*February 4–11.* Stalin, Churchill and Roosevelt meet at the Yalta Conference in the Crimea. Among the questions discussed are the military occupation of Germany, the westward shift of Poland's borders, the installation of provisional governments and the organization of free elections in Eastern Europe, the meeting of the United Nations Conference in San Francisco and the entry of the Soviet Union into the war against Japan.

*February 13.* The Red Army enters Budapest.

*March 30.* Danzig (Gdansk) is taken.

*April 5.* The USSR abrogates the neutrality treaty it signed with Japan in 1941.

*April 9.* Königsberg capitulates.

*April 11.* A treaty of mutual assistance and friendship is signed with Yugoslavia.

*April 13.* Vienna is taken.

*April 21.* A treaty of friendship, mutual assistance and cooperation is signed with the provisional government in Warsaw.

*April 25.* Berlin is encircled. On the same day, American and Soviet troops meet at Torgau, on the Elbe River.

*May 2.* Berlin capitulates.

*May 8.* Breslau (Wroclaw) is taken.

*May 9.* At 12:16 A.M., Field Marshal Wilhelm Keitel, Admiral Hans von Friedeburg and General Hans-Jürgen Stumpff sign a document signifying Germany's unconditional military surrender at Karlshorst. The Soviets enter Prague.

*June 5.* A quadripartite administration of Berlin and Germany by the United States, Great Britain, France and the Soviet Union is declared.

*June 26.* The Charter of San Francisco creates the United Nations. The USSR (together with the Ukraine and Belorussia) is accorded three votes and becomes a permanent member of the Security Council.

*June 29.* Czechoslovakia cedes Ruthenia to the USSR; the territory will be reincorporated into the Ukraine.

*July 17–August 2.* Stalin, President Harry Truman of the United States, and Churchill meet at the Potsdam Conference. (Churchill will be voted out of office during the conference and replaced by Prime Minister Clement Attlee.) Tensions escalate amongst the three Allies. The questions they discuss include the status of Germany, reparations, the transfer of German populations and the territories to be placed under Soviet and Polish administration. An ultimatum is issued to Japan for its surrender.

*August 6.* Diplomatic relations are reestablished with Romania and Finland.

*August 8.* Following the dropping of an atomic bomb by the United States on the Japanese city of Hiroshima on August 6, the USSR declares war on Japan. On August 9, Soviet forces begin operations against Japanese troops in Manchuria, in northern Korea, on southern Sakhalin and on the Kuril Islands.

*August 14.* Japan capitulates. The USSR reestablishes diplomatic relations with Bulgaria and signs a treaty of friendship and alliance with China.

*August 16.* A Soviet-Polish accord is reached on Poland's eastern borders, which approximate the "Curzon Line."

*August 21.* The United States ends its "Lend-Lease" program of assistance to the Soviet Union. The USSR protests.

*September 2.* Japan signs a formal surrender.

# Civilization and Culture

## 1939

*Shchors*, a film by Alexander Dovzhenko. The director Vsevolod Meyerhold is arrested; he will die in prison in 1940. The writer Isaac Babel is imprisoned; he will die in 1941.

*January 27.* Mikhail Glinka's opera *A Life for the Czar* is produced under the name *Ivan Susanin*.

## 1940

Anna Akhmatova begins her *Poem without a Hero*. Mikhail Bulgakov completes *The Master and Margarita* in the year of his death. Sergei Eisenstein directs Richard Wagner's *Die Walküre*.

## 1941

The poet Marina Tsvetaeva, who returned from abroad in 1939, commits suicide. *The Fall of Paris*, a novel by Ilya Ehrenburg (1941–1942). *The Holy War*, a choral composition by Alexander Alexandrov. *The Outskirts of Moscow, November 1941*, a painting by Alexander Deineka. Dmitri Shostakovich composes his Seventh Symphony (known as the *Leningrad Symphony*) during the seige of Leningrad.

**1942**

*The Science of Hatred*, a story by Mikhail Sholokhov. *Vasili Terkin* (1942–1945), Alexander Tvardovsky's epic poem, meets with great success.

**1943**

*Days and Nights*, a novel recalling the Battle of Stalingrad, by Konstantin Simonov (1943–1944). Publication of *Before Sunrise*, by Mikhail Zoshchenko. *The Partisan's Mother*, a painting by Sergei Gerasimov.

**1945**

*The Young Guard*, by Alexander Fadeyev. Part One of *Ivan the Terrible*, a film by S. Eisenstein.

# Chapter 29          1945–1953

# Postwar Stalinism

The Second World War had severe consequences for the Soviet Union. Military and civilian deaths were set at 20 million (now believed to have actually been 27 million), and recaptured western territories were devastated (although the USSR was considerably enlarged by territorial annexations). The reconstruction of the country, launched with the Fourth Five-Year Plan (1946–1950), was carried out at an especially rapid pace in the industrial sector. But difficulties were encountered in agriculture, where peasants continued to resist measures that constrained their freedom (such as the forced surrender of lands taken by peasants during the war, the accelerated reconstitution of kolkhozes, Nikita Khrushchev's "agro-cities" projects and the forced collectivization of western regions).

The standard of living rose very slowly, and postwar Soviet life was characterized by increased political and social control. Centralization was strengthened as a result of the war, and Stalin, benefiting from the full-scale cult of personality that surrounded him, expanded his personal authority over the administration of the Party and the state.

In practice, Stalin's power remained highly repressive. Even before the war had ended, mass deportations of those accused of having collaborated with the enemy had begun. Once the war was concluded, a new round of purges and trials swept the Party. At the same time, the leaders of the newly created people's democracies in Central and Eastern Europe were attacked and undermined by Moscow; within a few years, they would be replaced by leaders who were completely obedient to the dictates of "Big Brother." Ideological constraints also became more severe within Soviet society. Any deviations from the Party line that might slow the drive toward communism were swept from all spheres, including culture and science.

Domestic tensions exacerbated tensions abroad, and as the divergences between the USSR and the West widened, the "cold war" began. At the time of the creation of the Communist Information Bureau (Cominform) in 1947, the Soviets were loudly proclaiming the insurmountable division between the capitalist and the socialist camps, as well as the necessity for the people's democracies and for the various Communist parties to closely align themselves with the USSR. When the master of the Kremlin died on March 5, 1953, in an atmosphere of tension created by the contrived "doctors' plot," confusion was mingled with expressions of grief that were often sincere.

# Politics and Institutions

## 1945

*September 4.* The State Committee for Defense (GKO) is dissolved.

## 1946

*January.* Lavrenti Beria gives over the leadership of the People's Commissariat for Internal Affairs (NKVD) to General Sergei Kruglov. Beria's protégé, Viktor Abakumov, is put in charge of the People's Commissariat for State Security (NKGB).

*February.* Elections are held for the Supreme Soviet.

*February 25.* The Red Army is renamed the Soviet Army.

*March.* Beria and Georgi Malenkov are elected full members of the Politburo, and Nikolai Bulganin and Alexei Kosygin are elected candidate members. Mikhail Suslov takes charge of agitprop for the Central Committee.

*March 15.* The Council of People's Commissars becomes the Council of Ministers of the USSR. It is presided over by Stalin, who also has charge of the armed forces.

*March 19.* Mikhail Kalinin, taken ill, resigns his post as president of the Presidium of the Supreme Soviet. He is replaced by Nikolai Shvernik.

## 1947

*February.* Nikolai Voznesensky becomes a full member of the Politburo.

*March.* Bulganin is named defense minister.

*March–December.* Nikita Khrushchev is temporarily replaced by Lazar Kaganovich as leader of the Communist Party of the Ukraine.

*May 26.* The death penalty is abolished.

## 1948

A revolt breaks out among detainees in the labor camps in the Pechora region. The population of the camps increased rapidly after the war. Among those sent to the camps were Soviet prisoners of war in Germany; many inhabitants of territories annexed during the war (the Baltic states and parts of Poland and the Ukraine); and members of armed resistance movements, many of which were still operating against Soviet authorities as late as 1950.

*January 13.* Solomon Mikhoels, the president of the Jewish Anti-Fascist Committee, is murdered in Minsk by Soviet intelligence agents.

*February.* Bulganin and Kosygin become full members of the Politburo.

*August 31.* Andrei Zhdanov dies. Malenkov and his supporters appear to be victorious in their struggle for control of the Party apparatus.

## 1949

*March.* A ministerial reshuffling occurs: Anastas Mikoyan loses the foreign commerce portfolio, Vyacheslav Molotov is replaced by Andrei Vyshinsky as minister of foreign affairs, Bulganin gives up the Defense Ministry in favor of Marshal Alexander Vasilevsky.

The "Leningrad affair" begins, allowing the Malenkov faction to solidify its hold on power. Purges are instituted, followed by the executions of, among others, Nikolai Voznesensky (a member of the Politburo and the head of Gosplan), Alexei Kuznetsov (secretary of the Central Committee), Peter Popkov (secretary of the Leningrad Party) and Mikhail Rodionov (chairman of the Council of Ministers of the Russian Republic).

*December.* Khrushchev becomes secretary of the Central Committee and first secretary of the Moscow Party organization.

*December 21.* The cult of personality reaches its highest point on the 70th birthday of Stalin.

## 1950

*January 12.* The death penalty is reinstated for espionage, treason and sabotage.

## 1951

*November.* The "Mingrelian affair" begins. The arrest of a group of Mingrelian cadres in Georgia seems to be directed against Beria.

## 1952

A campaign against "cosmopolitanism" is unleashed. Many Jews are executed.

*October 5–14.* The Nineteenth Congress of the Communist Party is held. Party membership is 6,882,000 (including members and candidate members). The Politburo is replaced by a Presidium of 25 full and 11 candidate members. In addition, the Orgburo (Organizational Bureau) is abolished and the Central Committee Secretariat is expanded from 5 to 10 members.

## 1953

*January 13.* The discovery of a "doctors' plot" is announced: Nine Kremlin physicians, most of them Jewish, are accused of murdering Zhdanov, of attempting to assassinate Party and army leaders, and of Zionist plotting.

*March 5.* Stalin dies.

# Foreign Affairs

## 1945

The USSR seizes industrial installations in Germany and the former German satellites as reparations for its war losses. The "Sovietization" of the countries of Central and Eastern Europe begins. These countries will be essentially under Communist control by 1947.

*September 11–October 2.* The USSR participates in a conference of foreign ministers in London.

*September 25.* Diplomatic relations are reestablished with Hungary.

*November 10.* Diplomatic relations are reestablished with Albania.

*December 16–26.* A foreign ministers' conference is held in Moscow.

## 1946

*February 27.* A treaty of friendship and mutual assistance is signed with Mongolia.

*March 26.* The USSR agrees to withdraw its troops from northern Iran.

*April 25–May 15 and June 15–July 12.* The USSR participates in a conference of foreign ministers in Paris.

*July 29–October 15.* The Paris Peace Conference is held. It decides the conditions to be imposed on Italy, Romania, Bulgaria, Hungary and Finland.

*August.* The USSR demands joint Soviet-Turkish control of the Dardanelles and the Bosporus straits. With the support of Great Britain and the United States, Turkey rejects the Soviet demand.

*November 4–December 12.* The USSR participates in a foreign ministers' conference in New York.

## 1947

*February 10.* In Paris, peace treaties are signed with Nazi Germany's former allies (Italy, Romania, Bulgaria, Hungary and Finland). Romania and Finland recognize their new borders with the USSR.

*March 10–April 24.* A conference of foreign ministers is held in Moscow. The East-West split emerges. On March 12, President Harry Truman asserts the vital importance of blocking Communist expansion in Europe and of assisting Greece and Turkey (the Truman Doctrine).

*June 5.* American Secretary of State George Marshall announces his plan to aid in the reconstruction of Europe. The "Marshall Plan" will be criticized and then rejected by the USSR at the Paris Conference (June 27–July 2). The Soviet Union will force Czechoslovakia to renounce its earlier acceptance of the plan, and Moscow will block participation by other Central and Eastern European countries.

*September 22–27.* The Cominform (the Communist Information Bureau) is established at a conference in Poland attended by Communist Party representatives from the Soviet Union, the Central and Eastern European countries, France and Italy. Zhdanov declares the division of the world into two rival camps: the imperialist camp, led by the United States; and the anti-imperialist camp, led by the Soviet Union.

*November 25–December 15.* In London, a conference of foreign ministers (the "Last Chance Conference") fails to resolve problems in East-West relations. The break between the two rival camps is complete.

## 1948

*February 25.* In the "Prague Coup," Communists seize power in Czechoslovakia.

*February–March.* The USSR signs treaties of friendship, cooperation and mutual assistance with Romania (February 4), Hungary (February 18) and Bulgaria (March 18).

*March 20.* Soviet Marshal Vasili Sokolovsky walks out of the Allied Control Council in Berlin to protest against Western plans for the future of Germany.

*April 6.* The USSR signs a treaty of friendship and mutual assistance with Finland.

*May 15–18.* The USSR recognizes the State of Israel.

*June 24.* The Soviets impose a blockade on all land routes into the sectors of Berlin controlled by the Western powers, cutting off their supply lines to these sectors. The West will provision these sectors by an airlift until May 1949.

*June 28.* The split between the Soviet Union and Yugoslavia becomes public when the Cominform condemns Yugoslav Communists for their anti-Sovietism and deviationism.

*September.* The USSR recognizes the People's Republic of Korea (North Korea).

## 1949

*January 25.* A communiqué is issued announcing the establishment of Comecon (the Council for Mutual Economic Assistance). The announcement is made following the close of an economic conference in Moscow (January 5–8) attended by delegations from the Soviet Union, Bulgaria, Hungary, Poland, Romania and Czechoslovakia.

*March 31.* The Soviets deliver a diplomatic note protesting the proposed North Atlantic Treaty (which will be signed on April 4). The Treaty will lead to the creation of the North Atlantic Treaty Organization (NATO), a military alliance between the United States and its allies in Western Europe.

*May 12.* The Berlin blockade is lifted.

*May 23–June 20.* A conference of foreign ministers meets in Paris. Talks on the future of Germany are unproductive. The Federal Republic of Germany (West Germany) is founded on May 23, and the German Democratic Republic

(East Germany) will be established on October 7.

*September 6.* Soviet Marshal Konstantin Rokossovsky is named defense minister of Poland. Purges against Communist cadres with "nationalist" leanings are unleashed in Soviet satellite countries.

*September 28.* The Soviet Union abrogates its treaty of friendship and mutual assistance with Yugoslavia.

*October 1.* The USSR recognizes the establishment of the People's Republic of China and breaks relations with the Chiang Kai-shek regime.

## 1950

*February 14.* The USSR and China sign a 30-year treaty of friendship and mutual assistance. In 1952, the Soviets will restore Chinese sovereignty over the naval base at Port Arthur. China is granted a credit of $300 million.

*June 25.* The Korean War begins when North Korean forces cross the 38th Parallel to invade South Korea. The Security Council of the United Nations will condemn this aggression and vote to send United Nations forces to Korea. (The USSR does not veto this action because it has boycotted meetings of the Security Council since January to protest the Council's failure to recognize the People's Republic of China.)

*August 1.* The USSR rejoins the Security Council of the United Nations.

## 1951

*June 23.* Jacob Malik, the Soviet delegate to the United Nations, proposes an armistice in Korea. Negotiations will begin on July 10.

## 1952

*March 10.* In an effort to dissuade West Germany from participating in the proposed European Defense Community, the Soviet Union delivers a diplomatic note proposing the reunification of Germany.

## 1953

*February 11.* Following an attack on Soviet diplomats in Tel Aviv, the USSR breaks relations with Israel. (Relations will be reestablished in July.)

# Economy and Society

## 1945

Preparations are made for the Fourth Five-Year Plan.

## 1946

The economy performs badly: Industrial production declines, and the grain harvest is a disaster because of a drought.

*March 8.* A synod of the Uniate Church is held in Lvov. It proclaims the end of the Church's union with Rome and its return to Orthodoxy.

*March 18.* The Fourth Five-Year Plan (1946–1950) is adopted. Its broad goal is "rebuilding and developing the economy of the USSR." The Plan's key objective is to reach and then surpass the level of production attained in 1940.

*September 19.* A Council on Kolkhoz Affairs is established under the direction of Andrei Andreyev. Central control over privately farmed plots of land is strengthened, and the size of such plots is strictly limited.

## 1947

*February 15.* Soviet citizens are prohibited from marrying foreigners.

*February 28.* New measures for the renewal and reorganization of agriculture are taken.

*March.* The first turbine at Dnieproges resumes service. (The hydroelectric power station on the Dnieper River was destroyed during World War II.)

*May 21.* The Central Committee adopts a resolution on the collectivization of agriculture in the annexed Baltic regions. Active peasants resistance to the introduction of the kolkhoz system will continue for three years.

*December 14.* The rationing of food and industrial products is ended. Inflation and speculation are halted by a monetary reform involving an exchange of paper currency.

## 1948

*October.* A plan for the "transformation of nature" is adopted. In particular, the plan calls for digging canals and planting trees as windscreens in the southern steppe.

## 1949

The coal-bearing Donets region reaches its prewar level of production.

*September 25.* TASS announces the first detonation of a Soviet atomic bomb. The detonation took place on August 29.

## 1950

*February 19.* *Pravda* publishes an article that criticizes the agricultural policies of Andrei Andreyev, who favors the use of small groups rather than large brigades to do the work on kolkhozes.

*March 1.* The value of the ruble is detached from the dollar and set at 0.222 grams of gold.

*May 30.* The Central Committee decided to merge kolkhozes. As a result of this restructuring, the number of kolkhozes will drop from 250,000 to 121,000 in one year. (By 1953, the number of kolkhozes will have fallen to 94,000.)

*September 21.* The construction of the Great Turkmenian Canal is approved.

## 1951

*January 1.* The construction of the Don-Volga Canal is approved. (The canal will open on July 27, 1952.)

*March 4.* *Pravda* publishes Khrushchev's plan for the gradual elimination of traditional villages and the creation of immense "agro-cities."

## 1952

*October 5–14.* The Nineteenth Party Congress approves the directives for the Fifth Five-Year Plan (1951–1955), which has been under way for more than a year. The plan calls for an increase of 80 percent in heavy industrial production, an increase of 60 percent in consumer goods production and an increase of 40 to 50 percent in grain production.

# Civilization and Culture

## 1946

*August 14.* The Central Committee condemns the literary reviews *Leningrad* and *Zvezda* ("Star"). This marks the emergence of Zhdanov's dictatorship (the *Zhdanovshchina*) over all of Soviet cultural life. Authors (including Anna Akhmatova), filmmakers (including Sergei Eisenstein) and composers (including Dmitri Shostakovich) will be denounced for producing "bourgeois" and ideologically hostile work.

*September 4.* The Central Committee criticizes the film *A Great Life*, by Leonid Lukov. The second part of *Ivan the Terrible*, completed by S. Eisenstein in 1946, will not appear until 1958.

## 1948

*February 10.* The Central Committee adopts a resolution criticizing "the decadent tendencies in Soviet music."

*August.* The views of the botanist Trofim Lysenko concerning the influence of environment and heredity on acquired traits become scientific orthodoxy in the Soviet Union.

## 1949

A massive campaign denouncing "cosmopolitanism" in Soviet art and science takes place.

## 1950

*June 20.* *Pravda* publishes Stalin's article "Marxism and Problems of Linguistics."

## 1951

In Novgorod, inscriptions dating from the 11th century are discovered on birch bark.

## 1951–1952

A systematic attack on the national epics of the Moslem peoples of the Soviet Union is carried out.

Chapter 30                          1953–1964

# De-Stalinization and the Beginning of the Thaw

Stalin's death triggered swift changes in the USSR and revealed the presence of significant reformist tendencies within the Party. Nikita Khrushchev soon became the spokesman for reform.

In the power struggle that followed Stalin's death, Khrushchev condemned the excesses of Stalinism and placed some of the blame for those excesses on his adversaries. But the initial denunciations of Stalinist absolutism were also intended to reestablish a political consensus within Soviet society. That Khrushchev had become the master of this process became clear after the Twentieth Party Congress, where he denounced the crimes of the Stalinist regime in his famous "secret speech." The speech ushered in a relaxation of domestic tensions, and the leadership hoped for a new level of social cohesion and commitment that would facilitate the country's development.

Political changes were equally evident in foreign affairs. After 10 years of the cold war, the Party sought to bring the USSR out of its isolation from the world community. The concept of "peaceful coexistence" with the capitalist world, unveiled at the Twentieth Party Congress, backed up Khrushchev's efforts to open a dialogue with the West.

Khrushchev's radical orientation, however, provoked opposition from members of the conservative wing of the Party. From 1957 onward, Khrushchev's hold on power was threatened by these conservatives, many of whom themselves felt threatened by his policies. The failure of his economic reforms also generated broader opposition within Soviet society at large. In addition, Khrushchev's program of de-Stalinization did not go far enough to satisfy the intelligentsia, who withdrew their support from him during the early 1960s.

Khrushchev's foreign policies also began to suffer serious reversals. The construction of the Berlin Wall and then the Cuban Missile Crisis led to a new deterioration in the USSR's relations with the West. During this period as well, China broke off its alliance with the Soviet Union.

Khrushchev's dismissal was unanimously voted by the Presidium in October 1964. The Soviet people reacted to this event with indifference, perhaps even with satisfaction.

# Politics and Institutions

## 1953

*March 6.* Georgi Malenkov, secretary of the Central Committee and chairman of the Council of Ministers, appears to be the likely successor to Stalin.

*March 14.* Malenkov gives up his post as secretary of the Central Committee but keeps the chairmanship of the Council of Ministers, where he is assisted by four vice chairmen, among them Vyacheslav Molotov and Lavrenti Beria. Meanwhile, Khrushchev's importance increases within the Secretariat of the Central Committee.

*March 27.* Amnesty is granted for minor administrative and economic crimes. Prison sentences of less than five years are suspended. The sick, the elderly, adolescents under the age of 18, and mothers are released from prison.

*April 4.* The Ministry of Internal Affairs issues a communiqué clearing the doctors who were accused in January 1953 of plotting against Stalin.

*April 10.* The Central Committee adopts a resolution condemning "the violation of legality by the state security organs." This resolution is directed against Beria.

*June 26.* Beria is arrested during a session of the Presidium of the Central Committee. (His trial and execution will be announced officially in December.) The "triumvirate" of Malenkov, Molotov and Khrushchev is formed.

*Summer.* Internees at the Vorkuta labor camp stage a revolt.

*September.* The rehabilitation of the victims of the Stalinist terror begins.

*September 13.* Khrushchev becomes first secretary of the Central Committee.

## 1954

*February 19.* The Crimea, until now part of the Russian Socialist Federal Soviet Republic (RSFSR), is incorporated into the Ukrainian Republic.

*March.* The Ministry of State Security (MGB) is reorganized and given a new name, the Committee of State Security (KGB). General Ivan Serov, an ally of Khrushchev, becomes head of the KGB.

*April–June.* Internees at the Kengir labor camp stage an uprising.

*July.* Mikhail Ryumin, a former deputy minister for state security, is put on trial. Accused of having staged the bogus "doctors' plot," he is condemned to death and executed.

*December.* Viktor Abakumov, the former minister of state security, is held responsible for the "Leningrad affair" and is executed. Malenkov's position is further undermined.

## 1955

*January 25.* A plenum of the Central Committee condemns the policies of Malenkov.

*February 8.* Admitting his management errors, Malenkov resigns. Nikolai Bulganin succeeds him as chairman of the Council of Ministers and cedes the Ministry of Defense to Marshal Georgi Zhukov.

*March.* Lazar Kaganovich, an ally of Malenkov, is forced out as director of the industrial planning administration.

*July.* Molotov, who had opposed the reconciliation with Yugoslavia as well as the Soviet Union's approval of the treaty restoring Austrian sovereignty, is forced to repudiate his positions and recognize his "errors."

*October.* Molotov makes a public self-criticism for having declared that the USSR had only "laid down the foundation" for a socialist society.

# 1956

*February 14–25.* The Twentieth Party Congress is held. Khrushchev emphasizes the importance of international détente and the plurality of paths to socialism. Khrushchev strengthens his position within the Party by putting his partisans, including Leonid Brezhnev, Dmitri Shepilov and Marshal Zhukov, onto the Presidium.

*Night of February 24–25.* Khrushchev presents a secret report to a closed session of the Party Congress. He reveals Stalin's crimes and denounces the cult of personality, but he does not call into question the economic policies of the preceding 30 years. Khrushchev's "secret speech" will be published by the United States government on June 4.

Following the Twentieth Party Congress, more political prisoners are released and rehabilitated.

*June 30.* The Central Committee passes a resolution to "eliminate the cult of personality and its consequences."

*July 16.* The Karelian-Finnish Soviet Socialist Republic becomes the Autonomous Republic of Karelia within the RSFSR.

*November.* Molotov returns to government in the capacity of minister of state control.

# 1957

*February.* Certain nationalities that were deported by Stalin to other regions of the USSR are rehabilitated and allowed to return to their region of origin (the Chechens, the Ingush, the Balkars, the Karachai and the Kalmyks).

*May 10.* Against the wishes of Party conservatives, a law decentralizing the administration of industry is adopted.

*May 22.* Khrushchev increases tensions within the Party by declaring that the USSR should match American levels of production for beef, milk and butter within the next four years.

*June 19.* During an impromptu meeting of the Presidium convened by Khrushchev, the participants call for his resignation by a vote of 7 to 4. Khrushchev refuses to accept this decision and demands that a plenary session of the Central Committee be convened.

*June 22–29.* A plenary session of the Central Committee confirms Khrushchev in his post as first secretary of the Party and condemns the factional activities of the "antiparty" group. Molotov, Malenkov, Kaganovich and Shepilov are ousted from the Presidium and the Central Committee. A new 15-member Presidium is formed; included among the nine Presidium members considered to be partisans of Khrushchev are Brezhnev, Frol Kozlov and Marshal Zhukov. Alexei Kosygin becomes a candidate member of the Presidium.

*October 26.* Khrushchev, fearful of Zhukov's growing popularity, replaces him as minister of defense with Marshal Rodion Malinovsky.

# 1958

General Serov hands over the leadership of the KGB to the first secretary of Komsomol, Alexander Shelepin.

The academician Andrei Sakharov makes his first request to Khrushchev for an end to nuclear weapons testing.

*March 27.* Bulganin resigns as chairman of the Council of Ministers. Khrushchev replaces him, thereby obtaining the same Party and government leadership positions that Stalin held after 1941.

*August.* Ethnic unrest between Chechens and Russians breaks out in Grozny.

*December 25.* A new penal code for the USSR and its republics is adopted. Sentences are reduced, the expression "enemy of the people" is abolished, the minimum age for criminal responsibility is raised from 14 to 16, the exceptional nature of capital punishment is reaffirmed, and prison sentences are limited to 15 years instead of 25. Labor camps are replaced by "corrective labor colonies." The GULAG is succeeded by the GUITK (Main Administration of Corrective Labor Colonies).

## 1959

*January 27–February 5.* The Twenty-first Party Congress is held. Khrushchev declares that the USSR has completed the construction of communism.

*October.* Alexei Kirichenko, a key ally of Khrushchev, is declared responsible for the bad harvests and is dismissed from the Presidium of the Central Committee. Kosygin, Nikolai Podgorny and Dmitri Polyansky become full members of the reorganized Central Committee Presidium.

## 1960

*January 14.* The Ministry of Internal Affairs (MVD) is dissolved; its functions are taken over by the Ministries of Internal Affairs in the 15 federal republics.

*May 5.* Kozlov is named to the Secretariat of the Central Committee. Kosygin replaces Kozlov as vice chairman of the Council of Ministers.

*May 7.* Kliment Voroshilov is replaced as president of the Presidium of the Supreme Soviet by Brezhnev.

## 1961

*May.* The application of the death penalty is extended to certain economic crimes.

*October 17–31.* The Twenty-second Party Congress is held. Khrushchev reveals new crimes committed by Stalin and announces that communism will be achieved by 1980. A new Party program is adopted, as are new Party bylaws that provide for greater turnover on ruling bodies (at each election, one-third of all seats must be contested).

*October 31.* Stalin's body is removed from the mausoleum on Red Square. The city of Stalingrad is renamed Volgograd.

## 1962

*June 2.* Workers riot in Novocherkassk to protest a cut in wages. The army violently crushes the rebellion. Social unrest will occur in several cities throughout the USSR during 1962–1963.

*November 19–23.* A plenum of the Central Committee is held. Strong opposition to Khrushchev develops, reflecting the discontent within the Party apparatus over his economic policies. Khrushchev prevails upon the plenum to adopt a plan that divides Party authority into two sectors (agricultural and industrial) at all echelons.

## 1963

Brezhnev and Podgorny, now adversaries of Khrushchev, become members of the Secretariat of the Central Committee.

*February–March.* Khrushchev fights off an attack led by Kozlov.

*April.* Following an illness, Kozlov is removed from his public duties.

*June.* After a debate, a plenum of the Central Committee reaffirms the necessity of maintaining Marxist orthodoxy.

## 1964

*April 17.* Khrushchev's 70th birthday is celebrated ostentatiously; a new cult of personality is in the making.

*July.* Brezhnev relinquishes the presidency of the Presidium of the Supreme Soviet to devote himself entirely to the Secretariat of the Central Committee.

*August 29.* The Volga Germans are rehabilitated.

*October 12.* While Khrushchev is vacationing on the Black Sea, the Presidium of the Central Committee meets to plan his removal.

*October 13.* The Presidium convenes a plenum of the Central Committee and calls Khrushchev back to Moscow to demand his resignation.

*Night of October 13–14.* The plenum of the Central Committee strips Khrushchev of all of his party and state functions. Brezhnev becomes first secretary of the Party, and Kosygin becomes chairman of the Council of Ministers.

*October 15.* TASS announces officially that Khrushchev has left office "for reasons of health."

# Foreign Affairs

## 1953

*March 26.* A commercial accord with China is signed.

*June 17.* A popular insurrection in East Berlin is suppressed with the aid of Soviet tanks.

*July 27.* An armistice is signed, bringing an end to the Korean War.

*August 20.* The USSR officially announces the detonation of its first hydrogen bomb.

## 1954

*March 25.* The USSR recognizes the sovereignty of East Germany.

*April 26–July 21.* The Soviets participate in the Geneva Conference, which ends the French Indochina War.

*September 29–October 12.* Khrushchev visits China. A new Sino-Soviet accord is signed, providing for a Soviet withdrawal from Port Arthur.

## 1955

*March 7.* The Soviet Union agrees to adhere to The Hague Conventions.

*May 14.* In response to West Germany's entry into the North Atlantic Treaty Organization (NATO), the Soviet Union announces the establishment of the Warsaw Pact, an organization of political and military cooperation between the USSR, Albania, Bulgaria, Hungary, Poland, East Germany, Romania and Czechoslovakia.

*May 15.* The USSR and the Western powers sign a State Treaty restoring Austrian sovereignty.

*May 27–June 2.* Khrushchev, Bulganin and Anastas Mikoyan travel to Belgrade and achieve a Soviet-Yugoslav reconciliation.

*July 18–23.* A summit meeting of the major powers is held in Geneva. Attended by Bulganin, Khrushchev, President Dwight Eisenhower of the United States, Edgar Faure of France, and Anthony Eden of Great Britain, the meeting evidences a new spirit of international détente.

*September 9–13.* West German Chancellor Konrad Adenauer visits Moscow. Diplomatic relations between the USSR and the Federal Republic of Germany are established.

*September 20.* A treaty of friendship and cooperation is signed by the Soviet Union and East Germany. The treaty specifies the conditions for the stationing of Soviet troops on East German soil.

*November 18–December 19.* Khrushchev and Bulganin travel to India, Burma and Afghanistan, where they reaffirm the principle of neutrality.

## 1956

*January.* A Permanent Commission of the Warsaw Pact is established and charged with the formulation of foreign policy recommendations. The decision is made to integrate the East German army into the forces of the Warsaw Pact.

*February 14–25.* At the Twentieth Party Congress, Khrushchev agrees to halt the export of armed revolution in an effort to promote peaceful coexistence.

*April 17.* The Cominform (Communist Information Bureau) is dissolved.

*June 1–23.* Marshal Josif Tito of Yugoslavia makes a state visit to the Soviet Union.

*October 19.* Khrushchev, Molotov, Mikoyan and Kaganovich make a surprise visit to Warsaw. They attempt to dissuade the Central Committee of the Polish Communist Party from electing Wladislaw Gomulka Party chief. Faced with the determination of the leadership and the populace, the Soviets acquiesce to the "Polish path to socialism."

*October 23.* An insurrection in Budapest will provoke the first intervention of Soviet troops in Hungary (October 26).

*October 30.* The Soviet Union declares its intention to redefine its relations with the socialist countries of Eastern Europe on the basis of full equality, which it recognizes it has not always respected in the past.

*November 4.* A second Soviet military intervention takes place in Hungary. The Soviets crush the Hungarian uprising.

*November 5.* In the United Nations Security Council, the USSR condemns the French-British-Israeli attack against Egypt during the Suez crisis.

*December 17.* The USSR proposes a nonaggression pact between NATO and the Warsaw Pact.

## 1957

*February 15.* Andrei Gromyko becomes minister of foreign affairs.

*March 28.* The Moscow accords legitimate the stationing of Soviet troops in Hungary.

*November 14–16.* A conference of Communist parties of socialist countries meet in Moscow. The parties condemn dogmatism and revisionism. The unity of the socialist camp is reaffirmed in the wake of the events of 1956.

## 1958

*May 10.* The USSR demands that Yugoslavia submit to the authority of the socialist camp.

*July.* A coup d'état takes place in Iraq. The pro-Soviet general Abdul Karem Kassim takes power.

*November 27.* Khrushchev delivers an ultimatum to the United States, France and Great Britain on the status of Berlin. He seeks to make it a free, demilitarized city, and proposes that negotiations begin in six months or he will take unilateral action.

## 1959

*April 6.* The Soviets propose the creation of a demilitarized zone in Asia and the Pacific.

*Summer.* The USSR ends its nuclear cooperation with China.

*July 13–August 3.* A conference in Geneva on the Berlin question fails to arrive at a solution, but Gromyko softens the Soviet demands.

*September 15–27.* Khrushchev makes the first visit to the United States by a

Soviet head of government. He presents his plan for disarmament to the United Nations and meets with President Eisenhower at Camp David. *September 30–October 1.* Khrushchev visits Beijing, where he preaches détente to Mao Zedong.

## 1960

*February 4–13.* Mikoyan visits Cuba, where Fidel Castro took power the previous year. Commercial agreements are signed, and the Soviets announce they will provide Cuba with economic assistance.

*March 23–April 3.* Khrushchev travels to France. Scientific and technical cooperation agreements are signed.

*April. People's Daily,* the Chinese Communist Party newspaper, publishes a long indictment of Yugoslav revisionism that is also directed at the USSR.

*May 1.* An American U-2 spy plane is shot down over the Soviet Union. Khrushchev uses this event to torpedo the Paris summit meeting between the USSR, the United States, Great Britain and France. The meeting was to have addressed European security, arms control and the status of Berlin.

*June 20–25.* Khrushchev denounces the Chinese Communists at the Romanian Communist Party Congress in Bucharest.

*July.* Following the imposition of an American embargo of Cuba, the USSR promises to buy Cuban sugar. Khrushchev threatens war in the event of armed aggression against Cuba.

*July 15.* Khrushchev puts himself forward as protector of the regime of Patrice Lumumba in the Congo.

*August 18.* All Soviet technicians and specialists are recalled from China.

*September 23.* At the United Nations General Assembly in New York,

Khrushchev takes up the question of the Congo. He also proposes replacing the Secretary General of the United Nations with a triumvirate composed of one representative each from the Western powers, the Communist powers and the neutral countries.

*November 10–December 3.* In Moscow, a world conference of 81 Communist parties is held. Despite the growing differences between the Soviets and the Chinese (who are supported by the Albanians), Khrushchev succeeds in having his theses ratified by the conference in the name of the necessary unity of the international Communist movement.

## 1961

*April 18.* After the American-sponsored anti-Castro invasion fails at the Bay of Pigs in Cuba, Khrushchev sends a message of protest to President John Kennedy.

*April 26.* The USSR breaks its credit agreements with Albania.

*June 3–4.* Khrushchev and Kennedy meet in Vienna; the problem of Berlin remains unresolved.

*August 13.* Construction of the Berlin Wall begins.

*October 17–31.* The Twenty-second Party Congress approves the break in Sino-Soviet relations.

## 1962

*March 19.* The Soviet Union recognizes the provisional Algerian government.

*April 11.* The Soviets express their support for Castro publicly for the first time.

*Spring.* Clashes occur on the Sino-Soviet border.

*October 22.* The United States having discovered Soviet nuclear missile installations in Cuba, President Kennedy announces a naval blockade of the island and demands that the missiles be removed immediately, under the threat of armed conflict.

*October 26.* Khrushchev promises to remove the Soviet missiles in Cuba in exchange for an American promise not to invade the island.

*December.* In a heated speech before the Supreme Soviet, and with Mao Zedong present, Khrushchev denounces dogmatism as the principal danger facing communism.

## 1963

*March.* Sino-Soviet relations worsen. The Chinese leaders label Khrushchev's policies "adventurist" and "defeatist," and question the borders imposed by "unjust treaties" dating from the time of the czars.

*June 14.* China sends Moscow a 25-point indictment that justifies a possible eventual recourse to war and refuses to recognize the leading role of the Soviet Union in the Communist bloc.

*June 20.* An American-Soviet agreement is reached to set up a "hot line" between Washington and Moscow. The special communications link is intended for use in the event of a crisis involving the two nuclear superpowers.

*July 14.* The Soviet Communist Party issues an open letter replying to the 25 points raised by the Chinese in June; an ideological break occurs between the two countries.

*July 25–26.* The member countries of Comecon meet in Moscow. Faced with strong opposition from Romania, the Soviets drop their plan under which each member state would have assumed a different economic specialization.

*August 5.* In Moscow, a treaty prohibiting nuclear weapon tests in the atmosphere, in outer space or underwater

is signed by the USSR, the United States and Great Britain.

## 1964

*April.* The Central Committee of the Romanian Communist Party affirms Romania's independence from the USSR.

*June 12.* A treaty of friendship, mutual aid and cooperation is signed by the Soviet Union and East Germany.

*July 28.* China refuses to participate in the world conference of Communist parties proposed by Khrushchev.

# Economy and Society

## 1953

*September 3–7.* Khrushchev casts himself as the patron of agriculture at a plenum of the Central Committee devoted to that sector of the economy. Past difficulties are criticized, prices for agricultural products are raised, the obligatory deliveries of produce are reduced, kolkhoz debts are forgiven, and the role of Machine Tractor Stations is strengthened.

## 1954

*February 23–March 2.* A plenum of the Central Committee passes a resolution on the production of wheat and on the exploitation of uncultivated virgin and fallow lands. A massive cultivation project encompassing 13 million hectares of land is launched in Kazakhstan and southern Siberia.

*June 27.* The first Soviet atomic power plant is put into operation.

*Summer.* As many as 300,000 volunteers depart for the virgin lands of northern Kazakhstan, the Altai region, southern Siberia and the Urals.

## 1955

*January.* Khrushchev launches a major campaign to promote the planting of corn.

*March 9.* Agricultural planning is reformed, and greater autonomy is given to the kolkhozes. Plans will henceforth establish the amounts of production to be delivered to the state but not the production levels themselves.

*November.* Abortion, which was outlawed in 1936, is again made legal.

## 1956

*February 14–25.* The Twentieth Party Congress approves the Sixth Five-Year Plan. The highest priorities continue to be accorded to heavy industry and energy, but new efforts are planned as well in the areas of agriculture, consumer goods and housing construction.

*April 25.* The "antiworker" law of 1940 is abolished; absenteeism ceases to be a criminal offense.

*July 14.* A law on retirement is passed. Pensions are increased, and kolkhozniks are extended the right of retirement under certain conditions.

*July 31.* The Central Committee and the Council of Ministers decide to promote the construction of apartment housing.

*September 8.* A minimum wage is established.

## 1957

*February 13–14.* A plenum of the Central Committee approves a plan to decentralize the administration of enterprises. The large industrial ministries are abolished and replaced by 100 *sovnarkhozes* (regional economic councils) that are to manage industry at the local level.

*May 3.* The transformation of kolkhozes into sovkhozes is halted.

*August 3.* The first successful test flight of an intercontinental ballistic missile (ICBM) takes place in the Soviet Union; Sergei Korolev is the missile's chief designer.

*October 4. Sputnik,* the first manmade satellite, is launched into orbit around the earth.

## 1958

*March 31.* Machine Tractor Stations are abolished.

*December 24.* The educational system is reformed. Compulsory education is increased to eight years, and the ties between education and industry are strengthened.

## 1959

A massive antireligion campaign is launched.

People's militias (*druzhiny*) are formed; members are recruited from factories and workplaces to maintain public order.

*January.* A census sets the total population of the Soviet Union at 208.8 million; 48 percent of the inhabitants live in urban areas.

*January 2. Lunik I,* the first space probe to reach the moon, is launched.

*January 27–February 5.* The Twenty-first Party Congress meets in extraordinary session. It adopts a Seven-Year Plan (1959–1965) that modifies the Sixth Five-Year Plan already under way. The production goals for oil and natural gas are increased. New resources in Siberia and Central Asia are to be developed, as is the chemical industry. The railways are to be converted to electric and diesel power.

## 1960

*May 7.* A law is passed limiting the workday to seven hours.

## Late 1960–Early 1961

The *sovnarkhozes* are organized. Their total number will decline from 100 in 1960 to 47 in 1963. State committees responsible for production and organization are created to replace the abolished economic ministries.

## 1961

*January 1.* A monetary reform is energetically pursued. The new ruble is valued at 10 old rubles within the USSR, but it is sharply devalued in relation to gold.

*April 12.* The first manned space flight is made by Yuri Gagarin.

*May 4.* The Presidium of the Supreme Soviet of the RSFSR issues a decree on the struggle against "parasitic elements."

*July 18.* A council of the Russian Orthodox Church, held in Zagorsk, is required to recognize the increased control of the state over parish associations. The antireligious campaign continues.

## 1962

*June.* Agricultural prices rise sharply.

*September 9. Pravda* publishes an article by Evsei Liberman recommending a relaxation of planning, more autonomy for individual enterprises, and a return to modified competition.

## 1963

A serious agricultural crisis occurs.

The first great ecological catastrophes take place in the "virgin lands" when soil is eroded by the wind.

Soviet authorities officially acknowledge a serious drop in the rate of economic growth in 1963–1964.

## 1964

*Summer.* Khrushchev proposes a new agricultural reform project that would create State Committees to direct each sector of agricultural production. This project will become the pretext for the October meeting of the Central Committee Presidium that will force Khrushchev from office.

# Civilization and Culture

## 1953

"On Sincerity in Literature," a critical article by Vladimir Pomerantsev.

## 1954

Publication of *The Thaw,* by Ilya Ehrenburg; the novel is one of the key literary texts of the de-Stalinization process.

*December 15–26.* The Second Congress of Writers shows evidence of a relative relaxation in the control exercised over literature. The rehabilitation of writers begins.

## 1956

*Not by Bread Alone,* a novel by Vladimir Dudintsev. *The Forty-First,* a film by Grigori Chukhrai. The Nobel Prize in chemistry is awarded to Nikolai Semenov. Trofim Lysenko is removed from his post as president of the Academy of Agricultural Sciences under pressure from the scientific community.

*May 13.* After the revelations of the Twentieth Party Congress, Alexander Fadeyev, secretary of the Writers' Union, commits suicide.

## 1957

*The Cranes Are Flying,* a film by Mikhail Kalatozov.

*November. Doctor Zhivago,* by Boris Pasternak, is published in Italy.

## 1958

The liberal Alexander Tvardovsky returns as editor of the review *Novy Mir.*

The Nobel Prize for physics is awarded to Pavel Cherenkov, Ilya Frank and Igor Tamm. B. Pasternak is awarded the Nobel Prize for literature; under pressure from the Soviet regime, he refuses to accept the award.

**1959**

Konstantin Fedin is made head of the Writers' Union.

**1960**

The University of the Friendship of Peoples is opened in Moscow. (In 1961, it will be renamed Patrice Lumumba University.) *Lady with the Little Dog*, a film by Iosif Heifitz.

*May 30.* B. Pasternak dies.

**1961**

*Kira Georgievna*, a novel by Viktor Nekrasov.

**1962**

*Silence*, a novel by Yuri Bondarev on the cult of personality. The Nobel Prize for physics is awarded to Lev Landau.

*October 21. Pravda* publishes Yevgeni Yevtushenko's poem "Stalin's Heirs."

*November.* Alexander Solzhenitsyn's novel *One Day in the Life of Ivan Denisovich*, an unvarnished portrayal of Stalinist labor camps, is published.

*December 1.* Khrushchev indignantly walks out of an exhibition of modern art. The authorities will soon condemn abstract art and tighten ideological control over artists and intellectuals.

**1963**

A. Tvardovsky publishes *Vasili Terkin in the Other World*.

*March.* Khrushchev reaffirms the necessity of conforming to the principles of socialist realism and rejects any "ideological coexistence."

**1964**

*The Merry Drummer*, a collection of poems by Bulat Okudzhava. The Nobel Prize for physics is awarded to Nikolai Basov and Alexander Prokhorov.

*February.* The poet Joseph Brodsky is put on trial; he will be convicted of "social parasitism" and sentenced to five years in a labor camp.

# Chapter 31            1964–1982

# The USSR under Brezhnev

After the political upheavals of the Khrushchev era, the ascension of Leonid Brezhnev to the post of general secretary of the Communist Party marked the return of normalcy to political life. This was evidenced by the extreme stability of the political leadership, in sharp contrast with the frequent turnover in Party and government posts during the preceding period. During the 18 years of the Brezhnev era, the Soviet Union also pursued a more realistic policy. The leadership abandoned Khrushchev-style prognostications about the arrival of pure communism in favor of the more modest concept of "developed socialism" (which happened to coincide, according to the Soviet leadership, with the level of development already attained by the USSR).

Fundamentally conservative in their politics, Brezhnev and his associates placed particular emphasis on the economic development of the country. Beginning in 1965, they put through new reforms that gave some management autonomy to enterprises. These reforms resulted in an amelioration of the Soviet standard of living that was especially noticeable in the countryside. After an early period of real economic growth, however, the Soviet economy showed signs of stagnation from the mid-1970s onward.

Brezhnev's opposition to change was conducive to the development of a *nomenklatura* (a class of individuals appointed to jobs by the Party) that was primarily interested in preserving its own prerogatives and privileges. The Party's pretension to leadership in all aspects of life was especially evident in its constant effort to exercise an obsessive control over the Soviet intelligentsia. But the image of an all-powerful regime was shattered by the emergence of dissidents who, while only a tiny minority, symbolized the gulf that now divided Soviet society from the Party and the state.

In foreign affairs, Brezhnev continued to pursue the policy of East-West dialogue inaugurated by Khrushchev. An agreement on the status of Berlin, international recognition of borders in Eastern Europe and, above all, the negotiation of the first arms control treaties were some of the results of the period of détente that was to culminate in the signing of the Helsinki Accords in 1975. These successes, however, were compromised by the Soviet Union's actions in Africa and then by its invasion of Afghanistan, which led, in 1979, to a new sharpening of international tensions.

# Politics and Institutions

## 1964

*October 14.* Leonid Brezhnev succeeds Nikita Khrushchev as first secretary of the Central Committee. Alexei Kosygin becomes chairman of the Council of Ministers.

*November 16.* A plenum of the Central Committee ousts V. Poliakov from the post of Party secretary for agriculture and appoints Nikolai Podgorny secretary responsible for cadres. Peter Shelest is promoted to full membership on the Presidium, and Alexander Shelepin also enters that body as a full member. The Central Committee abandons the reform of 1962 that created a firm division between the management of industrial and agricultural sectors.

## 1965

*December 9.* Podgorny replaces Anastas Mikoyan as president of the Presidium of the Supreme Soviet.

## 1966

A federal ministry for the maintenance of public order is reestablished.

*February 10–14.* The writers Andrei Sinyavsky and Yuli Daniel are convicted of "agitation and propaganda" and sentenced to seven and five years of hard labor, respectively.

*March 29–April 8.* The Twenty-third Party Congress is held. Brezhnev is appointed general secretary of the Party, the post once held by Stalin. A new law relaxes the policy on the turnover of cadres imposed by Khrushchev.

*September 16.* The Penal Code is amended in order to facilitate the prosecution of dissidents.

## 1967

*April 12.* Marshal Andrei Grechko becomes minister of defense following the death of Marshal Rodion Malinovsky.

*May 18.* Vladimir Semichastny is ousted as head of the Committee of State Security (KGB). He is replaced by Yuri Andropov.

*September 15.* A decree rehabilitates the Crimean Tatars.

## 1968

*January 8–12.* A trial of four dissidents (Yuri Galanskov, A. Dobrovolsky, V. Lashkova and Alexander Ginzburg) is held.

*April 30.* The first issue of the *Chronicle of Current Events*, a clandestine publication (*samizdat*) that exposes breaches of civil liberties, appears.

*June. Progress, Peaceful Coexistence and Intellectual Freedom*, by the physicist Andrei Sakharov, appears as a *samizdat*.

*August 25.* Dissidents stage a demonstration in Red Square to protest the Soviet invasion of Czechoslovakia. The participants are condemned to exile or terms in labor camps.

## 1969

*May.* The Group for the Defense of Civil Rights in the Soviet Union, led by the dissidents Peter Yakir and Leonid Plyushch, is founded.

## 1970

*March 19.* Sakharov, Valentin Turchin and Roy Medvedev send an open letter to Brezhnev, Kosygin and Podgorny calling for the democratization of the regime.

*November 4.* The Human Rights Committee is established by Sakharov, Valeri Chalidze and Andrei Tverdokhlebov.

# 1971

*March 14.* The Central Committee issues a resolution strengthening the power of the soviets.

*March 30–April 9.* The Twenty-fourth Party Congress is held. Brezhnev announces "the emergence of a new historic community, the Soviet people."

*September 11.* Khrushchev dies. He will be buried at Novodevichy Cemetery in Moscow.

# 1972

*January 5.* The trial of Vladimir Bukovsky is held. He is sentenced to two years imprisonment, five years in a labor camp and five years of internal exile.

*January 11–15.* Mass raids and arrests are carried out in Moscow and in the Ukraine, in an effort to prevent the appearance of clandestine publications.

*May 14.* A young Lithuanian, Roman Kalanta, commits suicide by self-immolation to protest against persecutions launched against the Catholic Church in Lithuania.

*May 20.* Shelest is removed as first secretary of the Ukrainian Communist Party. He is replaced by Vladimir Shcherbitsky.

*October.* Most of those responsible for the publication of the *Chronicle of Current Events* are imprisoned.

# 1973

*February 3.* Dmitri Polyansky replaces V. Matskevich as minister of agriculture.

*April 26–27.* A plenum of the Central Committee is held. Shelest resigns from the Politburo while Andropov, Andrei Gromyko and Grechko become full members of that body.

*July 11.* Brezhnev receives the International Lenin Prize for his contribution to friendship among peoples and to peace.

*August.* The trial of the dissidents Peter Yakir and Viktor Krasin is held.

# 1974

*February 12–13.* Alexander Solzhenitsyn is arrested and expelled from the Soviet Union.

# 1975

*May 22.* Shelepin, already ousted from the Politburo on April 16, resigns from the presidency of the Central Council of Trade Unions.

*October 9.* The Nobel Peace Prize is awarded to Andrei Sakharov.

# 1976

*February 24–March 5.* The Twenty-fifth Communist Party Congress is held.

*April 26.* Marshal Grechko dies. Dmitri Ustinov becomes minister of defense.

*May 13.* Helsinki Watch, a dissident group, is created on the initiative of Yuri Orlov. The group will attempt to monitor Soviet compliance with the human rights provisions of the 1975 Helsinki Accord.

*December 18.* Vladimir Bukovsky is freed and exiled in exchange for the imprisoned general secretary of the Communist Party of Chile, Luis Corvalan.

*December 19.* A lavish celebration is held for the 70th birthday of Brezhnev.

# 1977

*January 8.* An attack takes place in the Moscow subway, for which three Armenians will be sentenced to death in a secret trial and executed.

*January 9.* Marshal Viktor Kulikov succeeds Marshal Ivan Yakubovsky as commander in chief of Warsaw Pact forces. General Nikolai Ogarkov becomes chief of the Soviet General Staff.

*February–March.* A wave of arrests is unleashed. (Those arrested include Alexander Ginzburg, Yuri Orlov and Anatoli Shcharansky.)

*June 16.* Brezhnev replaces Podgorny as president of the Presidium of the Supreme Soviet.

*October 7.* A new Soviet Constitution is adopted. It substitutes the notion of "a state of one people" for the "dictatorship of the proletariat."

## 1978

*April 14.* At Tbilisi (Tiflis), a demonstration by several thousand inhabitants takes place. The demonstrators call for the recognition of Georgian as the official language of the Georgian Republic.

*July 6.* A special law on "collegiality in the work of the Council of Ministers of the USSR" leaves Alexei Kosygin, the Council's chairman, with only a nominal role.

## 1979

Five political prisoners (including Alexander Ginzburg, Edvard Kuznetsov and Valentin Moroz) are exchanged for two Soviet spies held by the United States.

## 1980

*January 22.* Sakharov is assigned to internal exile in Gorky.

*June.* Father Dmitri Dudko, a figure in the dissident Orthodox movement, is freed after having publicly disavowed his activities.

*August.* Father Gleb Yakunin, the founder of the Committee for the Defense of the Rights of Believers, is convicted and sentenced.

*October 21.* Mikhail Gorbachev becomes a full member of the Politburo.

*October 22–23.* Kosygin, who is gravely ill (he will die on December 18),

is retired as chairman of the Council of Ministers. He is replaced by Nikolai Tikhonov.

## 1981

*February 23–March 3.* The Twenty-sixth Communist Party Congress is held. No modification is made in the composition of any of the ruling bodies.

## 1982

*January 19.* General Semyen Tsvigun, first vice chairman of the KGB and brother-in-law of Brezhnev, dies. Rumors circulate in Moscow attributing his death to suicide and implicating those close to Brezhnev (particularly his daughter Galina and his son-in-law Yuri Churbanov) in vast schemes of corruption.

*January 25.* Mikhail Suslov, chief ideologist of the Party, dies at the age of 79.

*May 24.* At a plenum of the Central Committee, Yuri Andropov is named secretary of the Central Committee.

*September 8.* The Moscow branch of Helsinki Watch is shut down, its members having been arrested.

*November 10.* Brezhnev dies.

# Foreign Affairs

## 1964

*November.* Zhou Enlai visits Moscow and a slight thaw in Sino-Soviet relations occurs.

## 1965

*March 1–5.* An international conference of Communist parties is held in Moscow. The assembled representatives declare their solidarity with North Vietnam.

*April 5.* The Soviet Union furnishes surface-to-air missiles to North Vietnam for defense against American air bombardments.

## 1966

*March 29.* The Twenty-eighth Party Congress opens. No delegation from the Chinese Communist Party attends.

*April 27.* Pope Paul VI meets with Foreign Minister Gromyko in the Vatican. It is the first private audience accorded by a Catholic pontiff to a Soviet government official.

*June 20–July 1.* Following the withdrawal of France from NATO's military command structure, President Charles de Gaulle is given a triumphal welcome in Moscow.

## 1967

*January 27.* A treaty on the peaceful use of outer space is signed in Moscow, Washington and London.

*June 10.* The USSR breaks diplomatic relations with Israel following the Six-Day War. The Soviets will increase their military aid to Egypt and Syria.

## 1968

*July 1.* The Nuclear Nonproliferation Treaty is signed in Moscow, Washington and London.

*July 15.* Representatives of five of the members of the Warsaw Pact (the Soviet Union, Bulgaria, Hungary, Poland and East Germany) meet in Warsaw. A sharp warning is issued to Czechoslovakia, which is seen as being menaced by "counterrevolution."

*July 29–August 1.* Soviet-Czechoslovak discussions are held in the Slovak town of Cierna-on-Tisa. The Soviets demand that Czech leaders put an end to the "Prague Spring."

*August 21.* A military intervention by five Warsaw Pact nations (the Soviet Union, Bulgaria, Hungary, Poland and East Germany) in Czechoslovakia begins. Protests against this action are lodged by Romania, Yugoslavia, China and Albania (which will officially quit the Warsaw Pact on September 13). It will take more than a year of Soviet pressure before a "normalization" of the situation in Czechoslovakia that is suitable to the Soviet Union is achieved.

*September 26.* The "Brezhnev Doctrine" is published in *Pravda.* The Doctrine declares that the full sovereignty of individual socialist states is not bound to be completely respected in cases where internal events pose a danger to the world socialist system as a whole.

*October 16.* A Soviet-Czechoslovak treaty providing for the "temporary stationing" of foreign troops in Czechoslovakia is signed in Prague.

## 1969

*March 2.* The first of several bloody border clashes between Soviet and Chinese forces on the Ussuri River takes place.

*June 5–17.* A world-wide conference of Communist parties meets in Moscow. Numerous disagreements within the international Communist movement are revealed.

*September 11.* Kosygin meets with Zhou Enlai in Beijing. The Soviets and the Chinese decide to open negotiations on their border dispute.

*November 17.* The Strategic Arms Limitation Talks (SALT) between the United States and the Soviet Union open in Helsinki.

## 1970

*May 6.* A new treaty of friendship, cooperation and mutual assistance is signed by the USSR and Czechoslovakia.

*July 1.* The Soviet Union reestablishes diplomatic relations with China.

*July 7.* The Soviet Union signs a new treaty of friendship, cooperation and mutual assistance with Romania. This treaty leads to a relative normalization of relations between the two countries, which had been at odds since the intervention in Czechoslovakia.

*August 12.* The "Treaty of Moscow," an agreement by West Germany to respect postwar borders, is signed. This is a manifestation of the *Ostpolitik* of Chancellor Willy Brandt.

*October 6–13.* French President Georges Pompidou visits the USSR.

## 1971

*February 11.* An international treaty barring the emplacement of nuclear weapons on the seabed and the ocean floor is signed in Moscow, Washington and London.

*May 27.* A treaty of friendship and cooperation is signed by the Soviet Union and Egypt.

*July 27–29.* The 25th meeting of Comecon is held in Bucharest. Economic integration among its member states is strengthened.

*August 9.* The Soviets sign a treaty of friendship and cooperation with India.

*September 3.* The four occupying powers—the USSR, Great Britain, France and the United States—announce the conclusion of a treaty on the status of Berlin. The Soviet Union guarantees unhindered access to West Berlin.

*September 24.* Great Britain expels 105 Soviet diplomats accused of espionage.

*October 25–30.* Brezhnev visits France.

## 1972

*April 9.* The Soviet Union and Iraq sign a treaty of friendship and cooperation.

*April 10.* An international convention barring the development, production and stockpiling of bacteriological weapons is signed in Moscow, Washington and London.

*May 22–30.* President Richard Nixon visits Moscow. On May 26, Nixon and Brezhnev sign the SALT I agreements, which place limits on the deployment of strategic offensive missiles and on antiballistic missile systems. The two leaders also sign an agreement on basic principles of relations between their countries on May 29.

*July 18.* Because of what he calls Soviet "passivity" in the face of the hostility between Egypt and Israel, Egyptian President Anwar al-Sadat announces the expulsion of all Soviet advisors in Egypt.

*October 18.* A trade agreement is signed by the USSR and the United States.

*November 22.* Preliminary discussions open in Helsinki in preparation for the Conference on Security and Cooperation in Europe (CSCE).

## 1973

*May 18–22.* Brezhnev visits West Germany.

*June 18–25.* Brezhnev visits the United States. On June 22, he and President Nixon sign an agreement on the prevention of nuclear war.

*July 3.* The CSCE convenes in Helsinki.

*October.* During the Yom Kippur War between Israel and its Arab neighbors, the Soviet Union criticizes Israel and presents itself as the defender of Arab interests.

*October 30.* The Mutual and Balanced Force Reduction Talks (MBFR) between NATO and the Warsaw Pact open in Vienna.

## 1974

*January 28–February 3.* On a visit to Cuba, Brezhnev reaffirms Soviet support for the Castro regime.

*March 12–13.* Brezhnev and French President Pompidou meet at Pitsunda, in the Caucasus.

*July 3.* During a visit by President Nixon to the Soviet Union, a U.S.-Soviet treaty limiting the explosive yield of underground nuclear weapons tests is signed.

*November 23–24.* Brezhnev and President Gerald Ford meet at Vladivostok, where they agree in principle to new limitations on strategic nuclear weapons.

## 1975

*January 15.* The Soviets disavow the U.S.-Soviet trade agreement because they consider the Jackson-Vanik amendment to American trade legislation to constitute interference in the Soviet Union's internal affairs. (The amendment would require the Soviet Union to permit the free emigration of Jews in return for U.S. trade concessions.)

*August 1.* The Final Act of the CSCE (the "Helsinki Accord") is signed in Helsinki by 35 countries, including the USSR. In addition to recognizing existing borders in Europe, the Act also includes provisions for the observance of certain human rights.

*October 7.* The Soviet Union signs a treaty of friendship, cooperation and mutual assistance with East Germany.

*October 14–18.* French President Valéry Giscard d'Estaing visits the Soviet Union.

*November.* The Soviet Union provides assistance to the Popular Movement for the Liberation of Angola. (The United States lends its support to a rival group in the Angolan civil war.)

## 1976

*March 15.* Egypt abrogates the Soviet-Egyptian friendship treaty of 1971.

*May 28.* The United States and the Soviet Union sign a treaty limiting the yield of peaceful underground nuclear explosions.

*June 8–13.* Indian Prime Minister Indira Gandhi visits the USSR.

*July 16.* The USSR and France sign an agreement on the prevention of the accidental launching of nuclear weapons.

*October 8.* A treaty of friendship and cooperation is signed by the Soviet Union and Angola in Moscow.

*November 15–17.* Brezhnev makes an official visit to Yugoslavia.

## 1977

*August 16–24.* Marshal Josif Tito of Yugoslavia visits the Soviet Union.

*October 2.* A U.S.-Soviet declaration calls upon Israel to withdraw from the territories it has occupied since 1967.

*October 4.* The Belgrade Conference, which will examine the application of the Helsinki Accord, opens. The final resolution of this conference will be signed on March 8, 1978.

*November 13.* Somalia breaks its 1974 treaty of friendship with the USSR.

## 1978

*April 20.* A South Korean passenger plane is forced down by Soviet fighter aircraft in northern Russia (2 passengers are killed and 13 are injured).

*April 27.* A pro-Soviet coup in Afghanistan brings to power Nur Mohammad Taraki and his Afghan Communist Party (Khalq). A massive influx of Soviet advisors begins.

*June 21–25.* Turkish Prime Minister Bulent Ecevit visits the Soviet Union.

*December 5.* The Soviet Union signs a treaty of friendship and cooperation with Afghanistan.

## 1979

*June 18.* In Vienna, President Jimmy Carter and Brezhnev sign the SALT II Treaty limiting strategic offensive arms.

*September 16.* In Afghanistan, a coup brings Hafizullah Amin to power. The Soviet Union supports the new regime.

*October 6.* Brezhnev announces the unilateral withdrawal of 1,000 tanks and 20,000 troops from East Germany.

*December 12.* Responding to the installation, since 1977, of Soviet SS-20 ballistic missiles targeted on Western Europe, the NATO alliance announces that it intends to deploy American Pershing II and ground-launched cruise missiles in Europe.

*December 26–27.* The Soviet Union invades Afghanistan. Hafizullah Amin is killed and replaced by Babrak Karmal. The Soviet Union will send massive amounts of military personnel and weapons into the country.

## 1980

*January.* As a result of the Soviet invasion of Afghanistan, the U.S. Congress suspends consideration of the ratification of the SALT II Treaty. President Carter announces an embargo on the sale of grain and high-technology equipment to the Soviet Union (January 4). He also calls for a boycott of the Moscow Olympic Games, which are scheduled for later in the year.

*January 14.* The General Assembly of the United Nations calls for the im-

mediate withdrawal of "foreign troops" from Afghanistan.

*March 19.* An agreement of cooperation is signed by the Soviet Communist Party and the Sandinista National Liberation Front of Nicaragua.

*June 30–July 1.* West German Chancellor Helmut Schmidt visits the Soviet Union.

*August 31.* In Poland, the Gdansk Agreement is signed by the Polish government and the striking workers who have formed the independent trade union Solidarity. The Soviet Union increases its pressure on the Polish government.

*September 9–11.* A meeting of representatives of nearly thirty Moslem countries is held in Tashkent.

*October 8.* A treaty of friendship and cooperation is signed by the USSR and Syria.

*November 11.* The second CSCE conference to examine the application of the Helsinki Accord opens in Madrid.

*December 8–11.* Brezhnev visits India.

## 1981

*April 24.* President Ronald Reagan lifts the grain embargo on the Soviet Union.

*October 19–20.* Yasir Arafat visits the Soviet Union and signs an agreement whereby the USSR accords diplomatic status to the Palestine Liberation Organization (PLO).

*November 18.* President Reagan offers to reverse the NATO decision to deploy Pershing II and cruise missiles in Europe, in exchange for a Soviet agreement to dismantle SS-20, SS-4 and SS-5 missiles (the "zero option").

*November 20.* The Soviets sign a commercial accord with West Ger-

many for the sale of Siberian natural gas.
*November 22–25.* Brezhnev visits West Germany.
*November 30.* The Intermediate-range Nuclear Forces (INF) talks between the United States and the Soviet Union begin in Geneva.
*December 29.* Following the imposition of marshal law in Poland (December 13), President Reagan criticizes the Soviet Union for its "direct responsibility" for the Polish crisis and announces economic and diplomatic sanctions against the USSR and Poland.

## 1982

*January 23.* The Soviet Union signs a commercial accord with France for the sale of Siberian natural gas.
*June 29.* Strategic Arms Reduction Talks (START) between the United States and the Soviet Union open in Geneva.

# Economy and Society

## 1965

*March 24–26.* Central control over the kolkhozes is relaxed.
*September 27–29.* A plenum of the Central Committee approves a major industrial reform plan (inspired by the ideas of Evsei Liberman). The *sovnarkhozes* (regional economic councils) are abolished. State control over enterprises is relaxed, and "stimulation funds" are set aside for use as subsidies and to finance social measures and the development of new production techniques.

## 1966

*July 1.* Monthly salaries for kolkhozniks are introduced.

## 1967

*April 12.* A decree on the financial autonomy of the sovkhozes is issued.
*September 16.* A decree authorizes artisanal enterprises on the kolkhozes.

## 1968

*June 27.* A basic law on marriage and the family is promulgated. It reinforces the requirement that marriages be registered with the state.

## 1969

*November 25–27.* The Third Congress of Kolkhozniks is held. Kolkhoz Councils are established; their members will be elected from different echelons in the kolkhozes' administrative hierarchy.
*November 28.* New regulations for kolkhozes are adopted.

## 1970

*January.* A census is taken. The population of the Soviet Union is set at 241.7 million.
*July 14–15.* A basic law on labor legislation is adopted.

## 1971

*March 30–April 9.* The Twenty-fourth Party Congress approves the Ninth Five-Year Plan (1971–1975). Its key objective is to "perceptibly increase the well-being of the workers."
*June.* Metropolitan Pimen becomes head of the Orthodox Church, succeeding Patriarch Alexis, who recently died.

## 1972

*July 30.* The Krasnoyarsk Hydroelectric Station goes into operation.
*December 13.* A huge canal project intended to connect the Irtysh River with the Aral Sea is announced.

## 1973

*January 29.* A huge irrigation project that will cover an area of 200,000 square kilometers to the north of the Caspian Sea is announced.

*March 2.* A decree on "the perfection of industrial management" is issued. An industrial reorganization program that, in theory, will lessen the control of state ministries over enterprises is put into effect.

## 1974

A huge soil-improvement project is launched; it will cover those areas of European Russia that lack "black earth."

*March 27.* Enterprises are reorganized into "production associations." The policy favoring the establishment of extremely large enterprises is abandoned, and enterprises are granted some autonomy in order to better utilize stimulation funds and to rationalize management.

## 1975

The grain harvest, totaling only 140 million tons, is a disaster.

*May 8.* The first section of the BAM (the Baikal-Amur Railway) is completed.

*December 30.* In an effort to stimulate research, a decision is made to create "scientific production associations" that link research laboratories with factories.

## 1976

*February 25–March 5.* At the Twenty-fifth Party Congress, Brezhnev stresses the need to raise the Soviet standard of living during the Tenth Five-Year Plan (1976–1980).

## 1977

*April 14.* A law is promulgated promoting the integration of common services (such as construction, production, marketing) among kolkhozes and sovkhozes.

*September 6.* Inhabitants of Gorky demand that churches be reopened.

## 1978

The Soviet Union has a record harvest of 237 million tons of grain.

*February 1.* The Free Association of Soviet Workers (SMOT), an independent trade union, is established illegally in Moscow.

*November 1.* The use of the Tupolev TU 144, the first supersonic transport aircraft, is halted because of technical flaws in its design.

*December 7.* Model regulations concerning "production associations" in agriculture are adopted: Basic units within production associations are reorganized to integrate them with the food industry and with research laboratories.

## 1979

*January.* A census sets the population of the USSR at 262.4 million.

*July 12.* A decree strengthens control over enterprises.

## 1980

*April 14.* A Central Committee Conference is held on the acceleration of the pace of construction projects connected with the oil and natural gas complex in western Siberia.

## 1981

*January 8.* A decree is issued setting forth measures intended to augment agricultural production in marginal areas.

*February 23–March 3.* The Twenty-sixth Party Congress sets the objectives for the Eleventh Five-Year Plan (1981–1985).

## 1982

*January 1.* A reform of wholesale industrial prices goes into effect.

# Civilization and Culture

## 1964

The Taganka Theater is established in Moscow by Yuri Lyubimov. *The Sun of the Incas*, by E. Denisov.

## 1965

Mikhail Sholokov is awarded the Nobel Prize for literature. After the publication of *Bratsk Station*, Yevgeni Yevtushenko's privileges are restored. Films: *War and Peace*, by Sergei Bondarchuk (1965–1967); *The First Teacher*, by A. Mikhalkov-Konchalovsky.

## 1966

*Kolyma Tales*, by Varlam Shalamov. *Phoenix 66*, a *samizdat* by Yuri Galanskov. *Babi Yar*, a novel by Anatoli Kuznetsov.

## 1967

*My Testimony*, published in *samizdat*, by Anatoli Marchenko. *Andrei Rublev*, a film by Andrei Tarkovsky (it will not be released until 1971). I. Ozerov begins work on the film *Liberation* (1967–1971).

## 1968

Alexander Solzhenitsyn's *Cancer Ward* and *The First Circle* are published abroad.

## 1969

The novelist A. Kuznetsov leaves the Soviet Union. A. Solzhenitsyn is expelled from the Soviet Writers' Union. Andrei Amalrik's essay "Will the Soviet Union Survive until 1984?" is published in *samizdat*. Films: *Sayat Nova*, by S. Paradzhanov; *Gentry Nest*, by A. Mikhalkov-Konchalovsky.

## 1970

Viktor Yerofeyev completes *Moskva-Pitushka*, which circulates in *samizdat*. *Khrushchev Remembers*, the first volume of N. Khrushchev's memoirs, is published in the West (a second volume will be published in 1974, and a third in 1990). Films: *There Was a Singing Blackbird*, by the Georgian O. Ioseliani; *King Lear*, by Grigori Kozintsev.

*February.* Alexander Tvardovsky is dismissed as editor of the literary review *Novy Mir*.

*October 8.* A. Solzhenitsyn is awarded the Nobel Prize for literature.

## 1971

The first issue of *Veche*, Vladimir Osipov's clandestine nationalist journal, appears. A. Solzhenitsyn's *August 1914* and Vladimir Maximov's *The Seven Days of Creation* are published in the West.

## 1972

The poet Y. Galanskov dies in detention. The poet Joseph Brodsky is forced to emigrate.

*January 25.* The Central Committee emphasizes the need to wage an ideological war against nonconformist tendencies.

## 1973

The first volume of *The Gulag Archipelago*, by A. Solzhenitsyn, appears in the West. The writers Andrei Sinyavsky and Zhores Medvedev (who is also a biologist) leave the Soviet Union. *The Red Guelder Rose*, a film by Vasili Shukshin.

## 1974

The writers Viktor Nekrasov and Vladimir Maximov, and the poet and singer Alexander Galich, leave the Soviet Union.

*February.* A. Solzhenitsyn is expelled from the Soviet Union.

## 1975

The novel *The Life and Extraordinary Adventures of Private Ivan Chonkin*, by Vladimir Voinovich, is published in the West. Films: *Bonus*, by S. Mikaelian; *Agony*, by Elem Klimov.

*October 17.* Leonid Kantorovich is awarded the Nobel Prize for economics.

## 1976

Valentin Rasputin's *Farewell to Matyora* enjoys great success. Yuri Trifonov's *House on the Embankment* and Alexander Zinoviev's *The Yawning Heights* are published in the West. Films: *I Wish to Speak*, by Gleb Panfilov; *Twenty Days Without War*, by A. German. The historian Andrei Amalrik and the mathematician Leonid Plyushch leave the Soviet Union. The sculptor Ernst Neizvestny is expelled from the country.

## 1978

A. Zinoviev is forced to emigrate. *Pushkin House*, by Andrei Bitov, and *Faculty of Useless Things*, by Yuri Dombrovsky, are published in the West. *Siberiade*, a film by A. Mikhalkov-Konchalovsky.

## 1979

Yevgeni Yevtushenko's *Ivan the Terrible and Ivan the Fool* is published. Films: *Stalker*, by A. Tarkovsky; *A Few Days in the Life of Oblomov*, by N. Mikhalkov.

## 1980

The novel *Life and Fate*, by Vasili Grossman, appears in the West.

*July–August.* The XXII Olympic Games are held in Moscow. Approximately 60 nations, including the United States, boycott the Games to protest the Soviet invasion of Afghanistan.

*December.* The writers V. Voinovich, Vasily Aksyonov and Lev Kopelev are forced into exile.

## 1982

*July 30.* The Central Committee issues a decree on "cultural reviews and the building of socialism."

# The Andropov-Chernenko Interregnum

The election of Yuri Andropov as general secretary in 1982 did not result in any fundamental alteration of the political line adopted by Leonid Brezhnev, although initially it seemed that a change was in the making. In reality, however, the former KGB chief who was promoted to head the Soviet state was more concerned with changing the image of the leadership than its policies: He was anxious to reestablish discipline within a Party that had been compromised by scandal during Brezhnev's last years. Although the new general secretary often spoke of reform, he did not initiate any basic structural change, whether of institutions or the economy. Those new measures that he did introduce were primarily aimed at reinforcing labor discipline. While putting himself forward as the leader of a modern state, Andropov adhered to the ideological line of his predecessor and actually increased the level of repression, especially against dissidents and religious movements.

On Andropov's death in February 1984, Konstantin Chernenko, who had been Brezhnev's heir apparent, was elected general secretary. Chernenko's selection was quickly seen as a transitional arrangement. In contrast to the previous rule of silence always observed in such matters, the serious illness of the head of state was often publicly invoked to justify his frequent absences.

Standing in the wings was Mikhail Gorbachev, who had already been suggested as a possible successor to Andropov. Gorbachev's influence was immediately confirmed by his role in the electoral campaign for a new Supreme Soviet, and then by his nomination to head a commission on foreign affairs. When Chernenko died on March 10, 1985, the rapidity of Gorbachev's elevation to the top leadership post surprised only Western observers.

## Politics and Institutions

### 1982

*November 12.* A plenum of the Central Committee unanimously elects Yuri Andropov to the post of general secretary of the Party.

*November 22.* A plenum of the Central Committee is held. Nikolai Ryzhkov becomes a member of the Secretariat, Geidar Aliyev (first secretary of the Party in Azerbaijan) is made a full member of the Politburo, and Andrei Kirilenko is removed from his positions on the Secretariat and the Politburo. The city of

Naberezhnye Chelny is renamed Brezhnev.

*November 24.* Aliyev becomes first vice chairman of the Council of Ministers.

*December 8.* *Literary Gazette* attacks the "Group for the Reestablishment of Trust between the USSR and the USA."

*December 17.* Nikolai Shchelokov, the minister of the interior, is replaced by Vitali Fedorchuk, who until then had been chairman of the KGB. Viktor Chebrikov is named head of the KGB. With Andropov leading the way, the regime manifests its desire to fight corruption and to clean up public life while at the same time repressing dissidents of all stripes.

*December 21–22.* A joint session of the Supreme Soviet and the Central Committee is held to commemorate the 60th anniversary of the founding of the USSR. Andropov uses the occasion to reaffirm Soviet policy with respect to the nationalities that make up the Soviet Union: "It is not only a question of bringing nations together, but of fusing them."

## 1983

*January 26.* Alfonsas Svarinskas, a priest and member of the Committee for the Defense of the Rights of Believers, is arrested in Lithuania. The antireligion campaign intensifies.

*February 18.* Sergei Grigoryants, a specialist in Russian literature, is arrested in Borovsk (near Moscow) and accused of participating in the publication of the clandestine information bulletin *V.*

*March 24.* Andrei Gromyko, the foreign minister, is given the additional title of first vice chairman of the Council of Ministers, with special responsibility for the coordination of foreign policy.

*April 12.* V. Gershuni, a member of SMOT (an illegal free trade union) and the former editor of the *samizdat* review *Poiski,* is institutionalized in a psychiatric hospital.

*Night of May 31–June 1.* A peace demonstration organized in a Moscow park is dispersed.

*June 14–15.* A plenum of the Central Committee is held. Konstantin Chernenko gives a report on "the current problems of ideological work and politics with respect to the masses." Andropov intervenes in the preparation of a revised Party program. Grigori Romanov, the first secretary of the Leningrad Party organization, joins the Secretariat of the Central Committee.

*June 16.* Andropov is elected president of the Presidium of the Supreme Soviet.

*October 24.* The Ukrainian philologist and journalist Anatoli Marchenko is arrested and accused of "anti-Soviet propaganda."

## 1984

*February 9.* Andropov dies, the victim of an illness whose existence was officially denied until the end.

*February 13.* Chernenko is unanimously elected general secretary by a plenum of the Central Committee.

*March 4.* Elections are held for the Supreme Soviet, with 99.9 percent of registered voters reportedly participating. The candidates (one per office) for the Soviet of the Union obtain 99.94 percent of the vote, and the candidates for the Soviet of the Nationalities get 99.95 percent of the vote.

*March 15.* The city of Rybinsk is renamed Andropov.

*April 10.* A plenum of the Central Committee adopts resolutions on increasing the authority of the soviets and on the broad outline of a reform of education.

*April 11.* Chernenko is elected president of the Presidium of the Supreme Soviet.

*May 2.* Andrei Sakharov begins a hunger strike in order that his wife, Yelena Bonner, be allowed by the authorities to go abroad for medical treatment.

*July.* Vyacheslav Molotov is reinstated in the Communist Party.

*August 17.* Bonner is sentenced to five years of internal exile in Gorky for "calumnies against the state."

*September 7.* Marshal Nikolai Ogarkov, chief of the General Staff of the armed forces since 1977, is dismissed. He is replaced by Marshal Sergei Akhromeyev.

*December 10.* A national conference is held "on the improvement of advanced socialism and the ideological work of the Party."

*December 20.* Marshal Dmitri Ustinov, the defense minister, dies. He will be replaced by Marshal Sergei Sokolov on December 22.

## 1985

*February 24.* Elections are held for local soviets and republic soviets. Brezhnev's son and his son-in-law, Yuri Churbanov (the former deputy minister of the interior), are not reelected as deputies of the Russian Federation.

*March 10.* Chernenko dies of an illness that had been acknowledged by high officials since January.

# Foreign Affairs

## 1982

*November 13.* President Ronald Reagan lifts the sanctions that were imposed on the USSR following the decla-

ration of martial law in Poland in December 1981.

*December 3.* Meetings are held in Moscow between Andropov and a delegation of Arab leaders led by King Hussein of Jordan. Soviet policy on the Middle East is reaffirmed, and "Israeli aggression in Lebanon" is condemned.

## 1983

*January 1.* TASS issues a statement on the war in Afghanistan reaffirming that "the limited contingent of Soviet forces will not be withdrawn until foreign intervention ceases." The statement denies President Reagan's allegation that the Soviets are using chemical weapons in Afghanistan.

*January 4–5.* The Political Consultative Committee of the Warsaw Pact meets in Prague. The great challenge for the Soviet Union in 1983 will be to avert the scheduled deployment of American Pershing II and cruise missiles in Western Europe.

*January 16–19.* Andrei Gromyko visits West Germany.

*January 27.* The INF talks (on limiting intermediate-range nuclear forces in Europe) resume in Geneva.

*February 2.* The Strategic Arms Reduction Talks (START) resume in Geneva.

*February 16–21.* French Foreign Minister Claude Cheysson visits Moscow.

*March 1–15.* Soviet and Chinese officials meet in Moscow to discuss the possibility of normalizing relations between their two countries.

*April 5.* France expels 47 Soviet diplomats and residents accused of espionage.

*May 28.* The Soviet government declares that it will be compelled to take "countermeasures" should NATO proceed with the planned deployment of American missiles in Western Europe.

*July 4–6.* West German Chancellor Helmut Kohl visits Moscow.

*August 25.* A new grain agreement with the United States is signed in Moscow. It calls for the purchase by the Soviet Union of a minimum of 9 million tons of American grain each year.

*Night of August 31–September 1.* Soviet fighter aircraft shoot down a South Korean airliner that flies over Sakhalin Island (269 passengers and crew are killed). The Soviet Union accuses the United States of having deliberately directed the aircraft off its normal route, putting it on an espionage mission over Soviet territory.

*September 7–8.* The final meeting of the Madrid Conference on the application of the Helsinki Accords takes place.

*September 7–15.* Deputy Foreign Minister Mikhail Kapitsa visits Beijing (Peking).

*September 9.* Foreign Minister Gromyko visits Paris.

*October 6–20.* Sino-Soviet political consultations take place in Beijing.

*October 18–20.* The heads of the Comecon member states meet in East Berlin. They approve a plan for cooperation through the year 2000, and they issue a declaration on the planned deployment of American missiles in Europe.

*October 25.* TASS issues a statement condemning the American invasion of Grenada.

*November 24.* Following the deployment of the first Pershing II missiles in Europe, Andropov breaks off arms control negotiations in Geneva. He also ends the Soviet moratorium on the deployment of intermediate-range nuclear weapons, and accelerates the deploy-

ment of tactical missiles in East Germany and Czechoslovakia.

# 1984

*January 17.* The Conference on Disarmament in Europe (CDE) opens in Stockholm.

*May 8.* The Soviet Olympic Committee announces that the USSR will not participate in the 23rd Olympic Games that will be held in Los Angeles that fall.

*May 23.* Marshal Kim Il Sung, the president of North Korea, visits Moscow.

*May 26–30.* Australian Foreign Minister Bill Hayden visits Moscow. It has been 20 years since an Australian official of this high a level has come to the Soviet Union.

*June 12–14.* A summit conference of Comecon countries is held in Moscow.

*June 21–23.* French President François Mitterrand visits the Soviet Union. Differences are expressed on several issues (Afghanistan, Cambodia, Poland, human rights and the deployment of missiles in Europe).

*June 29.* The Soviet government issues a declaration directed at the American government on the urgent necessity of taking measures to prevent the militarization of outer space. The statement reflects Soviet anxiety over the American Strategic Defense Initiative (the SDI or "Star Wars" program).

*June 30.* The Soviets advance a proposal for peace in the Middle East.

*September.* Under Soviet pressure, East German leader Erich Honecker cancels his planned visit to West Germany.

*September 17.* The French journalist Jacques Abouchar is captured in Afghanistan. Sentenced to 18 years imprisonment, he will be freed on October 25

274

following French entreaties to the Soviet leadership.

*September 28.* President Reagan meets with Foreign Minister Gromyko at the White House. This marks the reopening of the Soviet-American dialogue following the deployment of American missiles in Europe.

*October 9.* The USSR signs a treaty of friendship and cooperation with South Yemen.

*November 23.* The resumption of arms control negotiations in Geneva in January 1985 is announced by the Soviet Union and the United States.

*December 15–21.* Mikhail Gorbachev visits Great Britain.

*December 21–28.* The first vice chairman of the Council of Ministers, Ivan Arkhipov, visits China. The countries agree to cooperate in several areas.

## 1985

*January 7–8.* In Geneva, Foreign Minister Gromyko meets with American Secretary of State George Schultz. They announce the reopening of nuclear arms reduction talks (the negotiations will resume in Geneva on March 12).

*February 11–14.* Greek Prime Minister Andreas Papandreou visits Moscow.

*February 25–March 1.* Gromyko visits Italy (where he will meet with Pope John Paul II on February 27) and Spain.

*March 3–13.* A Chinese parliamentary delegation visits the Soviet Union.

# Economy and Society

## 1982

Jewish emigration hits its lowest point since 1970 (2,670 departures, compared with 9,460 in 1981, and 51,300 in 1979).

*December 10.* Model regulations are issued on "agro-industrial unions."

## 1983

*January 7.* The Central Committee holds a meeting to discuss "the strengthening of labor discipline." Since his accession to power, Andropov has launched a major campaign (involving party organizations, administrative offices, trade unions and the Komsomol) against absenteeism and "parasitism."

*February 9.* Criticized for its abuse of psychiatric internment as a political tool, the Soviet Union withdraws from the World Psychiatric Association.

*June 17.* A law is adopted on "work collectives and their increasing role in the management of enterprises." Work collectives participate in the discussion and elaboration of planning projects, in the negotiation of collective agreements, and in the determination of measures to boost labor productivity. The collectives also assist in maintaining control over the labor force.

*July 26.* A decree expands the role of trade unions in planning and in other spheres of economic activity. Greater autonomy is granted to enterprises in the management of their day-to-day affairs. Trial programs will soon be established in several sectors; they will be extended throughout industry in 1987.

*August 7.* A decree is issued on the "strengthening of socialist labor discipline." The productivity of individual workers is to be taken into account when calculating vacation time, wages are to be withheld for defective output, and a struggle against alcohol consumption on the job is launched.

## 1984

For the first time since World War II, Soviet oil production declines. A major energy development program that is already under way is seriously hampered by difficulties in exploitation, by lack of needed technology and by delays.

*March 26–27.* A national conference is convened to explore problems of industrial agriculture. Since 1981 the USSR has not published the production figures for grain; harvests have fallen well short of the goals set in the economic plans.

*April 12.* A law sets the guidelines for a major reform of general and professional education. It mandates an improvement of training programs for technical careers (such programs are to include 70 percent of all students within 10 years), an improvement of education in rural schools, and an improvement of teaching conditions. Schools are also required to contribute to the "ideological and patriotic" education of youth.

*July 13.* The execution of the former director of the best-known food store in Moscow is announced. He was convicted of economic crimes.

*September 30.* The eastern and western segments of the Baikal-Amur (BAM) Railway are joined. The railway will not become fully operational for another five years.

*October 23.* A plenum of the Central Committee is devoted to problems of agriculture. A long-term program for soil improvement is discussed. Among the projects unveiled is one that would reverse the flow of Siberian rivers toward the south.

# Civilization and Culture

## 1983

*February 8.* The caricaturist V. Sysoyev is arrested.

## 1984

The filmmaker Andrei Tarkovsky emigrates.

*March.* Yuri Lyubimov loses his post as director of the Taganka Theater; he will be deprived of his Soviet citizenship in July.

# Chapter 33        1985-1991

## Gorbachev and *Perestroika*

Upon his accession to power, Mikhail Gorbachev engaged in a policy of reform. This policy, which was accelerated in 1989, led the USSR along a path of radical change that ultimately brought about the country's dissolution. Faced with an inflexible system, he affirmed the need for a new basis of political legitimacy, one founded on the assent of civil society, in order to pull the country out of its "stagnation."

With the key words *glasnost* (openness) and *perestroika* (restructuring), Gorbachev launched a program of political and economic reform that quickly exceeded its initial goals. The creation of a "state of law," the democratization of institutions, and the influence given to public opinion led to a genuine redistribution of power. The Party abandoned its leading role, the soviets and the new Congress of People's Deputies were endowed with real popular legitimacy, and the presidential system of government conferred on the head of state an unprecedented power.

But certain habits from the past remained. These continued to take their revenge in the economic domain, where projects ran aground because of hesitation and uncertainty, the resistance of the bureaucracy, and the persistence of a way of life anchored in decades of administrative control. The announcement of a shift to a market economy (whose consequences were unforeseeable) provoked more uneasiness than enthusiasm from a population already weary of constant shortages.

Gorbachev's "revolution from above" nevertheless found real support in a society where change had been kept hidden for so long. His revolution was also accompanied by a spectacular reopening of issues from the past whose complexity and sensitivity simply added to the challenges of reform. Meanwhile, other challenges, these from abroad, had to be met. The sudden yet peaceful upheaval of Central and Eastern Europe, made possible by a renewed international détente, also made necessary a redefinition of the Soviet Union's place in "the common European home" that had figured so prominently in Gorbachev's speeches.

Gorbachev's crucial role in ending the cold war was not enough, however, to prevent the spectacularly sudden collapse of Soviet communism and the Soviet Union itself at the end of 1991. Gorbachev never recovered after an unsuccessful coup was launched against him in August 1991 by his own hard-line appointees. This seminal event resulted in the Soviet president being eclipsed by his Russian counterpart, Boris Yeltsin. Ultimately, it seemed that while *perestroika* had failed to rescue the economy, *glasnost* had succeeded in opening the eyes of the Soviet people to such an extent that a return to the old ways was impossible. The 74-year-old experiment that was the USSR ended with a whimper, not a bang, and the periphery of the empire won its independence—at least for now—from a center that could not hold.

# Politics and Institutions

## 1985

*March 11.* Mikhail Gorbachev succeeds Konstantin Chernenko in the post of general secretary of the Party. Within a year, Gorbachev will profoundly transform the composition of the country's political officialdom (70 percent of the ministers at the national level, and 50 percent of the cadres in the federated republics, will be replaced).

*April 23.* A plenum of the Central Committee is held. Gorbachev makes a programmatic speech. The top leadership is altered: Viktor Chebrikov (chairman of the KGB), Yegor Ligachev (Central Committee secretary in charge of ideology and cadres), and Nikolai Ryzhkov (Central Committee secretary in charge of the economy) become full members of the Politburo.

*July 1.* A plenum of the Central Committee is held. Grigori Romanov leaves the Politburo, while Eduard Shevardnadze becomes a full member. Boris Yeltsin and Lev Zaikov join the Secretariat of the Central Committee.

*July 2.* Shevardnadze becomes minister of foreign affairs, replacing Andrei Gromyko, who is elected president of the Presidium of the Supreme Soviet.

*July 21.* Alexander Yakovlev, a close associate of Gorbachev, is named chief of propaganda on the Central Committee.

*September 27.* Ryzhkov replaces Nikolai Tikhonov as chairman of the Council of Ministers.

*October 14.* Nikolai Talyzin replaces Nikolai Baibakov as head of Gosplan.

*December 2.* Yelena Bonner receives permission to travel to the United States for medical treatment.

## 1986

*February 11.* The Jewish dissident Anatoli Shcharansky is freed in Berlin in exchange for Eastern bloc intelligence agents.

*February 25–March 6.* The Twenty-seventh Party Congress is held. Gorbachev denounces the "stagnation" of the Brezhnev era. He insists on the necessity of profound reforms in the management of the economy and on the need to democratize society. The Party program and bylaws are revised.

*April 26.* An explosion at a nuclear power plant in Chernobyl, 80 miles north of Kiev, is followed by a release of radioactive gases. Moscow will not acknowledge the accident until April 28. One hundred thousand persons will be forced to evacuate the areas affected by the nuclear radiation.

*August 28.* The Council of Ministers issues a decree specifying conditions for the granting of entry and exit visas.

# Breakup of the Soviet Union and Formation of the Commonwealth of Independent States

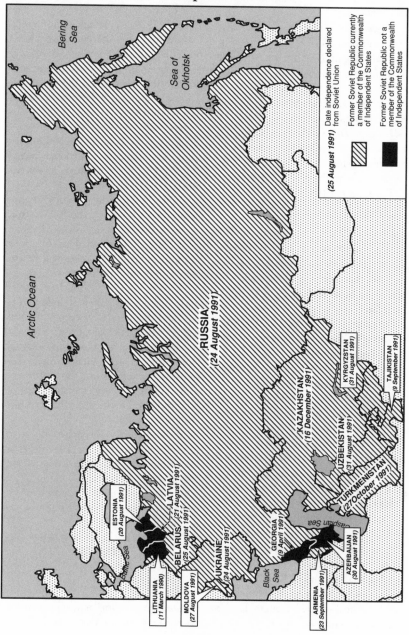

*(25 August 1991)* Date independence declared from Soviet Union

Former Soviet Republic currently a member of the Commonwealth of Independent States

Former Soviet Republic not a member of the Commonwealth of Independent States

Bering Sea

Sea of Okhotsk

Arctic Ocean

RUSSIA (24 August 1991)

KAZAKHSTAN (16 December 1991)

KYRGYZSTAN (31 August 1991)

TAJIKISTAN (9 September 1991)

UZBEKISTAN (31 August 1991)

TURKMENISTAN (27 October 1991)

ESTONIA (20 August 1991)

LATVIA (21 August 1991)

BELARUS (25 August 1991)

UKRAINE (24 August 1991)

GEORGIA (9 April 1991)

Caspian Sea

AZERBAIJAN (30 August 1991)

Baltic Sea

Black Sea

LITHUANIA (11 March 1990)

MOLDOVA (27 August 1991)

ARMENIA (23 September 1991)

*October 5.* Yuri Orlov, founder of the Helsinki Watch group, arrives in New York. He had been in exile in Siberia since 1984.

*November 30.* The Central Committee issues a decree on the "strengthening of socialist legality and the protection of the legitimate rights and interests of citizens."

*December 9.* The dissident Anatoli Marchenko dies in prison.

*December 16.* Gorbachev personally announces that Andrei Sakharov is free to return to Moscow. Sakharov had been living in exile in the city of Gorky since the beginning of 1980.

## 1987

*January 27–28.* A plenum of the Central Committee is held to discuss policy with respect to cadres. Gorbachev proposes that elections to the soviets be carried out by secret ballot with multiple candidates.

*February 3.* Yuri Churbanov, Brezhnev's son-in-law, is arrested and accused of corruption.

*February 9.* The freeing of approximately 100 dissidents is announced.

*February 14–16.* In Sakharov's presence, Gorbachev affirms the "irreversible" nature of *perestroika*.

*May 6.* The organization *Pamyat* holds a demonstration. This group will be characterized increasingly by an aggressive nationalism and anti-Semitism.

*May 28.* A small airplane piloted by a West German youth, Mathias Rust, lands in Red Square after penetrating Soviet air defenses. On May 30, Marshal Sergei Sokolov (the defense minister) and Marshal Alexander Koldunov (the commander in chief of antiaircraft defense) will be dismissed. General Dmitri Yazov will become defense minister.

*June 21.* Elections for local soviets are held. Multiple candidates run for office in approximately 4 percent of the local districts.

*June 25–26.* A plenum of the Central Committee strengthens Gorbachev's position. Nikolai Slyunkov, Alexander Yakovlev and Viktor Nikonov are appointed full members of the Politburo, while General Yazov becomes a candidate member.

*July 7–29.* A trial is held for three individuals accused of being responsible for the nuclear accident at Chernobyl. Each is sentenced to a 10-year term in a labor camp.

*August 20–23.* A meeting of 47 "sociopolitical action groups" is held in Moscow.

*September 4.* The West German pilot Mathias Rust is sentenced to four years in a labor camp. (He will be released on August 4, 1988.)

*October 12–13.* Gorbachev vigorously defends his policy of "restructuring" and threatens to "sweep out" local leaders who do not support it.

*October 21.* A plenum of the Central Committee is held. Geidar Aliyev resigns from the Politburo for health reasons. Yeltsin criticizes the slow pace of *perestroika* and accuses Ligachev of obstructing reform.

*November 2.* Gorbachev declares himself in favor of a "socialism that is unencumbered by the slag of dogmatism and that can prove itself economically." The establishment of a commission of inquiry on the victims of Stalin is announced.

*November 11.* Yeltsin loses his post as first secretary of the Moscow Party. He is succeeded by Lev Zaikov.

## 1988

*January 8.* Gorbachev calls for a compromise between the "right" and the "left," between the "conservatives" and those who are "impatient."

*February 4.* The Supreme Court of the USSR posthumously rehabilitates the 10 individuals who were condemned at the third Moscow show trial in March 1938, including Nikolai Bukharin, Alexei Rykov and Christian Rakovsky.

*February 5.* Nikolai Talyzin is replaced by Yuri Masliukov as head of Gosplan.

*February 17–18.* A plenum of the Central Committee is held. Yeltsin is removed from the Politburo; Masliukov and Georgi Razumovsky become candidate members of that body.

*March 13.* An article that is very critical of Gorbachev's policies is published in *Sovietskaia Rossia.* Signed by Nina Andreyeva, the article is considered to be the manifesto of forces hostile to *perestroika.*

*May 7–9.* A group calling itself "Democratic Union" is formed in Moscow. Defining itself as a political party, the group will be condemned by the Communist Party Conference the following month.

*June 3.* Sakharov holds a press conference, where he reviews the progress that has been made with respect to human rights in the USSR.

*June 13.* The Supreme Court announces the rehabilitation of Grigori Zinoviev, Lev Kamenev, Grigori Piatakov and Karl Radek.

*June 21.* Bukharin and Rykov are posthumously reinstated in the ranks of the Communist Party.

*June 28–July 1.* Approximately 5,000 delegates attend the Nineteenth Communist Party Conference in Moscow (the first such meeting since 1941). Resolutions are adopted on institutional reform, *glasnost,* the struggle against bureaucracy, *perestroika,* judicial reform and the nationalities question. The Party approves the erection of a monument to Stalin's victims.

*September 30.* A plenum of the Central Committee approves a vast reform of the Party's structure, including a reorganization of the Central Committee apparatus. The conservative "old guard" is forced out: Andrei Gromyko is removed from his posts as head of state and member of the Politburo; Mikhail Solomentsev, Vladimir Dolgikh and Peter Demichev also leave the Politburo. Vadim Medvedev becomes responsible for ideology, while Ligachev takes over responsibility for agriculture.

*October 1.* The Supreme Soviet holds an extraordinary session. Gorbachev is elected president of the Presidium and becomes head of state. He announces an acceleration of the program of reform. Vladimir Kryuchkov replaces Viktor Chebrikov as head of the KGB.

*October 20.* Sakharov is elected to the Presidium of the Academy of Sciences.

*December 1.* The Supreme Soviet adopts a reform of the Soviet Constitution and a new election law for people's deputies. A Congress of People's Deputies, with 2,250 members, is created. A true presidency is established (the president of the Supreme Soviet, who will be elected by the Congress of People's Deputies), and multiple-candidate elections are introduced at every level.

*December 17.* A fundamental reform of the penal code is announced: The duration of sentences is reduced, the application of the death penalty is restricted, and internal exile is abolished.

## 1989

*March 15–16.* The Central Committee opens an inquiry on Boris Yeltsin because of his proposals for a multiparty system.

*March 18.* In Moscow, 10,000 persons demonstrate in support of Yeltsin.

*March 26.* The first round of elections for the Congress of People's Deputies is held. Numerous reformers and nationalists are elected. Yeltsin is elected by Moscow voters in a landslide.

*April 9.* The second round of legislative elections confirms the victory of the reformers.

*April 25.* One hundred and ten members and deputy members of the Central Committee and of the Commission on the Revision of the Party resign. Gorbachev's position vis-à-vis the conservatives is strengthened.

*May 25.* The Congress of People's Deputies convenes. Gorbachev is elected head of state by a vote of 2,123 to 87, but the reformers will be in the minority in the Supreme Soviet that the Congress elects the following day.

*June 8.* The Congress of People's Deputies ratifies the nomination of Ryzhkov as chairman of the Council of Ministers (prime minister).

*July 2.* Gromyko dies.

*July 30.* An interregional parliamentary group is formed. Among its 388 members are Yuri Afanasiev, Yeltsin, Sakharov and Gavril Popov. The group proposes an acceleration of the tempo of reform.

*July 31.* A law is adopted on penal responsibility for "crimes against state."

*September 20–21.* A plenum of the Central Committee is held to discuss the nationalities problem. Five members of the Politburo resign, among them the last Brezhnevite, the Ukrainian Vladimir Shcherbitsky. A Russian Communist Party is to be reconstituted.

*November 7.* The anniversary of the October Revolution is marked by counterdemonstrations.

*December 12–24.* The second session of the Congress of People's Deputies is held. At Gorbachev's behest, the Congress refuses to discuss the abolition of the leading role of the Party (the vote to table this discussion is 1,138 to 839).

*December 14.* Sakharov dies. Tens of thousands of Muscovites pay homage to him.

## 1990

*January 20–21.* The most reform-minded Communists devise a "democratic platform" in Moscow.

*February 4.* In Moscow, 200,000 persons gather to demonstrate in favor of *perestroika.*

*February 5–7.* An enlarged plenum of the Central Committee adopts the platform that will be officially presented at the Twenty-eighth Party Congress. The platform calls for the abolition of the leading role of the Party, the establishment of a multiparty system and the creation of a true executive government with separation of powers.

*February 25.* More mass demonstrations in favor of reform take place in Moscow and other large cities.

*March 4.* The reformers and the radicals are successful in the first round of local elections in Russia, the Ukraine and Belorussia.

*March 11, 14 and 16.* At a plenum of the Central Committee, Gorbachev proposes a modification of the articles of the Constitution that deal with the leading role of the Party.

*March 12–15.* An extraordinary session of the Congress of People's Deputies is held. The Congress approves the constitutional amendments that introduce a multiparty system, thereby abolishing the leading role of the Communist Party. The Congress also approves the establishment of a presidential government. On March 14, Gorbachev is elected president for a five-year term, despite the opposition of the "interregional group," which denounces what it sees as the excessive power being conferred on the head of state.

*March 23.* A Presidential Council is created.

*April 11.* In an "Open Letter to Communists," the Central Committee calls for the exclusion of the most radical reformers.

*April 16.* The reformer Gavril Popov is elected mayor of Moscow.

*May 1.* Gorbachev is booed by thousands of demonstrators at the closing of the official May Day celebration.

*May 23.* The reformer Anatoli Sobchak is elected mayor of Leningrad.

*May 29.* Yeltsin, the leader of the radicals, is elected president of the Russian Federation.

*June 20–23.* The Communist Party of the Russian Federation, which was dissolved in 1925, is reconstituted at a special congress. Gorbachev's policies are violently attacked by the conservatives, who elect Ivan Polozkov as leader of the new Party.

*July 2–14.* The Twenty-eighth Party Congress is convened. Gorbachev's policies are hotly contested. He is, however, reelected general secretary of the Party, and he also succeeds in having the Ukrainian Vladimir Ivashko elected deputy general secretary over Yegor Ligachev, the leader of the conservatives. New bylaws authorize the creation of "platforms" while still maintaining the principle of "democratic centralism." The Politburo is reformed and stripped of many of its powers.

*July 12.* Yeltsin announces his resignation from the Communist Party. He is followed by the mayors of Moscow and Leningrad, Popov and Sobchak.

*July 15.* A decree ends the Communist Party's control over radio and television.

In Moscow, 40,000 persons demonstrate against the Communist Party.

*July 17.* Vadim Medvedev, the former Party ideologist, is added to Gorbachev's Presidential Council.

*July 18.* Seven prominent Soviets, including Sergei Stankevich, Yuri Ryzhov and Mikhail Bocharev, resign from the Communist Party.

*July 20.* Formal negotiations begin on a new union treaty between the republics and the central government.

*August 22.* Thousands of statues of Lenin are reportedly being removed from public squares throughout the country, by orders of local officials.

*August 30.* Gorbachev hosts a joint meeting of the Federation Council (the leaders of the republics) and the Presidential Council. First Deputy Prime Minister Vladilen Nikitin is fired.

*September 10.* The Supreme Soviet opens its fall session. Gorbachev rejects the demands of reformist deputies that Prime Minister Ryzhkov resign.

*September 14.* A constitutional watchdog committee overturns Gorbachev's decree giving him the right to ban political demonstrations in Moscow.

*October 9.* The Supreme Soviet passes a law placing all political parties on the same footing as the Communist Party, thereby laying the groundwork for a true multiparty system. The law also removes the Communist Party's legal authority over such institutions as the military, the KGB and government-sponsored unions. It is also announced that 682,000 persons have renounced their Party membership so far this year; officially, the Party still has more than 18 million members.

*October 20–21.* More than 2,000 persons attend the first congress of "Democratic Russia," a group of fledgling political parties based in the Russian Republic.

*November 5.* The Moscow City Council begins renaming streets, squares and landmarks that had been named after Communist heroes.

*November 16.* Gorbachev receives a cold reception when he addresses a crisis session of the Supreme Soviet and dismisses rumors of an impending famine or military coup. The next day, the legislature will give tentative approval to Gorbachev's proposals to place the entire executive branch under the president's control and to give the republics a greater say in the central government. (The proposals will gain final approval, with some modifications, on December 27.)

*November 23–24.* Gorbachev formally unveils his plan for a new union treaty. The republics react cooly.

*November 27–30.* Amid growing turmoil, presidential decrees are issued sanctioning the use of force to combat a "breakdown" in order and authorizing the creation of worker vigilante committees to curb theft and speculation.

*December 2.* Interior Minister Vadim Bakatin, a moderate, is replaced by Boris Pugo, a conservative.

*December 17.* The fourth session of the Congress of People's Deputies opens.

*December 19.* Gorbachev threatens to impose direct presidential rule on disorderly areas of the USSR.

*December 20.* Foreign Minister Shevardnadze resigns, warning that the nation is moving toward dictatorship.

*December 26.* The Russian parliament votes to withold 80 percent of its scheduled contribution to the 1991 Soviet central budget. Prime Minister Ryzhkov suffers a heart attack.

*December 27.* The Congress of People's Deputies approves Gorbachev's choice of Gennadi Yanayev, a Party apparatchik, as vice president on the second ballot.

## 1991

*January 14–15.* The Supreme Soviet confirms Finance Minister Valentin Pavlov as prime minister, replacing the ailing Ryzhkov. Alexander Bessmertnykh replaces Shevardnadze as foreign minister. (Vladimir Orlov will be named finance minister on February 25.)

*January 25–26.* It is announced that the army has been ordered to join the police in street patrols to combat unrest, and that the KGB has been given sweeping new powers to battle "economic sabotage."

*February 19.* Russian President Boris Yeltsin demands that Gorbachev resign. The challenge prompts a strong anti-Yeltsin campaign in the official media and unsuccessful moves by conservative politicians to oust the Russian president.

*March 10.* More than 100,000 persons stage a pro-Yeltsin rally in Moscow. A similar demonstration will be held on March 28 in defiance of an official ban.

*March 17.* Approximately 76 percent of the people participating in the USSR's first national referendum vote in favor of a Gorbachev proposal to preserve the union. Only nine of the 15 republics officially participate in the plebiscite.

*April 5.* The Russian parliament votes to give Boris Yeltsin emergency powers to rule by decree.

*April 6.* The arch-conservative Soyuz (Union) bloc in the Soviet Congress of People's Deputies launches a petition drive to gain a no-confidence vote in Gorbachev's leadership.

*April 9.* Gorbachev unveils an "anti-crisis program" to reassert central authority. Among other steps, he urges sanctions against those republics that fail to meet their obligations to the Soviet government or that refuse to sign the union treaty. He also calls for a moratorium on labor strikes.

*April 24–25.* Gorbachev successfully faces down hard-liners maneuvering to oust him at a plenum of the Communist Party Central Committee.

*June 12.* Having received 60 percent of the vote, Yeltsin is elected to the newly created executive presidency of the Russian Republic. He becomes Russia's first popularly elected leader. Moscow Mayor Popov and Leningrad Mayor Sobchak, both Yeltsin allies, are reelected. Some 55 percent of Leningrad's citizens vote to change the city's name to St. Petersburg, its prerevolutionary name.

*June 17.* Prime Minister Pavlov, backed by hard-liners, asks the Supreme Soviet for temporary emergency powers. Gorbachev complains bitterly, and the power play will be squelched on June 21.

*July 1.* Shevardnadze and other prominent moderates and liberals found the Democratic Reform Movement. Shevardnadze will quit the Communist Party on July 3.

*July 20.* Yeltsin issues a decree banning political activity in workplaces and in government institutions within the Russian Republic. The measure is aimed at the Communist Party.

*July 23.* Twelve prominent Party conservatives appeal to the military and to other "healthy forces" to save the country from "humiliation."

*July 24.* Gorbachev announces that he and the heads of 10 of the 15 republics have agreed on power-sharing provisions in the proposed union treaty.

*July 25–26.* At a plenum of the Central Committee, Gorbachev urges the Party to scrap "outdated ideological dogma" and to embrace "world socialist and democratic thought." He supports a market-oriented rather than a command economy, and he questions the relevance of the Leninist doctrine of violent "class struggle."

*August 16.* The reformer Alexander Yakovlev, a former close aide to Gorbachev, warns that a "Stalinist clique" within the Party is preparing for a "party and state coup."

*August 19.* A group of eight senior Party hard-liners launches a coup d'état. Gorbachev and his wife Raisa are detained while vacationing at their dacha in the Crimea on the Black Sea. An eight-man State Committee on the State of Emergency announces that it is replacing Gorbachev, who is described as suffering from an unspecified illness. The key plotters are Vice President Gennadi Yanayev, Prime Minister Valentin Pavlov, KGB Chairman Vladimir Kryuchkov, Defense Minister Dmitri Yazov and Interior Minister Boris Pugo. The claim they will continue Gorbachev's reforms while at the same time restoring law and order, public morality, economic stability, territorial integrity and national honor.

*August 19–20.* Opposition to the coup is led by Russian President Yeltsin.

Thousands of prodemocracy protesters rally at the Russian parliament building in Moscow and face down Soviet army tanks with a minimum of bloodshed. Hundreds of thousands of demonstrators also rally against the coup in cities around the country.

*August 21.* The putsch, evidently poorly planned, collapses amid widespread popular defiance and uncertainty about the support of the military, many of whose units refuse to commit themselves to either side in the struggle. Gorbachev is released unharmed and declares that he is back in charge.

*August 22.* Most of the plotters are in custody. Pugo commits suicide by shooting himself before he can be arrested. Gorbachev returns to Moscow, declares the failure of the coup a "serious victory for the *perestroika* process," and hails Yeltsin for "standing up" to the conspirators.

*August 23.* Yeltsin emerges as the country's most popular politician. He assumes the role of power broker and coleader, with Gorbachev, of the USSR. Rejecting Gorbachev's interim appointments of General Mikhail Moiseyev as defense minister and Leonid Shebarsin as KGB chairman, Yeltsin compels Gorbachev to appoint General Yevgeni Shaposhnikov and Vadim Bakatin, respectively, to those positions. Viktor Barannikov replaces Pugo as interior minister. Foreign Minister Bessmertnykh, who kept a low profile during the coup, is fired and replaced by Boris Pankin, the Soviet ambassador to Czechoslovakia and one of the few Soviet diplomats to have denounced the coup while it was in progress.

*August 24.* Reacting to the role that senior Communist Party officials played in the coup, Gorbachev resigns as general secretary of the Party but not from the Party itself. He also issues decrees disbanding the Central Committee, placing all of the Party's property under the control of the Soviet parliament, and banning political activity in public institutions and government agencies.

Up to 100,000 persons gather in Moscow for a funeral procession in honor of the three men who died on August 21, when army tanks tried to break through a civilian barricade near the Russian parliament building.

*August 25.* Defense Minister Shaposhnikov announces a plan to replace approximately 80 percent of the nation's top military officers with younger men chosen for their "moral qualities and professionalism" rather than their "personal loyalty" to superiors.

*August 27.* Gorbachev notifies the Supreme Soviet that a full-scale purge of the KGB is under way.

*August 28.* The Russian prosecutor's office charges 13 former officials with high treason for their alleged involvement in the coup. Anatoli Lukyanov, the former chairman of the Supreme Soviet, will be added to the list of those charged on September 5.

*August 29.* The Supreme Soviet, following up on Gorbachev's decrees, votes to suspend all activities of the Communist Party, effectively ending its 74-year reign in the USSR.

*September 5.* The Congress of People's Deputies approves a plan proposed by Gorbachev to establish an interim political structure to run the country. The plan calls for a sweeping transfer of power from the Kremlin to the republics while both sides redefine their relationship. The plan also provides for the creation of a State Council that will serve as an executive committee of government. The council will be headed by Gorbachev and include the heads of all the republics that wish to remain in the Soviet Union.

*September 20.* In published remarks, Gorbachev admits that the central government has lost most of its political control over the Soviet republics.

*October 2.* It is reported that Vadim Bakatin, the new KGB chief, has disbanded the directorate responsible for monitoring Soviet dissidents and has dismissed one-third of the section that handled domestic electronic surveillance.

*October 14.* It is announced that all restrictions on travel within the USSR will end at the beginning of 1992.

*November 7.* More than 10,000 persons hold an illegal pro-Communist parade in Moscow to mark the 74th anniversary of the Bolshevik Revolution. Many demonstrators denounce Gorbachev as a traitor to Marxism.

*November 14.* Seven republics— Russia, Belorussia, Kazakhstan, Azerbaijan, Kirghizia, Tadzhikistan and Turkmenistan—reach preliminary agreement on a Gorbachev-backed plan for a loosely confederated Union of Sovereign States. On November 25, however, representatives of the seven republics will decide not to sign the treaty but instead to submit it to their parliaments for review.

*November 19.* Eduard Shevardnadze is reappointed foreign minister, succeeding Boris Pankin.

*December 8.* The leaders of the three Slavic republics—Russia, Belorussia and the Ukraine—representing 80 percent of the Soviet Union's territory and 73 percent of its population, sign an agreement forming a Commonwealth of Independent States (CIS) to replace the

USSR. Gorbachev will denounce the move as illegal on December 9. The five Central Asian republics will agree to join the Commonwealth on December 13.

*December 17.* After a two-hour private discussion between the Russian and Soviet presidents, Yeltsin announces that Gorbachev accepts the demise of the USSR as imminent.

*December 19.* Yeltsin issues decrees ordering the Russian government to seize the Kremlin and to take over or replace the functions of the entire Soviet central government, with the exceptions of the ministries of defense and atomic energy.

*December 21.* Eleven former Soviet republics sign agreements creating the Commonwealth of Independent States. The three former Baltic republics, which have already declared their independence, and Georgia, which is wracked by civil war, do not join the CIS.

*December 25.* Gorbachev resigns as Soviet president in a nationally televised speech. "The old system collapsed before the new one had time to begin working," he laments. With little ceremony, 33 minutes later the Soviet flag atop the Kremlin is replaced by the flag of pre-revolutionary Russia, and the Soviet Union formally dissolves.

# Foreign Affairs

## 1985

*March 12.* Soviet-American talks on nuclear and space weapons open in Geneva.

*April 26.* The Warsaw Pact nations hold a meeting in Warsaw. The treaty that created the alliance is renewed for 20 years.

*April 28–30.* Daniel Ortega, the president of Nicaragua, visits Moscow.

The USSR reaffirms its support of the Sandinista revolutionary government.

*July 30.* The Soviet Union, the United States and Japan conclude an accord on civilian airline security in the Pacific.

*October 2–5.* Gorbachev visits France.

*November 19–21.* An American-Soviet summit meeting is held in Geneva. Gorbachev and President Ronald Reagan hold talks on the problems of disarmament.

## 1986

*January 15–19.* Soviet Foreign Minister Shevardnadze visits Japan. Disagreements persist on the status of the Kuril Islands.

*April 15.* The Soviets "categorically condemn" the American military raid on Libya.

*May 27.* The USSR expels 119 American nationals.

*June 10.* The Political Consultative Committee of the Warsaw Pact meets in Budapest. A program to reduce forces and conventional weapons in Europe is proposed.

*July 7–10.* French President François Mitterrand visits the USSR.

*July 28.* Gorbachev announces the opening of a new era in Soviet relations with China and other Asian countries. He also announces that the USSR intends to withdraw six regiments from Afghanistan by year's end.

*July 28–August 1.* Turkish Prime Minister Turgut Ozal visits the USSR.

*September 22.* The Stockholm Conference on Disarmament in Europe concludes. Accords are signed dealing with confidence-building measures and the verification of military activities from the Atlantic Ocean to the Ural Mountains by land and air inspections.

*September 29.* Nicholas Daniloff, an American journalist who was arrested in Moscow on August 30, is exchanged for Gennadi Zakharov, a Soviet scientific attaché at the United Nations who was arrested for espionage in New York on August 23.

*October 11–12.* An American-Soviet summit meeting is held in Reykjavik, Iceland. Reagan and Gorbachev reach a tentative understanding to reduce their strategic nuclear arsenals by 50 percent within five years and to remove all of their intermediate-range missiles from Europe; because the two leaders disagree on limiting the American SDI program, however, no arms control agreement is reached.

*November 4.* In Vienna, the Third Conference on Security and Cooperation in Europe opens; the conference will review the Helsinki Accord.

*November 25–28.* Gorbachev visits India, an important South Asian ally.

## 1987

*January 15.* Moscow announces that Soviet troops stationed in Mongolia will be withdrawn between April and July.

*February 9.* The Soviet Union and China renew negotiations on their border disputes.

*March 28–April 1.* British Prime Minister Margaret Thatcher visits the USSR.

*April 9–11.* Gorbachev visits Czechoslovakia.

*May 14–16.* French Prime Minister Jacques Chirac visits Moscow.

*May 25–27.* Gorbachev visits Romania.

*December 7–10.* Gorbachev makes an official visit to Washington. He and Reagan sign the Intermediate-range Nuclear Forces (INF) Treaty on December 8. The treaty calls for the removal and destruction of more than 2,600 such weapons in Europe.

## 1988

*February 8.* Gorbachev announces that Soviet troops will withdraw from Afghanistan beginning May 15, 1988, if a peace agreement is signed in Geneva before March 15.

*March 14–18.* Gorbachev visits Yugoslavia.

*April 14.* The Geneva accords on Afghanistan are signed. The USSR promises to withdraw its troops from that country within nine months, beginning May 15, 1988. (The West estimates that the Soviet Union has 115,000 troops in Afghanistan.) The Afghan resistance movements reject the accords.

*May 15.* Soviet troops begin their withdrawal from Afghanistan. On May 25, the Soviet Union will announce that 13,310 of its troops were killed in the conflict, and 35,478 were wounded.

*May 29–June 2.* Reagan and Gorbachev hold a summit meeting in Moscow. Talks are held on the proposed Strategic Arms Reduction Treaty (START), regional conflicts and human rights.

*July 11–16.* Gorbachev visits Poland. He publicly alludes to the "gaps" in the history of the relations between the two countries.

*October 4–6.* Romanian President Nicolae Ceausescu visits Moscow. In Ceausescu's presence, Gorbachev insists on the necessity of respecting human rights.

*October 24–27.* West German Chancellor Helmut Kohl makes his first official visit to the USSR.

*November 18–20.* Gorbachev travels to India.

*November 25–26.* French President Mitterrand visits the USSR.

*December 1–3.* Chinese Foreign Minister Qian Qichen visits Moscow.

*December 6–8.* Gorbachev visits New York, where he presents to the United Nations the "new principles" of Soviet foreign policy. He announces a reduction of the Soviet armed forces (by 500,000 men in two years) as well as the withdrawal of troops and armaments from Central Europe and Mongolia. Gorbachev also meets with President Reagan and President-elect George Bush.

## 1989

*January 17–19.* The Conference on Security and Cooperation in Europe, meeting in Vienna, adjourns. A document on human rights is adopted.

*February 2.* The Mutual and Balanced Force Reduction (MBFR) talks, held in Vienna since 1973, conclude without producing an agreement.

*February 2–4.* Foreign Minister Shevardnadze visits China.

*February 15.* The withdrawal of Soviet troops from Afghanistan is completed.

*March 6.* The Conventional Forces in Europe (CFE) talks open in Vienna. The participants include members of NATO and the Warsaw Pact.

*April 2–4.* Gorbachev makes an official visit to Cuba, where he reaffirms to Fidel Castro the "fraternal and indomitable nature" of the friendship between the Soviet and Cuban peoples.

*April 5–7.* Gorbachev makes an official visit to Great Britain.

*May 11.* Gorbachev meets with American Secretary of State James Baker and announces the unilateral withdrawal of 500 tactical nuclear warheads from Eastern Europe.

*May 18–19.* Gorbachev's visit to Beijing coincides with the start of the "democracy movement" in China. He has a historic meeting with Deng Xiaoping.

*June 12–15.* Gorbachev visits West Germany.

*June 20–23.* The president of the Iranian parliament, Hashemi Rafsanjani, visits Moscow and signs a number of bilateral cooperative agreements.

*July 4–6.* Gorbachev visits France, where President Mitterrand calls on the West to support *perestroika.* Gorbachev sets out his idea of a "common European home" before the Council of Europe.

*September 22–23.* The USSR withdraws its demand that the United States abandon its SDI, or "Star Wars," program before an accord can be reached on the limitation of strategic weapons in the Strategic Arms Reduction Talks (START).

*October 6–7.* Gorbachev visits Berlin on the occasion of the 40th anniversary of the establishment of the German Democratic Republic. He reaffirms that the status quo must be maintained in Europe, but he also encourages reform in East Germany.

*November.* The USSR affirms its desire not to interfere in the internal affairs of its "fraternal countries." The Berlin Wall is opened on November 9. Todor Zhivkov is ousted as Communist leader of Bulgaria on November 10. The Politburo of the Czech Communist Party resigns en masse on November 24. The Hungarian opposition is victorious in legislative elections on November 26.

*November 23–27.* Polish Prime Minister Tadeusz Mazowiecki visits the USSR. He agrees with Gorbachev on the necessity of maintaining the existing borders and alliance systems in Europe, and makes a visit to Katyn, where thousands of captured Polish military officers

were executed by Soviet security forces in 1940.

*November 27.* The Soviet Union signs an accord on commerce and cooperation with the European Economic Community.

*December 1.* A historic meeting takes place between Pope John Paul II and Gorbachev at the Vatican. They announce their intent to reestablish diplomatic relations between Moscow and the Holy See.

*December 2–3.* American President George Bush and Gorbachev hold a summit meeting in Malta. Discussions focus on regional conflicts, disarmament, economic relations and the future of Europe.

*December 4.* The leaders of the Warsaw Pact nations meet in Moscow, where they insist on the necessity of maintaining existing borders and alliances. They also condemn the entry of Warsaw Pact troops into Czechoslovakia in 1968.

*December 6.* Gorbachev and French President Mitterrand hold talks in Kiev. Gorbachev considers discussions concerning the reunification of Germany to be premature.

*December 24.* Following the popular overthrow of the Ceaüsescu regime, the Soviet government announces its support for the Romanian National Salvation Front and offers humanitarian aid to the country.

## 1990

*January 9–10.* The leaders of Comecon member states meet in Sofia, Bulgaria. They affirm the need for a radical reform of the organization.

*January 15.* Authorities in Prague raise the possibility of talks with the USSR about the withdrawal of the 95,000 Soviet troops stationed in Czechoslovakia.

*January 23.* Budapest announces that Moscow has agreed to withdraw its 52,000 troops stationed in Hungary by the end of 1991.

*January 30.* East German Prime Minister Hans Modrow visits Moscow. Gorbachev accepts the idea of the unification of the two German states.

*February 10.* Gorbachev and West German Chancellor Kohl hold talks on the future of Germany.

*February 26–27.* Czechoslovak President Václav Havel visits Moscow. An accord is signed on the withdrawal of Soviet troops from Czechoslovakia.

*March 15.* The Vatican and the USSR establish limited diplomatic ties for the first time since 1923.

*April 11–14.* Polish President Wojciech Jaruzelski visits the USSR. Gorbachev officially acknowledges Soviet responsibility for the Katyn massacre.

*April 23–26.* Chinese Prime Minister Li Peng visits the USSR.

*April 28–29.* East German Prime Minister Lothar de Maizière visits Moscow. Gorbachev opposes the possibility of a future unified Germany becoming a member of NATO.

*May 5.* The USSR participates in the first ministerial meeting on the international consequences of German reunification (the Two-Plus-Four Conference). The USSR reaffirms its opposition to unified Germany's membership in NATO. In Moscow on May 8, Gorbachev will refuse to sign a peace treaty, and on May 17, he will suspend the withdrawal of the Soviet Union's 380,000 troops from East Germany.

*May 25.* French President Mitterrand visits Moscow.

*May 30–June 3.* The second summit meeting between President Bush and President Gorbachev takes place in the United States. On June 1, they sign a treaty on chemical weapons disarmament and a declaration on the reduction of strategic weapons. A commercial accord is concluded. Gorbachev refuses to make concessions on the question of Lithuania or on the military status of Germany.

*June 7.* The seven members of the Warsaw Pact meet in Moscow. They decide to revise the nature and the function of the alliance, transforming it into more of a political rather than a military grouping. Hungary announces its wish to withdraw from the Warsaw Pact at the end of 1991.

*June 7–10.* British Prime Minister Margaret Thatcher visits the USSR and expresses strong support for Gorbachev's reforms.

*June 22.* The second round of the Two-Plus-Four talks on German reunification is held in East Berlin.

*July 15–16.* West German Chancellor Helmut Kohl visits the USSR. In exchange for a number of concessions, Gorbachev on July 16 agrees that a reunified Germany can become a member of NATO, thus removing the last major obstacle to German reunification.

*August 1–2.* Foreign Minister Shevardnadze and U.S. Secretary of State Baker meet in the Siberian city of Irkutsk to discuss arms control, Afghanistan and other regional issues. In Moscow, the two men on August 3 will issue a joint statement condemning Iraq's "brutal and illegal invasion of Kuwait."

*September 9.* Gorbachev and Bush hold a one-day summit in Helsinki, Finland, to demonstrate superpower solidarity against the Iraqi invasion of Kuwait.

*September 12.* The foreign ministers of East Germany and West Germany, together with those of the four victorious Allies in World War II—the United States, the Soviet Union, Great Britain and France—meet in Moscow and sign the Treaty on the Final Settlement with Respect to Germany. The agreement paves the way for German reunification the following month. A separate German-Soviet friendship pact will be signed on September 13.

*September 30.* Moscow establishes full diplomatic relations with South Korea and substantially upgrades its ties with Israel.

*October 3.* East Germany and West Germany are reunited as one state.

*October 15.* Gorbachev is awarded the Nobel Peace Prize for his role in peacefully reforming the USSR and ending the cold war.

*October 26–29.* Gorbachev visits Spain and France. He obtains additional economic and political support for his reforms, and cites Soviet diplomatic efforts to defuse the Persian Gulf crisis.

*November 9.* One year after the opening of the Berlin Wall, Gorbachev becomes the first foreign leader to visit reunified Germany. He and Chancellor Kohl sign several agreements, including a nonaggression pact.

*November 18.* Gorbachev meets Pope John Paul II at the Vatican for the second time in less than a year.

*November 19–21.* The leaders of the Conference on Security and Cooperation in Europe, including Gorbachev and Bush, meet in Paris and sign the Conventional Forces in Europe (CFE) treaty and the Charter of Paris for a New Europe. The gathering marks the formal end of the cold war.

*November 29.* The USSR joins other members of the United Nations Security Council in approving a resolution authorizing the use of force against Iraq if it does not withdraw from Kuwait. (Allied countries will begin an air war against Iraq on January 16, 1991.)

*December 12.* President Bush approves up to $1 billion in loan guarantees to allow the USSR to purchase American food. He also pledges U.S. emergency shipments of food and medical supplies to the Soviet Union.

## 1991

*February 12.* Yevgeni Primakov, Gorbachev's special envoy, meets with Iraqi President Saddam Hussein in Baghdad.

*February 21.* Iraqi Foreign Minister Tariq Aziz meets in Moscow with Gorbachev and accepts a Soviet plan for an Iraqi withdrawal from Kuwait. Because the plan does not satisfy the United States and its allies, a successful ground attack against Iraqi forces will begin the following week.

*March 4.* British Prime Minister John Major visits Moscow for talks with Gorbachev. (Major will visit Moscow again on September 1.)

*March 13.* Against the wishes of the German government, former East German Communist leader Erich Honecker is flown to Moscow by the Soviet military for medical treatment.

*March 14–16.* U.S. Secretary of State Baker visits Moscow to discuss arms control, postwar developments in the Persian Gulf and other issues.

*March 31.* Meeting in Moscow, the Warsaw Pact formally disbands its military structure.

*April 9.* The withdrawal of Soviet troops from Poland begins.

*April 17–19.* Gorbachev meets with Japanese Prime Minister Toshiki Kaifu in Tokyo during the first visit by a Soviet president to Japan. The two sides fail to resolve their differences on the Kuril Islands, which the Soviet Union seized from Japan at the end of World War II.

*April 20.* Gorbachev becomes the first Soviet leader to visit South Korea, where he signs diplomatic and economic accords.

*May 9–14.* Foreign Minister Alexander Bessmertnykh tours the Middle East in support of U.S. efforts to convene an Arab-Israeli peace conference.

*May 16.* Chinese Communist Party leader Jiang Zemin visits Moscow and signs an agreement resolving some aspects of the Sino-Soviet border dispute.

*May 22.* Gorbachev formally asks for an invitation to the upcoming summit meeting of the Group of Seven (G-7), the leading industrial nations, and pleads for Western economic aid.

*June 11.* President Bush approves up to $1.5 billion in U.S. loan guarantees to allow Moscow to buy American grain.

*June 18–21.* Russian President Boris Yeltsin visits the United States and meets with President Bush on June 20.

*June 19–21.* The last trainloads of Soviet troops and their dependents leave Hungary and Czechoslovakia.

*June 28–July 1.* The Council for Mutual Economic Assistance (Comecon) formally disbands on June 28, and the Warsaw Pact follows suit on July 1. These organizations were the last vestiges of the cold war–era Soviet bloc.

*July 5.* German Chancellor Kohl visits the USSR.

*July 17.* Gorbachev meets with the leaders of the G-7 industrial nations in London. He obtains pledges of technical assistance and political support, but receives no direct economic aid.

*July 30–31.* The first post–cold war superpower summit meeting is held in Moscow. Presidents Bush and Gorbachev sign the long-awaited Strategic Arms Reduction Treaty (START) and announce U.S.-Soviet sponsorship of an Arab-Israeli peace conference in October.

*August 1.* Bush visits Kiev, where he receives a warm welcome.

*August 19–21.* Western nations condemn the abortive coup against Gorbachev.

*August 25–27.* Scandinavian countries and the European Community recognize the independence of the three Baltic states (Estonia, Latvia and Lithuania). The United States will follow suit on September 2.

*September 10.* The foreign ministers of the member states of the Conference on Security and Cooperation in Europe meet in Moscow to open an international conference on human rights.

*September 10–16.* U.S. Secretary of State Baker tours the USSR; he visits the three independent Baltic states on September 14.

*September 11.* Gorbachev announces that the Soviet Union will soon begin talks with Cuba on the withdrawal of Soviet troops from the island.

*September 13.* The United States and the Soviet Union agree to halt their military aid to Afghan rebel and government forces, respectively.

*September 19.* Announcing that the USSR will need $14.7 billion in foreign food aid and credits in 1991–1992, a Soviet official asks the European Community to provide half of the aid.

*September 27.* President Bush announces a unilateral cut of approximately 2,400 U.S. nuclear weapons and asks Moscow to respond in kind.

*October 5.* In his last major arms control initiative, Gorbachev responds to President Bush's September 27 announcement by offering a broad package of unilateral arms reductions, including the destruction of all Soviet ground-based tactical nuclear weapons.

The USSR becomes an associate member of the International Monetary Fund (IMF); as such, Moscow now qualifies for technical assistance but not for IMF credits.

*October 13.* The G-7 nations agree to help the USSR formulate a plan for economic reform.

*October 18.* The USSR and Israel agree to restore full diplomatic relations.

*October 29.* Presidents Bush and Gorbachev hold a brief summit meeting in Madrid, Spain, where they will attend the opening of the U.S.- and Soviet-sponsored Middle East peace conference the next day.

*November 21.* The finance ministers of the G-7 nations agree to defer payment of $3.6 billion in foreign debts accumulated by the USSR.

*November 21–23.* Russian President Yeltsin receives a lukewarm reception during his visit to Germany.

*December 15–19.* U.S. Secretary of State Baker visits the USSR and is reassured by key republic leaders that the Soviet nuclear arsenal will remain under some form of central control when the USSR devolves into the Commonwealth of Independent States (CIS). The leaders also pledge that the CIS countries will honor all U.S.-Soviet arms control agreements, and ask for U.S. technical assistance in dismantling their nuclear weapons.

*December 25.* On the day the Soviet Union ceases to exist, President Bush hails the departing Gorbachev and announces that the United States will recognize the independence of all 12 remaining former Soviet republics; formal diplomatic relations will be established initially with only six of them: Russia, Ukraine, Belarus, Armenia, Kazakhstan and Kirghizia.

# Economy and Society

## 1985

*May 17.* The Communist Party Central Committee issues a decree on measures intended to eliminate drunkenness and alcoholism.

*November 23.* The creation of a State Committee for the Agricultural Food Products Industry (Gosagroprom) is announced. The Committee is given control of all ministerial departments relating to agriculture.

## 1986

*February 1.* A decree instituting measures intended to develop consumers' cooperatives is issued.

*March 5.* The Twenty-seventh Party Congress adopts broad guidelines for a plan for economic and social development for the years 1986–1990 and through the year 2000.

*March 21.* A State Committee on Computer Technology is created.

*May 12.* A decree is issued on "measures aimed at radically elevating the quality of production." *Gospriomka* is created to oversee quality control.

*August 14.* A decree is issued halting the project to reverse the flow of Siberian rivers.

*August 19.* A decree is issued on the improvement of the administration of foreign economic relations.

*November 19.* A law on the exercise of economic activity by individuals is promulgated; the law will take effect on May 1, 1987. Private activity will be allowed in artisanal production, trades and services.

*November 24.* In Tashkent, Gorbachev insists on the necessity of an unrelenting and resolute struggle against religious demonstrations.

## 1987

*January 1.* A wage reform is put into effect. Because remuneration is to be more closely tied to work actually accomplished, wage differences will increase.

*January 13.* A decree is issued setting out the principles for the establishment of mixed enterprises in the USSR; such enterprises would include partners from capitalist and developing countries.

*February 5.* Three decrees are issued permitting the creation of privately owned cooperatives in the following sectors: the production of consumer goods, the restaurant and catering business, and services.

*June 25–26.* A plenum of the Central Committee is devoted to the "radical restructuring of the economy." Ten decrees will be published in July: Power will be redistributed vertically (central organs—ministries—enterprises) and horizontally (regional decentralization); central planning will be reduced; prices will be revised, and the mechanism by which they are set will be reformed; reliance on the market will gradually replace the centralized system of allocation; credit and banking activities will be expanded.

*June 30.* A law on state enterprises is promulgated. This law, which will take effect on January 1, 1988, will replace the law of 1965. Directors of state enter-

prises will be elected, independent accounting and financing will be employed, and the possibility of bankruptcy will be established.

*August 3.* The introduction of checking accounts, effective January 1, 1988, is announced.

*August 25.* A decree is issued mandating the systematic testing of "at-risk individuals" and foreigners for the AIDS virus.

*December.* A decree is issued on the creation of employment agencies by local soviets. Approximately 16 million layoffs are predicted by the year 2000 in the industrial sector (out of a total of 75 million workers).

## 1988

*January 15.* The federal Ministry for Foreign Economic Relations is created.

*February 11.* The administration of "special psychiatric hospitals" is placed under the Health Ministry; these hospitals had previously been administered by the Interior Ministry. Approximately 2 million persons are removed from the list of the mentally ill (30 percent of the total number).

*April 29.* A reception is held at the Kremlin for Moscow Patriarch Pimen. Gorbachev announces the restoration of a number of places of worship and the anticipated promulgation of a law on freedom of religion.

*May 26.* A law on cooperatives encourages more individual economic activity.

*June 6–11.* The millennium of Russia's conversion to Christianity is celebrated. A council of the Russian Orthodox Church meets in Zagorsk, and a solemn ceremony is held in the Kremlin.

*July 28.* A decree is issued on public assemblies, meetings, parades and demonstrations. A number of restrictions are maintained on these gatherings.

*September 30.* A decree is issued on measures to improve the environment in the region of the Aral Sea. The gradual drying up of the Aral Sea constitutes one of the largest ecological catastrophes facing the Soviet Union.

*November 15.* The unmanned space shuttle *Buran* is launched.

*December 20–21.* A national congress of teachers convenes. It is decided to publish several manuals in each discipline, with individual teachers granted the right to choose what materials to use.

## 1989

The budget deficit for 1989 increases to 120 billion rubles.

*January 12–19.* A census is taken. The first results, available in April, indicate a population of 286,717,000.

*March 15–16.* A plenum of the Central Committee is held to consider agricultural policy. A Gorbachev reform plan is adopted that will lead to a partial decollectivization.

*June 3.* A rail accident in the western Urals leaves several hundred dead.

*July 10.* A strike begins among the miners of the Kuzbas region; it will gradually spread to the areas of the Donets, Pechora and Karaganda. More than 180,000 miners will walk off their jobs, and their demands will take on a political character.

*August 26.* The minister of the interior announces a serious rise in crime (32 percent in one year).

*September 9.* Gorbachev details a program for the overhaul of the economy that will include "painful and unpopular measures."

*October 9.* A law on labor disputes is promulgated. It recognizes the right to strike while at the same time regulating

strikes. Strikes are prohibited in key sectors of the economy.

*November 2.* A law on pensions and retirement is passed; benefits are increased by 40 percent.

*November 13.* A law requires a jury trial for crimes punishable by death.

*November 23.* Legislation on long-term leases is passed.

*December 12–24.* After a spirited debate, the Congress of People's Deputies adopts the Thirteenth Five-Year Plan.

## 1990

*February 28.* The Supreme Soviet adopts guidelines for new legislation on land ownership.

*March 6.* A new law on property is passed.

*March 23.* An Independent Federation of Trade Unions of the Russian Republic is formed.

*May 2.* Patriarch Pimen dies.

*May 24.* Prime Minister Ryzhkov presents an economic reform plan to the Supreme Soviet. The plan, which envisages the eventual passage of the USSR to a "planned market economy," sparks consumer panic. The Supreme Soviet asks Ryzhkov to revise his plan.

*June 7–8.* A council of the Russian Orthodox Church elects Alexis, the metropolitan of Leningrad, as the new patriarch.

*June 12.* A law prohibiting censorship in the media and the press is promulgated.

*June 14 and 17.* Inmates in Dnepropetrovsk and Chelyabinsk stage a revolt.

*July 11.* A 24-hour strike is staged at more than 100 mines in the Donets region. The strikers call for an improvement in their living conditions, the resignation of Prime Minister Ryzhkov, the nationalization of Party property and the abolition of Communist cells in enterprises.

*July 13.* The Russian parliament passes a resolution asserting sole authority over all banks within the republic and directing that, with the exception of the Russian State Bank, they be reorganized as commercial banks.

*July 29.* In response to the Russian parliament's action of July 13, Gorbachev issues a decree reaffirming the control of Gosbank, the Soviet State Bank, over all of the nation's banks.

*August 1.* Gorbachev and Russian President Yeltsin agree to cooperate in transforming the Soviet Union's centrally planned economy into one governed by market forces.

The Soviet government lifts restrictions on the spending or saving of "hard" (convertible) foreign currencies.

*August 10.* The Russian parliament passes a resolution asserting the republic's control over all of the natural resources within its borders.

*August 15.* Russia and Lithuania sign a treaty on trade and economic cooperation. It is the first of its kind between two Soviet republics.

*August 30–31.* Gorbachev hosts an economic summit in Moscow; the Federation Council and the Presidential Council approve the Shatalin plan to reform the economy.

*August 30–September 3.* Widespread shortages of bread and cigarettes are reported.

*September 5.* Details of a draft program to radically transform the Soviet economy are reported. The program was drawn up by a working group of aides to both Gorbachev and Yeltsin headed by Stanislav Shatalin. Based on Russia's own "500-day" plan, the draft

plan aims to dismantle most central economic controls within 500 days.

*September 6.* It is reported that Soviet oil production has declined by half a million barrels a day since 1989.

*September 11.* In a debate in the Supreme Soviet, Gorbachev voices support for the radical 500-day Shatalin plan for economic reform. Prime Minister Ryzhkov, whose own reform program is more moderate, denounces the Shatalin plan.

*September 14.* Gorbachev offers the "president's plan," a slightly amended version of the Shatalin plan that would preserve central government authority over banking, currency, taxation and foreign exchange.

*September 17.* Gorbachev proposes a nationwide referendum on whether to allow private ownership of land in the USSR.

*September 21.* Gorbachev asks the Supreme Soviet for sweeping new powers to meet the worsening economic crisis. The parliament will respond on September 24 by voting to give the president the power to rule by decree.

*October 16.* Gorbachev offers a more detailed version of the "president's plan," one which lacks the strict timetable of the Shatalin plan for the transition to a market economy. The Supreme Soviet will adopt Gorbachev's plan on October 19.

*October 22.* The Supreme Soviet passes a law stiffening penalties for "speculation," or black market activities, which are described as rampant.

*October 26.* Gorbachev issues emergency decrees aimed at stimulating foreign investment, boosting exports and encouraging citizens to save.

Coal miners meeting in the Ukraine establish the USSR's first nationwide independent labor confederation.

*November 4.* Thirteen radical Soviet economists, including Shatalin, assail Gorbachev's economic plan as inadequate.

*November 17.* The first Soviet stock exchange is founded in Moscow.

*December 3.* The Russian parliament passes legislation allowing the private ownership of farmland in the republic.

*December 19.* Prime Minister Ryzhkov tells the Congress of People's Deputies that *perestroika* has failed, and he takes personal responsibility for the country's economic collapse.

*December 22.* KGB Chairman Vladimir Kryuchkov warns against Soviet acceptance of Western aid, claiming that it is a "screen" behind which the West is stealing Soviet secrets, dumping contaminated food, cheating Soviet businesses and seeking to impose capitalism.

# 1991

*January 8.* Gorbachev and Yeltsin settle their disagreement over Russia's contribution to the 1991 Soviet central budget.

*January 16.* Nikolai Petrakov resigns as Gorbachev's personal economic advisor in protest against the president's economic policies.

*January 22.* Large denomination ruble notes are abolished as legal tender in an effort to curb inflation and undermine the black market.

*February 18.* Prime Minister Valentin Pavlov unveils a plan to raise prices on most goods and services by an average of 60 percent.

*March 1–April 3.* Coal miners in the Ukraine's Donets region go on strike for higher pay. The strike spreads until it has shut down 25 percent of the country's 600 mines. The strikers ignore a back-to-work order issued by the Supreme Soviet on March 26. The government

and the strikers reach an agreement on April 3 to double the miners' pay in return for higher production.

*March 19.* Gorbachev issues a decree formally authorizing price hikes.

*April 2.* State price controls are relaxed. Retail prices on many goods and services will rise by 200 percent to 1,000 percent, sparking widespread consumer resentment.

*April 4–26.* Thousands of workers in Minsk, Belorussia, strike in protest against the price increases. The nationwide coal miners' strike continues, despite the wage accord of April 3, with strikers around the country demanding Gorbachev's resignation. The Minsk workers give up their walkout on April 26, while on the same day an estimated 50 million Russian workers stage a "warning strike."

*May 1.* Russian President Yeltsin signs a decree bringing all of the republic's coal mines under the control of his government. The Soviet government will acquiesce to the move on May 6.

*May 8.* The central strike committee of Russian coal miners votes to end their nine-week-old walkout. Miners in the Ukraine, where the strike began, have already begun returning to work.

*May 13.* Gorbachev issues a decree outlawing strikes in vital sectors of the economy, such as coal mining, while also offering special economic incentives to workers in those sectors.

*June 14.* An unofficial plan drafted by Grigori Yavlinsky, an aide to Gorbachev and Yeltsin, and by Harvard University economists is unveiled. It calls for a "Grand Bargain": In exchange for massive Western aid, the USSR would undertake fundamental political and free-market economic reforms.

*July 1.* The Supreme Soviet passes a law allowing for the first time the sale of state-owned enterprises. The new policy is called "denationalization" rather than privatization. To placate Communist Party traditionalists, the law favors the sale of state property to Soviet rather than foreign citizens, and stresses collective ownership and leasing arrangements over individual ownership.

*September 6–11.* Details of a plan drafted by Yavlinsky for a Soviet economic union are revealed. The plan proposes a relatively strong central authority in Moscow, a dominant Soviet central bank and a continuation of the ruble as the national currency.

*September 11.* Statistics for 1991 show that industrial and food production have fallen 8 percent compared with the same period in 1990. Oil production has declined 10 percent.

*October 18.* Eight of the 12 remaining Soviet republics sign an economic union treaty based on the Yavlinsky plan. (After initial hesitation, the Ukraine will sign the treaty on November 6 in response to Western pressure. Moldavia will also sign, leaving Azerbaijan and Georgia as the only remaining holdouts.)

*October 29.* The 12 republics formally agree to share responsibility for repaying the USSR's foreign debts.

*October 30.* The 1991 Soviet grain harvest is reported to be 30 percent less than the 1990 harvest.

*November 1.* The Russian parliament grants President Yeltsin sweeping powers to carry out radical economic reforms.

*November 15–17.* Yeltsin issues decrees giving the Russian government control over the extraction and export of natural resources within its territory. He also offers a plan for economic and monetary liberalization.

*December 8–25.* The Commonwealth of Independent States is formed to replace the USSR. The member states pledge "allegiance to cooperation in the formation and development of the common economic space." The states will assume ownership of all former Soviet government civilian facilities on their soil.

# Nationalities

## 1986
*December 16.* The first secretary of the Kazakhstan Communist Party, Dinmukhamed Kunayev, is replaced by a Russian; this will lead to revolts in Alma Ata on December 17–19.

## 1987
*June 24.* The news agency TASS reports demonstrations by the Crimean Tatars on Red Square in Moscow. A commission of inquiry is formed to examine their situation and their claims. (It will reject their demand for an autonomous republic in June 1988.)

*August 23.* Nationalist demonstrations are staged in the three Baltic republics to mark the 48th anniversary of the Nazi-Soviet Pact.

*October 17–19.* Demonstrations are held in Yerevan, the capital of Armenia.

## 1988
*February 11–26.* In Armenia, demonstrators call for the incorporation of the autonomous region of Nagorno-Karabakh into Armenia. The region, with a population 75 percent Armenian, has been part of Azerbaijan since 1923.

*February 28.* An anti-Armenian pogrom takes place in Sumgait, Azerbaijan. The official reports indicate 32 dead.

*March 17.* Approximately 75,000 Armenians demonstrate in Stepanakert, the capital of Nagorno-Karabakh. The regional committee of the Communist Party will declare its support for incorporation into Armenia on March 20.

*March 23.* The Presidium of the Supreme Soviet rejects the Armenian demand concerning Nagorno-Karabakh.

*April.* A "Popular Front for *Perestroika*" is formed in Estonia.

*May 21.* The first secretaries of the Armenian and Azerbaijani Communist Parties are removed.

*June 15.* The Supreme Soviet of Armenia demands the incorporation of Nagorno-Karabakh into Armenia. The Supreme Soviet of Azerbaijan refuses.

*July 12.* The Regional Soviet of Nagorno-Karabakh proclaims the region's unilateral withdrawal from Azerbaijan and its incorporation into Armenia. The decision will be rejected on July 18 by the Presidium of the Supreme Soviet.

*September.* In Lithuania, a Central Council of the nationalist movement Sajudis is formed.

*September 11.* In Tallin, Estonian is declared the official language of Estonia.

*September 18.* New clashes occur between the Armenians and the Azerbaijanis in Nagorno-Karabakh.

*November 16.* The Supreme Soviet of Estonia declares the primacy of its laws over those of the USSR.

*November 19–24.* Clashes take place between Armenians and Azerbaijanis in Kirovabad, Azerbaijan.

*November 22–23.* Nationalist demonstrations are organized in Tbilisi (Georgia), Baku (Azerbaijan) and Yerevan.

*November 26.* The Presidium of the Supreme Soviet rejects the declaration of Estonian sovereignty.

*December 7.* An earthquake hits Armenia, destroying the cities of Spitak (100 percent) and Leninakan (80 percent), and seriously damaging the city of Kirovakan.

*December 10.* Most of the members of the Karabakh Committee are arrested in Armenia.

# 1989

*January 12.* The administration of Nagorno-Karabakh is taken over by Moscow.

*February 16.* The Lithuanian nationalist movement Sajudis declares its support for the republic's self-determination.

*March 10.* With the agreement of the Soviet authorities, the Pope names two archbishops and one bishop in Lithuania.

*April 9.* A peaceful demonstration in Tbilisi is violently repressed. Approximately 20 persons are killed.

*May 31.* The members of the Karabakh Committee, imprisoned since January in Moscow, are authorized to return to Armenia.

*June 3.* Interethnic troubles are stirred up in Uzbekistan. More than 100 Meskhets are killed in conflicts with Uzbeks.

*June 17.* Revolts break out in Kazakhstan against the Caucasian minority.

*July 15.* Clashes break out in the autonomous republic of Abkhazia, which is part of Georgia; almost two dozen persons die.

*July 27.* The Supreme Soviet declares its willingness to accept limited economic autonomy in the Baltic republics beginning in 1990.

*August 23.* An immense human chain 348 miles long is formed across

Lithuania, Latvia and Estonia to denounce the Nazi-Soviet Pact of 1939.

*August 31.* After numerous demonstrations, the Supreme Soviet of Moldavia declares Moldavian to be the official language of the republic.

*September 4.* A general strike begins in Azerbaijan. A blockade of road and rail links to Armenia is imposed (it will be lifted on October 12).

*September 8.* A congress of the Popular Movement of the Ukraine in Support of *Perestroika* opens.

*September 17.* A demonstration in Lvov by 100,000 Greek Catholics demands the legalization of the Uniate Church, which was forcibly integrated into the Orthodox Church under Stalin.

*September 19–20.* A plenum of the Central Committee is held to discuss the nationalities question. It declares its support for a new federal pact and for the self-determination of the republics.

*October 5.* The Supreme Soviet of Azerbaijan declares its sovereignty over the entire republic and proclaims Azerbaijani to be the official language.

*November 5.* In Yerevan, an Armenian National Movement is formed with the goal of Armenian independence.

*November 7.* On the anniversary of the October Revolution, counterdemonstrations are staged in Tbilisi, Yerevan and Kishinev (Moldavia).

*November 28.* A special committee charged with the direct administration of Nagorno-Karabakh is abolished. Unrest breaks out again in Armenia and Azerbaijan.

*December 20.* The Lithuanian Communist Party declares its autonomy from the Soviet Communist Party.

*December 30.* Azerbaijani nationalists stage demonstrations for the relax-ation of travel restrictions between the USSR and Iran.

# 1990

*January 11–13.* Gorbachev visits Lithuania. The Lithuanian Communist Party does not retract its proclamation of autonomy.

*January 19.* Following new anti-Armenian violence in Baku, a state of emergency is declared. The army takes control of the city by force, with the official casualty count indicating 125 dead.

*March 4.* In Lithuania, the independence movement Sajudis is victorious in local elections.

*March 11.* The Lithuanian parliament votes 124-9 to restore the independence of the republic, and elects the leader of the Sajudis movement, Vytautas Landsbergis, as president.

*March 12.* Gorbachev declares that the Lithuanian declaration of independence "affects the vital interests and the future of the Soviet state."

*March 23.* Soviet troops and tanks arrive in Vilnius, Lithuania's capital.

*March 25.* The Estonian Communist Party declares its autonomy from the Communist Party of the Soviet Union.

*March 30.* The new Estonian parliament votes in favor of Estonian independence but does not break immediately with Moscow.

*April 3.* A law governing the secession of Soviet republics is promulgated. It sets up a number of restrictive conditions for secession from the USSR.

*April 13.* Gorbachev issues an ultimatum to Lithuania. He demands within two days the abrogation of many laws passed by the Lithuanian parliament and threatens Lithuania with economic sanctions.

*April 18.* Moscow imposes an economic blockade on Lithuania.

*May 4.* The Latvian parliament votes in favor of independence, but it recognizes the need for a period of transition.

*May 14.* The declarations of independence by Estonia and Latvia are rendered illegal by Gorbachev's presidential decree.

*May 27.* Violent armed clashes occur between Armenian nationalists and Soviet troops. A climate of civil war engulfs most of the Caucasus.

*June 4.* Clashes between the Kirghiz and the Uzbeks break out. The official toll is 186 dead.

*June 12.* The parliament of the Russian Federation proclaims its sovereignty by a vote of 907 to 13.

Gorbachev proposes negotiations for a new union treaty.

*June 20.* Uzbekistan's parliament declares sovereignty.

*June 29.* The Lithuanian parliament suspends its declaration of independence. Economic sanctions are lifted by Moscow.

*July 14.* Interethnic clashes break out again in Kirghizia.

*July 16.* The Ukrainian parliament declares the sovereignty of the Ukraine.

*July 17.* The Lithuanian parliament passes a law allowing the formation of security forces made up of Lithuanian conscripts.

*July 17–21.* Deadly ethnic riots resume between the Kirghiz and the Uzbeks.

*July 19.* It is reported that Latvia has decided to form its own customs service to guard its borders.

*July 23.* The Ukrainian parliament elects Leonid Kravchuk, a nationalist Communist, to succeed Vladimir Ivashko as president.

*July 25.* Gorbachev issues a decree giving ethnic militants 15 days to disarm voluntarily or face confrontation with Soviet security forces. (He will extend the deadline for two months on August 11.)

*July 27.* The Belorussian parliament passes a sovereignty resolution.

*July 28.* The three Baltic republics reject participation in negotiations for a new union treaty.

*August 5.* The Armenian parliament elects Levon Ter-Petrosyan, a fervent nationalist, as president.

*August 10.* A bomb blows up a bus in Azerbaijan, killing 17 people.

*August 21.* It is reported that Karelia, an autonomous region within Russia on the border with Finland, has declared sovereignty.

*August 23.* The Armenian parliament votes to declare independence and asserts Armenian control over Nagorno-Karabakh. It also drops "Soviet Socialist" from the republic's name, and declares that all Armenians living abroad are entitled to citizenship.

*August 23–24.* Sovereignty is declared by Turkmenistan and then by Tadzhikistan.

*August 29.* The Armenian parliament declares a state of emergency and outlaws the Armenian National Army, the republic's largest paramilitary group.

*September 1.* It is reported that the parliament of the Tatar Autonomous Republic, a part of the Russian Republic, has voted to declare sovereignty and to seek status as an independent republic.

*September 18.* The exiled writer Alexander Solzhenitsyn calls for the creation of a non-Communist Slavic state made up of Russia, Ukraine, Belorussia and a large part of Kazakhstan.

*September 30.* Azerbaijan holds multiparty local elections.

*October 1.* It is reported that authorities in Kazakhstan, citing health and environmental concerns, have banned nuclear weapons tests at the USSR's main underground testing range.

*October 15.* Ethnic Russian-speakers and Gagauz (Turkic-speaking Orthodox Christians) in Moldavia are reported to have formed their own unofficial republics and declared sovereignty.

*October 17.* Ukrainian Prime Minister Vitali Masol tenders his resignation in response to student-led nationalist protests in Kiev.

*October 19.* The Soviet Interior Ministry announces that three tons of explosives and 20,200 firearms have been confiscated under Gorbachev's decree targeting ethnic militants.

*October 24.* The Chuvash, a people of mixed Finnish-Turkish ancestry, proclaim an independent republic within the Russian Republic.

*November 2.* Moldavian militiamen kill six people in a clash with Russian-speaking protesters in the latters' self-proclaimed Trans-Dniester Republic.

*November 12.* Kirghizia becomes the last of the 15 Soviet republics to declare itself a sovereign state.

*November 14.* Zviad Gamsakhurdia is elected Georgia's president. The parliament also removes the words "Soviet Socialist" from the republic's name.

*November 30.* The parliaments of the three Baltic republics hold their first ever joint session in Vilnius. The lawmakers pass a joint resolution seeking the withdrawal of Soviet troops.

*December 11.* The Georgian parliament abolishes South Ossetia as an autonomous region of Georgia, effectively annexing the enclave, and declares a state of emergency after three people are killed in clashes between Ossetians and Georgians.

*December 30.* The Moldavian parliament accedes to veiled threats and demands from Gorbachev to curb ethnic turmoil. Among other steps, it says it will review a 1989 law making Moldavian the republic's official language.

## 1991

*January 7.* The Soviet Defense Ministry announces it is sending thousands of army paratroopers to seven restive republics—Estonia, Latvia, Lithuania, Armenia, Georgia, Moldavia and parts of the Ukraine—to enforce military conscription and round up draft dodgers.

*January 10.* Gorbachev warns Lithuania to "immediately" obey Soviet central authority or risk the consequences. Supporters of Moscow launch a series of strikes in Lithuania.

*January 11.* The pro-Kremlin wing of the Lithuanian Communist Party announces the creation of a "National Salvation Committee" whose stated purpose is to replace the republic's elected pro-independence leadership. Soviet troops seize key buildings in Vilnius, injuring seven people.

*January 13.* Soviet paratroopers storm the central broadcasting complex in Vilnius and kill 14 Lithuanian protesters. The violence outrages Soviet liberals and is widely condemned abroad. Russian President Yeltsin will sign a mutual security pact with representatives of the three Baltic republics.

*January 14.* Gorbachev denies any responsibility for the army attack in Vilnius. He claims that the local military commander acted on his own initiative in response to pleas from the National Salvation Committee.

*January 15–16.* Elite "Black Beret" troops of the Soviet Interior Ministry seize a police academy in Latvia. A National Salvation Committee, made up of loyal pro-Moscow Communists, is formed in that republic as well.

*January 20.* Soviet Black Berets, reportedly acting at the behest of the Latvian National Salvation Committee, storm the Latvian Interior Ministry in Riga, killing four people.

*February 9.* Lithuania holds a nonbinding plebiscite that shows overwhelming popular support for secession from the USSR. Gorbachev had decreed the vote illegal, and Lithuania, to avoid further antagonizing Moscow, calls it an unofficial "public opinion poll."

*March 3.* Latvia and Estonia hold similar nonbinding plebiscites. These also indicate widespread support for independence, including (to a surprising degree) among the republics' ethnic Russian minorities.

*March 31.* Georgians support independence by a reported margin of 99 percent in a republic-wide referendum that excludes South Ossetia.

*April 8.* Georgia threatens a general strike unless Moscow recalls the 100,000 Soviet troops sent to quell ethnic violence between Georgians and Ossetians. At least 60 persons have died in the violence thus far in 1991.

*April 9.* Georgia's parliament votes unanimously to declare independence from the USSR.

*April 23.* Gorbachev and the leaders of nine of the USSR's 15 republics agree to cooperate on finding ways to solve the country's economic and political problems. (The meeting is boycotted by the three Baltic republics, Armenia, Georgia and Moldavia.)

*April 29.* An earthquake rocks Georgia, killing more than 100 people.

*May 26.* Georgia's Zviad Gamsakhurdia becomes the first leader of a Soviet republic to be elected by direct popular vote; he reportedly wins by a margin of 86 percent.

*June 3.* The Soviet prosecutor general issues a preliminary report exonerating Soviet troops for the killing of 14 Lithuanians in January. The report blames drunken Lithuanian nationalists for the shootings.

*June 17.* Gorbachev and the leaders of seven republics sign a new draft union treaty that would decentralize many of the powers of the Soviet government and remove "Socialist" from the USSR's name. Two other republics promise to sign the treaty later. The document is sent to the federal and republic parliaments for debate. All of the republics favor swift ratification, but the Ukrainian parliament on June 27 postpones debate until the fall.

*July 24.* Gorbachev announces that he and the leaders of 10 republics (Armenia has joined the original group of nine) have reached agreement on disputed power-sharing provisions in the draft union treaty.

*August 19–21.* Soviet army, KGB and Interior Ministry troops seize broadcasting facilities and telephone exchanges in the Baltic republics during the attempted coup against Gorbachev in Moscow. The Baltic republics respond to the coup by declaring their full independence from the USSR (Estonia on August 20, and Lithuania and Latvia on August 21).

*August 20.* The attempted coup delays the scheduled signing by five republics of Gorbachev's new union treaty. Opposition to the treaty by hard-liners is said to be a major motivation behind the coup.

*August 24–27.* In the wake of the failed coup and the secessions of the Baltic republics, the parliaments of three more republics swiftly approve declarations of independence: the Ukraine on August 24, Belorussia on August 25, and Moldavia on August 27.

*September 5.* The parliament of the Crimean region votes to declare independence from the Ukraine.

*September 6.* The USSR formally recognizes the independence of Estonia, Latvia and Lithuania.

*September 8.* Azerbaijan holds its first direct presidential election. The current president, the parliamentary chairman Ayaz Mutalibov, wins easily (there are no other names on the ballot). The opposition boycotts the election, calling it a "sham."

*September 9.* Tadzhikistan's parliament declares independence.

*September 14.* The Communist Party of Uzbekistan keeps de facto power and circumvents the nationwide ban on Communist Party activity by changing its name to the Popular Democratic Party and appropriating all property held under its former name.

*September 23.* Armenia and Azerbaijan agree to settle their conflict over Nagorno-Karabakh through negotiations. The accord is brokered by Russian President Yeltsin and Kazakhstan President Nursultan Nazarbayev. The fighting will continue despite the agreement.

The Communist-dominated parliament of Tadzhikistan declares a state of emergency and fires the republic's non-Communist, reformist acting president.

*September 24.* Georgian President Gamsakhurdia declares a state of emergency and urges his supporters to come

to Tbilisi to "liquidate" the "nest of bandits" that opposes him. There have been increasingly violent protests against the president, who is accused by critics of dictatorial behavior and paranoia. By the end of 1991, the turmoil will develop into virtual civil war.

*October 9–22.* The Azerbaijan parliament on October 9 authorizes the formation of an independent army for the republic. The Ukraine follows suit on October 22.

*October 11–November 6.* Gorbachev and the leaders of 10 republics commit themselves on October 11 to form an economic union. Eight republics sign the treaty on October 18. After initially holding out, the Ukraine and Moldavia sign it on November 6, leaving only Georgia and Azerbaijan outside the pact.

*October 27.* Turkmenistan's parliament votes a declaration of independence.

*October 27–November 11.* Soviet air force General Dzhokhar Dudayev, the leader of an armed independence movement, on October 27 is elected president of the Chechen-Ingush autonomous region, a self-governing enclave in southern Russia. President Yeltsin on November 8 decrees a state of emergency in the enclave and dispatches troops, but the Russian parliament overturns the decree on November 11.

*October 29.* The Ukrainian parliament votes to shut down and dismantle the Chernobyl nuclear power plant by 1993.

*November 24.* Tadzhikistan's voters elect former Communist Party leader Rakhman Nabiyev president of the republic. The opposition charges fraud.

*November 25.* In a setback to Gorbachev, seven republics refuse to sign a new treaty on political union.

*December 1.* Ukrainian voters overwhelmingly approve a republic-wide referendum calling for independence from the USSR. The voters also make former Communist Party leader Leonid Kravchuk Ukraine's first popularly elected president.

Kazakhstan's voters elect their incumbent president, Nursultan Nazarbayev. He is the lone candidate on the ballot.

*December 8.* Incumbent Moldavian President Mircea Snegur, running unopposed, wins popular election.

*December 8–25.* The Commonwealth of Independent States is formed to replace the USSR. It will eventually comprise 11 states, including all of the former Soviet republics except the Baltic states and Georgia.

*December 12.* Ukrainian President Kravchuk declares himself commander in chief of all Soviet armed forces on Ukrainian territory, including the Black Sea Fleet.

# Civilization and Culture

## 1985

*My Friend Ivan Lapshin*, a film by A. German, opens.

## 1986

The poet Nikolai Gumilev, who was executed in 1921, is rehabilitated. *The Defense*, written in 1930 by Vladimir Nabokov, is published. *Dictatorship of Conscience*, a play by Mikhail Shatrov. *Is It Easy To Be Young?*, a film by J. Podnieks.

*May 13–15.* The Fifth Congress of the Cinematographer's Union elects Elem Klimov as its leader and decides to "liberate" the films that were long prohibited by censorship.

*December 5–6.* The First Congress of the Union of Theatrical Societies of the USSR is held. It declares its objective to be the renewal of theater and its transformation into a "tribunal of truth."

## 1987

*Children of the Arbat*, a novel by Anatoli Rybakov. Publication in the Soviet Union of *The Pit*, by Andrei Platonov; *The Heart of a Dog*, by Mikhail Bulgakov; and *Pushkin House*, by Andrei Bitov. Films: In Moscow, *Repentance*, by Tengiz Abuladze, opens; *The Commissar*, filmed in 1967 by A. Askoldov, opens. A rock music festival is held in Moscow. The Nobel Prize for literature is awarded to the poet Joseph Brodsky.

## 1988

The following are published in the Soviet Union: *Doctor Zhivago*, by Boris Pasternak; *Life and Fate*, by Vasili Grossman; *Chevengur*, by A. Platonov; *Kolyma Tales* (excerpts), by Varlam Shalamov; *Faculty of Useless Things*, by Yuri Dombrovsky; *Disappearance*, by Yuri Trifonov; *Speak, Memory*, by Vladimir Nabokov. Films: *Little Vera*, by Vasili Pichul; *The Power of the Solovki*, by Marina Goldovskaya. A virtual rewriting of the history of the USSR begins.

*October 25.* Kazakhstan's parliament adopts a sovereignty resolution.

*October 28.* The Georgian Round Table, a coalition of non- Communist parties favoring swift secession from the USSR and led by Zviad Gamsakhurdia, wins parliamentary elections.

*November 1.* The Ukraine becomes the first Soviet republic to issue its own currency, in the form of coupons.

## 1989

Deep splits occur in all cultural enterprises, reviving in some cases the old debates of the Slavophiles and the Westernizers. Kazimir Malevich's abstract art is exhibited in Moscow.

*August.* *Novy Mir* begins publishing Alexander Solzhenitsyn's *The Gulag Archipelago, Cancer Ward* and *The First Circle.*

Publication of *Everything Flows,* a novel written in 1960 by V. Grossman.

## 1990

*Taxi Blues,* a film by P. Lungin.

Cellist Mstislav Rostropovich returns to play his first concert in the USSR in 16 years.

# Chapter 34                                    1991–1992

# The Commonwealth of Independent States

The Commonwealth of Independent States (CIS) came into being in December 1991 as the successor to the dissolved Union of Soviet Socialist Republics. The historic collapse of the Soviet state came with stunning rapidity in the wake of the August coup against President Mikhail Gorbachev. Although the coup failed, it led to the downfall of the Communist Party, the unravelling of Gorbachev's power and the rise to prominence of Russian President Boris Yeltsin. With Gorbachev's failure to cobble together a new union treaty, the way was cleared for Yeltsin and the leaders of the other republics to form the CIS, which brought together 11 of the 15 former Soviet republics (excluding Georgia, which was engulfed in civil war, and the three already independent Baltic states).

The main questions facing the peoples of the former Soviet Union as 1992 progressed concerned the future of the CIS: Would it be able to constitute itself as a meaningful supranational entity? Would it continue to exist in name only, and slowly wither away? Or would it collapse completely under the same strains that had torn the old USSR apart? On this issue, optimists were hard to find, while there were doomsayers aplenty, both within the CIS and abroad.

The raison d'être of the CIS was to establish joint security policies and to regulate trade and economic ties between the states. In their early meetings, however, the leaders of the new states were able to hammer out few substantive agreements to flesh out the original CIS charter. One reason for this lack of progress was the instinctive fear of the non-Russian states that Moscow would use the CIS as an instrument for reasserting its traditional political, economic and military dominance over the rest of the commonwealth. Since the former Soviet military establishment that would make up the bulk of a common CIS defense force was largely Russian in composition and command, such fears were not entirely misplaced. In addition, the already prickly relations between Russia and Ukraine were strained even further by the unresolved status of Crimea and the Black Sea Fleet.

An even more basic stumbling block to greater cooperation was the persistent unrest within—and, in the case of Armenia and Azerbaijan, between—the states themselves. The Transcaucasian and Central Asian states, in particular, were riven by interethnic bloodshed and political strife; their governments often seemed more concerned with day-to-day survival than with strengthening the CIS. These states on the periphery of the old Soviet empire also found themselves increasingly looking south, to such countries as Turkey and Iran, rather than north to Moscow, for aid and guidance.

Domestic political unrest also plagued Russia itself. While some Russian nationalists talked about going to the aid of embattled ethnic Russian minorities in the other former republics, the attention of most politicians and citizens remained focused on domestic problems and, in particular, on the floundering economy. Here the main power struggle was between Yeltsin's Western-oriented technocratic government, which was pushing a wrenching, radical free-market plan, and the conservatives in parliament and industry, mostly former Communists, who favored a slower transition to a market economy with a larger state role. The contest was bitter and marked by frequent confrontations, but both sides seemed willing to reach for last-minute compromises that kept the jury-rigged, post-Soviet system from complete collapse. Similarly, and despite dire predictions of food riots and social chaos, the long-suffering Russian people continued to muddle through stoically, enduring the rigors of a system that was no longer Communist but not yet capitalist.

# Politics and Institutions

## 1991

*December 30.* The 11 presidents of the CIS's Council of Heads of State hold their first full meeting since the dissolution of the USSR on December 25. Gathering in Minsk, the capital of the CIS and of Belarus (formerly Belorussia), the leaders formally agree to place the strategic nuclear arsenal of the former USSR under central control, in effect, under Russian President Boris Yeltsin. In the event of war, however, the agreement requires the CIS nuclear states—Russia, Ukraine, Belarus and Kazakhstan—to jointly agree on the use of the weapons and to consult with the other members of the CIS. No agreement is reached on control of the former Soviet Union's conventional forces, al-

though there is a consensus that any state can form its own army or national guard.

## 1992

*January 4.* Ukraine's president, Leonid Kravchuk, declares that all former Soviet military personnel on his country's territory must swear allegiance to Ukraine.

*January 9.* Yeltsin declares that the former Soviet navy's Black Sea Fleet, which is based at the Ukrainian port of Sevastopol, on the Crimean Peninsula, and is claimed by Ukraine, "was, is and will be Russia's."

*January 11.* Russia and Ukraine reach a tentative preliminary agreement on the Black Sea Fleet; the details of the agreement remain to be worked out.

*January 14.* Mikhail Gorbachev makes his first public appearance in Moscow since his resignation three weeks earlier. He begins work as chairman of the International Foundation for Social, Economic and Political Research, a private "think tank."

*January 18.* Approximately 5,000 military officers of the former Soviet armed forces gather in the Kremlin to demand that the old USSR's conventional armed forces remain under a unified CIS command. Their concerns are heard by Yeltsin, Kravchuk and Marshal Yevgeni Shaposhnikov, who remains the interim commander of all ex-Soviet forces pending a new agreement on a CIS military structure.

*February 1.* The CIS agrees to begin withdrawing the estimated 100,000 ex-Soviet troops from the three Baltic states. Lithuania, Latvia and Estonia had demanded an immediate pullout, but the CIS agreement does not include a timetable for completing the withdrawal.

*February 12.* In what amounts to a "defection," the crews of six SU-24 bombers fly their planes from their base in Ukraine to Russia.

*February 14.* The CIS's Council of Heads of State, meeting in Minsk, fails to reach an agreement on the formation of a common defense force under a unified command. Azerbaijan, Moldova (the former Moldavia) and Ukraine each reassert their intention to form their own separate armed forces under civilian control.

*March 20.* Ten of the 11 CIS leaders meet in Kiev, Ukraine, but again fail to resolve any major military, political or economic issues. Ukraine's Kravchuk accuses his fellow presidents of avoiding crucial decisions. "If the situation does not change, the Commonwealth is doomed," he says.

*April 2–3.* In a gesture to his critics, Yeltsin removes Yegor Gaidar, the architect of radical economic reform, as

finance minister, and strips Gennadi Burbulis of his position as a first deputy prime minister. These moves are seen as cosmetic: Vasili Barchuk, Gaidar's deputy, succeeds him as finance minister; Gaidar retains his post as first deputy prime minister for economic policy; and Burbulis remains as state secretary, effectively Yeltsin's chief aide.

*April 6.* The first post-Soviet session of Russia's parliament, the Congress of People's Deputies, opens in the Kremlin's Grand Palace. At issue are Yeltsin's radical economic reforms and his desire to permanently entrench his emergency powers to rule by decree. In a 447-412 vote, with 70 abstentions, Yeltsin escapes a conservative-sponsored motion to bring a no-confidence vote to the floor.

*April 11–15.* Russia's parliament adopts a resolution aimed at softening Yeltsin's reforms; the resolution also orders him to step down as prime minister by the end of July. (In addition to the presidency, Yeltsin had assumed the post of Russian prime minister in November 1991.) Gaidar announces the resignation of the entire cabinet in protest. After the deputies approve a compromise declaration of conditional support for Yeltsin's policies, the cabinet declares victory and rescinds its resignation.

*April 17–21.* The Russian parliament votes to give "Russia" and "Russian Federation" coequal status as the country's official name. The deputies then formally ratify the 1991 accord creating the CIS. They also vote to delete all references to the USSR from Russia's constitution (which is an updated version of the old Soviet Constitution), but they add a statement declaring Russia's willingness to form a "renewed union" with other ex-Soviet republics.

*April 29–30.* Russian and Ukrainian negotiators meet in Odessa but fail to reach agreement on the fate of the Black Sea Fleet. Earlier in the month, both governments issued decrees claiming the fleet for their respective states.

*May 1.* About 25,000 persons—Russian right-wing nationalists in alliance with Communists—march in Moscow on the "Day of Spring and Labor" (formerly May Day) to denounce Yeltsin, U.S. and Israeli "imperialism," and other targets.

*May 7.* Yeltsin issues decrees creating Russia's own armed forces and naming himself supreme commander. He also appoints Colonel General Pavel Grachev as Russia's acting defense minister.

Ukraine confirms that all of its tactical nuclear weapons have been transferred to Russia for destruction.

*May 15.* CIS leaders and representatives meet in Tashkent, Uzbekistan, where 6 of the 11 states sign a mutual security treaty. Those signing include Russia, Armenia, Kazakhstan, Turkmenistan, Uzbekistan and Tajikistan. Those declining to sign include Belarus, Azerbaijan, Ukraine, Moldova and Kyrgyzstan (formerly Kirghizia). The treaty pledges a collective military response should one state be attacked by a foreign power, and the signatories vow never to wage war against one another. They also agree to form a joint force to patrol their external borders. The accord tacitly acknowledges the demise of the ex-Soviet armed forces as a jointly run entity. On other matters, the members of the CIS agree in principle to create a commonwealth peace force to keep warring nationalist forces apart, to establish an interrepublic banking system, and to share the former Soviet space program.

*June 6.* Yeltsin accepts the resignation of Moscow Mayor Gavril Popov, who had earlier said he would resign in December 1991. Popov had battled with the Moscow city council over his radical reform policies.

*July 6.* The CIS holds a summit meeting in Moscow. Although constructive in tone, the meeting produces no major new accords.

*July 16.* CIS foreign and defense ministers agree on mechanisms for organizing an armed volunteer peacekeeping force on a permanent basis. The planned force would not engage in military action, and its deployment would require the invitation of all parties directly involved in a conflict.

*July 20.* Belarus and Russia sign a military cooperation agreement that allows Moscow to maintain Russian strategic nuclear forces units on Belarusian soil for an undetermined period.

# Foreign Affairs

## 1992

*January 22–23.* The U.S. State Department hosts a conference of aid donors to the CIS. Forty-seven nations and five financial institutions attend. President George Bush pledges $645 million in new U.S. aid, and Secretary of State James Baker announces that the U.S. Air Force will begin an emergency airlift of food and medicine—dubbed "Operation Provide Hope"—to needy CIS institutions.

*January 26.* In an interview, Yeltsin vows that CIS strategic nuclear missiles would no longer be targeted on U.S. cities, although he does not say what the missiles' new targets might be.

*January 28–29.* Bush and Yeltsin offer new initiatives aimed at dramatically reducing their countries' nuclear arsenals.

*January 30.* The 10 other states in the CIS join Russia as members of the Conference on Security and Cooperation in Europe (CSCE).

*January 31.* Yeltsin and the leaders of the other countries on the United Nations Security Council meet in New York. This is the first such summit meeting ever held.

*February 1.* Yeltsin meets with President Bush for private talks at the presidential retreat at Camp David, Maryland.

*February 6.* U.S. Vice President Dan Quayle visits the three Baltic states to formally reopen U.S. embassies there. He offers a total of $18 million in American aid.

*February 7.* Yeltsin and French President François Mitterrand, meeting in Paris, sign a landmark treaty calling for unprecedented political, economic and military cooperation between Russia and France.

*February 10.* An international airlift of food and medicine to the CIS begins. The United States, Japan and several European countries participate.

*February 11–16.* U.S. Secretary of State Baker visits Moldova, Armenia, Azerbaijan, Turkmenistan, Tajikistan and Uzbekistan. (Of these six states, the United States has thus far extended diplomatic recognition only to Armenia.)

*February 16–17.* Azerbaijan, Turkmenistan, Uzbekistan, Kyrgyzstan and Tajikistan join Iran, Turkey and Pakistan in the Economic Cooperation Organization during a summit meeting in Teheran.

*February 17–18.* Baker confers in Moscow with Yeltsin and Russian Foreign Minister Andrei Kozyrev on arms control issues. During the visit, the

United States, Germany and Russia agree to set up an international program that will employ former Soviet nuclear weapons scientists in nonmilitary projects.

*March 25.* Twenty-one nations in North America and Europe, and four in the former USSR (Russia, Belarus, Ukraine and Georgia), sign an "open skies" treaty allowing reconnaissance flights over their territory by foreign planes.

*March 31.* The International Monetary Fund (IMF) formally endorses Russia's economic reforms.

*April 1.* President Bush and German Chancellor Helmut Kohl separately announce a $24 billion aid package for Russia from the Group of Seven (G-7) leading industrial nations.

*April 27–May 5.* The IMF and World Bank formally offer membership to all of the former Soviet republics. Russia will be officially admitted to the IMF on June 1.

*May 6.* Ukrainian President Kravchuk meets with President Bush in Washington and vows that his country will cut its nuclear arsenal as required by the 1991 U.S.-Soviet Strategic Arms Reduction Treaty (START). President Nursultan Nazarbayev of Kazakhstan will meet with Bush on May 19 and make a similar pledge.

*May 18.* Kazakhstan and the Chevron Corporation, an American oil company, sign a joint-venture agreement to develop the huge Tengiz oil field and other sites. The pact calls for an estimated $20 billion investment over 40 years.

*May 25–26.* U.S. Secretary of State Baker visits Georgia for talks with its new leader, Eduard Shevardnadze, the former Soviet foreign minister.

*June 8–9.* Baker and Russian Foreign Minister Kozyrev meet in Washington but fail to settle presummit arms control issues.

*June 16–17.* Yeltsin visits Washington for the first official American-Russian summit meeting. He and Bush reach a surprise agreement on sweeping strategic nuclear arms reductions that go well beyond the 1991 START accord. Yeltsin also addresses the U.S. Congress and creates a controversy by raising the possibility that American servicemen missing in action during the Vietnam War might have been transferred to the USSR.

*July 2.* The U.S. Senate approves an aid package for Russia, the other CIS states and Georgia. The House of Representatives will pass similar legislation on August 6.

*July 8.* Yeltsin addresses the leaders of the G-7 nations during their summit meeting in Munich, Germany. Although he wins promises of support, he receives little in the way of specific aid pledges.

*July 16.* The heads of the U.S. and Russian space agencies announce plans for a series of joint missions: A Russian will travel aboard a U.S. space shuttle in 1993, an American will visit the Russian space station *Mir*, and the shuttle will link up with *Mir* in 1994.

# Economy and Society

## 1992

*January 2.* In the first major step of Yeltsin's radical economic reform plan, Russia eliminates state subsidies for most goods and services, causing prices to soar. Ukraine, Belarus and Moldova also begin lifting price controls.

*January 6–7.* The Russian people mark Christmas as an official state holiday (on the Russian Orthodox Church's Julian calendar) for the first time in more than 70 years.

*January 7.* Shoppers in nearly a dozen cities protest the lifting of price controls by smashing windows.

*January 13.* Georgi Matyukhin, chairman of Russia's Central Bank (the successor to the USSR's Gosbank), warns that Yeltsin's policies could lead to social upheaval. Parliament Chairman Ruslan Khasbulatov calls for Yeltsin's resignation.

*January 16.* Yeltsin hits back at his critics by vowing to continue his reforms while saying he will review some aspects of his economic plan.

*January 16–19.* At least six persons die when police open fire on students protesting high prices in Uzbekistan; Azerbaijan and Turkmenistan roll back their own price increases to head off unrest.

*April 6–21.* Yeltsin continues to spar with his critics at the first post-Soviet session of the Russian Congress of People's Deputies. It is widely reported that Yeltsin's requests for Western aid and his willingness to subscribe to the IMF's "shock-therapy" approach to economic reform (involving high prices and growing unemployment) have alienated even some of his close democratic allies.

*April 22.* The Ukrainian official in charge of the Chernobyl cleanup asserts that the 1986 nuclear power plant accident has caused between 6,000 and 8,000 deaths.

*June 20.* Estonia introduces its own currency, the *kroon*, thereby becoming the first former Soviet republic to replace the Russian ruble with a new, convertible currency.

*July 20.* Latvia makes its own non-convertible ruble the only legal tender in the country. It is regarded as an interim currency, to be replaced by a new, convertible Latvian ruble by the end of the year.

# Events in Other CIS States

## 1992

*January 6.* Georgian President Zviad Gamsakhurdia flees his capital, Tbilisi, after months of civil war. A loose coalition of rebel forces takes control.

*January 16–28.* After first seeking refuge in Armenia, Gamsakhurdia returns to western Georgia and exhorts his followers to wage war to return him to power. Troops of the new Georgian government capture the rebellious towns of Poti and Zugdidi.

*January 23.* Estonian Prime Minister Edgar Savisaar falls into a feud with parliament over food and fuel shortages. He will be replaced on January 30 by Tiit Vahi.

*January 28–March 17.* Escalating warfare between Armenia and Azerbaijan over Nagorno-Karabakh claims the lives of hundreds. (Guerrilla warfare, terrorist acts and massacres of civilians by both sides have killed an estimated 1,500 persons since 1988.) Mediation efforts are launched by Iran, Turkey, Britain, the Islamic Conference Organization, the United Nations and the CSCE.

*March 2.* Yeltsin signs a decree allowing Russians of German descent to resettle in two areas along the Volga River that were once populated by ethnic Germans. The Germans were moved from the region to Siberia during World War II.

*March 6.* Azerbaijan's president, Ayaz Mutalibov, is accused of being too conciliatory toward Armenia and is forced to resign. Yakub Mamedov, the speaker of the parliament, becomes acting president until new elections can be held.

*March 10.* Georgia's ruling military council names Eduard Shevardnadze to head a newly created State Council. Shevardnadze, a former Soviet foreign minister, had served as Georgia's interior minister and the head of the former republic's Communist Party from 1972 to 1985.

*March 17.* The Moldovan government and Slavic separatists in the eastern Dniester region agree to a cease-fire after two weeks of clashes during which at least 30 persons are killed. Violence will continue, however, and Moldova will declare a state of emergency on March 28.

*April 11.* Yeltsin issues a decree nationalizing the CIS military forces in Moldova and placing them under his personal command.

*April 29–May 21.* The Ukrainian government offers the Crimean region the status of autonomy within Ukraine. The Crimean parliament responds by declaring independence, but it is forced to back down in the face of Ukrainian threats. The Russian Supreme Soviet on May 21 votes to nullify the 1954 transfer of Crimea from the Russian to the Ukrainian Republic.

*May 11.* Tajikistan's president, Rakhman Nabiyev, agrees to form a power-sharing cabinet with an opposition coalition composed of secular antiCommunists and Islamic fundamentalists. The concession comes after months of protests during which more than 100 persons died.

*May 18–19.* Armenian forces capture Shusha, the last Azerbaijani stronghold in Nagorno-Karabakh, and attack Nakhichevan, an autonomous Azerbaijani enclave within Armenia. The Armenian successes lead to political chaos in Baku, the Azerbaijan capital, where the parliament is forced to turn over power to an ad hoc National Council dominated by the opposition Popular Front.

*June 24.* Georgian security forces crush an attempted coup by rebels loyal to the ousted president, Gamsakhurdia. Shevardnadze and Yeltsin meet and agree to jointly deploy Georgian and Russian peacekeeping troops along the border with South Ossetia, a region of Georgia within which secessionists have been waging armed struggle. The unrest has spread to North Ossetia, which is part of Russia, and has increased tensions between Georgia and Russia. (The peacekeepers will be deployed on July 14.)

*June 28.* Estonia holds a nationwide referendum on its first post-Soviet constitution. Under new citizenship laws, only pre-1940 residents and their descendants are allowed to vote; these measures are aimed at curbing the rights of ethnic Russians, who make up about one-third of Estonia's population.

*July 17.* The Russian parliament passes a resolution condemning "human rights violations" in Estonia and considers possible sanctions.

*July 27.* Estonian and Russian soldiers exchange shots in Tallin, Estonia's capital; a Russian officer and a civilian are wounded.

*August 7.* It is reported that Russia has asked for $7.7 billion in relocation payments from the Baltic states in return for the withdrawal of all Russian troops from the region by 1994.

# Civilization and Culture

## 1992

*August.* The "Unified Team," which consists of athletes from 12 former Soviet republics who are competing together for perhaps the last time, wins more medals (112) than any other nation at the Summer Olympic Games in Barcelona, Spain.

# GLOSSARY

**apparatchik** An official; a member of the Communist Party or state apparatus.

**archimandrite** The highest rank for monastic superiors.

**artel** A crew of artisans or tradesmen (e.g., boatmen, fishermen).

**ataman** The cossack leader; also, the leader of a gang of brigands.

**barin** A Russian landlord, usually one with large land holdings; the word *barshchina* is derived from this word.

**barshchina** Corvée; unpaid labor that serfs were obligated to render to a landlord.

**bezdorozhie.** A term meaning "a lack of roads," indicating the difficulties of transportation in Russia, often connected with the spring thaw.

**Black Hundreds** In Russian, *Chernosotentsy;* extreme rightist groups that organized pogroms in late-czarist Russia.

**boyar** In Russian *boyarin;* a dignitary of the first rank in the hierarchy of the Muscovite aristocracy, followed by the *okolnichi.*

**Boyar Duma** An assembly.

**Bund** The Union of Jewish Workers in Lithuania, Russia and Poland at the turn of the 20th century (1897–1921).

**Cadets (Kadets)** From the Russian abbreviation *K.D.;* members of the Constitutional Democratic Party.

**Cheka** From the Russian *Chrezvychainaia Komissiia;* the Extraordinary Commission, organized as a network to combat counterrevolutionaries and saboteurs.

**chistka** Purge; characteristic of the Stalin era.

**Comecon** An English acronym corresponding to the Russian *S.E.V.;* the Council for Mutual Economic Assistance.

**Cominform** The Communist Information Bureau (September 1947–April 1956).

**Comintern** The Communist International (March 1919–May 1943).

**desyatina** A measure of land approximately equivalent to 2.7 acres.

**Domostroi** A household manual from the 16th century.

**Duma** The legislative assembly at the end of the czarist period (1905–1917).

**dusha** Soul; a peasant under poll tax obligation.

**Gosplan** The Russian acronym for *Gosudarstvennaia Planovaia Komissiia pri Sovete Ministrov SSSR;* the commission set up in February 1921, charged with the drafting of state economic plans and the verification of their execution.

**GPU**  The Russian abbreviation for *Glavnoe Politicheskoe Upravlenie;* the central administration of the political police, which replaced the Cheka in February 1922. It became the OGPU beginning in July 1923. It was the equivalent of a People's Commissariat, and as such was not subordinate to the People's Commissariat of Internal Affairs, the NKVD.

**Gulag**  The Russian acronym for *Glavnoe Upravlenie Lagerei;* the principal administration of the "archipelago" of labor camps. It was set up by the decrees of September 5, 1918, and April 15, 1919; it reached its most tragic dimensions under Stalin.

**hegumen**  A priest; the head of an Orthodox monastery or his assistant.

**hetman**  From the German *Hauptmann;* a cossack leader.

**Holy Synod**  The council created by Peter the Great to exercise state control over the Orthodox Church.

**ispolkom**  The executive committee of a soviet.

**ispravnik**  A district police chief in the czarist period.

**KGB**  The Russian abbreviation for *Komitet Gosudarstvennoi Bezopastnoi;* the state security committee established as an independent entity in 1954.

**kharakteristika**  A personal evaluation, essential for nominations and promotions in the cadres of the Communist Party or the state.

**kolkhoz**  The Russian acronym for *kollektivnoe khoziaistvo;* a collective farm.

**Kombedy**  The Russian acronym for *Komitety bednoty;* a committee of poor peasants, organized in 1918.

**Komsomol**  The Russian acronym for *Kommunisticheskii soiuz molodezhi;* the Communist youth organization (for those 14 years old and up).

**kopek**  One hundredth of a ruble.

**kulak**  In the context of prerevolutionary Russia, a kulak was a well-to-do peasant accused of being a "monopolizer" and a usurer; during the era of agricultural collectivization, it became a label to be used against the more independent peasants in order to justify their arrest. Stalin decided to "liquidate them as a class" beginning in December 1929.

**malozemlie**  "Land hunger"; a lack of land that was suffered in particular by peasants after the 1861 agrarian reform.

**mestnichestvo**  The system of official appointments, based on hierarchical family rankings, in Muscovite Russia; a term for "laziness" in the former USSR.

**metropolitan**  The primate of the Orthodox Church (the "patriarch" beginning in 1589). In the 19th century, a metropolitan resided in each of the historic capitals of the Russian Empire: Kiev, Moscow and

St. Petersburg. Today, this title designates the bishop of a provincial capital.

**mir**  The rural assembly that administered an agricultural community (which did not always correspond to one village); generally it refers to the rural community and its inhabitants.

**MTS**  An abbreviation for the Russian *Machino-traktornaia stantsiia*, the Machine Tractor Station; stations comprised of agricultural machines and tractors, instituted by decree on June 5, 1929.

**narodniki**  The populists; revolutionaries who turned "to the people," the *narod*, in the years 1860–1890.

**nepman**  An entrepreneur, sometimes considered a profiteer, during the period of the New Economic Policy.

**NKVD**, later **MVD**  The People's Commissariat of Internal Affairs, later the Ministry of Internal Affairs.

**nomenklatura**  The upper echelons in Communist Party and state organizations.

**obrok**  Payment in cash and, more rarely, in kind, owed by the peasant to the landlord.

**Octobrists**  Moderates who supported the October Manifesto of 1905.

**Okhrana**  The political police of the czarist period; from the Russian word *okhrana*, meaning "protection."

**oprichnina**  The extraordinary regime put into place by Ivan IV between 1565 and 1584. The term *"zemshchina"* designated the part of Russia that was not under the *oprichnina* administration.

**patriarch**  The title conferred on the head of the Russian Orthodox Church since its independence in 1589 until the era of Peter the Great. It was reestablished in November 1917 and, after a break, has been used again since 1943.

**Politburo**  The Political Bureau of the Central Committee of the Communist Party. It was called the Presidium from October 1952 to April 1966, and was supplanted by the Presidential Council beginning in the spring of 1990.

**pomeshchik**  A landed proprietor; from the Russian word *pomestie*, meaning an estate granted in reward for service rendered to the czar, from 1478 until the 17th century.

**pood**  A measure of weight equivalent to 36 pounds.

**posadnik**  The head of a district or suburb (*posad*) in ancient Russia, particularly in Novgorod and Pskov; the first civil magistrate.

**prikaz**  An administrative bureau in the Muscovite era.

**Primary Chronicle**  One of the first written accounts of Russia's earliest history, beginning with the year 852; also known as the *Tale of Bygone Years*.

**Profintern**  The Red Trade Union International (July 1921–late 1937).

**profsoyuz**  Trade unions, considered in the USSR as the means to empower the masses; they were also charged with the task of parcelling out fringe benefits.

**Rada**  The General Assembly of cossacks; the Assembly of the independent Ukraine.

**Raskolniki** or **Staroobriadtsy**  The "Old Believers," adherents of the traditional Orthodox Church who opposed the reforms carried out by Patriarch Nikon in the 17th century.

**RSDLP**  The Russian Social Democratic Labor Party; founded in Minsk in 1898, it split into Mensheviks and Bolsheviks after 1903.

**Russkaia Pravda** (Russian Justice)  The legal code of the Kievan era.

**skhod**  A peasant assembly that directed the affairs of the commune or village; it was composed of the heads of families, and was therefore not an elective assembly.

**sloboda**  A village or settlement inhabited by free peasants.

**sokha**  A wooden plough with a simple iron ploughshare, in contrast to the *plug*, an iron plough; a unit of taxation in the ancient period.

**soviet**  A council; a political organization of the masses (during the Revolution of 1905, and then from February 1917 onward).

**sovkhoz**  From the Russian term *sovetskoe khoziaistvo;* a large-scale state farm in which the farmers are wage-earning employees.

**sovnarkhoz**  From the Russian *sovet narodnogo khoziaistvo;* a regional economic council.

**Sovnarkom**  From the Russian *Sovet Narodnykh Komissarov;* the Council of People's Commissars. This was the key administrative body of the state from shortly after the Bolshevik Revolution until, in March 1946, it was transformed into the Council of Ministers of the USSR.

**SR**  A member of the Socialist Revolutionary Party.

**stakhanovism**  A movement for the rationalization of labor and increased productivity, which was begun in 1935 and based on the alleged exploits of the miner Alexei Stakhanov.

**starets**  An elder; a spiritual guide.

**starosta**  An elected village mayor.

**starshina**  A district mayor; a sergeant-major.

**Stoglav**  A legal code made up of 100 chapters (*sto:* 100, *glava:* chapter), which resulted from the work of the council convened in Moscow by Ivan IV in 1551.

**streltsy**  Regiments of musketeers added to the Russian army in 1550; their mutiny in 1698 was put down by Peter the Great, who then abolished the regiments.

**Strigolniki**  A heretical sect (the "cutters") that denied the authority of the Church and most of the sacraments. They were active in Novgorod and Pskov from the mid-14th century to the beginning of the 15th century.

**Sudebnik**  The Russian legal code in the 15th and 16th centuries.

**taiga**  The Siberian forests.

**trudoden**  Literally "workday," a unit by which compensation to the kolkhoznik was calculated. The amount of time necessary to earn one unit varied according to the type of work performed.

**tundra**  Marshy regions in northern Russia and Siberia, sparsely covered with mosses, lichens and small shrubs.

**uchastok**  Under the kolkhoz system, a plot of land that the peasant could cultivate for his or her own benefit.

**udel**  The separate landholding of an individual prince in medieval Russia, known in English as an appanage.

**ukase**  A decree or edict; a term used during the czarist period as well as during the Soviet era.

**Ulozhenie**  The Russian code of laws of 1649.

**uravnilovka**  "Leftist" egalitarianism denounced by Stalin beginning in 1931–1932.

**veche**  The popular assembly in the towns of ancient Russia.

**verst**  A unit of distance equivalent to approximately two-thirds of a mile.

**voevoda**  The commander of an army; later a provincial governor in Muscovite Russia.

**VSNKh**  From the Russian *Vyschii Sovet Naradnogo Khoziaistva;* the Supreme Council of the National Economy, established in December 1917.

**VTsIK**  The All-Russian Central Executive Committee.

**vykhod**  A tribute paid to the Tatars.

**Zemlia i Volia**  Land and Freedom, a terrorist organization that grew out of the populist movement.

**Zemskii Sobor**  "An assembly of the land," a consultative body convened by the first czars, from the mid-16th century through the mid 17th-century.

**zemstvo**  A local assembly established in 1864 in every district and province in the Russian empire, responsible for local administration.

# INDEX

The index headings are filed letter-by letter. Some entries are filed by date to reflect the chronology. Maps are indicated by "*m*" following the page number; tables by "*t*" and glossary items by "*g*".

# Great Dates in Russian and Soviet History

All-Muslim Conference (1917) 177
*All Quiet at the Shipka Pass* (Vereshchiagin) 133
All-Russian Academy of Arts (Leningrad) 218
All-Russian Association of Proletarian Writers (VAPP) 193
All-Russian Central Executive Committee see Central Executive Committee of the Soviets (VTsIK)
All-Russian Committee for the Salvation of the Country and of the Revolution 181
All-Russian Committee of Railway Workers (Vikzhel) 181
All-Russian Conference of Mensheviks (1917) 175
All-Russian Conference of Soviets of Workers' and Soldiers' Deputies (1917) 174
All-Russian Conference of Trade Unions (1917) 177
All-Russian Congress of Peasants' Deputies (1917) 177
All-Russian Congress of Soviets of Workers' and Soldiers' Deputies (1917) 175
All-Russian Moslem League 153
All-Russian Peasant Union 153
All-Russian Union of Towns 167
All-Russian Union of Zemstvos 167
*All Sorts of Things* (periodical) 88
All-Soviet Agricultural Exhibition (1939) 230
aluminum 225
Alvensleben, Count Constantine 129
Amalrik, Andrei 270
Amin, Hafizullah 266
*Ammalat Bek* (Bestuzhev) 119
amnesty
    by czars 91, 95, 123, 153
    by Provisional Government 171, 173
    by Soviet government 213, 249
*Among People* (Donskoi) 226
*Among the People* (Gorky) 170
*Amphitryon* (Molière) 61
Anastasia (daughter of Iaroslav the Wise) 9
*Ancient Russian Library, The* (Novikov) 89
Anders, Wladyslaw 235
"Anders army" 235
Andrei I (Hungary) 9
Andrei II 22
Andrei III Alexandrovich of Gorodets 22
*Andrei Rublev* (Tarkovsky) 269
Andrei the Big 32
Andrew I (Hungary) 25
Andrew II (Hungary) 25
Andrew, Saint 15
Andreyev, Andrei 213, 245–246
Andreyeva, Nina 281
Andropov, Yuri 260–262, 271–275
Andrusovo, Peace of (1667) 54
Andrusovo, Treaty of (1667) 56–57
*Angel, The* (Lermontov) 119
Angola 265
aniline dye 120
*Anna Karenina* (Tolstoy) 133

*Annals of the Fatherland* (journal) 107, 120, 133, 136
Anne (daughter of Constantine IX Monomamakh) 10
Anne (daughter of Iaroslav, prince of Kiev) 10
Anne (sister of Basil II, Byzantine emperor) 8
Anne I (Anne Ivanovna) 67, 71–73, 78, 80
Anne, Grand Duchess 98
*Anno Domini MCMXXI* (Akhmatova) 200
*Answer to A.S. Khomiakov, An* (Kireevsky) 120
Antes (Slavic tribe) 2
anthems 120, 231
Anthony (hermit/monk) 14–15
Anthony, Archbishop of Novgorod 26
antiballistic missiles 264
*Antidote, The* (Catherine II) 89
antireligious campaigns 199, 208, 230, 256–257, 272
anti-Semitism 135, 143, 149, 153, 280 see also pogroms
Antonescu, Ion 237
*Apology of a Madman* (Chaadaev) 120
*Apostol* (printed by Federov and Mstislavets) 43
*Apotheosis of War* (Vereshchiagin) 133
apparatchik 316g
*Appearance of Christ before the People, The* (Ivanov) 120
Apraksin, Admiral Fedor 66
Apraksin, Stepan 76
April Crisis (1917) 174
"April Theses" (Lenin) 174
*Arabesques* (Gogol) 120
Arafat, Yasir 266
Aragon, Louis 218
Araia, Francesco 78
Arakcheev, Count Aleksei 96, 103–104, 106
Aral Sea 296
Arcade, Bishop of Novgorod 17
archaeology 133
archimandrite 316g
architecture see culture and the arts; *specific style* (*e.g.*, modernism); *architect* (*e.g.*, Shekhtel)
Arkhipov, Ivan 275
"armed neutrality" 85
Armenia
    antireligious actions in 145
    as autonomous republic 190
    Azerbaijan conflict 300–301, 305, 308
    CIS treaty signed 311
    demonstrations 299
    ethnic conflict 152
    political organizations 137
    resistance to Soviet rule 182, 302–304
    as Soviet Republic 192, 221
    terrorist attacks 261
    in Transcaucasian federation 195
    US diplomacy and 294, 312
Armenian National Army 302
Armenian National Movement 301
"Armored Train 14-69" (Ivanov) 200

dance see ballet
Daniel (abbott) 16
Daniel (son of Alexander Nevsky) 22
Daniel (son of Roman of Volynia) 19, 25–27
Daniel, Yuli 260
Danielson, N. 131, 137
Daniel the Black 35
Danilevsky, Nikolai 126
Daniloff, Nicholas 288
Danubian principalities 97, 105, 114–115, 128
Dargomyzhsky, Alexander 132
Dashkova, Princess Catherine 89, 91
Dashnaktsutuin (Armenian socialist party) 137
Das Kapital (Marx) 131
Days and Nights (Simonov) 240
Days of the Turbins, The (Bulgakov) 209
Dead Souls (Gogol) 120
Death of the Commissar, The (Petrov-Vodkin) 209
Death of the Poet (Lermontov) 120
death penalty 174, 177, 213, 216, 220, 242–243, 281
Deceiver, The (Catherine II) 89
Decembrist Rebellion (1825) 103, 109–110
"Declaration of Rights of the Peoples of Russia" 181
"Declaration of the Rights of the Toiling and Exploited People" 186
"Declaration of the Thirteen" 204
Dedinovo dockyards (Oka River) 58
Defense, The (Nabokov) 306
Defense of Petrograd, The (Deineka) 209
deforestation 77
deformed children 68
de Gaulle, Charles 237, 263
Deineka, Alexander 209, 239
Delcassé, Théophile 146
Delegate, The (Ryazhsky) 209
Delianov, Ivan 137
Deluded, The (Catherine II) 89
Delvig, Baron A. 108, 119
Demichev, Peter 281
Demidov, Prince Anatoly 117
Demidov Gymnasium (Iaroslavl) 100
Democratic Centralism (Communist faction) 187, 204
Democratic Reform Movement 285
Democratic Russia 284
Democratic Union 281
Demon (Vrubel) 141
Demon, The (Lermontov) 119
Demons, The (Dostoyevsky) 126, 133
Deng Xiaoping 290
Denikin, General Anton 189–191
Denisov, E. 269
Denmark
  armed neutrality policy 85, 90, 93
  friendship treaties 85
  military alliances 41, 66–67, 84
  territorial agreements 160

Department for Safeguarding Public Security and Public Order (Okhrana) 136
Department for the Affairs of Non-Orthodox Sects 231
Department for the Affairs of the Russian Orthodox Church 231
Department of Appanages 91
Department of Commerce 58
Department of Foreign Affairs 54
Department of Secret Affairs 54
Der Blaue Reiter (group of painters) 163
Description of Moscow (Cantemir) 70
desyatina (measure of land) 316g
détente 259
Development of Capitalism in Russia, The (Lenin) 147
Diaghilev, Sergei 150, 163
Diary of a Superfluous Man (Turgenev) 121
Dictatorship of Conscience (Shatrov) 306
Diderot, Denis 80, 88–89
Diebitsch-Zabalkansky, Marshal Hans von 110
Diet (Finland) 175
Diet (Poland) 103–104, 110–111
Die Walküre (Wagner) 239
Dilettantism in Science (Herzen) 120
Dionysius, Abbot 47
Dionysius, Archimandrite 59
Dir (Varangian leader) 4
Disappearance (Trifonov) 306
disarmament see arms control
dissident movements 259–260, 271–272, 287
distilleries 77
divine right 37
divorce 184, 207, 225, 231
"Dizzy with Success" (Stalin) 214
Dmitri (first civil magistrate of Novgorod) 24
Dmitri (son of Ivan IV) 44–45
Dmitri, Grand Duke 168
Dmitri, Prince "Donskoi" 19, 23–24, 29, 35
Dmitri Alexandrovich of Pereiaslavl 22
Dmitri Cantemir of Moldavia, Prince 70
Dmitri Mikhailovich of Tver 22–23
Dmitri Shemiaka 30–31
Dmowski, Roman 144
Dnieproges (hydroelectric station) 216
Dobroliubov, Nikolai 124
Dobrovolsky, A. 260
"doctors' plot" 241, 243, 249
Doctor Zhivago (Pasternak) 257, 306
Dokuchaev, N. 201
Dokuchaev, Vasili 141
Dolgikh, Vladimir 281
Dolgoruky, Catherine 72
Dolgoruky, Maria 53
Dolgoruky, Yuri 11, 13, 16–17
Dombrovsky, Yuri 270, 306
Dominicans 25
Domostroi ("the Household Manager") 42, 316g
Don Cossacks 37, 42, 55, 189
Donkey's Tail Exhibition (1912) 164
Don Ossetians (Slavic tribe) 5

# Index

*Two Tactics of Social Democracy in the Democratic Revolution* (Lenin) 153
Tynyanov, Yuri 200, 209

## U

Uborevich, Jeromin 222
uchastok 320*g*
udels (landholdings) 33, 91, 320*g*
uezdy (districts) 83
Ufa Conference (1918) 190
Ugedey, Great Khan 21
ukase 320*g*
Ukraine 38*m*, 56, 74, 127, 175, 189–192, 298–306, 309–314
Ukraintsev, Emelian 66
"Ulozhenie" (legal code) 54, 320*g*
Ulyanov, Alexander 137
*Uncle Vanya* (Chekhov) 150
*Under Northern Skies* (Balmont) 142
Uniate Church 25, 46, 49, 117, 131, 245, 301
Unified Team 315
Union Bureau (Menshevik organization) 212
Union of Brest-Litovsk 49, 56
Union of Florence 34
Union of Jewish Workers in Lithuania, Russia and Poland (the Bund) 144
Union of Liberation 143, 145, 152–153
Union of Proletarian Architects of Russia 210
Union of Russian Social Democrats Abroad 144
Union of Salvation 104
Union of Socialist Revolutionaries 145
Union of Soviet Architects 218
Union of Soviet Musicians 218
Union of Soviet Writers 218
Union of Struggle 144
Union of the Russian People 153
Union of the 17th of October 154
Union of Towns 169
Union of Unions 153
Union of Welfare (secret society) 104
Union of Zemstvos 169
unions *see* trade unions; Zubatovshchina
union treaty 283–285, 287, 304, 308
United Kingdom *see* Great Britain
United Nations (UN)
  actions of 245, 253, 266, 292, 314
  founding of 237–239
  reform proposals 254
  Security Council 239, 245, 253, 292
United Opposition 202, 204
United States
  Alaska sold to 105, 129
  arms control 254, 263, 267, 275, 290–294, 311–313
  Berlin status question 239, 253–254, 264
  commercial agreements 116, 223, 264–265, 274
  diplomatic relations 97, 176, 214
  Khrushchev period and 250, 252–255
  trade with 149*t*

in WWII 235–239
Universal Exposition in Paris (1900) 147
universities *see also specific university* (*e.g.*, University of Moscow)
  legal restrictions 116–118, 136, 161–162
  liberalization 100, 125, 153
  purges 103, 106
  quotas for Jewish students 139, 161
  unrest at 144, 162
University of Dorpat (Tartu) 93, 100, 140
University of Helsingfors (Helsinki) 116
University of Kazan 100, 106
University of Kharkov 100
University of Kiev 117
University of Moscow 107
University of Saratov 161
University of the Friendship of Peoples (Moscow) 258
University of Tomsk 139
University of Vilna 111
University of Vilnius 100
University of Warsaw 106, 111, 131
Unkiar Skelessi, Treaty of (1833) 113–114
"Ural-Siberian method" 207
uravnilovka (egalitarianism) 320*g*
Uritsky, Moisei 186
*Urn, The* (Bely) 163
Ushakov, Admiral Fedor 90, 92
Uspensky, Gleb 141
Ustinov, Dmitri 261, 273
U-2 spy plane 254
Uvarov, Count Serge 109, 111
Uzbekistan 203, 300, 302, 305, 311–313
Uzbeks 52*m*

## V

Vahi, Tiit 314
*Vampire, The* (Tolstoy) 120
VAPP *see* All-Russian Association of Proletarian Writers
Varangians 1–7
Vasilevsky, Alexander 242
"Vasili Terkin" (Tvardovsky) 240
*Vasili Terkin in the Other World* (Tvardovsky) 258
Vaska (Cossack leader) 58
Vasnetsov, Viktor 150
Vassiliev, Georgi and Sergei 218
Vatican 114, 129, 138, 263, 290–292
Vatsétis, Ioakim 186
Vatutin, Nikolai 236
veche (popular assembly) 11, 17, 32, 320*g*
*Vedomosti* (newspaper) 69
*Vekhi* (Signposts) (essay collection) 163
velvet 57
Venedi (Slavic tribe) 2
Venetsianov, Alexei 107
Venevitinov, Dmitri 108
Venice 65–66
Vereshchiagin, Vasili 133

355